# JAMAICA

OLIVER HILL

# JAMAICA

Caribbean Sea

North West Point
Lucea
Sandy Bay
Dias
HANOVER
Long Bay
WESTMORELAND
Negril
Little Bay
Little London
St. Johns Point
Savanna-la-Mar
Bluefields Bay
Grange Hill
B9
A1
Ramble
Bethel Town
B8
Darlinston
Auchindown
A2
B7
Luana Point
Black River Bay
Parotee Point
Black Spring Point

MONTEGO BAY INTERNATIONAL AIRPORT
Montego Bay
Montego Bay
A1
Realing
Cambridge
B7
B6
Black River
Black River

SAINT JAMES
Queen of Spain Valley
Cockle Bar Point
Falmouth
Mountain Spring Bay
QUEENS HWY
Mangrove Point
Duncans
Discovery Bay
A1
Philadelphia
Clarks Town
TRELAWNY
Nassau Mountains
A3
SAINT ELIZABETH
MANCHESTER
Mandeville
Santa Cruz
A2
Spur Tree
Santa Cruz Mountains
Treasure Beach
May Day Mountains
Alligator Pond Bay
Cuckhold Point
Long Bay
Rest
Macarr Bay

0   10 mi
0   10 km

© AVALON TRAVEL

# Contents

DISCOVER

# Jamaica

It's hard to argue when Jamaicans assert that their island is blessed. Simple luxuries abound, like picking a mango from a tree for breakfast, watching hummingbirds flit about tropical flowers, or bathing in a crystal-clear waterfall on a hot day. It's no wonder that for more than a century visitors have come to Jamaica to escape cold northern winters and bask in the island's tropical climate and calm Caribbean waters.

Jamaica's resorts have supplemented these simple pleasures with luxury: hot stone massages, candlelit gourmet dinners, soft reggae music, and lapping waves are just the beginning. Many resorts have perfected the art of indulgence to such a degree that it's entirely possible to miss the depth and color of the country's culture beyond their walls.

Outside the hotel gates you'll find the tenacious evolution of a nation barely 50 years old, where preachers—religious, musical, and political—lend vibrancy to everyday life. Jamaica's vibrant culture and resilient spirit can be felt throughout the country, from small villages to bustling urban centers like Kingston.

Ironically, it wasn't the tropical climate or endless natural beauty that brought worldwide attention to Jamaica in the 20th century. It was a young man

---

**Clockwise from top left:** San Michele at Bluefields Villas; grilling lobster at 3 Dives Jerk Centre in Negril; I-Octane at Rebel Salute; The HouseBoat Grill in Montego Bay; cliffs on Negril's West End; the beach at the mouth of Dunn's River Falls.

growing up with the odds stacked against him in the ghetto of Trench Town, who managed to make his truthful message heard above the din of political violence and clashing Cold War ideologies of the 1970s. Robert Nesta Marley, along with band members Peter McIntosh and Bunny Livingston, became a beacon of hope, not just for disenfranchised Jamaicans, but for the oppressed the world over. Today, countless singers keep Marley's legacy alive and fuel Jamaica's music industry, the most prolific on the planet.

Whether you're seeking to explore the country's rich history, soak in the sunshine and the clear, warm waters of the Caribbean, or just go with the flow, you'll come to understand what makes this island and its inhabitants so exceptional.

**Clockwise from top left:** San San, an upscale enclave just east of Port Antonio; the red-billed streamertail, Jamaica's national bird; Gabre Selassie at Kingston Dub Club; ziplining at Mystic Mountain in Ocho Rios.

# Planning Your Trip

## Where to Go

### Negril and the West Coast

Jamaica's westernmost parish has the country's **most popular beach resort town,** Negril. Once a quiet fishing village, Negril is known as the capital of casual, where recreational activities like **water sports** and **cliff jumping** complement the inactivity of **relaxing in the sun.** A wetlands area inland from the beach is backed by gentle hills suitable for **hiking and bird-watching.**

### Montego Bay and the Northwest Coast

Known the island over as Mobay, Jamaica's leading resort town offers **beaches, great house tours,** and top-notch **music festivals.** Rivers along the eastern and western borders of St. James offer **rafting,** and Mobay has an active yacht club with a lively social calendar. Neighboring Trelawny encompasses a rugged inland terrain known as **Cockpit Country,** riddled with caves and underground rivers.

### Ocho Rios and the North Central Coast

Throngs of travelers disembark cruise ships each week in Ocho Rios, many headed for Jamaica's most popular attraction, **Dunn's River Falls.** Less trafficked river gardens abound and **world-class hotels and villas** dot the coast to the east and west. Contrasting bustling Ochi, **St. Mary** is laid-back, with **quiet hills, hidden waterfalls,** and **sleepy fishing villages.**

### Port Antonio and the East Coa

Portland's parish capital and the biggest towr the east, Port Antonio has an **Old World cha** lingering in **luxurious villas** and **hilltop** **sorts.** Despite its claim as the first Caribbe tourist destination, it has, for better or wor been spared from large-scale development, a the area's **natural beauty** remains its prir pal draw with singular **beaches, lush fores** and **waterfalls.**

### Kingston and the Blue Mountains

The boisterous capital city has **remarkable r taurants, pulsating nightlife,** and **histori treasures.** There's no sugarcoating the juxta sition of poverty and wealth, but their coexiste inspires a prolific **music industry** and **vibra arts scene.** Beaches, waterfalls, and cool air just a short drive away, and in the Blue Mounta visitors enjoy the **world's finest coffee, h ing,** and **bird-watching.**

### The South Coast

The South Coast defines **off-the-beate track,** where **waterfalls, crocodile-infest wetlands,** and **seafood** are the main dra **Treasure Beach,** a string of bays and fish villages, is a favored destination for those w of crowds looking to get away from it all, wh **Mandeville's cool highland air,** historic g **course,** and **fine restaurants** represen chance to experience the island's quiet interic

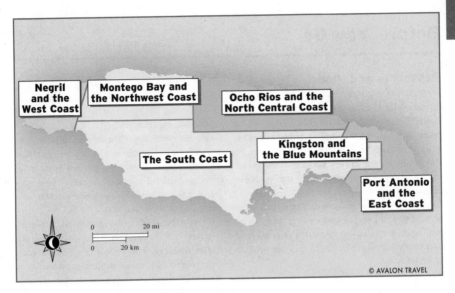

Map labels:
- Negril and the West Coast
- Montego Bay and the Northwest Coast
- Ocho Rios and the North Central Coast
- The South Coast
- Kingston and the Blue Mountains
- Port Antonio and the East Coast

0 — 20 mi
0 — 20 km

© AVALON TRAVEL

# When to Go

Jamaica has typically been marketed as a destination for escaping the winter blues, but it can be just as good, or better, in the summer, when temperatures are comparable or even cooler than in places as far north as New York.

Jamaica's **hurricane season,** with regular low pressure systems accompanied by rain, runs **June through October.** In the absence of a large front, however, rainfall usually lasts only a few minutes and shouldn't be cause for concern in planning a trip.

The high season and low season should be of more concern in planning a trip, as many establishments set rates according to demand. **High season** runs **December 15 to April 15,** when accommodations can be twice as expensive as during the low season. Some establishments set

their own specific dates, and others vary pricing throughout the year, raising them for Easter, Thanksgiving, or the week between Christmas and New Year's. If escaping the winter blues is not your first priority, visiting during the **low season** can be much more cost-effective. Check with each establishment when planning a trip to see how prices vary seasonally.

The Jamaican calendar is filled with **annual events,** many of which are worth considering in planning a trip. A music festival like Rebel Salute or Sumfest is one of the best ways to jump out of the tourism box and appreciate Jamaica's culture alongside Jamaicans from all walks of life. If music isn't your thing, there are several other annual events, like the Calabash Literary Festival, food festivals, and fishing tournaments.

# Before You Go

## Passports and Visas

Jamaica now requires **passports** for all visitors, including those from the United States and the United Kingdom. A **tourist visa** is required for many nationalities. A complete listing of visa requirements can be found on the website of the Consulate General in New York (www.congenjamaica-ny.org/visas). Visitors must also be able to demonstrate sufficient funds to cover their stay and be in possession of an onward or return ticket or itinerary. It helps to know where you will be staying on arrival, as immigration officials tend to detain visitors on entry until they can provide an address.

## Vaccinations

The Jamaican government recently began requiring documentation demonstrating visitors from certain countries have been vaccinated against Yellow Fever. Ensure you can provide documentation for required vaccinations upon entry. Check with the **Jamaica Tourist Board** (tel. 876/929-9200, www.visitjamaica.com) or **Passport Immigration and Citizenship Agency** (PICA) (25C Constant Spring Rd., tel. 876/754-7422, www.pica.gov.jm) for current requirements.

Note that the CDC has issued an alert for pregnant women or women who plan to conceive, advising that they postpone travel to many parts of the Caribbean, including Jamaica, due to the spread of the Zika virus.

All other travelers should practice enhanced precautions to avoid mosquito bites. Always be sure to use insect repellent, wear protective clothing when venturing into the outdoors, and keep mosquitoes outside.

## What to Pack

Most Jamaican **ATMs** will dispense cash with foreign debit cards. The best exchange rates are found at foreign exchange traders like Scotia Investments and FX Trader. **Banks** accept traveler's checks, but typically have long lines and offer less competitive rates.

Where **clothing** is concerned, what to take depends entirely on the nature of your trip. Most all-inclusive hotels have semiformal dress codes (a collared shirt, dress shoes) for their fine-dining restaurants; if church or a business meeting is in order, formal attire is a must.

If nobody needs to be impressed, however, Jamaica can be the **most casual place on earth,** where certain esteemed members of society refuse to wear shoes for greater proximity to Mother Earth, and nude beaches abound at hotels like Couples and Hedonism. However, outside the beach resort towns like Negril, entering a place of business without a shirt will be frowned upon.

Cool, light-colored cotton clothes are best for the heat and humidity, and bring your favorite bathing suit. For cool evenings, pack a long-sleeved shirt and long pants.

Many travelers to Jamaica are surprised to find that Jamaicans rarely wear shorts on a normal day, while jeans and full suits are common everyday attire. It is not necessary to buy an entire wardrobe of Hawaiian shirts before your trip, and in a pinch plenty are sold in gift shops across the island with the requisite "Jamaica, no problem" printed across the front.

You'll definitely want to bring your most flashy getup if you're planning a **night on the town.** In nightclubs such as Fiction and Privilege in Kingston, women are remarkably dressed up; men will come dressed in their shiniest shoes and most "criss" jacket to "flex" in the corner till the dance floor heats up.

For **hiking** and overnights in the higher elevations of the Blue Mountains, you'll want a sweatshirt, parka, boots, and warm socks.

the Blue Mountains

a rope swing at YS Falls

# The Best of Jamaica

Ten days is a good length for a trip to Jamaica and provides enough time to relax on the beach while also venturing beyond the sun and sand for a mix of adventure and culture. Highlights include the cliff-jumping and scrumptious food of Negril's West End, the culture and nightlife of Kingston, the coffee plantations in the Blue Mountains, and the beaches in Portland.

## Day 1

Arrive at the airport in **Montego Bay** and check in for two nights at **Wharf House**. Splurge for a dinner at **The Sugar Mill** or **HouseBoat Grill**, or keep it casual and affordable at **Scotchies** for some authentic roadside jerk. Hit up **Mobay Proper** for an evening drink to gauge the scene along **the Hip Strip**.

## Day 2

Tour **Rose Hall Great House** in the morning, then spend the afternoon lazing at **Doctors Cave Beach** or try your hand at kiteboarding

by **Sea Castles** in the afternoon, wind permitting. Dine at **Day-O Plantation** followed by a play at **Fairfield Theatre** or a night out at **Margaritaville**.

## Day 3

Head west to **Negril** for cliff jumping on the West End or a splash at Brighton's **Blue Hole Mineral Spring** by late morning. Head to **Chill Awhile** for lunch and soak up some rays before taking a sunset stroll down **Seven-Mile Beach.** Try **Hungry Lion** or **Pushcart Restaurant and Rum Bar** for dinner before checking out some live reggae music on the beach at night.

## Day 4

In the morning, drive to **Savanna-la-Mar** and then turn inland to **Mayfield Falls** or **Blue Hole Gardens.** Spend the morning exploring the falls and gardens, then head over to nearby **Paradise Park** for horseback riding or a swim in the river followed by a picnic. Alternatively,

# Boutique Spas

Jamaica has world-class spas, based predominantly at the high-end resorts. These spas strike the right balance between high-end and rootsy: even the most expensive among them draw from Jamaica's panoply of natural products and soothing vibes.

## NEGRIL

- **The Spa Retreat** draws on the vast experience of one of Canada's leading day-spa operators with a full range of pampering and invigorating treatments as well as educational couples massage sessions that can enhance a relationship with practical skills (page 42).

- **Rockhouse Spa** offers massage treatments in cliff top cabanas, signature foot ceremonies, detox pedicures and revitalizing scrubs in a temple-like garden pavilion and deep soak baths seaside, utilizing indigenous, mind-, body-, and soul-stimulating ingredients (page 43).

- **The Caves Spa** is the only place where you can get a massage inside a cavern glowing with candles and sprinkled with flower petals. Follow that with a relaxing soak in the private whirlpool-tub chamber carved into the cliff side while gazing out to sea (page 43).

- **Kiyara Spa on the Cliff,** located at The Cliff on Negril's West End, prides itself on offering natural herbal remedies made from seasonal local ingredients applied in treatment rooms near the water's edge to the tune of crashing waves. Or opt for the convenience and privacy of in-room treatments (page 43).

## MONTEGO BAY

- **Fern Tree Spa at Half Moon Resort,** Montego Bay's leading boutique hotel and villa complex pulls out all the stops, offering massage in a gazebo overhanging the soothing surf, and facials, manicures, and pedicures in a state-of-the-art treatment room surrounded by rejuvenating plunge pools (page 83).

## OCHO RIOS

- **FieldSpa at Goldeneye** is uniquely situated overhanging a magical lagoon, where guests are pampered with products and treatments not even Ian Fleming enjoyed when he sought

bubbling plunge pools at Fern Tree Spa

solitude at this seaside estate to pen his James Bond classics. The spa is located on the wooded lagoon banks in and around a cozy two-story cottage with soaking tubs and massage tables hidden amid the tropical foliage (page 145).

## BLUE MOUNTAINS

- **The Strawberry Hill Living Spa** marries deep tissue treatments and ayurvedic healing philosophies. The spa features five treatment rooms, hydrotherapy, a sauna, a yoga deck, and a plunge pool with spectacular panoramic views of the Blue Mountains surrounded by lush cloud forests and rejuvenating mountain air that naturally promotes health and tranquility (page 248).

## THE SOUTH COAST

- **Jake's Driftwood Spa** features seaside cabanas facing the water where the surf lulls visitors into a trance as they receive treatments that merge holistic techniques and philosophies from around the globe into a potent blend of Caribbean concoctions developed by wellness guru Laura Henzell (page 269).

grab a bite at **Sweet Spice** in Sav, then stop at **Eldin Washington Ranch** for **Reggae Horseback Riding** in the afternoon on the way back to Negril.

## Day 5
Drive east to **YS Falls** in **Middle Quarters** for a splash in the river and an adrenaline-fixing zipline. Grab some jerk chicken at YS before heading to nearby **Appleton Estate** to sample Jamaica's best rum. Continue on to **Treasure Beach** in the late afternoon to check in for the night and sample the conch soup and fried fish at **Jack Sprat.**

## Day 6
Wake up with a dip at the beach in **Great Bay** before a mid-morning stroll to **Back Sea Side.** In the afternoon catch a canoe boat to **Black River** to spot alligators and birds or head straight to **Pelican Bar,** a one-of-a-kind watering hole and ramshackle fried fish joint built on stilts 1.5 kilometers (1 mile) offshore, for some snorkeling and Red Stripe. Cruise back to Treasure Beach for a second night.

## Day 7
Leave early for **Kingston** to get there by late morning, sightsee downtown with a visit to the **National Gallery** followed by a stroll along **Ocean Boulevard** and around **Coronation Market.** Stop by **Liberty Hall** or **Culture Yard** before heading uptown for lunch at **Opa!** or **Chilitos.** After lunch, take a tour at nearby **Bob Marley Museum.** Pick up some souvenirs and grab an ice cream at **Devon House** and prepare for a night out at a club or street dance.

## Day 8
Head up to the **Blue Mountains** before the late morning clouds roll in for a tour of **Old Tavern Coffee Estate.** Continue over to Portland to reach **Port Antonio** in time for an afternoon dip at **Winnifred Beach** or **Frenchman's Cove** before dinner at **Mockingbird Hill** and a night out at **Cristal Night Club** or **Natural Mystic Bar.**

## Day 9
Depart for **Ocho Rios,** stopping at **Firefly** on the way to check out Noël Coward's island digs. Lunch at **Dor's Fish Pot** in Race Course or at **Chris Café** in Oracabessa and then head up to **Mystic Mountain** for a bobsled run and zipline tour through the canopy, or swim with dolphins and pet the sharks at **Dolphin Cove.** Take a late-afternoon dip and tube ride down the **White River** before dinner at **Passage to India** or **Toscanini's.**

## Day 10
Get up and on the road early to beat the crowds for a climb up **Dunn's River Falls** before heading west toward **Montego Bay** for an afternoon departure. Stop by **Green Grotto Caves** or **Greenwood Great House** on your way, time permitting.

# Roots and Culture

Delve into the pulsating cultural milieu that shapes and defines Jamaican society. The roots of Jamaican popular music will become vivid with this tour, designed to immerse visitors in the island's singular musical gold mine. Keep tabs on the weekly events calendars in Kingston and Negril to plan your time in these areas.

## Day 1
Arrive in **Montego Bay** for one night at the **Spanish Court.** If you arrive in the morning, visit **Rose Hall Great House** or **Bellefield Great House** for a step back in time with a stop at **Scotchies** for jerk either before or after the tour. Visit the **Gallery of West Indian Art** for some inspiration before dinner at **Pier 1** or the

reggae artist Sizzla performing at St. Mary Mi Come From

**HouseBoat Grill.** Hit up **Margaritaville** to mingle and "wine" with visitors and locals if you still have the energy before bed.

## Day 2

Head to **Doctors Cave Beach** in the morning and then to **Negril** in the afternoon stopping at **Niah's Patties** for a bite before catching sunset and dinner on the cliffs at **Tensing Pen** or **Pushcart Restaurant and Rum Bar.** Check out the night's live reggae band on the beach or hit the club at **The Jungle.**

## Day 3

Make a loop from Negril to **Blue Hole Gardens** or **Mayfield Falls** before swinging back around to **Half Moon Beach** along the Hanover coast. Head back to Negril for dinner at **Hungry Lion** or **Zest Restaurant** at **The Cliff.**

## Day 4

Leave for **Kingston** in the morning, stopping in Belmont to pay respects to a reggae legend at **Peter Tosh Memorial Garden.** Make a pit stop in **Middle Quarters** for "swimps," or pepper shrimp, and then take a break at **Scott's Pass, Clarendon,** to meet the Rasta elders at the headquarters of the **Nyabinghi House of Rastafari** before continuing on to Kingston for the night.

## Day 5

Hit Kingston's cultural sights, or any combination of the **Bob Marley Museum, Tuff Gong Recording Studio, Culture Yard,** and the **National Gallery.** Visit **Cap Calcini** to pick up some oldies reggae vinyl before heading out to **Hellshire Beach** for an early supper of fried fish, festival, and bammy at **Shorty's** or dine at **Gloria's** in Port Royal before a night out on the town at **Fiction Fantasy** or at a street dance.

## Day 6

Leave in the morning for **Jamnesia Surf Club** in **Bull Bay** to ride waves with Billy "Mystic" Wilmot and his family, followed by dinner and an overnight stay in one of their bungalows. Time your stay to fall on the last Saturday of the month to witness the musical talents of the host family and friends riffing at **Jamnesia Sessions.**

# Adrenaline Junkie Fix

## KITEBOARDING

- **Water Network Jamaica,** based at Sea Castles in Rose Hall, Montego Bay, offers kiteboarding lessons for the uninitiated and gear rentals for the experienced (page 71).

## SURFING

- **Jamnesia Surf Club,** located east of Kingston in Bull Bay, has professional surfing equipment and respectable waves on a good day. A skateboard park entertains when the seas are flat (page 236).

## WHITE-WATER RAFTING

- Raft the Rio Bueno in Montego Bay with **Braco Rapids Adventures** (page 97)

- **Chukka Caribbean** offers rides down the White River (page 112).

## ZIPLINING

- **Mystic Mountain** in Ocho Rios offers canopy zipline tours (page 109).

- **Chukka Caribbean** also offers canopy zipline tours at Good Hope Plantation in Montego Bay (page 99) and YS Falls in Cockpit Country (page 276).

## CLIFF JUMPING

- Cliff jumping on Negril's West End is the cheapest adrenaline fix in Jamaica. Several locations are suitable for jumping into the azure waters,

kiteboarding with Water Network Jamaica

but **Rick's Café** is the most famous for having the highest cliffs around, about 18 meters (60 feet) above the water (page 25).

## MOUNTAIN BIKING

- The annual **Fat Tyre Festival** draws biking enthusiasts locally and from abroad to Ocho Rios (page 116).

- Also in Ocho Rios, **Single Track Jamaica** offers guided tours to more serious mountain bikers (page 115).

## Day 7

Spend the morning sampling the ritualized Rasta life at **Bobo Hill** if you're in the mood for some serious worship. Visit **Reggae Falls** or **Cane River Falls** in the afternoon before heading back to Kingston. Dine on Indian cuisine at **Pushpa's** or **Tamarind** and then head up to skyline drive for some roots music and a drink at **Gabre Selassie's Kingston Dub Club,** especially lively on Sundays.

## Day 8

Leave in the morning for **Port Antonio,** checking in at **Great Huts, Drapers San,** or **Goblin Hill.** Spend the afternoon at **Reach Falls** or on the beach with a quick visit to **Folly Mansion,** a dilapidated old mansion located between the Folly Oval cricket field and the sea.

## Day 9

Depart first thing for **Ocho Rios,** stopping in **Charles Town** to take in some Maroon history, hiking, and swimming at **Asafu Yard.** In Ocho Rios, visit **Konoko Falls** to check out the

iguanas and take an evening dip before dinner at **Tropical Vibes** on **Fisherman's Beach.**

## Day 10

Visit **Blue Hole River** for swimming and a bit of light hiking in the morning before making your way to **Montego Bay** for an evening departure. Stop by **Burwood Beach** in Trelawny on the way for a quick dip, time permitting.

# Hidden Beaches and Hillside Hikes

Hikes, bird-watching, secluded beaches, and mangrove tours are indispensable to a greater appreciation of Jamaica's natural wonders.

Transportation is an important consideration when planning an eco-vacation, as many of the less-visited sights are remote and require a **rental car** or car and driver. Excursions into remote parts of Cockpit Country and the Blue Mountains require a **4WD vehicle,** but for most places, SUVs are not necessary and the extra expense is not justified.

## Day 1

Arrive in **Montego Bay** and head directly to your rental villa at **Good Hope Plantation** or **Silver Sands** in Trelawny. Spend a few hours at **Good Hope's** private beach in Bounty Bay or at **Harmony Cove** in nearby Braco before a relaxing dinner back at the ranch.

## Day 2

Explore **Cockpit Country** on horseback in the morning or go tubing down the river with **Chukka Caribbean,** followed by lunch back at the villa. Head to **Sea Castles** in the afternoon for **kiteboarding** before a casual dinner at **Far Out Fish Hut** in nearby **Greenwood.**

## Day 3

Depart in the morning for **Negril,** stopping at **Half Moon Beach** for lunch and a dip. Continue

on to **Tensing Pen** to spend the afternoon **jumping off the cliffs** and **relaxing by the pool.**

## Day 4

Depart for **Belmont,** stopping at Brighton's **Blue Hole Mineral Spring** before heading to **Blue Hole Gardens** for a refreshing dip and walk through the gardens. Catch the sunset at **Bluefields Beach** and overnight in **Belmont** at the **Luna Sea Inn.**

## Day 5

On your way to the **Blue Mountains,** make a stop in **Black River** for a morning kayak or pontoon boat safari to see the crocs, and then stop by **YS Falls** for an early afternoon dip. Push on through Kingston to overnight at **Forres Park** in **Mavis Bank, Lime Tree Farm,** or **Whitfield Hall,** if you can make it that far before dark.

## Day 6

Rise early to hike up to **Blue Mountain Peak.** Descend by early afternoon stopping at **Crystal Edge** for lunch before checking in to **Woodside** for your last two nights.

## Day 7

Hike the trails of **Holywell,** or up to **Cinchona Gardens** in the morning. Afterward, visit the Twyman's **Old Tavern Coffee Estate** for a tour

# Jamaica's Top Beaches

Harmony Cove

## NEGRIL

- **Seven-Mile Beach** is full of Negril's quintessential beach town vibes with fine white sand and gentle surf (page 26).

- **Bluefields Beach** is a tranquil spot practically unvisited by tourists, but popular with locals on the weekends (page 55).

## MONTEGO BAY

- **Burwood Beach** in Bounty Bay is one of the best places for kiteboarding, free of corral and shallow enough to stand 100 meters (330 feet) out (page 94).

- **Silver Sands** in Duncans is ideal for families, reserved for guests of the gated community and completely free of hustlers (page 94).

- **Harmony Cove** in Braco is one of Jamaica's best kept secrets and will soon be home to a mega resort and casino (page 94).

## OCHO RIOS

- **Laughing Waters,** just west of Ochi, has a breathtaking waterfall that cascades onto its gentle surf (page 113).

## PORT ANTONIO

- **Frenchman's Cove** in San San has a chilly meandering river that meets the warm, formidable surf, creating an invigorating mix (page 172).

- **Boston Beach** consistently gets some of the best waves for surfing, with boards for rent on site (page 175).

- **Long Bay Beach** has nice breakers for boogie boarding and surfing and a few kilometers of fine white sand (page 176).

## KINGSTON

- **Lime Cay,** offshore Port Royal, is a sandbar barely rising above sea level, popular with boaters and bathers, especially on weekends (page 233).

## SOUTH COAST

- **Great Bay** in Treasure Beach is protected by Great Pedro Bluff, and has one of the safer beaches on the South Coast with gentle surf and fine, golden sand (page 268).

# Vital Vittles

## JAMMIN' JERK

- Negril: **Best in the West** (page 34); **3 Dives Jerk Centre** (page 36)
- Montego Bay: **Scotchies** (page 78); **The Pork Pit** (page 78); **MVP Smokehouse** (page 79)
- Ocho Rios: **Scotchies Too** (page 127)
- Kingston: **Scotchies Tree** (page 216); **Jo Jo's Jerk Pit and More** (page 219)
- The South Coast: **All Seasons Restaurant Bar & Jerk Centre** (page 262)

## POWERFUL PATTIES

- Negril: **Niah's Patties** (page 34)
- Kingston: **Devon House Bakery** (page 224)

## DELECTABLE CURRY GOAT

- Port Antonio: **Soldier's Camp** (page 163)
- The South Coast: **Claudette's Top Class** (page 262)

## SUMPTUOUS SEAFOOD

- Negril: **Dervy's Lobster Trap** (page 49)
- Montego Bay: **Far Out Fish Hut & Beer Joint** (page 90)
- Ocho Rios: **Dor's Fish Pot** (page 143)
- Port Antonio: **Cynthia's** (page 163); **Gurley Aston Wine & Grill Bar and Boston Jerk Stop** (page 175)

Scotchies has deliciously spicy jerk.

- Kingston: **Gloria's Seafood Restaurant** (page 234); **Shorty's** (page 240)
- The South Coast: **Oswald's** (page 266)

## DESTINATION DINING

- Montego Bay: **The Sugar Mill Restaurant** (page 80); **Day-O Plantation** (page 80); **The HouseBoat Grill** (page 79)
- Ocho Rios: **Toscanini Italian Restaurant & Bar** (page 119) Port Antonio: **Mille Fleurs** (page 163); **Mike's Supper Club** (page 164)

and to pick up some beans to carry home. Dine at **The Gap Café, Strawberry Hill,** or back at Woodside.

## Day 8

Rise early for the drive back to **Montego Bay,** stopping in Ocho Rios for a dip in the **White River** or at **One Love Trail** by the sea, or take a garden tour at **Konoko Falls.** Leave Ochi in time for an evening departure from Mobay's Sangster International Airport.

# Negril and the West Coast

# Highlights

★ **Rick's Café:** Negril's West End runs along limestone cliffs, making many places suitable for thrilling leaps into the turquoise sea (page 25).

★ **Seven-Mile Beach:** Jamaica's longest beach is great for long walks into the sunset (page 26).

★ **Half Moon Beach:** Escape to this crescent-shaped cove with fine sand, undeveloped coastline, and a beach bar and grill (page 46).

★ **Blue Hole Mineral Spring:** Cool off with a jump into this popular swimming hole, just a short drive from Negril (page 51).

★ **Mayfield Falls:** Spend an afternoon at one of the best waterfall attractions in Jamaica. Take a dip in the river or walk upstream along a series of gentle cascades and pools (page 52).

★ **Blue Hole Gardens:** Visit one of Jamaica's most picturesque swimming holes and enjoy the unreal turquoise water, lush garden surroundings, and bubbling wellheads of Turtle River (page 53).

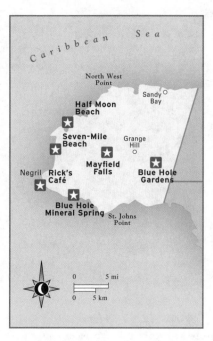

# Negril is Jamaica's most popular beach town, embodying the "Jamaica No Problem" spirit plastered on T-shirts sold in souvenir shops across the island.

It's a place where visitors and locals alike can easily forget what day of the week it is.

Live music blasts from beachfront bars virtually every night—and once in a while, one of the island's top-ranking artists passes through town to perform. Negril is split between the iconic Seven-Mile Beach, with its fine white sand stretching from the Negril River to Point Village, and the iconic cliffs of the West End. It's as much a raucous beach town for the mass tourism market as it is a secluded enclave for the well-heeled vacationer.

After the Jamaican government decriminalized marijuana in 2015, the spliff-infused, Red Stripe-soaked, laid-back lifestyle espoused by so many in this coastal community has finally been officially embraced; the Cannabis Cup has even been added to the line-up of annual events. For those with some pep in their step, Negril also provides a good base for exploring Westmoreland and its neighboring parishes without having to sacrifice the town's spectacular sunsets, enjoyed every evening like a ritual. For those who prefer to vacation without being surrounded by other travelers, sleepy coastal communities around Negril like Little Bay, Bluefields, Belmont, and Whitehouse offer fewer distractions and a variety of lodging options, from rustic clapboard cottages to boutique hotels and luxury villas.

## PLANNING YOUR TIME

Negril is the ultimate place to kick back on the beach with plenty to do by day or night, and for many, it's the only destination they'll visit during their stay in Jamaica. For those looking to experience what Negril has to offer and move on to see other parts of the island, two or three nights is sufficient. The general area has many worthwhile attractions that make great day trips and can help break up long days under the sun to avoid overexposure while providing a glimpse of the "real" Jamaica—with all the allure of its countryside lifestyle and lush scenery. Most visitors to Negril come specifically to laze on the beach in the dead of winter, but there are special events throughout

---

**Previous:** The Caves; a glass bottom boat at Seven-Mile Beach. **Above:** Rick's Café.

# The West Coast

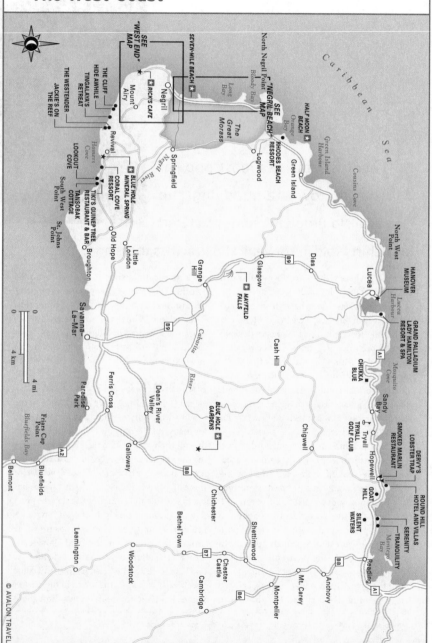

SEE "WEST END" MAP

"NEGRIL BEACH" MAP

SEVEN-MILE BEACH

THE CLIFF
HIDE AWHILE
TINGALAYA'S RETREAT
THE WESTENDER
JACKIE'S ON THE REEF

RICK'S CAFE

North Negril Point

Caribbean

Mount Airy

Long Bay

Bloody Bay

Negril

North Negril Point

HALF MOON BEACH

Orange Bay

Green Island Harbour

Green Island

Sea

Cousins Cove

Revival

Homers Cove

LOOKOUT COVE

TANSOBAK COTTAGE

South West Point

St. Johns Point

South West Point

CORAL COVE RESORT

BLUE HOLE MINERAL SPRING

TIKI'S GUINEP TREE RESTAURANT & BAR

The Great Morass

Springfield

Logwood

RHODES BEACH RESORT

Old Hope

Little London

Broughton

Grange Hill

Glasgow

B9

Dias

MAYFEILD FALLS

Cabarita River

B9

Cash Hill

Lucea

North West Point

HANOVER MUSEUM

Lucea Harbour

GRAND PALLADIUM LADY HAMILTON RESORT & SPA

A1

CHUKKA BLUE

Mosquito Cove

Savanna-La-Mar

Ferris Cross

Dean's River Valley

Galloway

Paradise Park

Friars Cap Point

Bluefields Bay

Belmont

Bluefields

A2

Leamington

Woodstock

Bethel Town

Chichester

B8

Chigwell

BLUE HOLE GARDENS

Shettinwood

Chester Castle

Cambridge

B7

Montpelier

B6

Mt. Carey

Anchovy

B8

Reading

A1

Sandy Bay

TRYALL TRYALL GOLF CLUB

Hopewell

DERVY'S SMOKED MARLIN RESTAURANT

DERVY'S LOBSTER TRAP

ROUND HILL HOTEL AND VILLAS

GOAT HILL

SILENT WATERS

SERENITY

TRANQUILITY

Montego Bay

0    4 km

0    4 mi

© AVALON TRAVEL

the year to be considered if you're planning a trip with flexibility. Apart from the Christmas and New Year's period, when it can be difficult to find accommodations, Negril is completely overrun by local and international visitors during the first week of August for the national holidays that fall on the 1st and the 6th.

## ORIENTATION

Life in Negril is focused on the west-facing coastline divided between **Seven-Mile Beach** and the **West End,** or the **Cliffs.** Seven-Mile Beach runs the length of **Long Bay** from a small peninsula separating it from **Bloody Bay** on its northern end to the mouth of the Negril River at the southern end. There are three main roads that meet at the roundabout in the center of Negril: **Norman Manley Boulevard,** which turns into the A1 as it leaves town heading northeast toward Montego Bay; **West End Road,** which continues along the coast from the roundabout hugging the cliffs well past the lighthouse, until it eventually turns inland, rejoining the main south coast road (the A2) in the community of Negril Spot; and **Whitehall Road,** which extends inland from the roundabout toward the golf course, becoming the A2 as it passes the Texaco gas station. Whitehall Road turns south just before the Texaco station, climbing a hill and passing the ruins of Whitehall Great House, before continuing through the communities of Mount Airy

and Orange Hill and then rejoining the A2 in Negril Spot. A sharp turn due south between Orange Hill and Negril Spot leads to Brighton and Little Bay, before the road continues east, rejoining the A2 in Little London and continuing east toward Savanna-la-Mar.

## SAFETY

As Jamaica's foremost tourism mecca, Negril attracts some of the island's most aggressive hustlers. Many will feign friendship and generosity only to demand, often with aggression and intimidation, exorbitant compensation for whatever good or service is on offer, whether it's a CD of one of the countless "up-and-coming artists," a marijuana spliff handed to you as someone extends their hand in greeting, or a piece of jewelry. As a rule, don't accept anything you don't actually want, and clarify the expected compensation if you do want it before allowing anyone to put something in your hand or mouth. Though not commonplace, it's not unheard of for hustlers to draw a knife to intimidate, and there's generally little fear of repercussions from the police, who tend to be slow-moving if responsive at all. The police are unlikely to be sympathetic, especially if a quarrel or skirmish involves drugs, even if the mix-up was unprovoked. Do your best to stay in well-populated areas and try to avoid unsolicited approaches from strangers offering something you don't want.

# Sights

## ★ RICK'S CAFÉ

**Rick's Café** (tel. 876/957-0380, www.rickscafejamaica.com, info@rickscafejamaica.com, noon-10pm daily, free) buzzes with visitors every afternoon, especially just before sunset, thanks to the tall precipice jutting out over a protected cove with deep turquoise water. Adrenaline junkies can choose from three different heights to launch into the sea:

3 meters (10 feet), 7.6 meters (25 feet), and 10.6 meters (35 feet). A pool area surrounded by lounge chairs and cabanas (US$75 per day, 10 guests max.) is suitable for children and those with no appetite for heights. Live bands belt out reggae classics throughout the evening, occasionally sounding true to the originals. The café serves beer, spirits, and bar food, and the gift shop sells T-shirts and souvenirs.

This is a mandatory stop for every tour bus and sunset catamaran cruise in Negril.

## WHITEHALL GREAT HOUSE

**Whitehall Great House** (unmanaged, free) is little more than the ruins of a former mansion. Located on the old Whitehall Estate on the ascent to Mount Airy, it's a great vantage point for a panoramic view of Seven-Mile Beach and the large swampy expanse known as the Negril Morass. To get here, take a right immediately before the Texaco Station on Good Hope Road heading east from the Negril roundabout toward Savanna-la-Mar. The ruins are about 1.5 kilometers (1 mile) up the hill on the left. One of the largest cotton trees in Jamaica stands on the property.

## NEGRIL LIGHTHOUSE

**Negril Lighthouse** is located near the westernmost point of Jamaica on West End Road just past The Caves. The lighthouse dates from 1894 and stands 30 meters (100 feet) above the sea. The site is seldom visited by travelers and is a more tranquil alternative to Rick's Café for a dip.

# Beaches

## ★ SEVEN-MILE BEACH

Jamaica's longest beach, **Seven-Mile Beach** is no longer the undisturbed fishing spot it was in the 1960s, but there are plenty of benefits that have come as a result of the unbridled development of the last 30 years. The sand remains beautifully golden, and the water remains crystal clear. A bar is never more than arm's length away, and every kind of water sport is offered by determined captains and their countless freelance promoters. Expect come-ons from all manner of peddler and hustler until your face becomes known and your reaction time to these calls for attention slows to island speed. The northern end of the beach is cordoned off by security in front of the all-inclusive resorts, while at the southern end the Negril River forms a natural border by the fishing village and craft market. Also on the southern end of Seven-Mile Beach

Seven-Mile Beach

is Norman Manley Sea Park Beach, where dances and daytime events are often held.

## LONG BAY BEACH PARK

**Long Bay Beach Park** (tel. 876/957 3159, or 876/957-5260, longbaybeachpark@udcja.com, 9am-5pm daily, US$3 adult, US$1 children 4-11) is found just past Cosmos towards the northern end of Seven-Mile Beach, where the unspoiled coastline is dotted with sea grape trees providing ample shade and lifeguards keep watch. The four-hectare Long Bay Beach Park I lies just south of the two-hectare Long Bay Beach Park II.

## BLOODY BAY

**Bloody Bay** is located just north of the piece of land jutting out toward Booby Cay that is home to Hedonism II, Point Village, and Royalton Negril. All-inclusive resorts dominate the waterfront, beginning with Royalton at the southern end, then Couples Negril, Sunset at the Palms, and two Riu properties to the north. The beach on Bloody Bay is accessible to nonguests at several points along the road, most easily just past the fenced-off private beach reserved for guests of Sunset at the Palms. Here you can buy lobster and fish at the **Office of Nature** (11am-sunset daily, US$10-30) or hire **Ackee** (Roydel Reid, cell tel. 876/868-7312) for snorkeling excursions (1.5 hours, 2-person minimum, US$25 pp) and glass-bottomed boat tours.

# Sports and Recreation

## WATER SPORTS
### Diving
**Dream Team Divers** (Sunset on the Cliffs, tel. 876/957-0054 or 876/831-0435, info@ dreamteamdiversjamaica.com, www.dream-teamdiversjamaica.com, 8am-4pm daily) has English- and German-speaking dive instructors. Master Instructor Ken Brown ran every dive shop in town since he landed in Negril in 1991 and finally opened his own shop in 2008. Dream Team offers free pickup and drop-off from any lodging in Negril. The outfit sets itself apart by visiting dolphin dive sites and locations not visited by others. Rates range from the Discover Scuba intro course (US$80) to dive master certification (US$600). Certified divers can rent equipment (US$5 per dive) and suits (US$6) and tank up (from US$40).

**Sun Divers** (Travelers Beach Resort, tel. 876/405-6872, seabossdivers@yahoo.com, www.sundiversnegril.com, US$55, US$65 with equipment, 2-tank dive US$100) offers a great intro class for beginners lasting about three hours with classroom and pool time and one open-water dive. The dive outfit is owned by Christian Rance, who also runs Jamaica Scuba Divers in Runaway Bay.

### Snorkeling
**Captain Junior's Glass Bottom Boat Tours** (cell tel. 876/849-2301, juniorkir-lew@gmail.com, US$30 pp) takes guests on a clean boat on snorkel trips to reefs about 15 minutes offshore or along the coast. Junior parks his boat next to Negril Palms Hotel on Norman Manley Boulevard, but he can pick you up from your hotel anywhere along Seven-Mile Beach.

### Parasailing
**Premium Water Sports** (Norman Manley Blvd., next to Footprints, tel. 876/957-3928, owner Trevor Forbes cell tel. 876/383-2906, premiumairparasail@hotmail.com, www.pre-miumparasailjamaica.com) offers parasailing (8-10 minutes in the air US$60 single, US$100 double, US$150 triple), tubing (10-15 minutes US$30 pp) and glass-bottom boat tours (US$25, US$30 with snorkeling gear).

**Negril Treehouse** has a water sports center offering parasailing (US$40), Jet Skis (US$50 per half hour), and fishing trips (US$150 up to 4 people).

## Fishing

The waters just off Negril's shoreline are severely overfished, with very low counts found in surveys conducted by the Negril Area Environmental Protection Trust. Nevertheless, a bit farther offshore in deeper waters it's possible to catch wahoo, tuna, mahimahi, and even marlin.

**Stanley's Deep Sea Fishing** (tel. 876/957-6341, cell tel. 876/818-6363, deepseafishing@cwjamaica.com, www.stanleysdeepseafishing.com) is a professional trolling outfit run by Captain Stanley Carvalho offering a good mix of options that include half-day (US$500), three-quarterday (US$750), and full-day trips (US$1,000) for up to four people. Up to eight passengers (US$50-100 per additional person) can participate. Stanley's also offers the option of charter sharing on four-hour half-day excursions, where individuals can team up with others to fill the boat (US$125 pp) rather than charter exclusively. Transport from anywhere in Negril to the boat is included. Billfish are tagged and released, but other fish can be taken for dinner.

## Kool Runnings Waterpark

**Kool Runnings Waterpark** (tel. 876/957-5400, info@koolrunnings.com, www.koolrunnings.com, 11am-5:30pm Tues.-Sun. May 21-Aug., over 122 cm/4 feet tall US$25, under 122 cm/4 feet US$19, free under age 3) is a water park with several slides, a wave pool, a lazy river for gentle tubing, and a kiddie pool. It's located across from Sensatori Hotel. Three restaurants serve Jamaican dishes (US$6) and a juice bar serves natural smoothies. Outside food is not permitted.

The Adventure activities at the park include the **Kool Kanoe Adventure** (US$48 for one or two), which takes visitors on a guided tour of the Great Morass, Jamaica's largest wetland

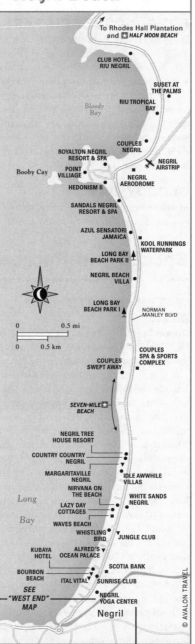

area, located in the water park's back yard. Visitors share a large inflatable "kanoe" to paddle a guided tour through the canals of the morass. **Jamboo Rafting** (US$48 single or double) is similar but on a bamboo raft. Those favoring a more independent experience can opt for the **Kayaking Adventure** (US$20 double) through the morass. You are likely to encounter yellow snakes, land crabs, mongooses, turtles, and birds.

With a 2,500-person capacity, the water park regularly hosts events that include wild parties during Emancipation-Independence celebrations in early August. The in-house DJ provides entertainment throughout the season, and there are Soldier Crab Derbies, allowing visitors to bet on the winners, and a snake show as well as **Paintball** (US$25), **Laser Tag** (US$20), and **Go-Kart Racing** (3 minutes US$8).

## HORSEBACK RIDING

**Rhodes Beach Resort** (tel. 876/957-6422 or cell tel. 876/431-6322, info@rhodesresort.com, www.rhodesresort.com) has good horseback riding (US$70, under age 12 US$35) that takes riders through the coconut groves, mangrove swamp with crocodiles, up the hill for a panoramic view of Negril, and back to the beach.

The resort is five minutes northeast of Negril toward Montego Bay.

**Reggae Horseback Riding** (contact Paul Washington, cell tel. 876/881-6917, paul@reggaehorsebackriding.com, www.reggae-horsebackriding.com, 1 hour US$60 pp, 2 hours US$80, ages 6-10 US$50, including transportation from Negril) based at Eldin Washington Ranch on the main road from Negril to Savanna-la-Mar, features horseback riding on a 365-hectare (900-acre) farm populated by peacocks, ostriches, donkeys, and goats. Schedule a tour with up to 15 riders. The two-hour ride ends on a 1.6-kilometer (1-mile) stretch of private beach.

**Chukka's Horseback Ride 'N' Swim** (tel. 876/953-5619, montegobay@chukkacaribbean.com, US$73) in Sandy Bay, Hanover, offers two-hour rides through forest and along the shore before swimming on horseback. Remember to bring a change of clothes, and a waterproof camera if you don't want to buy photos from Chukka. The Sandy Bay location also offers two-hour ATV tours (over age 15, US$115 pp) and dune buggy tours (over age 15 to drive, US$130 single, US$230 double). Canopy zipline tours (US$79), river tubing (US$65), and kayaking (US70) are

Reggae Horseback Riding

staged from Chukka's Montpelier location in St. James, about 45 minutes from Sandy Bay.

**Paradise Park** (tel. 876/955-2675, ehaclarke@gmail.com, US$5 admission, US$40 horseback riding) is one of the best places in Jamaica for down-to-earth small-group (up to 10 at a time) rides on an expansive seaside ranch a few kilometers east of Savanna-la-Mar in Ferris Cross. Riders are led through beautiful countryside to a river park and private beach on an hour-and-a-half loop. The river park area has BBQ grills and tables, ideal for a picnic and refreshing dip.

## GOLF

**Negril Hills Golf Club** (Sheffield, east of the roundabout along the A2, tel. 876/957-4638, www.negrilhillsgolfclub.com, 7:30am-3pm daily) has reasonable rates for nonmembers on a quiet course. Greens fees are for 9 holes (US$28.75) or 18 holes (US$57.50), and carts (US$17.25-34.50), caddies (US$7-14), and clubs (US$18-40) are available.

# Entertainment and Events

The great thing about Negril is that no matter the season, you can forget what day of the week it is in a hurry. Weekends remain going-out nights, and important acts that draw large Jamaican audiences generally perform on Friday or Saturday, but big artists also perform Monday, Wednesday, and Thursday nights. Because Negril is so small, the handful of clubs that monopolize the regular live entertainment market have made a tacit pact where each takes a night or two of the week, so that the main clubs are guaranteed a weekly following, and it's easy to know where to go on any particular evening.

## NIGHTLIFE
### Bars and Venues

Negril has an overwhelming number of bars and grills. This section covers establishments recommended as nightlife spots rather than for food.

**The Jungle** (Norman Manley Blvd., tel. 876/954-4005 or cell tel. 876/997-5750, thejunglenegriljamaica@gmail.com, www.the-jungle-negril.com) is Negril's only off-the-water club, located in an old bank toward the middle of the beach on the morass side of Norman Manley Boulevard. It is generally only open two nights a week, Thursday Ladies Night (US$10, women free before midnight) and Inclusive Saturdays (US$15), when patrons can opt to upgrade to top-shelf spirits (US$30).

**Margaritaville** (Norman Manley Blvd., tel. 876/957-4467, www.margaritavillecaribbean.com) hosts a beach party (5pm-9pm Wed.) and a drinks-inclusive night (10pm-2am Fri., US$55) with complimentary round-trip transportation from any hotel in Negril. Margaritaville has been a venue for spring-break parties for a number of years and is one of the most successful bar chains on the island; the Jimmy Buffet franchise also has locations in Montego Bay and Ochi.

**Juju Tours** (tel. 876/957-0767, 876/789-4309, JuJuTours@gmail.com, www.jujutours.com), led by American expat Angela Eastwick, operates under the tag line, "Don't Be Such a Tourist!", offering chaperoned nightlife excursions with its "Negril After Dark" tour and a host of other activities to fill the days in Negril and beyond with off-the-beaten path adventures.

## Live Music
**Roots Bamboo Beach Resort** (Norman Manley Blvd., tel. 876/957-4479, denise.plummer64@hotmail.com, www.rootsbamboobeach.com) is run by Denise and Jerome Plummer, the children of the late Ted Plummer. It's been in business since 1979, when Ted bought the property and constructed bamboo bungalows. When Hurricane Gilbert destroyed the bungalows in 1988, he built the current concrete-and-wood

# West End

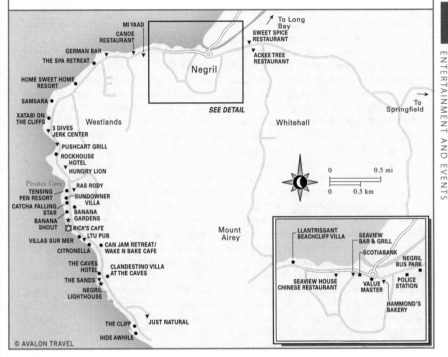

houses. Care should be taken to secure your belongings if you stay here: Security has been an issue, as the bar hosts live music a few nights per week and nonguests flood the property. Live performances are typically on Monday and Wednesday. The Wednesday shows have featured some of Jamaica's top musicians, from Freddie McGregor to Luciano and the late John Holt.

**Bourbon Beach** (Norman Manley Blvd., tel. 876/957-4432, info@bourbonbeach-jamaica.com, www.bourbonbeachnegril.com) took over from Debuss and is managed by Jimmy Morrell. Monday, Tuesday, and Saturday nights feature up-and-coming acts from all over Jamaica. Bounty Killa and Marcia Griffiths are among the internationally acclaimed artists to recently grace the stage. Bourbon Beach serves the best jerk on the beach from mid-morning until 2am. Nine rooms with queen beds are available.

**Alfred's Ocean Palace** (Norman Manley Blvd., tel. 876/957-4669 or 876/957-4375, info@alfreds.com, www.alfreds.com) has live music Sunday, Tuesday, and Friday featuring predominantly local acts and some bigger names. The beach bar and restaurant (8am-10:30pm daily high season, 8am-9pm low season, US$10-15) serves Jamaican and international cuisine including chicken, shrimp, and fish dishes. Alfred's also has eight double and triple rooms (US$60).

**No Name Bar** (West End Rd., cell tel. 876/287-0667) occasionally hosts live music events.

## FESTIVALS AND EVENTS

The weekends around Emancipation Day (Aug. 1) and Independence Day (Aug. 6) bring party animals to Negril en masse for Dream

Weekend (www.jamaicadreamweekend. com), a series of parties typically sponsored by a brewery or spirits brand held over the course of several days. Promoters from "yaad" (home) and abroad draw partygoers from near and far to indulge in booze, ganja, general debauchery, and a few stage shows. It's the only time of year when Negril is almost completely taken over by Jamaicans, who make spring breakers appear tame in comparison.

The **Reggae Marathon, Half Marathon, and 10K** (race director Alfred "Frano" Francis, tel. 876/922-8677, racedirector@reggaemarathon.com, marketing director Diane Ellis, frandan@cwjamaica.com, www.reggaemarathon.com) held the first Saturday in December, is a popular event drawing locals and expats from abroad and "a yaad" for a race on a mostly flat IAAF-certified route starting at Long Bay Beach Park on Seven-Mile Beach. Registrations and package pick-up begins on Thursday, continuing on Friday with a pasta party and village bash. Races start at dawn Saturday, with a ceremony later in the day. Prizes total US$10,000. You must be age 18 to run the marathon (US$120) and at least age 10 for the 10K (US$85). Fees are lower if you register earlier.

The **Rastafari Rootz Fest** was quick to celebrate the Jamaican government's move to decriminalize ganja by hosting the first **Cannibus Cup Jamaica** (www.cannabiscup.com/jamaica) at Long Bay Beach Park I in December 2015. The event is now an annual affair in December, bringing friendly competitiveness, crafts and wares, and great music to Bloody Bay Beach.

**Stepping High Festival** (Cayenne Beach, tel. 876/957-0186, cell tel. 876/296-1719 or 876/549-5606, negrilsteppinghigh@yahoo. com, www.steppinghighfestival.com), held

the first weekend in March, is a celebration of Rastafarian culture aimed at building the ganja nation, featuring the sacred herb in great bounty, ital food, the requisite irie music and crafts.

**Painted Negril** (Cayenne Beach, Norman Manley Blvd., info@blackgoldjamaica.com, www.blackgoldjamaica.com, tel. 876/528-5527), held annually on the last Saturday in June, was launched in 2010 by Glenton Rowe with high-energy soca, EDM, and dancehall music. Paint, water, and debauchery add to the music.

**Miami Linkup** (contact Robert "Dozer" Williams, U.S. tel. 954/479-0202, tel. 876/815-2198, rebeltsound@gmail.com, www.rebeltsound.com), an event promotions group, hosts an annual spring break party around the second weekend in March that draws large crowds to a stage show brimming with the hottest dancehall and reggae artists.

**Rotary Club of Negril Donkey Races** (held at Wavz Entertainment Centre, organized by Negril Rotary Club, contact Richard Warren, cell tel. 876/437-3735, www.rotarynegril.com, US$6) is a charity event held the second Sunday in February each year to finance community projects. Local organizations sponsor 25 donkeys dressed to compete in a number of categories for trophies and prizes. The family-friendly fun day features local food vendors and games.

**Western Consciousness** (contact promoter Worrel King, cell tel. 876/849-8426 or 876/821-8853, kingofkingspro@hotmail.com, www.westernconsciousness.com) is a not-to-be-missed reggae show, usually annually in April or May, for fans of conscious roots music put on by Kings Promotions. The last iteration was staged at Paradise Park on the outskirts of Savanna-la-Mar.

# Shopping

## CRAFTS

**One Stop Branzo Wood Sculptures** (cell tel. 876/867-4246, 8am-8pm daily), run by Abdel, aka Branzo, can be found on the beachfront at Wavz Entertainment Centre. Branzo is one of the most talented wood carvers around and also sells the work of other woodworkers in his little shop.

**Negril Crafts Market** (between Norman Manley Sea Park and the Negril River) has a wide variety of crafts, some better and more authentic than others. Sadly, an increasing proportion of the products on sale are made in China rather than locally produced.

**Errol Allen** (cell tel. 876/385-5399) is a talented local artist who makes unique silhouette sculptures and oil paintings. Allen's sculptures can be seen on the grounds of Whistling Bird.

**Rutland Point Craft Centre** is located next to the aerodrome just before the Petcom gas station, heading northeast toward Montego Bay.

**Kosmic Gift Shop & Boutique** (located on the beach next to Cosmos, Norman Manley Blvd., tel. 876/957-3940) has a mix of Rasta knit hats and "Jamaica No Problem" T-shirts among a plethora of crafts and trinkets.

## APPAREL

**Time Square Mall Plaza** (tel. 876/957-9263, 9pm-7pm daily, Mon.-Sat.) is located on Norman Manley Boulevard across from Bourbon Beach. The duty-free shopping center has jewelry, Cuban cigars, crafts, liquor, watches, and trinkets.

**A Fi Wi Plaza,** next to Scotia Bank by the roundabout, has crafts and T-shirts from Sun Island.

Branzo is among Negril's foremost wood carvers.

# Food

## SEVEN-MILE BEACH
### Breakfast and Cafés

★ **Sunrise Club** (tel. 876/957-4293, breakfast served 8am-noon daily) has a wide variety of welcome options to start the day off right, from omelets or eggs and bacon to Jamaican breakfast (ackee and salt fish, callaloo and fried dumpling), crepes, pancakes, French toast and fresh squeezed orange juice and proper Italian coffee made in a quality espresso machine.

**Hammond's Bakery** (at the roundabout, tel. 876/957-4734, 8am-6pm Mon.-Sat., US$3-10) serves patties, cakes, and deli sandwiches.

### Jerk and Jamaican

**Best in the West** (Norman Manley Blvd., across from Idle Awhile, contact owner Devon James, cell tel. 876/383-3981, 10:30am-11pm daily) is the most dependable spot on the beach for jerk chicken (US$7/quarter lb., US$12/half) and pork (US$9 half lb), served with bread and salad. It has a small seating area roadside and a bar.

**Rainbow Arch** (between Charela Inn and White Sands, contact Joy James, cell tel. 876/423-6760, tel. 876/957-4745, 10am-10pm daily, US$10-30) serves curry shrimp and curry goat, as well as fish and lobster dishes. The James family is one of oldest in Negril.

★ **Niah's Patties** (Wavz Entertainment Centre, tel. 876/399-6323, 10am-8pm daily Dec. 15-May 15, US$5-10) has been making the best patties in Negril, and perhaps all of Jamaica, since 2005. Filling choices include Italian pizza, fish, red bean, potato, chicken, vegetable, and lobster.

**Sonia's** (across from Roots Bamboo, cell tel. 876/377-7069, 8am-9pm daily, US$5-10) is well recognized for her delicious Jamaican cuisine and homemade patties.

★ **Sweet Spice** (Whitehall Rd., tel. 876/957-4621, 8:30am-10:30pm daily, US$5-25) is the best place along the main road heading toward Savanna-la-Mar for typical Jamaican fare at local prices. It is popular with locals for real-world value in a town where prices are usually on par with U.S. cities. Dishes like fried chicken, coconut curry,

Niah makes the best patties in Negril.

or escoveitch fish, conch, and lobster are representative of Jamaica's traditional cuisine.

**Ackee Tree Restaurant** (Whitehall Road, across from the Texaco station, cell tel. 876/871-2524, 8am-10pm daily, US$5-8) serves the best ital stew and local dishes and is frequented by artists in the know. Noel "Wall" Masters runs the joint.

★ **Cosmos Seafood Restaurant and Bar** (next door to Beaches Negril, tel. 876/957-4330, 9am-10pm daily, US$5-43) serves excellent Jamaican seafood dishes, including conch soup, shrimp, and fried fish—in addition to other local dishes like curry goat, stewed pork, fried chicken, and oxtail. The beach out front is wide and good for swimming. A mixed crowd weighted toward locals is testament to the reasonable prices and tasty Jamaican home-style cooking.

**Kuyaba** (tel. 876/957-4318, 7am-11pm daily, US$12-27) has consistently decent, but pricey, international and Jamaican fusion cuisine, including pork kebab, brown stew conch, peppered steak, and seafood linguine lobster for main courses.

**The Boat Bar** (between Rondel Village and Mariposa, tel. 876/957-4746, 8am-10pm daily, US$10-30) is a favorite that has been serving chicken, fish, shrimp, goat, pork, and steak since 1983. The garlic lobster gets rave reviews. Bunny and Angie are the proprietors.

## International

**Kenny's Italian Café** (Norman Manley Blvd., tel. 876/957-4032, kennykjohnson@ yahoo.com, 7am-2am daily) launched in 2010, giving Luca's down the road some heated competition. The setup is inviting with bamboo thatch ceilings, hanging lanterns and padded stools with seating for up to 200. A DJ spins mostly house music nightly. Complimentary appetizers are offered 4pm-7pm daily. The menu is Kenny's take on Italian, absorbed from his wife and trips to the motherland, with salads, pasta dishes, seafood, and pizza. Entrees range from US$9 for spaghetti with olive oil to $55 for a mixed seafood platter with whole lobster, fish fillets, calamari, and shrimp.

## Fine Dining

★ **The Lobster House** (Sunrise Club, beside Coral Seas Garden, tel. 876/957-4293, noon-11pm daily), owned and operated by Italian expat Luca, serves Italian and Jamaican fare such as pasta with tomato sauce (US$8), gnocchi (US$12), wood-fired pizza (US$10-16), and grilled lobster (US$26). Wines are about US$24-26, and great coffee is served.

**Chill Awhile** (Idle Awhile Resort, tel. 876/957-3303, 7am-9pm daily) offers lounge chairs and wireless Internet free to its customers. The charming beachfront deck restaurant serves a variety of light food items for lunch, including club sandwiches, burgers, fish-and-chips (US$6-8), and jerk chicken (US$10). For dinner, international and Jamaican-style entrées range from grilled chicken breast with peanut or Jamaican sauce (US$8.50) and coconut-breaded snapper with tartar sauce (US$12.50) to lobster thermidor (US$23.50) or a seafood platter with grilled lobster and coconut shrimp (US$25). There is also a full bar next to the restaurant.

# WEST END
## Breakfast and Cafés

**Canjam Wake N Bake Café** (West End Rd., across from Citronella, cell tel. 876/536-6642, 7:30am-3pm during high season, US$10-15, ganja edibles only available mid-April-Sept.) serves fresh fruit juices and breakfast items you can depend on, as well as famous ganja cookies that pack a punch far beyond their weight. Located just past Rick's Café.

**Just Natural** (Hylton Avenue, past lighthouse off West End Rd., tel. 876/957-0235 or cell tel. 876/354-4287, 8am-8:30pm Mon.-Sat., 8am-6pm Sun. in low season, closes at 9pm in high season from late November-April, US$6-30) serves breakfast, lunch, and dinner with items like callaloo or ackee omelets and fresh juices. Vegetarian dishes and seafood items are served for lunch and dinner. Phone service is unreliable, so clients are advised to simply "set out an' reach," or show up assuming it's open during regular business hours.

## Jerk and Jamaican

★ **Seaview Bar & Grill** (West End Rd., around the bend from Scotia Bank, tel. 876/957-9199, 4pm-2:30am daily), run by Anthony "Tony Montana" Dawson, does the best steam roast conch (US$4) in Jamaica, as well as steam roast fish (US$12), conch soup (US$2), and jerk or fried jerk chicken (US$5), among other local favorites.

**Canoe Beach Bar & Grill** (across from MX3, tel. 876/957-4814, Kirby's cell tel. 876/878-5893, canoebeachbar@gmail. com, 7am-10:30pm daily, US$10-30) serves Jamaican breakfast, pancakes, french toast, and eggs to order. Chicken, shrimp, lobster, and vegetarian fare are served for lunch and dinner in a dining room overlooking the beach.

**3 Dives Jerk Centre** (contact owner Lloydie, tel. 876/957-0845 or 876/782-9990, noon-midnight daily) offers a quarter chicken with bread (US$3.50) or with rice-and-peas and vegetables (US$4.50), half chicken with rice-and-peas and veggies (US$8), steamed or curried shrimp (US$17), and grilled lobster (US$34). This is *the* place to get jerk on the West End. Located right on the cliffs, the open-air restaurant has a nice outdoor barbecue vibe.

★ **Pushcart Restaurant and Rum Bar** (West End Rd., next door to Rockhouse, tel. 876/957-4373, www.rockhousehotel.com, 3pm-10pm daily, US$10-30) serves entrées including peppered shrimp, homemade jerk sausage, curry goat, and oxtail. Opened in 2009, Pushcart brings Jamaican street food to one of the West End's most exclusive resort enclaves. The menu is inspired by the pushcarts used by Jamaican street vendors across the island, selling produce or cooked food in open-air markets. A local mento band provides live entertainment several nights during the week. Pushcart offers casual dining in a breathtaking cliff-side setting made famous in the films *20,000 Leagues Under the Sea* and the Steve McQueen classic *Papillon.* Pushcart has great spots for cliff-jumping with less crowds.

**The Sands Bar** (tel. 876/957-0270, tel. 876/618-1081, 4pm-7pm Wed. and Fri.-Mon.) is one of the best bars for sunset cliff jumping away from the gawking crowds that convene at nearby Rick's Café each evening. Located inside The Caves, an exclusive boutique resort operated by Chris Blackwell's Island Outpost, a jerk pan is fired up each afternoon when nonguests are welcome to enjoy the 12-meter (40-foot) jump and the best view of Negril's lighthouse, right next door.

**Blue Mahoe Restaurant** (Negril Spa Retreat, West End Rd., cell tel. 876/399-3772, info@thespajamaic.com) is located at Negril Spa Retreat but welcomes non-guests and guests alike, serving breakfast, lunch, and dinner, seven days a week. The menu features a mix of Jamaica-inspired dishes like jerk fish tacos and jerk chicken pesto, as well as more traditional Jamaican fare like braised oxtails and beans, curried chicken, and curried goat. International standards include burgers, sandwiches and pizzas. The large indoor dining area extends outside onto the cliffs.

## International

**Seaview House Chinese Restaurant** (Cotton Tree Place, between Vendors' Plaza and the post office, tel. 876/957-4925, 10am-10pm daily) has decent Chinese food, with vegetable dishes (US$7-10), chicken (US$10), seafood (US$18), and roast duck and lobster variations (US$27).

**German Bar** (Mary's Bay Boathouse, West End Rd., cell tel. 876/471-6493, www.german-bar.com, 1pm-9:30pm Tues.-Sun.) safely claims its place as the only German restaurant in Jamaica, serving dishes like bratwurst, schnitzel and ham hock with sauerkraut in addition to pizza and sandwiches.

**No Name Bar** (West End Rd., cell tel. 876/287-0667, US$8-20) serves wood-fired pizza as well as jerk in an open-air waterfront bar and dining area. Live music is typically performed Tuesday evenings.

**Ahhh Bees** (West End Rd., cell tel. 876/871-5106), run by Aubie, serves homemade burgers in Negril in addition to his trademark breadfruit smoothies.

**LTU Pub & Restaurant** (tel. 876/957-0382, 7am-11pm daily, US$10-30) has good Jamaican and international food in a laidback setting perched on the cliffs. Specialties include crab quesadilla, stuffed jalapeño, and crab ball appetizers, plus schnitzel, surf-and-turf, pasta, chicken, and seafood dishes like grilled salmon and the snapper papaya boat. The name is taken from the German airline Lufthansa, of which founder Walter Bigge was a shareholder. Bigge was killed in 1992 and the restaurant closed until the present owner, Bill Williams, bought the place around 2000. Free Wi-Fi is available for customers.

Food and beer at **Rick's Café** (tel. 876/957-0380, noon-10pm daily, US$18-28) is mediocre and outrageously expensive, but nobody seems to mind. Choices include chicken, shrimp, fish, and lobster with rice-and-peas, French fries, or sweet potato sides; a beer costs US$5.

## Fine Dining

★ **Zest Restaurant** (tel. 876/632-0919, 7am-10pm daily), located at The Cliff past the lighthouse on West End Rd., showcases the creative hand of internationally acclaimed executive chef Cindy Hutson. Try singular starters like the shrimp ceviche with fried plantain and bean dip or mains like sautéed snapper with a side of cashew and jackfruit spiced rice. The dining area is split between a chic interior and clifftop al fresco, with crashing waves as a soundtrack. Reservations are required for guests not staying on property.

**The Hungry Lion** (West End, tel. 876/957-4486, 4pm-10:30pm daily Nov.-Sept., US$10-30), owned by Bertram Saulter, who also owns The Caves, is an excellent dinner spot with healthy-size entrées. The lobster burritos are delicious. The pleasant ambiance features soft reggae, intricate latticework, and mellow tones. It is good value for the money, and the drink special—the Lion Heart, made with mango, ginger, and rum—is not to be missed.

## Vegetarian

**Ras Rody Organics** (across from Tensing Pen, cell tel. 876/283-1421, truelove@gmail.com, 10am-6pm daily) is an ital roadside food shop run by Shadrock Whitter that specializes in red pea soup (US$3-10) and other vegetarian specialties of the day such as steam vegetables.

**Royal Kitchen** (just before Samsara, contact chef Errold Chambers, cell tel. 876/287-0549, by reservation only, US$5-8) is one of the best spots in Negril for ital vegetarian food, the signature dish being broad bean stew, veggie chunks, and tofu. Fresh juices (US$3) like pumpkin punch, beet, and cucumber as well as natural ginger beer accompany the meal.

# Accommodations

Negril has something for everyone when it comes to finding the ideal place to stay, from couples-only all-inclusive resorts to hip inexpensive independent cottages by the sea and exclusive villas. Low-season and high-season rates apply here, as at other tourism centers on the island. Some establishments increase rates in the middle of the low season for special events like Independence weekend at the beginning of August, when Jamaicans from "yaad" and abroad flock for a torrent of nonstop parties that last for days on end.

Accommodations are listed geographically from Negril's roundabout, which distinguishes properties on Norman Manley Boulevard from those on West End Road. Within each price category, the accommodations are organized from north to south.

Seven-Mile Beach starts at the mouth of Negril Rover and stretches the length of Long Bay, which is separated from Bloody Bay by the outcropping of land that is home to Hedonism II, Point Village and the Royalton. A multitude of small hotels face the beach on Long Bay with the all-inclusive resorts concentrated to the northern end of Long Bay and facing Bloody Bay further north.

## SEVEN-MILE BEACH
### Under US$100

★ **Da Fabio** (Good Hope district, cell tel. 876/247-3125, info@dafabio.net, www.dafabio.net, US$70 d), Italian for "Fabio's Place," offers eight bedrooms with queen beds, mini fridges, and en suite baths in a house in the hills overlooking Seven-Mile Beach. Proprietor Fabio offers a package with breakfast and dinner and round-trip shuttle service to Seven-Mile Beach (US$35 pp). The house has a pool and Wi-Fi.

**Negril Yoga Centre** (tel. 876/957-4397, negrilyoga@cwjamaica.com, www.negrilyoga.com, US$30-75), also known as The Little Oasis, has simple, clean rooms with single and double beds. The center is tasteful and secure, with a decent restaurant that specializes in vegetarian food cooked to order. The property boasts, "There is no bar, no pool, and no dance club at the Centre, which keeps our prices low and our ambience low-key."

**Sunrise Club** (tel. 876/957-4293, cell tel. 876/422-1818, info@sunriseclub.com, www.sunriseclub.com, from US$90) is a collection of 14 well-appointed rooms with wood furnishings, A/C safes, private verandas and bathrooms. B&B and all-inclusive plans are available. The full service on-site restaurant serves the best breakfast and Italian dishes in Negril.

**White Sands** (tel. 876/957-4291 or U.S. tel. 305/503-9074, info@whitesandsnegril.com, www.whitesandsnegril.com, from US$60 low season, US$78 high season) is a no frills hotel with five categories of rooms on either side of Norman Manley Boulevard, all with mini fridges, air-conditioning, and small balconies or porches. The hotel has a bar and dining area beachfront with a TV. A four-bedroom villa sleeps up to eight on the morass side of the road with a full kitchen, a living area, and a private pool. One-bedroom apartments also have kitchens.

**Indika Negril** (Norman Manley Blvd., contact Bill Blauer, U.S. tel. 617/529-1534, info@indikanegril.com, www.indikanegril.com) has a spacious four-bedroom main building called Devon House that sleeps up to seven, and another large structure with three bedrooms called Dolton House that also sleeps seven, both priced at US$150 low season, US$225 high season. Also on the property is a self-contained cottage with a full kitchen and two beds (US$40 low season, US$60 high season), as well as two rustic cabins (US$30 low season, US$50 high season), each with two beds, a small fridge, a shower, and a standing fan. Dolton House bedrooms all have exterior entrances and can rent separately (US$50 low season, US$65 high season) and share the kitchen and living area. Airport transfers are offered by the caretaker, Devon (up to 4 people US$120 round-trip).

**Cortina's Cottage** (cell tel. 876/382-6384, www.carolynscaribbeancottages.com, US$100) is actually a studio apartment located in the Point Village complex at the end of Seven-Mile Beach. It's a good option for independent travelers. The apartment is tastefully decorated with plenty of curtains.

### US$100-250

**Kuyaba** (Norman Manley Blvd., tel. 876/957-4318 or 876/957-9815, kuyaba@cwjamaica.com, www.kuyaba.com) is one of the longest-running rental options on the beach and has developed into a handful of tasteful cottages. The more rustic cottages (US$56-64 low season, US$70-77 high season) hold true to Negril's original rustic hippie vibe, while newer, more elegant cottages (US$77-85 low season, US$97-106 high season) have been added in recent years. All cottages have ceiling fans, air-conditioning, and private baths with hot water. A restaurant on the property has good food.

★ **Country Country** (Norman Manley Blvd., tel. 876/957-4273, countrynegril@gmail.com, www.countryjamaica.com, US$140-155 low season, US$170-190 high season) has 26 cottages on the beach side of Norman Manley Boulevard, and two self-contained apartments on the morass side. Built in 2000, the cottages are well laid out in a lush garden setting that promotes quiet and privacy. Rooms have air-conditioning, flat-screen TVs with cable, spacious private baths with hot water, and porches. The superior and premium rooms are close to the beach. An expansion is in the works. Rates include breakfast, and Wi-Fi is available in the communal lounge by the office.

**Boardwalk Village** (Norman Manley Blvd., tel. 876/957-4633, cell tel. 876/878-4308, www.theboardwalkvillagenegril.com, from US$110 low season, from US$130 high season) is a hotel run by the Wallace Family, one of Negril's most prominent in the hospitality industry. The family also owns and operates Jungle Nightclub and Negril Escape on the cliffs. One-bedroom apartments have air-conditioning and modern kitchens featuring granite countertops.

★ **Idle Awhile Resort** (Norman Manley Blvd., tel. 877/243-5352 or 876/957-3302, USD 300/400 low season/high season per bedroom, plus 20% taxes and gratuity) offers one-, two-, three-, four-, and five-bedroom villas clustered around a central shared pool. The property was taken over by Jamaican hoteliers Lee and Jane Issa in 2015 and is managed by Jane's boutique hotel group. The property underwent upgrades before being reopened to grace Seven-Mile beach with a top-notch villa offering. The villas come with all the amenities of home, and then some, like king-size beds, Wi-Fi, billiards tables, butlers, chefs, and housekeepers. Security guards monitor the beachfront 24 hours a day, ensuring peaceful days in the sun, and serene nights to the sound of lapping waves.

## Villas

**Idle Awhile Villas** (U.S. tel. 800/621-1120, info@moondancevillas.com) has an assortment of one- to five-bedroom villas (US$600-1,500 low season, US$700-1,900 high season) and is centrally located, with 90 meters (300 feet) of private sand on Seven-Mile Beach. Moon Dance rates (4-night minimum) include a chef, a bartender, a housekeeper, security, Internet access, a private pool and jetted

an aerial view of Llantrisant Beachcliff Villa

tub, and airport transfers, with an unlimited food option (US$115 pp daily). Moon Dance is an ideal option for families and small groups.

**Llantrisant Beachcliff Villa** (U.S. tel. 305/321-7458, info@beachcliff.com, www.beachcliff.com, from US$576 low season, from US$768 high season) is a one-hectare (two-acre) beachfront estate with a quaint colonial cottage that harkens back to the good old days. The property juts into the sea just west of the roundabout with an uninterrupted view of Seven-Mile Beach. A grass tennis court and two private beaches make the property unique, as do the 50-foot veranda, enormous cotton trees, and the colonial-era double canopy beds in the two ground-level master suites. Upstairs, the attic is three rooms that share a bath, with a king on the southern end, a single in the middle, and two single beds on the northern side of the house overlooking the bay. A friendly and committed staff include housekeepers, a groundskeeper, and night watchmen.

**Negril Beach Villa** (tel. 876/957-3500, www.negrilbeachvilla.com, US$800 nightly, min. three nights) is a secluded three-bedroom villa with a private pool on 1.5 acres and 400-feet of beachfront facing Bloody Bay. Rooms have king beds, A/C, and private bathrooms.

## All-Inclusive Resorts

**Sandals Negril** (Long Bay, www.sandals.com, US$818-2,454, 65 percent discount for 3 nights or more) is a 222-room resort with exclusive butler service in its top room category, a Red Lane Spa, and two-story loft suites with spiral staircases. A pro sports complex offering racquetball, squash, and tennis, and there are two pools, whirlpool tubs, and a scuba certification pool. Swim-up river suites have stairs descending from the veranda doors into a lazy river with views to the sea, and plantation suites have private plunge pools, outdoor showers, and private balconies. Rooms have full amenities that include cable TV, air-conditioning, and en suite baths.

★ **Couples Swept Away** (U.S. tel. 800/ COUPLES—800/268-7537, tel. 876/957-4061, from US$413 d low season, US$602 d high season) is an exceptional all-inclusive located toward the northern end of Seven-Mile-Beach with a new wing on the south end of the compound that has a wet bar, a grill, and a tastefully decorated lounge. Couples Resorts Chairman Lee Issa can often be found on the property, checking in with his guests and making sure everything is running smoothly. The gym facilities and tennis courts are the best in Negril. Eight-hour day passes (US$100) allow nonguests access to everything on the property.

**Couples Negril** (U.S. tel. 800/ COUPLES—800/268-7537, tel. 876/957-5960, from US$408 d low season, US$590 d high season) is in Hanover at the northern end of Long Bay. For proximity to off-site activities and an easy walk to Negril's nightlife, Couples Swept Away is the better option. To get away from it all, including public beaches, Couples Negril is the better option.

★ **Sunset at the Palms** (US$385/600 low/high season per couple for treetop deluxe, US$620/895 low/high season for the one-bedroom Suite) is a boutique adults only (18+) all-inclusive property featuring cozy one-bedroom treetop deluxe bungalows and one-bedroom suites spread out across lush, well-manicured grounds. The food offering is a mix of buffet style and a la carte meals at Lotus Leaf restaurant, as well as the open-air demonstrative kitchen known as The Chef's Table, where the cooks flex their culinary muscles as they feature seasonal fresh ingredients.

Inside the bungalow-style cottages, the wooden furniture, Bali-esque detailing and plush bedding are inviting. Bathrooms are well appointed with his and her showerheads and high quality finishing. Balconies feature day beds with views of lush gardens and the protected wetlands area known as the Negril Morass.

Sunset at the Palms is set back from the sea on the opposite side of Norman Manley Boulevard, its private beach smack dab in the center of Bloody Bay, a two-minute walk from the lobby. A bar and grill on the beach ensure guests are well fed and watered, and a water sports center offers catamarans and windsurfing equipment. The property's tennis court and weight room are located on the morass side of the property, along with the swimming pool, heated whirlpool and lounge.

**Club Hotel Riu Negril** (tel. 876/957-5700, www.riu.com, from US$228) is a 420-room all-inclusive resort on Bloody Bay with a large main building and four two-story annexes. The resort has a gym, a jetted tub, and an over-18 sauna. Rooms have minibars, king or two double beds, and a balcony or terrace. Four restaurants offer à la carte and buffet options, with bars spread across the property. The resort has two hard-surface tennis courts, table tennis, volleyball, and a variety of water sports. The hotel has a computer room available for an additional charge and a free Wi-Fi zone. The Renova Spa offers a variety of massages and treatments for an additional charge.

**Hedonism II** (tel. 876/957-5200, www.superclubs.com, US$135-215 low season, US$175-285 high season) is the original and notorious all-inclusive resort at the northern end of Negril's Long Bay, with 280 rooms and 15 suites, all with tiled floors, air-conditioning, TVs, and, of course, mirrored ceilings. Many of the suites have private whirlpool tubs right on the beach. It's a great place for couples and singles looking to unwind and let go, and potentially do things they would never do at home. Repeat guests don't return for the food but rather the sexually charged atmosphere. Two private beaches, one nude, offer activities from water sports to volleyball and acrobatics. The main terrace dining area is complemented by Italian-inspired Pastafari, Japanese-inspired Munasan, and Reggae Café, as well as beach grills. Premium liquor is served at bars throughout the property, which also has a spa, a fitness center, and tennis court facilities. An underwater disco boasts "anything goes." Hedonism hosts theme weeks throughout the year; be sure to inquire when making a reservation if any will coincide with your stay.

# WEST END
## Under US$100

**Xtabi** (tel. 876/957-0121, fax 876/957-0827, xtabiresort@cwjamaica.com, www.xtabi-negril.com) is one of the most unpretentious and well-situated properties in Negril in terms of the price range and value for money. Economy rooms (US$49 low season, US$65 high season) have fans, spacious suites (US$59 low season, US$90 high season) have air-conditioning and TVs, and stylish cliff-top cottages (US$120 low season, US$210 high season) ensure there is something for every budget. The restaurant and bar, also on the cliffs, serve up some of the best lobster (US$25) in Negril, and the conch burger is highly acclaimed. Xtabi is the most unpretentious, well-situated hotel on the West End. The name Xtabi is Greek for "meeting place of the gods."

★ **Banana's Garden** (across West End Rd. from Rick's Café, tel. 876/957-0909, cell tel. 876/353-0007, bananasgarden@gmail.com, www.bananasgarden.com, US$85-135 low season, US$100-165 high season), owned and operated by Nicole Larson, is a tasteful retreat with five quaint self-contained cottages surrounded by lush vegetation. Each cottage has unique hand-carved wood detailing, ceiling fans, louvered windows, hot water, and kitchenettes, making the property ideal for those seeking independence and the modest back-to-basics vibe that put Negril on the map. The pool is beautiful. Rates include continental or Jamaican breakfast. Banana's Garden is ideal for small groups looking to book the entire property, for which discounts can be negotiated. The Solar Wellness Spa on the property offers massage and treatments.

## US$100-250
★ **Tensing Pen** (tel. 876/957-0387, tensingpen@cwjamaica.com, www.tensingpen.com, from US$145 low season, US$193 high season) is the West End's crown gem. Luxurious, thatch-roofed, bungalow-style cottages adorn

the cliffs above turquoise waters. The absence of TVs is deliberate, as is every other meticulous detail that makes it so hard to leave. The staff exhibits the epitome of Jamaican warmth and conspire to make guests feel a sense of belonging, treating guests with utmost attentiveness and regard for minute details, from hibiscus flowers on your pillow to cool water at the bedside. A 30-foot saltwater infinity pool was recently installed in front of the dining area, fed by a rock fountain.

**Catcha Falling Star** (tel. 876/957-0390, stay@catchajamaica.com, www.catchajamaica.com, US$95-175 low season, US$120-250 high season) has five one-bedroom cottages, two two-bedroom cottages, and a thatch-roofed building on the cliffs with six units. With its cliff-top grounds well maintained with neat walkways and verdant gardens, this is one of the choice properties on the West End.

**Banana Shout** (tel. 876/957-0384, cell tel. 876/350-7272, reservations@bananashoutresort.com, www.bananashoutresort.com, US$80-100 low season, US$150-200 high season) is owned by Milo Gallico, named after the Mark Conklin novel of the same name about Jamaica. It is beautifully decorated and on one of the West End's most gorgeous stretches of cliffs. Four one- and two-bedroom cottages

adorn the cliffs with cozy furniture and an artsy vibe. A live band performs classic reggae covers every evening at Rick's Café next door for an earful of music to set the mood for sunset.

**Jackie's on the Reef** (tel. 876/957-4997 or 718/469-2785, jackiesonthereef@rcn.com, www.jackiesonthereef.com, US$125 d low season, US$150 d high season) is the place to go for a nature, yoga, or tai chi retreat. The rates include morning activity sessions and are a great value. The hotel is one of the farthest out along West End Road, where there's less development and it's easy to meditate undisturbed.

**The Westender Inn** (tel. 876/957-4991, U.S. tel. 800/223-3786, cell tel. 876/473-8172, westenderinn@yahoo.com, www.westender-inn.com, US$90-199) is a low-key lodging a bit farther out from Jackie's, deep on the West End. Rooms are comfortable with a variety of bed sizes, and layouts as studios, one-bedrooms, and ocean-side suites. By the main parking area the hotel has a raised pool and a deck with a restaurant and a bar where non-guests are welcome.

## Over US$250
**The Spa Retreat** (cell tel. 876/399-3772, info@thespajamaica.com, www.

Tensing Pen

thespajamaica.com, from US$250) is a luxurious adults-only boutique on the cliffs with expert pampering and great food at the Blue Mahoe Restaurant. The 18 rooms are comfortably dispersed along cut stone paths atop the cliffs on Negril's West End, all with air-conditioning, fridges, safes, Wi-Fi, Serta mattresses, room service, and cell phones. Garden Stone Cottages and Rooftop Stone Cottages have king beds and sleep up to four; Seaside Stone Cottages and Bridal Suites accommodate two on queens or kings. Best known for its outstanding Spa, treatments include manicures (US$45), pedicures (US$65), organic facial treatments (US$99-115), body wraps (US$110), body scrubs (US$110), reflexology (US$95), and massage (US$95-145). Couples massage classes (US$250) are offered.

**Rockhouse** (tel. 876/957-4373, fax 876/957-0557, info@rockhousehotel.com, www.rockhousehotel.com) is a favorite for hip New York weekenders looking to get away in style. The hotel is always full, testament to good marketing, quality service, well-maintained grounds, and competent management. The beautiful villas (US$295-350 low season, US$355-425 high season) are perched on the cliffs with views out to sea. The 34 rooms include standards (US$125 low season, US$160 high season) and studios (US$150 low season, US$185 high season). The restaurant has a nice evening ambience, and the coconut-battered shrimp are a must. The pool is notable for its assimilation with the cliffs. The eight-room **Rockhouse Spa** offers massages, wraps, scrubs and holistic treatments using all-natural local ingredients in two cliff-side treatment cabanas.

Upscale ★ **The Caves** (West End Rd., tel. 876/957-0270, tel. 876/618-1081, reservations@islandoutpost.com, www.islandoutpost.com) has Negril's best upscale yet rootsy vibe. Thatch-roofed, contoured cottages are seamlessly integrated with the cliffs. Conducive to spiritual relaxation, the hotel has a sophisticated African motif, soft music, and hot tubs carved into the cliffs. You can vault from the cliffs into the crystal-clear water up to 18

meters (60 feet) below. Everywhere you turn there are platforms for sunbathing or for diving. At night, a large grotto just above water level is strewn with flowers and set up as the most romantic dining room imaginable, lit with hundreds of candles.

Bertram and the late Greer-Ann Saulter teamed up with former Island Records boss Chris Blackwell to create their idea of paradise at The Caves. The rooms are all unique, with king beds, African batik pillow covers, classic louvered windows, and well-appointed baths. Love seats are nestled into the surroundings. The cottages are decorated with an assortment of Jamaican carvings and paintings. Every detail is consciously designed to put guests in relaxed mode—to the point of entrancement. Open bars (some staffed, some self-serve) dot the property, and a snack bar has gourmet food ready whenever you're hungry.

Rooms range from one-bedroom suites (US$615 low season, US$800 high season) to two-bedroom cottages (US$720 low season, US$915 high season). Perhaps the nicest two-bedroom cottage, Moon Shadow, is separated from the rest by The Sands bar, open to nonguests for sunset and featuring a balcony overlooking the lighthouse and an azure cove below. All suites have kings, while the two-bedroom cottages have queens downstairs.

★ **The Cliff** (www.thecliffjamaica.com, US$325 low season, US$500 high season) is a secluded upscale boutique hotel and villa complex just past Negril's lighthouse. The 33 spacious rooms, 22 in a hotel block and the rest in villas, wrap around a large open garden peppered with palm trees and criss-crossed by an enormous multilevel swimming pool and meandering paths. Zest Restaurant, the dining option, also caters to nonguests (by reservation), with some of the most inspiring meals in Negril and indoor and alfresco seating areas atop the limestone cliffs facing the sea, with a bar located just below. Rooms at The Cliff are well appointed with cushy sofas inside and simple wicker furniture on the balconies. Soft tones create a relaxing ambiance, encouraging romance. Soft cotton linens, firm mattresses and fluffy pillows ensure peaceful rest in four-poster mahogany beds. Showers have rain heads and Jamaican handmade soaps. The Wi-Fi signal is strong, and the bedrooms have flat-screen TVs. All rooms have mini fridges and air-conditioning.

### Cottages and Villas

**Sundowner** (cell tel. 876/382-9434, westendtommy@yahoo.com, US$120 low season, US$165 high season) is a four-bedroom two-story house sandwiched between Catcha Falling Star and Rick's Café. Ideal for two couples or a small family, the house has full kitchen, Wi-Fi, and a large outdoor area overlooking the sea.

**Villas Sur Mer** (tel. 876/957-0342, cell tel. 876/382-3717, reservations@villassurmer. com, www.villassurmer.com, from US$448) is a boutique hotel straddling both sides of West End Road on Negril's West End. A six-bedroom villa overhangs the crashing waves at the top of the cliff with a private pool and bedrooms with sea views. On the other side of the road, one-, two-, and three-bedroom cottages are laid out surrounding a large pool with a central dining area. The rooms are tastefully

designed with white sofa covers and louvered windows and polished cement countertops.

**Hide Awhile** (West End Rd., tel. 877/243-5352 or 876/957-3302, www.idleawhile.com, from US$228) is Negril's most exclusive and luxurious private villa complex away from the hustle and bustle. The three villas feature a duplex layout with a spacious master bedroom upstairs. Amenities include all the details expected in a top-end property, from flat-screen TVs to fully equipped kitchen, plush bedding, and a relaxing porch. The property is best if you have a car. Wireless Internet is available. Chisty is the Rastafarian caretaker who serves up excellent cooking.

**Tingalayas** (tel. 876/957-0126, reservations@tingalayasretreat.com, from US$122 low season and US$170 high season) is named after a donkey that lives on the property. It has a total of eight tasteful cottages and bungalows. It is a good place for a group or family, with accommodations for up to 14 people. Amenities include ceiling fans, hot water, wireless Internet, and a combination of queen and bunk beds. Breakfast is included, and resident Rasta cook Jubey does excellent lobster, jerk chicken, and rice-and-peas to order.

# Information and Services

## EMERGENCIES

The Negril **police station** (tel. 876/957-4268, emergency tel. 119) is located on Whitehall Road just east of the roundabout next to the Negril Transport Centre. The police advise travelers to stay away from dark secluded areas at night, as people have had bags snatched. Don't leave valuables on the beach while swimming.

## BANKS AND ATMS

Banking can be done at **NCB** (Sunshine Village, tel. 876/929-4622), with ATMs at Plaza Negril and Petcom, or **Scotiabank** (Negril Square, across from Burger King near

the roundabout, tel. 876/957-4236), with an ATM at the Petcom next to the airstrip across from the Royalton.

**FX Trader** (tel. 888/398-7233) has a branch at Hi-Lo supermarket in Sunshine Village Plaza by the roundabout (9am-5pm Mon.-Thurs., 9am-5:30pm Fri.-Sat.).

The Negril **post office** (tel. 876/957-9654, 8am-5pm Mon.-Fri.) is located on West End Road between Cotton Tree Hotel and Samuel's Hardware, just past Vendor's Plaza.

## VISITOR INFORMATION

The **Negril Chamber of Commerce** (Vendors Plaza, West End Rd., tel.

876/957-4067, www.negrilchamberofcommerce.com) has visitor information, including a regularly updated brochure full of ads for hotels and attractions.

## MEDICAL CLINICS

**Long Bay Medical & Wellness Centre** (Norman Manley Blvd., tel. 876/957-9028) is run by Dr. David Stair.

**Omega Medical Centre** (White Swan Plaza and Sunshine Plaza, tel. 876/957-9307 or 876/957-4697) has two branches run by husband-and-wife team Dr. King and Dr. Foster.

**Dr. Grant** (Sunshine Plaza, West End, tel. 876/957-3770) runs a private clinic.

# Transportation

## GETTING THERE
### By Air

Negril's Aerodrome can accommodate small private aircraft and charters, and **AirLink Express** (Sangster International Airport, Domestic Terminal, tel. 876/940-6660, reservation@flyairlink.net, www.intlairlink.net) offers scheduled daily flights between Montego Bay and Negril (US$140 pp) as well as charter service between any two airports or aerodromes in the island.

**TimAir** (Sangster International Airport, Domestic Terminal, tel. 876/952-2516, timair@usa.net, www.timair.net) offers charter service from Montego Bay to Negril, Treasure Beach, Boscobel (St. Mary), Ken Jones (Portland), and Kingston.

### By Land

Negril can be reached by several means, depending on your budget and comfort requirements. Most accommodations offer airport transfers at additional cost, and a host of private taxi operators generally charge around US$60 for two people, plus US$20 pp for extra passengers.

**Knutsford Express** (tel. 876/971-1822, www.knutsfordexpress.com, 8am-10pm daily) offers bus service between Negril and Montego Bay (US$15), Ocho Rios (US$23), and Kingston (US$30), among other routes, with onboard Wi-Fi and a lavatory. Reserve online in advance for discounted fares.

The **Jamaica Union of Travelers**

**Association** (JUTA) is the best option for budget-minded travelers booking an airport pickup or drop-off. Drivers use any kind of vehicle imaginable: sedans, vans, or buses carrying up to 45 passengers. JUTA's **Negril Chapter** (Norman Manley Blvd., tel. 876/957-4620 or 876/957-9197, info@jutatoursnegrilltd.com, www.jutatoursnegrilltd.com) offers the most affordable way to Negril from Montego Bay's Sangster International Airport, US$20 pp from the beach and US$25 from the cliffs. Reservations made by email get a US$2 discount. JUTA drivers take visitors on excursions to popular attractions across the island.

**Alfred's Taxi and Tour Company** (tel. 876/854-8016 or 876/527-0050, U.S. tel. 646/289-4285, alfredstaxi@aol.com, negriltracy@aol.com, US$50 for 2 people), led by proprietor Alfred Barrett, has a 15-seat vehicle for larger groups using his "Irie Airport Rides and Vibes" service, previously only offered in his tinted Toyota Corolla station wagon.

For those with less money and more time, there are **buses** from Montego Bay to Savanna-la-Mar (US$2) and then from Savanna-la-Mar to Negril (US$2), mainly served by **route taxis.** It is also possible to take a route taxi from Montego Bay to Hopewell (US$2), then another from Hopewell to Lucea (US$2), and then a third from Lucea to Negril (US$2), but these cars leave when full and won't have much room for luggage.

Negril has two main taxi stands: one next

to Scotiabank in Negril Square, where taxis depart for points along the West End following the cliffs; the other in the main park next to the police station on Whitehall Road, where taxis and buses depart for points along Norman Manley Boulevard and east toward Savanna-la-Mar.

## GETTING AROUND

Route taxis run up and down the coast from the beach to the West End, generally using the plaza across from Burger King by the roundabout as a connection point. Some negotiating will generally be required, as the route taxis always try to get a higher fare from visitors, especially at night when everyone is charged extra. From anywhere on the West End to the roundabout should never be more than US$2 during the day, and US$4 at night. From there to the beach should also not cost more than US$2. Excursions beyond the beach and the West End can be arranged with private taxi and tour operators.

## Car and Motorcycle Rentals

**Happy World Bike/Car Rental** (opposite Idle Awhile, Norman Manley Blvd., tel. 876/957-4004, cell tel. 876/336-4795, happyworldnegril@yahoo.com, www.carrentalnegril.com, 8am-6pm daily) rents Toyota Corolla (US$105), Suzuki Vitara (US$152), and BMW X5 (US$210) vehicles (deposit US$1,500) and Suzuki mopeds and Yamaha dirt bikes (US$41 per day, US$300 deposit).

**Jah B's Bike Rentals** (Norman Manley Blvd., tel. 876/957-4235 or 876/353-9533, 8am-6pm daily) rents 125-cc mopeds and scooters, 175-cc Yamahas (US$40), and 600-cc Honda Shadows (US$50). Deposit is US$200 on the smaller bikes, US$500 for the larger ones. The sign on the road says JB Bike Rental.

**Tykes Bike Rental** (West End Rd., across from Tensing Pen, just before Rick's Café, tel. 876/957-0388, cell tel. 876/441-2260, tonyvassell@yahoo.com, 8am-6pm daily) rents 21-speed cruiser bicycles (US$10) as well as 100-cc Activer (US$35) and 120-cc Suzuki scooters (US$45). A US$500 deposit is required for the scooters.

# Northeast of Negril

Several attractions have cropped up in recent years, bringing the popular tours around Ocho Rios closer to Negril. These include Dolphin Cove, where visitors can interact with dolphins, pet sharks, and snorkel with stingrays. Tour operators have set up outposts in Lucea, near Jamaica's largest all-inclusive resort, Grand Palladium's Lady Hamilton, about halfway between Negril and Montego Bay. History buffs shouldn't miss the ruins of Kenilworth, an old sugar estate; the Hanover Museum; and Fort Charlotte, all in the vicinity of Lucea, which at one time exported a large share of Jamaica's sugar and rum production. Closer to Negril, Rhodes Beach Resort offers horseback riding on the large seaside estate, and Half Moon Beach is a quiet little cove devoid of hustlers and with a beach

bar and grill. Golfers not satisfied with the club in Negril will surely find the greens at Tryall Club outstanding.

## GREEN ISLAND
★ Half Moon Beach

**Half Moon Beach,** located in Orange Bay, just west of Green Island, Hanover, is a quiet little private beach park managed by Andrew Marr (cell tel. 876/773-5257 or 876/531-4508, halfmoonbeach1@hotmail.com, www.halfmoonbeachjamaica.com) and preserved close to how nature made it. The beach bar and grill are set back from the pristine strip of white sand, its eight rustic cottages hidden on the far side of the property. A canoe boat takes visitors to Calico Jack's, a second bar and grill located on a small cay five minutes offshore at the center of the bay. Half Moon is a great place to come for a more low-key alternative to Negril's often-crowded Seven-Mile Beach.

## FOOD

**Half Moon Beach Bar & Grill** (9am-9pm daily, US$7-20) serves breakfast, lunch, and dinner in a laid-back beach shack setting with typical Jamaican favorites as well as creative international fusion dishes like coconut-encrusted shrimp, Green Island coconut chicken served in a pineapple bowl, and grilled lobster.

**Calico Jack's** (11am-sunset daily) serves grilled lobster, jerk chicken, veggie kebabs, and escoveitch fish, all done on the grill. The bar serves pirate's rum punch and beer. Calico Jack's hosts a Pirates Party (4pm-6pm Sat.).

## ACCOMMODATIONS

Accommodations are offered at Half Moon Beach in a number of cabins (cash only). Coconut Cabin (US$65) is a one-bedroom with a bath, a ceiling fan, and a mini fridge. Blue Moon Cabin (US$75) has two bedrooms that share a bath, sleeping up to four, plus ceiling fans and a mini fridge. Seagrape I (US$65) and Seagrape II (US$65) each have one bed and a bath with ceiling fans; they share a balcony. Half Moon Beach is one of the few places in Jamaica ideal for camping (US$15) for those with their own tents.

**Rhodes Beach Resort** (tel. 876/957-6422 or cell tel. 876/431-6322, info@rhodesresort. com, www.rhodesresort.com, from US$144 low season, US$180 high season), operated by owners Marcelle and David DeMichael, sits on a 223-hectare (550-acre) estate adjacent to Orange Bay, far enough from the hustle of Negril to feel neither the bass thumping at night nor the harassment during the day, and enough outdoor activities to feel like you're not missing anything. The Rhino Safari on inflatable speedboats takes you to cruise Seven-Mile Beach in no time. Other activities include horseback riding, hiking, birding, and snorkeling with some of the healthiest reefs in Jamaica. Modern comfortable rooms, suites, and villas all have verandas with sea views. Satellite TV, air-conditioning, cell phones, queen beds, and hot water are standard. Ignore the floral bedcovers and focus on the woodwork and bamboo detailing, much of which is handcrafted from materials sourced on the property. Rates vary depending on room size and amenities; the largest villa has three baths, a full kitchen, a dining room, and a whirlpool tub. Rates include breakfast and Wi-Fi.

Half Moon Beach

# LUCEA

Lucea, Hanover's capital, is located on a horseshoe-shaped harbor a few kilometers from the Dolphin Head Mountains. Dolphin Head is a small 545-meter (1,788-foot) limestone that overlooks some of the most biologically diverse forestland in Jamaica, with the island's highest concentration of endemic species. A few kilometers away, Birch Hill, at 552 meters (1,811 feet), is the highest point in the parish. The small range protects Lucea harbor from the dominant easterly winds. Both Lucea and Mosquito Cove are used as hurricane holes for small yachts.

Lucea is a quiet town with little to see beyond Fort Charlotte. The fort was built to protect a town that was busier than Montego Bay in its heyday, exporting molasses, bananas, and yams. The large Lucea yam, exported to Jamaican laborers in Cuba and Panama during the construction of railroads and the canal, is still an important product grown in the area, though the center of the island, from Trelawny to Manchester, grows more today. The clock tower atop the historic 19th-century courthouse was originally destined for St. Lucia, but the town's residents liked it so much they refused to give it up in favor of the less ornate version they had commissioned by the same manufacturer in Great Britain when it was mistakenly sent to Jamaica.

## Sights

Fort Charlotte (site is unmanaged but supervised by Jamaica National Heritage Trust, tel. 876/922-1287), located on the point of Lucea Harbor, is the most intact fort in western Jamaica, with three cannons in good condition sitting on the battlements. It was built by the British in 1756, with 23 cannon openings to defend their colony from any challenge from the sea. Originally named Fort Lucea, it was renamed during the reign of King George III after his wife. The Barracks, a large rectangular Georgian building next to the fort, was built in 1843 to house soldiers stationed at Fort Charlotte. It was given to the people of Jamaica in 1862 by the English War Office;

it became the town's education center and is now part of the high school complex.

Kenilworth was one of Jamaica's most impressive great houses, located on the former Maggoty Estate. Currently the property is home to the HEART Academy, a training skills institute. To get here from the east, pass Tryall and then Sandy Bay, then Chukka Blue; turn inland after crossing the bridge over the Maggoty River in the community of Barbican and look for the sign for HEART Trust NTA Kenilworth on the left. Turn in and look for the ruins behind the institute, which is painted blue and white.

Dolphin Cove Negril (Lucea, Hanover, tel. 866/393-5158, 876/974-5335, 876/618-0900, or 876/618-0901, www.dolphincoveja.com, 9am-5pm, daily) offers three different options: the Encounter program (US$99/99), consisting of a caress and a kiss in knee-deep water; the Swim Adventure program (US$149/99), where guests are pulled by a dolphin belly-to-belly; and the Royal Swim (US$199/99 adult/12 and under), where the guest is given a foot push or dorsal pull by two dolphins. Guests can also interact and snorkel with stingrays, pet camels and ostriches, and watch a shark show.

## Dolphin Head Eco Park and Trail

Dolphin Head Eco Park and Trail can be explored with the help of guides arranged by Project Manager Norma Gilzene (cell tel. 876/364-6699 or 876/798-5470, email normastennett@yahoo.com or dolphinhead.lfmc@gmail.com). A US$10 per person contribution to the guide will be appreciated. A trail that takes about an hour round-trip leads to a few lookout points on the northern slopes of the range where hikers can see views of Lucea, Montego Bay, and Negril. Hikes to Dolphin Head Peak can be arranged with Norma from the Askenish side of the range.

## Accommodations

Palladium Lady Hamilton Resort and Spa, a Fiesta Group, a Spain-based hotel chain, opened the 2,000-room **Fiesta Palladium Palace** (tel. 876/620-0000, www.fiestahotel-group.com, from US$304 d), a massive all-inclusive hotel just west of Lucea on Molasses beach, in 2008.

## HOPEWELL AND TRYALL

Just west of Montego Bay, the Great River marks the border of St. James and Hanover. The area is an enclave of high-end tourism. Round Hill is one of Jamaica's most exclusive club hotels, and Tamarind Hill and the surrounding coastline are dotted with luxury villas, most of them fetching upward of US$10,000 per week in the high season.

The town of Hopewell is not especially remarkable beyond its status as an active fishing community. There's a Scotiabank ATM, a small grocery store, and a few hole-in-the-wall restaurants in the heart of town for typical Jamaican fare. Sound systems and tipsy partygoers can bring traffic through the town to a snarl Friday evenings, which precede a busy market day on Saturday; if you're staying in the vicinity, it's worth a stop.

A few kilometers farther west of Round Hill and Hopewell is Tryall, a former sugarcane plantation destroyed during the Christmas Rebellion of 1831-1832. The old waterwheel, fed by an aqueduct from the Flint River, can be seen as you round the bend approaching from the east, but little else remains as a reminder of its past as a sugar estate. Today the hotel and villa complex, which fans out from the historic great house, sits on one of the Caribbean's premier golf courses; its winter residents include boxing champion Lennox Lewis among a host of international jet-setters.

### Food

★ **Dervy's Lobster Trap** (cell tel. 876/783-5046, by reservation daily, US$20-35), owned by the charismatic Dervent Wright and operated by the whole family, has some of the island's best lobster, plus a great view of Round Hill from its vantage point on the waterfront. Be sure to call ahead to make reservations. Reach it by taking the second right in Hopewell, heading west down Sawyer's Road to the sea's edge. A sign for "Lobster Trap" indicates the turnoff from the main road.

**Smoked Marlin** (Hopewell, tel. 876/609-4181, www.smokedmarlinrestaurant.com, US$6-30) has an affordable and well-conceived menu featuring smoked marlin on toast, of course, as well as other appetizers like shrimp cocktail, chicken satay, and

Fiesta Palladium Palace

wings. Soups include crayfish bisque, fish tea, and red pea, with mains like snapper, jerk conch, grilled lobster, lobster thermidor, and pasta dishes. Local dishes include stew pork, oxtail, and curry chicken. The waterfront location makes a nice venue for a romantic sunset dinner.

## Accommodations

★ **Round Hill Hotel and Villas** (U.S. tel. 800/972-2159, tel. 876/956-7050, reservations@roundhilljamaica.com, www.roundhilljamaica.com, suites from US$500), just west of the Great River, is an exclusive hotel and club on meticulously manicured grounds. The hotel's main Pineapple Suites, featuring plush lounge furniture, were designed by Ralph Lauren and boast an atmosphere of stately oceanfront elegance. A host of returning luminaries has sealed Round Hill's well-deserved reputation for excellence.

In the Pineapple Suites, a series of hinged louvered windows open to overlook an infinity pool and the sea beyond, perfectly aligned for dreamy sunsets. The baths feature rain showerheads above glass enclosures and large bathtubs. Just above the hotel suites, villas dot the hillside, each surrounded by a maze of shrubs and flowers, ensuring utmost privacy. Next to the small, calm beach there's a charming library with a huge TV (to make up for their absence in the suites) and an open-air dining area; a short walk down the coast leads to the spa, based in a renovated plantation great house. The 27 **Villas at Round Hill** (US$875-2,875 low season, US$1,250-4,100 high season) can be booked through the hotel office. Cottages 16, 20, and 21 are among the finest at Round Hill.

**Tryall Club** (tel. 876/956-5660, U.S. tel. 800/238-5290, reservation@tryallclub.com, www.tryallclub.com, 1-bedroom suites from US$395 low season, US$550 high season) has private suites adjoining the main house as well as villas scattered throughout the property that are pooled and rented through the club reservation office. **Tryall Villas** come in superior (US$630 low season, US$1,185 high season) and deluxe (US$785 low season, US$1,570 high season) and are fully staffed with excellent cooks, who prepare Jamaican favorites and are also adept at international cuisine. Most suites and villas have a one-week minimum stay during high season, reduced to three or four days in low season. The villas are privately owned, and owners establish their own season dates and discounts.

Tryall Club has one of the best golf courses

The spa at Round Hill Hotel and Villas is housed in a former plantation great house.

in the Caribbean; it sits on an 890-hectare (2,200-acre) estate that extends deep into the Hanover interior. Tennis and golf are offered to nonmembers (greens fees US$125 per day, carts US$30, caddy US$30, tip US$20). Tryall guests pay substantially less (greens fees US$70 low season, US$100 high season). There are nine tennis courts, two with lights.

The cushioned courts are less slippery than the faux clay. Courts are for members and guests only and are included in the stay. Fees include US$23 per hour for a hitting partner, US$48 to play with a club pro, and US$7 per hour for a ball boy. At night, courts cost US$20 per hour for the lights.

# Southeast of Negril

As you leave Negril heading southeast toward Savanna-la-Mar, the visible part of Jamaica's booming tourism industry quickly fades, replaced by low-key communities of Jamaicans going about their daily lives. Many visitors who head in this direction are seeking just that, the Jamaican iteration of normalcy. Look no farther than the first seafront community to the southeast, Little Bay, where Bob Marley famously sought solace and relaxation.

The fishing village has a few accommodations catering to off-the-beaten-track travelers. Savanna-la-Mar, another 20-minute drive in the same direction, is the Westmoreland parish capital, a congested little town full of traders and students. Mayfield Falls is located about 40 minutes north of Savanna-la-Mar, and Blue Hole Gardens is about half that distance to the northeast. Paradise Park, just a few minutes from Savanna-la-Mar along the coast, offers horseback riding and a nice picnic area along a meandering river, as well as a spectacular virgin beach. From there, the A2 turns northeast to Ferris Cross and then southeast past Cave to Bluefields, a quiet seafront community.

## LITTLE BAY AND AROUND
### ★ Blue Hole Mineral Spring
**Blue Hole Mineral Spring** (Brighton, U.S. tel. 954/353-5392, cell tel. 876/860-8805, info@blueholejamaica.com, www.bluehole-jamaica.com, 10am-6pm Mon.-Thurs., 9am-2am Fri.-Sun., US$10) is a swimming hole

located a few minutes' drive inland from Little Bay in Brighton and about 15 minutes from Negril. The deep swimming hole is about five meters (15 feet) below the surface, and daredevils can climb the overhanging tree to add another three meters (10 feet) of adrenaline to the drop. A constructed swimming pool is fed with mineral water from the spring.

The bar keeps visitors cool, even if they're not inclined to jump into either pool, and jerk chicken is served off the grill. The property offers comfortable accommodations (US$150 d, including breakfast, US$250 d for three meals) in 10 rooms featuring bamboo frame canopy beds for those who can't get enough of Brighton. The rooms have cable TV and private bathrooms. The property offers complimentary Wi-Fi.

### Broughton Beach
Broughton Beach is a secluded eight-kilometer (5-mile) stretch of sand located due east of Little Bay, reached by taking a right at the gas station in Little London, followed by a left at the T junction. Keep left at the Y junction, and drive to the parking lot of the old Lost Beach Hotel. Mostly a fishing beach, it has fine white sand and an open expanse free of peddlers and hustlers.

### Food
**Tiki's Guinep Tree Restaurant & Bar** (Little Bay, tel. 876/438-3496, 10am-9pm daily, US$5-10), run by Vernon "Tiki" Johnson, is a favorite with locals. It serves

dishes like stew conch, fried fish, fried chicken, and jerk pork, accompanied with rice-and-peas or French fries.

## Accommodations

**Purple Rain Guest House** (Little Bay, call Cug, pronounced "Cudge," cell tel. 876/425-5386, or Donna Gill Colestock, U.S. tel. 508/816-6923, greenbiscuit03@hotmail.com, US$60 pp, US$400 per week) is a small cottage set back from the beach owned by Livingston "Cug" Drummond. It's a basic cottage with two rooms downstairs and a loft with ceiling fans and lukewarm water. Rates include two meals per day.

**Tansobak** (Little Bay, U.S. tel. 608/873-8195, littlebaycottages@gmail.com, www.littlebaycottages.com, from US$120) is three tastefully appointed double rooms a few meters from the water's edge in Little Bay. It has simple comfortable decor, louvered windows, tiled floors, and hot water. Air-conditioning is available by request. Denis and Michele Dale have owned the property since the mid-1990s. A small saltwater pool overlooks the sea at the edge of the cliff.

★ **Coral Cove Beach Resort & Spa** (Little Bay, U.S. tel. 217/649-0619, cell tel. 876/457-7594, coralcovejamaica@gmail.com, www.coralcovejamaica.com, from US$179) is a secluded family-owned and operated boutique resort on the sea, with tasteful bamboo furniture and wood frame beds. The 17 beach houses and cottages are naturally ventilated with louvered windows and ceiling fans. The resort offers bed and breakfast or all-inclusive plans. The resort can sleep up to 40, making it ideal for weddings. Wi-Fi covers most of the property. The two-hectare (5-acre) property has 400 meters (0.25 miles) of ocean frontage and emphasizes fine cuisine and attentive service.

**Lookout Cove** (Little Bay, U.S. tel. 800/755-2693, www.lookoutcove.com, weekly rates from US$3,850 low season, from US$4,950 high season) has a three-bedroom villa and a two-bedroom cottage sleeping up to four, located on a 1.5-hectare

(3.5-acre) seafront estate with a tennis court and lush gardens, an ideal retreat for families or groups of friends looking for peace and tranquility.

# SAVANNA-LA-MAR

Savanna-la-Mar, or simply "Sav," as it is commonly referred to by locals, is one of the most subdued parish capitals in Jamaica, with two notable exceptions—the annual Curry Festival, held behind Manning's School in July, and **Western Consciousness,** held in April at Paradise Park, on the eastern outskirts of town. A free concert and symposium are also held in Sav in October every year to commemorate the life of the late Peter Tosh, who was born a few kilometers away in Grange Hill.

## Sights
★ MAYFIELD FALLS

Located in Flower Hill near the Hanover border, **The Original Mayfield Falls** (tel. 876/610-8612 or cell tel. 876/457-0759, info@mayfieldfalls.com, www.mayfieldfalls.com) is one of the best waterfall attractions in Jamaica, having been developed with minimal impact to the natural surroundings. It's a great place to spend an afternoon cooling off in the river and walking upstream along a series of gentle cascades and pools. Four- to five-hour tours (US$85 pp) include round-trip transportation from Montego Bay, entry fee with a guided hike up the river, and lunch afterward. The entry fee is significantly lower if you have your own vehicle and includes a guide (US$15). Lunch may be purchased separately (US$10-22).

Mayfield Falls can be reached from either the North or South Coasts. From the North Coast, turn inland before crossing the bridge at Flint River on the eastern side of Tryall Estate and follow Original Mayfield signs. From the South Coast, turn inland in Sav, keeping straight ahead at the stoplight by the gas station on the east side of town rather than turning right toward Ferris Cross, and head straight toward the communities of

Strathbougie, then take a left off Petersfield main road at the four-way intersection toward Hertford. From Hertford, head toward Williamsfield and then to Grange before making a right in the square to continue for about 10 minutes to the settlement of Mayfield. You'll see a sign on the right indicating the entrance to Mayfield Falls. The road from the north passes through Flower Hill before you see the Original Mayfield sign on the left.

## MANNING'S SCHOOL

The most architecturally appealing building in town, **Manning's School** is one of Jamaica's oldest schools, established in 1738 after local proprietor Thomas Manning left 13 slaves with land as the endowment for a free school. Now used as the area's leading high school, the attractive wooden structure, built in late-colonial style in 1910 on the site of the original school, stands in front of several newer, less stylish concrete buildings set around a large field. The annual **Westmoreland Curry Festival** (last Sun. in Apr., westmorelandcurryfestival@gmail.com) is hosted in this field and is definitely the best time to visit.

## ★ BLUE HOLE GARDENS

**Blue Hole Gardens** (Petersfield, www.blueholegardens.org, US$15 adults, free under age 13) is a lush and well-maintained attraction with diverse vegetation springing from manicured grounds surrounding a natural spring-fed pool brimming with surreal turquoise water most of the year. In the drier months, the water level falls. The spring that feeds the Blue Hole is one of more than 10 that combine within a few hectares, turning the gentle flow of subterranean rivers into the gushing Roaring River. It's definitely worth a visit for an afternoon splash, and for those who can't get enough, **Blue Hole Victorian Cottage** (Swiss tel. +41/79-615-9974, cell tel. 876/370-8033, www.blueholegardens.org, from US$220), located on the same property, accommodates up to eight guests.

## PARADISE PARK

One of the best places in Jamaica for down-to-earth small-group horseback rides (US$40) on an expansive seaside cattle ranch, **Paradise Park** (tel. 876/955-2675, paradise1@cwjamaica.com) is located a few kilometers east of Savanna-la-Mar in Ferris Cross. The 1.5-hour tours, offered for a maximum of 10 riders, cover diverse scenery and include a soft

Blue Hole Gardens

# Western Consciousness

Conscious Reggae is back in the limelight after 20 years thanks to steadfast artists and promoters like Worrell King who have stood by the principles established by the genre's early pioneers.

Starting around the time of Bob Marley's death in 1981, the reggae industry was taken over by dancehall artists like Shabba Ranks and Yellowman. The style of their lyrics signified a departure from roots reggae, with its messages of truth and progress, to an often violent and sexually explicit form of music that became known for its "slackness."

When Peter Tosh was killed in 1987, dancehall had taken over, and conscious reggae music was old news. Around that time Worrell King founded King of Kings Promotions to rescue the truth from the mire. King of Kings organized a very successful event at Titchfield High School in Port Antonio in 1988 dubbed **Eastern Consciousness,** which showcased several artists who displayed conscious leaning. "It was to attract people who needed to be uplifted, rather than just wasting away gyrating," King says.

After a second successful Eastern Consciousness the following year, King took the event to Westmoreland, the parish of his birth, where he says the people were yearning for it, thus putting on the first **Western Consciousness** in Paradise Park.

drink. Lunch can be prepared for groups of six or more (US$12 pp). Besides riding, the park features a lovely picnic area with a barbecue grill, baths, and a gentle river suitable for a refreshing dip (US$5).

## Food

**The Ranch Jerk Centre** cooks up Boston-style jerk on the western side of Sav.

**Sweet Spice** (Barracks Rd., beside the new bus park, tel. 876/955-3232, US$4.50-7.50) serves fried chicken, curry goat, oxtail, and fish fillet.

**Hammond's Pastry Place** (18 Great George St., tel. 876/955-2870, 8am-6:30pm Mon.-Fri., 8am-8:30pm Sat.) serves patties, cakes, and deli sandwiches.

**Hot Spot Restaurant** (23 Lewis St., contact Elaine Jagdath, cell tel. 876/848-6335, 7am-8pm Mon.-Sat., US$2.25-4.50) serves local dishes like fried chicken and curry goat. It is perhaps more mediocre than hot, but good enough to fill your belly in a crunch.

## Accommodations

**Blue Hole Gardens Victorian Cottage** (Swiss tel. +41/79-615-9974, cell tel. 876/370-8033, www.blueholegardens.org, from US$220), renovated in 2014, perches on a hill at the top of 94 steps ascending from a rustic

bar that belies the understated luxury above. Overlooking cane fields and the magical Blue Hole Gardens, the cottage has two bedrooms on the upper level, each with a full bath—an antique bathtub in one, an outdoor shower in the other, and two adjoining bedrooms below that share a full bath between them. Fixtures in the baths and appliances in the kitchen are of high quality. A housekeeper-cook-caretaker is on hand to prepare meals on request. The rental includes remarkably good Internet service, considering the remote location.

The drive to Blue Hole Gardens is not for the faint of heart, as the road is heavily potholed, ultimately turning to dirt as it passes through the impoverished rural community straddling the banks of the Turtle River. A stay at the Victorian Cottage offers a unique rural experience without sacrificing the comfort of soft linens and broadband.

## BLUEFIELDS AND BELMONT

This stretch of Westmoreland coast is as laid-back and "country" as Jamaica gets, with excellent lodging options and plenty of seafood. Bluefields public beach has more locals on it than travelers, with shacks selling fried fish, beer, and the ubiquitous herb. The windfall of jobs and revenue that Butch Stewart and

crab backs at Dor's Crab Shak

over the heavily laden branches. Peter Tosh was born in nearby Grange Hill before making his way to Kingston, where he became one of the original three Wailers along with Bob Marley and Bunny Livingston. His mother still lives in Belmont.

## Beaches

**Bluefields Beach Park** (tel. 876/957-5159) is a popular local hangout and sees few travelers. It has fine white sand and is lined with vendors. Music is often blasted on weekends when the beach fills up. There's no entry fee to use the beach, which is owned by the Urban Development Corporation in Kingston.

## Sports and Recreation

This Bluefields-Belmont area is perfect for activities like hiking, swimming, snorkeling, and relaxing. Nobody is touting parasailing or Jet Skis, and the most activity you will see on the water are fishing boats and an occasional yacht moored off the Luna Sea Inn or Bluefields Villas.

**Fishing excursions** can be organized by Lagga or Trevor, who can be contacted through Carolyn Barrett of Barrett Adventures (tel. 876/382-6384, info@barrettadventures.com).

**Reliable Adventures Jamaica** (tel. 876/955-8834, cell tel. 876/421-7449, rajtoursjm@gmail.com, www.jamaicabirding.com) organizes nature walks, community tours, birding, hiking, and marine excursions with local fishers led by Wolde Kristos. One-day bird tours (US$95 pp) include lunch. Transportation is available at additional cost.

the Jamaican government were to bring to the area from opening another monstrous all-inclusive resort, Sandals Whitehouse, has barely materialized, as the guests are not encouraged to venture off the compound and rarely do so.

## Sights

**Bluefields Great House,** located about 0.4 kilometers (0.25 miles) inland from the police station, was the home of many of the area's most distinguished temporary inhabitants, including Philip Henry Goss, an English ornithologist who resided in Jamaica 1844 to 1846, subsequently completing the work *The Birds of Jamaica.*

**Peter Tosh Memorial Garden** (US$5), where the remains of this original Wailer lie, is worth a quick stop, if only to pause amid the ganja seedlings to remember one of the world's greatest reggae artists. The entrance fee is assessed when there's someone around to collect it; otherwise the gate is unlocked, and a quick visit usually goes unnoticed. In mango season the yard is full of locals fighting

## Food

**The Belaire** (cell tel. 876/437-7593, www.belairjamaica.com) is a cut-stone bar overlooking the water in the heart of Belmont.

**Leroy's Beach Bar & Grill** (Belmont Main Road) is a rustic thatch hut bar serving fish and chicken.

★ **Dor's Crab Shak** (Belmont Sands, cell tel. 876/471-4984, 8am-10pm daily, US$4-15) serves delish crab backs, curried crab in the shell, grilled lobster, chicken, steam and escoveitch fish, curried or garlic conch, and stew pork. Desserts include bread pudding, sweet potato pudding, and ice cream. Occasional karaoke nights start at around 8pm on Friday and Sunday evening.

Doretta Hibbert is a much beloved fixture in Belmont who launched the **Belmont Crab Festival** (last Sun. in May) in 1998 at the Belmont Community Centre before moving to Belmont Sands in 2009. The annual festival is held the day after Busha's Crab Festival in Paradise Park.

**The Cracked Conch** (Luna Sea Inn, tel. 876/955-8099, 9am-9pm daily, US$5-15) serves creative takes on Jamaica's favorite green, like callaloo bundles or callaloo sticks, and classics like conch fritters and conch chowder. Mains include crab cakes, fish and chips, jerk chicken quesadillas, and pan seared mahimahi. For dessert, try the banana foster crepes or Dr. Linda's cheesecake.

## Accommodations
### UNDER US$100

**Nature Roots** (cell tel. 876/384-6610 or 876/315-3954, www.natureroots.de, US$30) is run by Brian "Bush Doctor" Wedderburn, also known locally as Rasta Brian, who leads hiking excursions (US$15-25) into the hills to learn about local flora and fauna. Wi-Fi and a shared kitchen are available.

**Rainbow Villas** (tel. 876/955-8078, cell tel. 876/872-9080 or 876/378-7853, www.rainbowvillas-jamaica.com, US$50 d), owned and managed by Carlene and her German husband, Ralph, is located across the road from the water along a little lane adjacent to Sunset Paradise Bar & Grill. The spacious and clean rooms have ceiling fans and kitchenettes, hot water, and air-conditioning. Carlene has a spa on property specializing in deep tissue and Swedish massage and reflexology (US$60 per hour).

**Good Hope Retreat** (Cave Mountain Rd., cell tel. 876/391-3775 or 876/855-8963, goodhoperetreat@gmail.com, goodhoperetreat. com, US$85) is a hilltop collection of three wooden cabins with outstanding views of the coast and surrounding hills set amidst natural beauty. The cabins have kitchenettes and desks, simple furnishings, and queen beds.

### US$100-250

★ **Horizon Cottages** (cell tel. 876/382-6384, info@barrettadventures.com, www.carolynscaribbeancottages.com, 3-night minimum stay, US$110) define rustic elegance, with two perfectly situated wooden cottages on Bluefields Bay. Each cottage is tastefully decorated with local artwork and has classic wooden louvered windows, queen beds, soft linens, attached baths with private outdoor showers, and cute functional kitchens. The porch steps of **Sea Ranch** cottage descend to the small, beautiful, private white-sand beach, and a pier off the manicured lawn makes the perfect dining room and cocktail bar. **Rasta Ranch** is a slightly larger cottage set farther back. Kayaks and snorkeling gear are on hand for excursions to the reef just offshore. Property manager Carolyn Barrett is a seasoned tour operator who runs Barrett Adventures, one of the island's best outfits, and can accommodate the interests of every kind of adventure seeker. Wi-Fi, hot water, and gentle waves make Horizon hard to leave.

**Luna Sea Inn** (Belmont Main Road, tel. 876/955-8099, cell tel. 876/383-6982, lchidester@lunaseainn.com, www.lunaseainn.com, from US$110, including breakfast) is a 10-room boutique hotel run by a congenial doctor, Linda Chidester, who became an innkeeper in retirement. The property juts out into the sea with a raised gazebo on the point. A small pool is located in the courtyard. Rooms have en suite baths with showers and hot water, air-conditioning, cable TV, and Wi-Fi.

**Shafston Great House** (contact Frank Lohmann, cell tel. 876/869-9212, mail@shafston.com, www.shafston.com) is one of the few plantation great houses that you can actually stay in. On a hill overlooking Bluefields Bay, Shafston has a large pool and rooms that range from basic with shared bath (US$140 d) in a side building to suites in the Great House (US$180 d) with hot water in private baths. Rates include meals and drinks. Frank also offers transfers from the airport in Montego Bay (US$75).

### VILLAS

★ **Bluefields Villas** (U.S. tel. 877/955-8993, vacations@bluefieldsvillas.com, www.bluefieldsvillas.com, 5-night minimum low season, 7-night minimum high season, from US$6,561 weekly for 2, includes food and beverages) is a collection of extravagant vacation homes set on prime seafront estates hugging the coast along Bluefields Bay. Each villa has a private pool and its own unique character and history, all impeccably appointed with antique furnishings, fine china, and silver. At San Michele in Belmont, a large gazebo stands by the pool for open-air dining; another juts out into the sea, ideal for evening cocktails.

Across the bay, the remaining villas are joined by a romantic sea walk leading down to Bluefields Beach, where fine white sand, lounge chairs, and kayaks await. Sundecks, pools, and luxurious linens make you feel like royalty. Wi-Fi coverage is strong throughout. Great care goes into preparation of lavish meals with quality ingredients.

# WHITEHOUSE

A quiet seaside town, Whitehouse has developed into a favored community for Jamaicans returning after years of working abroad thanks to a few developers who've built subdivisions and sold off lots and homes. The nicest beach in the area, Whitehouse Beach, was cordoned off and annexed by the most recent Sandals resort to be built in Jamaica, but the end of the beach closest to the road can be reached along a short path through the bush from the base of the hill in Culloden.

## Food

**Ruby's 24/7** (Whitehouse Square, tel. 876/453-0003, 24 hours daily) serves typical Jamaican dishes, around the clock, in a box to go or to stay.

**Jimmyz Restaurant and Bar** (tel. 876/390-3477, 6am-7pm Mon.-Sat., US$3.50-11), located next to the supermarket in White House Square and run by George "Jimmy" Williams, serves Jamaican breakfast items like ackee and saltfish accompanied by yam and boiled banana, with lunch and dinner dishes that include chicken and seafood staples. Fresh juices are also served.

The Hermitage, one of the villas associated with Bluefields Villas

## Accommodations

★ **Culloden Cove** (contact Andy McLean, tel. 876/472-4608, info@jamaicaholidayvilla.com, www.jamaicaholidayvilla.com, 2-5 bedrooms US$3,300-4,200 per week low season, US$3,950-5,100 high season), located at the former home of the Culloden Café, was renovated under new ownership in 2008. The property sleeps six in the villa and four in a separate cottage. An infinity pool is located seaside, at the bottom of a sloping lawn extending from the main house, with a gazebo at the water's edge. Mosquitos can be an issue seasonally, but shouldn't be a deterrent since there are screens on the windows and nets over the beds as well as air-conditioning.

The four-star **Sandals Whitehouse** (U.S. tel. 800/726-3257, from US$790, 65 percent discount for 3 nights or more) took about 15 years to complete at a cost of US$110 million—among the most expensive hotels ever built and nearly double the initial budget. At the high end of Sandals' many properties, it features premium drinks, a variety of dining options, and a beautiful cabaret bar. Rooms have all the amenities you could want. The property is stunningly grand, designed like a European village with a large central courtyard and an enormous pool with a wet bar. The beach is one of the best in the area. Day passes (until 6pm, US$85), evening passes (6pm-2am, US$100), and full-day passes (10am-2am, US$185) are also available.

**Kew Park Estate** (20 miles east of Montego Bay, tel. 202/364-4713, peter@kewpark.com, www.kewpark.com, US$25 per person per night) is a coffee farm in the hills of Westmoreland growing coffee and rearing cattle, pigs, and chickens. The 35-acre farm has a wide variety of fruit trees, shade-grown coffee, and wooded areas, creating an ideal environment for a diversity of birds. Kew Park is a birder's paradise, where rustic accommodations and caring staff make guests comfortable and days can be spent exploring the farm and surrounding hills, binoculars in hand. Bring bug dope and check your limbs for ticks. The list of birds sighted on the farm totals 44, including 16 endemic species. The list can be found on the Kew Park website. Bring food and the housekeeper will prepare it; make sure you leave a generous tip for her efforts.

## Getting There and Around

**Route taxis** ply the coast all day long from Savanna-la-Mar (US$2) and Black River (US$2) to Whitehouse. **Karl** (cell tel. 876/368-0508) is a JUTA-licensed driver based in the area who offers tours and taxi service.

# Montego Bay and the Northwest Coast

# Highlights

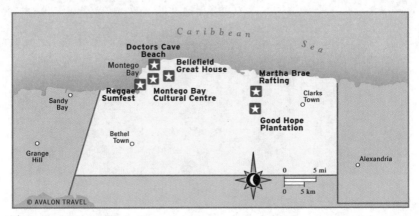

© AVALON TRAVEL

★ **Montego Bay Cultural Centre:** Check out historical and contemporary exhibits at the National Museum West and National Gallery West (page 66).

★ **Bellefield Great House:** Enjoy a historical tour of this colonial home that now houses Montego Bay elite. The tour doubles as a culinary treat (page 66).

★ **Doctors Cave Beach:** At the center of Mobay's Hip Strip, this beach is the best spot to see and be seen on weekends. It's also the site of a monthly live reggae series (page 69).

★ **Reggae Sumfest:** For three nights each July, the best reggae show on earth delivers top acts from Jamaica and abroad (page 75).

★ **Martha Brae Rafting:** Take a relaxing and romantic journey down a meandering river (page 92).

★ **Good Hope Plantation:** Chukka Caribbean offers culinary and adventure tours at this scenic citrus farm (page 98).

# Commonly referred to as "Mobay," Jamaica's second-largest city has the highest concentration of golf courses and all-inclusive resorts in the country, as well as a smattering of great restaurants and pulsating clubs.

Mobay is also home to Reggae Sumfest, arguably the best showcase of Jamaican music on the planet, held over three nights each July.

The city buzzes with cruise ships and international flights loaded with visitors. Many spend barely a day on land before climbing aboard to depart for the next port. While Mobay can't boast the island's best public beaches, it's a central base for day trips in Western Jamaica, from Ocho Rios to Negril and along the South Coast, all about 1.5 hours away on well-paved single-lane highways.

The Montego Bay Yacht Club is a lively hub of activity for sailing and sportfishing. Rivers in the area are popular for rafting, tubing, or a refreshing dip. History buffs will find plenty to discover in neighboring Trelawny and Hanover, strategic to the sugar-based economy of the colonial era. Inland, the rugged region known as cockpit country stretches east beyond Bob Marley's birthplace at Nine Mile in St. Ann. The rough-hewn limestone landscape gave refuge to the indomitable Maroons, and lush valleys are home to working plantations offering adventure and family-oriented tours.

## ORIENTATION

Montego Bay has several distinct tourist zones that are somewhat remote from the bustling and congested maze of downtown and not easy for pedestrians. Three roads lead from the roundabout as you exit Sangster International Airport: the A1, a double-lane highway leading past Flankers to Iron Shore, Rose Hall, Greenwood, and points east; Sunset Boulevard, leading directly to the so-called **Hip Strip** along Gloucester Avenue; and Queens Drive, which bypasses the hip strip toward downtown, Catherine Hall, Freeport, Bogue, Reading, and points west.

Most of the city's budget and mid-range hotels, as well as a few all-inclusive resorts, are concentrated along **Gloucester Avenue,**

**Previous:** Montego Bay; Margaritaville restaurant and bar. **Above:** ziplining with Chukka Caribbean.

# Mobay in One Day

As Jamaica's primary gateway, Montego Bay is likely to be a part of any Jamaican itinerary, even if it's just in passing. For those stepping off a cruise ship for a matter of hours, it may be the only part of Jamaica that fits in the itinerary. Here are some suggestions for how to spend one day in and around Jamaica's "second city."

- **Hit the beach: Doctors Cave Beach** (tel. 876/952-4355, info@doctorscave.com, www.doctorscave.com), located on Gloucester Avenue, aka Bottom Road, has a fine stretch of white sand, a restaurant, and a bar.

- **Charter a yacht: Lark Cruises** (contact Captain Carolyn Barrett, cell tel. 876/382-6384, info@barrettadventures.com, www.barrettadventures.com) and **Jamaica Water Sports** (cell tel. 876/381-3229 or 876/995-2912, dptgonefishing@hotmail.com, www.jamaicawatersports.com) offer day sail charters departing from Montego Bay Yacht Club on a 42-foot Beneteau and a 51-foot trimaran, respectively.

- **Tour a great house:** No visit to Jamaica is complete without stepping back in time to experience what life was like as a colony of the British Empire. **Rose Hall Great House** (tel. 876/953-2323, greathouse@rosehall.com, www.rosehall.com, day tours 9:15am-5:15pm daily, night tours 6:30pm-9pm daily, US$20 adults, US$10 children), perhaps the best-known and most foreboding, was the home of Annie Palmer, fearfully known as the White Witch of Rose Hall. Legend has it she murdered several lovers and ruled the plantation with an iron fist. Many visitors claim to feel the presence of spirits touring Rose Hall.

- **Visit the market:** There's no better way to get a feel for the real Jamaica than to visit an open-air market. Mobay's market is fittingly found on Market Street.

- **Kiteboard: Irie Kiteboarding** with **Water Network Jamaica** (cell tel. 876/540-4042, info@waternetworkjamaica.com, www.iriekiteboardingjamaica.com) is the best outfit to get you out on the water in no time, winds permitting.

as are many restaurants and bars catering to foreign visitors. The Hip Strip is overrun with souvenir shops. Extending north from the Hip Strip is Kent Avenue, which terminates at one end of the airport runway along the popular public Dead End Beach.

Queens Drive turns into Howard Cooke Highway as it bypasses downtown. The congested city is fraught with confusing one-way streets centered around **Sam Sharpe Square,** where a statue of the slave rebellion leader surrounded by a handful of followers stands to one side of a roundabout in front of the **Montego Bay Cultural Centre.**

A few stoplights south, Howard Cooke Highway meets Alice Eldemire Drive, which runs the length of **Freeport,** a peninsula jutting into the sea separating Bogue Lagoon to the south and the harbor to the north. Freeport is home to the city's cruise ship terminal, the yacht club, a few all-inclusive

resorts, and a handful of middle- and upper-income residential developments.

Heading inland along Alice Eldemire Drive from the junction with Howard Cooke Highway leads past the Fairview Shopping Centre to the junction of Barnett Street and Bogue Road. Barnett leads back into the city and Bogue Road heads south and turns into the A1 in Reading after it turns westward out of town toward Negril.

East of the airport along the A1, **Ironshore** is a middle-class area that covers a large swath of hill in subdivisions and oversize concrete houses. Farther east, **Spring Garden** is the most exclusive residential neighborhood in Mobay, bordering **Rose Hall Estate,** where many of the area's all-inclusive resorts are wedged between the main road and the sea and the city's top-notch golf courses are located.

# The Northwest Coast

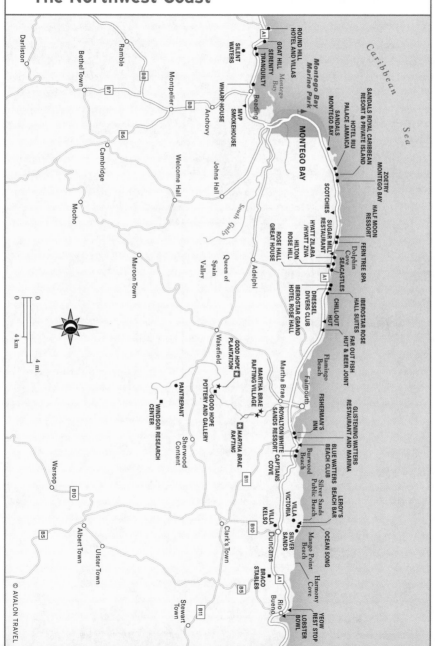

Caribbean Sea

Montego Bay Marine Park

Montego Bay

MONTEGO BAY

ROUND HILL HOTEL AND VILLAS
SILENT WATERS
GOAT HILL
SERENITY
TRANQUILITY
WHARF HOUSE
MVP SMOKEHOUSE
Reading
SANDALS ROYAL CARIBBEAN RESORT & PRIVATE ISLAND
HOTEL RIU PALACE JAMAICA
SANDALS MONTEGO BAY
ZOETRY MONTEGO BAY
HALF MOON RESORT
SCOTCHIES
SUGAR MILL RESTAURANT
HYATT ZILARA /HYATT ZIVA
FERN TREE SPA
HILTON ROSE HALL
ROSE HALL GREAT HOUSE
Dolphin Cove
SEACASTLES
IBEROSTAR ROSE HALL SUITES
DRESSEL DIVERS CLUB
IBEROSTAR GRAND HOTEL ROSE HALL
FAR OUT FISH HUT & BEER JOINT
CHILL-OUT HUT
Flamingo Beach
Falmouth
Wakefield
GOOD HOPE PLANTATION
MARTHA BRAE RAFTING VILLAGE
Martha Brae
PANTREPANT
GOOD HOPE POTTERY AND GALLERY
MARTHA BRAE RAFTING
WINDSOR RESEARCH CENTER
Sherwood Content
GLISTENING WATTERS RESTAURANT AND MARINA
ROYALTON WHITE SANDS RESORT
FISHERMAN'S INN
CAPTIANS COVE
Burwood Beach
BLUE WATTERS BEACH CLUB
LEROY'S BEACH BAR
Silver Sands Public Beach
SILVER SANDS
VILLA VICTORIA
VILLA KELSO
Duncans
OCEAN SONG
Mango Point Beach
Harmony Cove
BRACO STABLES
YEOW REST STOP
Rio Bueno
LOBSTER BOWL

Darliston
Ramble
Bethel Town
Montpelier
Anchovy
Cambridge
Welcome Hall
Johns Hall
Mocho
Maroon Town
Adelphi
Queen of Spain Valley
South Gully
Clark's Town
Warsop
Albert Town
Ulster Town
Stewart Town

A1
B8
B7
B8
B6

0 4 km
0 4 mi

B11
B10
B5
B10
B5
B11

© AVALON TRAVEL

# Montego Bay

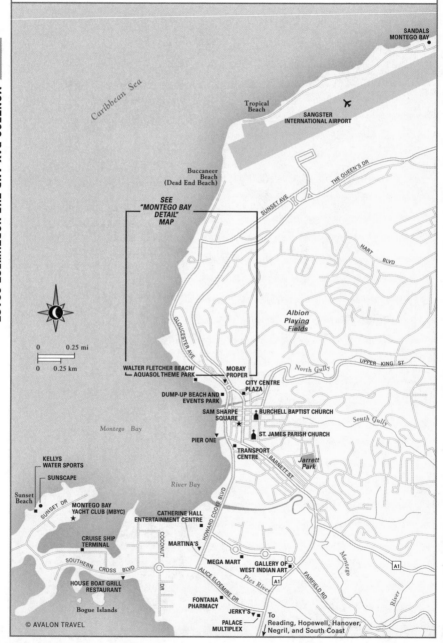

SANDALS
MONTEGO BAY

*Caribbean Sea*

Tropical
Beach

SANGSTER
INTERNATIONAL AIRPORT

THE QUEEN'S DR

Buccaneer
Beach
(Dead End Beach)

SUNSET AVE

SEE
"MONTEGO BAY
DETAIL"
MAP

HART BLVD

*Albion
Playing
Fields*

GLOUCESTER AVE

*North Gully*

UPPER KING ST

0    0.25 mi
0    0.25 km

WALTER FLETCHER BEACH/
AQUASOL THEME PARK

MOBAY
PROPER

CITY CENTRE
PLAZA

*South Gully*

DUMP-UP BEACH AND
EVENTS PARK

SAM SHARPE
SQUARE

BURCHELL BAPTIST CHURCH

ST. JAMES PARISH CHURCH

*Montego Bay*

PIER ONE

TRANSPORT
CENTRE

BARNETT ST

*Jarrett
Park*

KELLYS
WATER SPORTS

*River Bay*

HOWARD COOKE BLVD

SUNSCAPE

Sunset
Beach

SUNSET DR

MONTEGO BAY
YACHT CLUB (MBYC)

CATHERINE HALL
ENTERTAINMENT CENTRE

COCONUT

CRUISE SHIP
TERMINAL

MARTINA'S

*Montego
River*

SOUTHERN CROSS BLVD

MEGA MART

GALLERY OF
WEST INDIAN ART

A1

ALICE ELDEMIRE DR

*Pies River*

A1

FAIRFIELD RD

DR

HOUSE BOAT GRILL
RESTAURANT

FONTANA
PHARMACY

*Bogue Islands*

JERKY'S

PALACE
MULTIPLEX

To
Reading, Hopewell, Hanover,
Negril, and South Coast

*River*

© AVALON TRAVEL

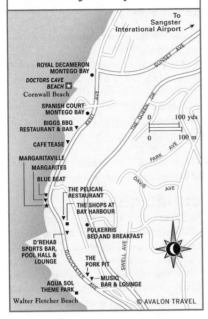

## Montego Bay Detail

To Sangster Interational Airport

ROYAL DECAMERON MONTEGO BAY

DOCTORS CAVE BEACH

Cornwall Beach

SPANISH COURT MONTEGO BAY

BIGGS BBQ RESTAURANT & BAR

CAFE TEASE

MARGARITAVILLE

MARGARITES

BLUE BEAT

THE PELICAN RESTAURANT

THE SHOPS AT BAY HARBOUR

POLKERRIS BED AND BREAKFAST

D'REHAB SPORTS BAR, POOL HALL & LOUNGE

THE PORK PIT

AQUA SOL THEME PARK

MUSIQ BAR & LOUNGE

Walter Fletcher Beach

© AVALON TRAVEL

0      100 yds

0      100 m

## PLANNING YOUR TIME

As a point of entry, Sangster International Airport is the best option if you're planning to spend most of your time in Western Jamaica. A night or two in Montego Bay, especially if you arrive on a weekend, can be a good way to enjoy some local culture before heading off to a more tranquil resort area. Ideally the area deserves three days, split between beaches, historical sites, natural attractions, and fine dining and entertainment around the city.

MoBay also makes a good base for nearby areas. Negril, Jamaica's foremost beach town, as well as attractions on the South Coast and in the neighboring parishes of Trelawny and Hanover, are only a few hours away from MoBay. Several great house tours and plantation tours closer to town make excellent half-day excursions, and if you prefer to relax on the beach, a few good options right in town and along the coast in either direction are only a few minutes away.

Historical places of interest include **Sam Sharpe Square** downtown as well as **Bellefield, Rose Hall,** and **Greenwood Great Houses**—at least one of which should be seen on a trip to Jamaica—and the Georgian town of **Falmouth.** All of these are close enough for half-day trips; tours and activities around Falmouth can easily consume the better part of an unhurried day. Natural attractions within easy reach include the **Martha Brae River, Windsor Caves,** Mayfield Falls, Blue Hole Gardens, and the **Great River.**

Mobay comes alive for the island's premier music festival, **Reggae Sumfest,** held in July.

## SAFETY

Montego Bay has many residential areas where it's not advisable to venture unless you know where you're going. As a rule of thumb, keep to well-heeled parts of town and be wary of overly friendly invitations and solicitations. If you've rented a vehicle, keep the doors locked while you're driving and don't let strangers inside the car. Stories abound of seemingly friendly residents offering to assist travelers with directions before entering vehicles without an invitation to "show the oblivious travelers the way," only to push overpriced ganja or otherwise lead the new arrivals off course in an effort to extract money.

The downtown area around Sam Sharpe Square and the Montego Bay Cultural Centre are well policed and perfectly safe, as is the Hip Strip. Nonetheless, expect to be offered every product or service imaginable; you're best off not taking the bait. Women should avoid walking alone in poorly lit and desolate areas, especially at night.

# Sights

## RICHMOND HILL INN

Whether or not you choose to stay at the hilltop **Richmond Hill Inn** (tel. 876/952-3859, info@richmondhillinnja.com, www.richmondhillinnja.com, nonguests 7am-7pm daily, admission US$2), you should visit the site for a sunset cocktail at the poolside terrace, which provides the best panoramic view of Mobay. As sun sets, the lights of the city begin to shimmer, the sea and sky merge into darkness, and cruise ships sail over the horizon.

The hotel has an illustrious history, and ancient relics pepper the property. Columbus is said to have stayed for a year around 1500 while he was stranded in Jamaica. A palatial abode was built by John Dewar of Scotch whisky fame in 1804. Today, the hotel is still appointed with many original antiques dating as far back as the 1600s. It's owned and operated by Stefanie Chin and her daughters, Gracie and Galey, Austrian expatriates in Jamaica since 1968.

## ★ MONTEGO BAY CULTURAL CENTRE

The **Montego Bay Cultural Centre** (Sam Sharpe Square, tel. 876/971-3920, 10am-6pm Tues.-Sun., US$6 adults, US$3 ages 5-16, free under age 5), previously known as the Montego Bay Civic Centre, houses a permanent exhibit featuring a history of St. James and Jamaica, with a collection of artifacts from the Taino to the postcolonial period. Tours are offered daily.

**National Museum West** is housed on the bottom floor of the main building, with the permanent collection in the southern wing and temporary exhibits in the northern wing. **National Gallery West** is located upstairs in the adjoining building, featuring a rotating exhibit lasting three-months. A town hall ballroom and performing arts space is located upstairs in the main building and rents out for functions.

A freedom monument stands at the back of the building, honoring those who were sentenced on the site when the building was a courthouse in the slave period. The names of condemned slaves appear alongside the punishment meted out by whipping, striping, or death. **The Cage,** just in front of the Cultural Centre in Sam Sharpe Square, was once used to lock up misbehaving slaves and sailors.

## CHURCHES

**St. James Parish Church** (Church St., tel. 876/971-2564) is one of the most attractive buildings in town. It's set on large grounds that house a small cemetery.

**Burchell Baptist Church** (Market St., tel. 876/971-9141) is a more humble church where Sam Sharpe used to preach. His remains are interred there.

## ESTATE GREAT HOUSES

Each of the area's estate great houses is worth visiting and quite distinct from the others. A visit to one or all of these historic properties is a great way to catch a glimpse of the island's glorious and tumultuous past.

## ★ Bellefield Great House

Five minutes from Mobay at Barnett Estate, **Bellefield Great House** (tel. 876/952-2382, info@bellefieldgreathouse.com, www.bellefieldgreathouse.com) offers two- to three-hour tours (10am-3pm Mon.-Thurs., US$40) that comprise a 45-minute visit of the great house and gardens and a one-hour lunch serving well-prepared Jamaican dishes. The tour can be arranged any day of the week for parties of 10 or more. A basic tour (US$20), without the delicious lunch, is also offered. Bellefield belongs to the Kerr-Jarretts, a family that still controls much of the land in and around Mobay as part of Fairfield Estate. To

# Sam Sharpe, National Hero

Sam Sharpe was the central figure of the Christmas Rebellion of 1831-1832, which many point to as the beginning of the end of slavery in Jamaica, officially granted in 1838. Sharpe was a Baptist deacon, respected across the deep societal divides. Despite this, he was executed in a public hanging on May 23, 1832, in what is now Sam Sharpe Square in the heart of Montego Bay. Over 300 slaves were also executed for their role in the rebellion. Sharpe had originally envisioned and promoted a peaceful rebellion of passive resistance, whereby the slaves would stage a sit-down strike until the planters agreed to pay them for their labor, in accordance with what was perceived as a royal decree from England being withheld in Jamaica.

The rebelling slaves were swept up in the excitement of the hour, however, as Sharpe's lieutenants swept across the western parishes to the sound of war drums in slave villages. Only 16 white people were killed during the rebellion, but around 20 large estates were torched, and the rebellion struck fear into the heart of the plantocracy. Sharpe took responsibility for the rebellion, relieving the white missionaries of the blame that was focused on them by the established powers of the day, including the Anglican Church, which, with a few isolated exceptions, even backed the landed elite, even organizing terror squads to target the Baptist missionaries who had made it their charge to foment discontent among the slaves. The Christmas Rebellion was consequently also known as the Baptist War.

get to Bellefield, take Fairfield Road from Catherine Hall, keeping right where the road splits to Chambers Drive until you reach the Granville Police Station. Take a right on Bellefield Road at the police station and proceed until you see the great house on the left.

## Rose Hall Great House

**Rose Hall Great House** (tel. 876/953-2323, greathouse@rosehall.com, www.rosehall.com, day tours 9:15am-5:15pm daily, night tours 6:30pm-9pm daily, US$20 adults, US$10 children) is the former home of Annie Palmer, remembered as the White Witch of Rose Hall in Herbert de Lisser's novel of that name. It's the most formidable and foreboding great house on the island today, with a bone-chilling history behind its grandeur. The tour

Montego Bay Cultural Centre

through the impeccably refurbished mansion is excellent.

Rose Hall was built in 1770 by John Palmer, who ruled the estate with his wife, Rosa. The property passed through many hands before ending up in possession of John Rose Palmer, who married the infamous Annie in 1820. A slight woman not more than five feet tall, Annie is said to have practiced voodoo, or black magic, and would eventually kill several husbands and lovers, starting with John Rose. Annie ruled the plantation brutally and was much feared by the estate's enslaved workers. She would ultimately taste her own medicine, as she was killed during the Christmas Rebellion of 1831.

Rose Hall was virtually abandoned with the decline in the sugar economy until an American rags-to-riches businessman, John Rollins, bought the estate in the 1960s and restored the great house to its old grandeur. Today the estate is governed by Michelle Rollins, who has upheld the ambitious development ethic of her late husband. Rose Hall Great House forms the historic centerpiece of the vast Rose Hall Estate, which encompasses three 18-hole golf courses, the Hyatt Zilara and Hyatt Ziva, Half Moon Resort and Hilton

Rose Hall, and the most desirable residential district of Montego Bay, Spring Farm.

Also on the Rose Hall Estate, Cinnamon Hill Great House was the home of the late Johnny Cash. Cinnamon Hill is not open to the public except during special events. Rose Hall is also the site of the Montego Bay Convention Centre and hosts the One Love Music Festival honoring Bob Marley around the time of his birthday on February 6.

## PLANTATION TOURS

Several plantations in the area offer visitors a chance to learn about Jamaica's principal agricultural products—from those that were historically important to crops adapted to the modern economy.

The birthplace of slave rebellion leader and national hero Sam Sharpe, 53-hectare (130-acre) **Croydon Plantation** (contact Tony Henry, tel. 876/979-8267, croydonplantationja@gmail.com, www.croydonplantation.com, Tues. and Thurs.-Fri. as well as days when cruise ships are in port) is a pineapple and coffee plantation located at the base of the Catadupa Mountains. The six-hour walking tour (US$65 pp) takes visitors through a working section of the plantation with an accompanying narrative, with three

Rose Hall Great House

refreshment stops for visitors to sample some of the 12 different kinds of pineapple grown here, in addition to other crops such as jackfruit, sugarcane, and Otaheite apples, depending on what's in season. The tour includes transportation, refreshments, and a typical Jamaican country lunch.

**John's Hall Adventure Tour** (tel. 876/971-7776 or 876/952-0873, johnshalltours@hotmail.com, www.johnshalladventuretour.com) offers a plantation tour (US$75 pp, includes jerk lunch and fruit) with a historical and contextual commentary by the guides. Stops along the way include the St. James Parish Church, Sam Sharpe Square, and Mt. Olive Basic School. John's Hall Adventure Tour also offers the Jamaica Rhythm Tour (by reservation, US$75, includes dinner), a musical show held at John's Hall featuring old-time heritage, from maypole dancing and limbo to mento. Both tours include transportation from Mobay hotels.

# Beaches

## ★ DOCTORS CAVE BEACH

**Doctors Cave Beach** (tel. 876/952-2566, www.doctorscavebathingclub.com, drscave@jamaica.com, 9am-5pm daily, US$5) is a private bathing club located at the center of Montego Bay's Hip Strip (Gloucester Ave.). The beach is well maintained, the sand is soft and white, and the water is crystalline. The beach is mostly used for sunbathing and swimming by visitors but is also frequented by Mobay's upscale crowd, who can purchase a yearly membership (US$150) that grants access to the clubhouse and its TV lounge, billiard table, and clean restrooms with showers. A gym offers membership on a daily (US$12), weekly (US$24), monthly (US48), and yearly (US$250) basis. The Beach Restaurant & Beach Bar at Doctors Cave hosts a live music series, We Are Reggae (US$25, US$20 in advance), the last Saturday of each month. Gates open at 8pm and shows start at 10pm with a local act opening for a major artist like Freddie McGregor, Sizzla Kalonji, and Romaine Virgo.

Doctors Cave Beach

## OTHER BEACHES

**Walter Fletcher Beach,** facing Mobay's harbor, is located on the Hip Strip, across from The Pork Pit. It is the location of **Aquasol Theme Park** (Gloucester Ave., tel. 876/979-9447 or 876/940-1344, 9am-6pm Mon.-Thurs., 9am-10pm Fri.-Sun., US$5 adults, US$3 under age 12), on a protected cove, with go-karts (US$3 single-seated, US$7 double), two tennis courts (operated by Steve Nolan, cell tel. 876/364-9293, 6:30am-10pm daily, US$6 per hour), billiard tables (US$0.50 per game), a video game room, glass-bottomed boat excursions to the coral reef (30-minute tour US$25 pp), and personal watercraft like Jet Skis ($75 for 30 minutes). There's also a sports bar with satellite TV and the Voyage restaurant (US$5-10), serving fried chicken, fried fish, and jerk. A gym on the property, **Mighty Moves** (tel. 876/952-8608, 7am-8pm daily, US$8), has free weights, weight machines, and aerobics classes included in the day pass.

**Tropical Beach** is a decent small strip of sand on the far side of the airport in White House, not a bad spot for a dip and with a few thatch umbrellas for shade. To get to Tropical Beach, turn left after passing the airport barrier fence, heading east toward Ironshore and Rose Hall.

**Dead End Beach** is the best free public beach in close proximity to the Hip Strip at the heart of Mobay's tourism scene. Sandals Carlyle faces the beach, which borders the end of the runway at the airport. The beach is located on Kent Avenue, better known as Dead End Road.

**One Man Beach** and **Dump-Up Beach,** located across from KFC and Mobay's central roundabout, are venues for occasional events and horse grazing. The beach here is not appropriate for swimming, as the city's effluent emerges from a neighboring gulley.

**Seawind Beach Club & Restaurant** (lot A59, Alice Eldemire Dr., Freeport, tel. 876/940-9660, beachclub2.sesmb@secretsresorts.com, 9am-6pm Mon.-Tues., 9am-10:30pm Wed.-Sun., US$10 adults, US$7 under age 12 Mon.-Fri., US$21 adults, US$14 under age 12 Sat.-Sun.) is a private beach club with a pool, changing rooms, and a bar and restaurant (last order 9pm) serving a mix of local Jamaican fare and Mexican tacos. Make a reservation to dine to avoid the admission fee.

**Old Steamer Beach** is 100 yards past the Shell gas station heading west out of Hopewell, Hanover. An embankment leads down to the skeleton of the USS *Caribou,* a steamer dating from 1887 that washed off its mooring in Mobay. You can hang your towel on the skeleton ship and take a swim at one of the nicest beaches around, which only gets busy on weekends when locals come down in droves to stir the crystal clear waters.

# Sports and Recreation

## WATER SPORTS
### Sailing

The **Montego Bay Yacht Club** (tel. 876/979-8038, fax 876/979-8262, mbyc@cwjamaica.com, www.mobayyachtclub.com) was refurbished in 2006 with a new building, landscaped grounds, and a small swimming pool. The club is a warm and friendly family environment with a great bar and restaurant, The Seahorse Grill, making it the place in western Jamaica for sailing, fishing, or just to hang out and make friends. A pool table and table tennis are available. Every Friday, the Seahorse Grill hosts a buffet dinner. Social and sailing membership (US$303 per year) grants members access to the Royal Jamaica Yacht Club in Kingston as well.

The Mobay Yacht Club is the finish line of the **Pineapple Cup Race** (www.montegobayrace.com), which covers 1,305 kilometers (810 miles) of water from its starting point in Fort Lauderdale. This classic race—a beat, a reach, and a run—is held in February every odd-numbered year. Other events include the annual Jamin **J-22 International Regatta** every December, and the Great Yacht Race, which precedes every Easter Regatta, a fun-filled, friendly, and competitive multiclass regatta. The **International Marlin Fishing Tournament** is held every fall, normally in September. Sailing camps for children are held during the summer, and courses are offered to adults based on demand.

If you arrive in Jamaica on a private vessel, the Mobay Yacht Club has some of the lowest docking fees anywhere (US$1.17 per foot per day up to 30 days), which are reduced for longer stays (US$0.82 per foot). Utilities are metered and charged accordingly, while boats at anchor can use the club facilities for the regular daily membership fee (US$10 pp). Mobay's mangrove areas in the Bogue Lagoon are often used as a hurricane hole for small vessels.

**The Lark Cruises** (contact Captain Carolyn Barrett, cell tel. 876/382-6384, info@barrettadventures.com, www.barrettadventures.com) operates half-day (US$400 for up to 3 people, US$100 for each additional person up to 15) and full-day (US$600, for up to 3, US$150 each additional person up to 10) cruises out of Mobay, with snorkeling and a Jamaican lunch included in the full-day charter. Weekly charters are also offered (US$3,500 for up to 4, plus provisions), inclusive of captain and cook. Charter destinations include Negril, Port Antonio, or even Cuba, contingent on favorable weather conditions.

**Dreamer Catamaran Cruises** (contact Donna Lee, tel. 876/979-0102, reservations@dreamercatamarans.com, www.dreamercatamarans.com, reservations required, 10am-1pm and 3pm-6pm Mon.-Sat., US$75 pp) has two three-hour cruises daily on its two 53-foot and three 65-foot catamarans, departing from Doctor's Cave Beach. The excursion includes an open bar and use of snorkeling gear during a 45-minute stop. The cruises stop at Margaritaville for lunch (not included). A five-hour cruise goes to Rick's Café (US$150 pp adult, US$120 pp under age 13) at 12:30pm

Wednesday and Sunday. The trip ends with an hour of cliff jumping (or watching) and includes lunch of jerk chicken, festival, veggie pasta, and an open bar. The return journey by bus takes an additional two hours.

**Jamaica Water Sports** (dptgonefishing@hotmail.com, www.jamaicawatersports.com) offers sailing charters (2-hour sails US$600 up to 10 people) on the 51-foot trimaran *Freestyle* for sailing and snorkeling around the Montego Bay Marine Park.

## Kiteboarding

**Irie Kiteboarding** with **Water Network Jamaica** (cell tel. 876/540-4042, info@waternetworkjamaica.com, www.iriekiteboardingjamaica.com) is your best bet for kite boarding, windsurfing, paddle boarding, and scuba in Mobay. Several IKO-certified instructors are on staff, including Jamaica's top kite boarder, Andrew Davis. It is based at Sea Castles, just past Rose Hall and the Montego Bay Convention Centre heading east. Introductory lessons start at US$180 for three hours; all-day rentals are US$290.

**Kiteboarding Jamaica** (tel. 876/781-2190, www.kiteboardingjamaica.com) operates out of Greenwood, offering lessons and CORE XR4 kite, control bar, harness and board rentals (from US$100).

## Scuba Diving

**Kelly's Water Sports** (Sunscape Splash, Freeport, cell tel. 876/893-2859 or 876/406-9380, kellyswatersports@gmail.com, kellyswatersportsjm.com) offers courses starting with the Discover Scuba Diving intro (US$120) and dives for certified divers, starting with a single tank (US$60) plus equipment rental (US$20).

## Fishing

**Ezee Sport Fishing** (Denise Taylor, cell tel. 876/381-3229 or 876/995-2912, dptgonefishing@hotmail.com, www.ezeesportfishing.com, half day US$650 for up to 6, full-day US$1,300) operates *Ezee*, a 39-foot Phoenix Sportfisher for deep-sea trolling, providing a good chance of catching big game like wahoo, blue marlin, or dorado, depending on the time of year. The crew assists in reeling them in with finesse.

**Lucky Bastard Fishing Charters** (cell tel. 876/572-0010, reservations@fishinginjamaica.com, www.fishinginjamaica.com), run by captain Howard Martin, boasts high catch rates on four-hour and eight-hour excursions deep-drop fishing, trolling, or a combination of both. Deep-drop fishing is done in around 300 meters (1,000 feet) of water and trolling from 60 meters (200 feet). *Lucky Bastard I* is a 30-foot cigarette boat converted for fishing; *Lucky Bastard II* is 28-foot Anacapri Flybridge.

## Snorkeling

**C-Jay's Watersports** (Pier 1 Marina, tel. 876/632-5824, cell tel. 876/881-7585 or 876/324-6065, contactus@cjwatersportsjm.com, www.cjwatersportsjm.com) offers glass-bottomed boat tours (US$25 adults, US$20 children), scuba diving (from US$110), parasailing (from US$60), waterskiing (US$30), wakeboarding (US$20), and tubing (US$25), as well as deep-sea fishing (4 hours, US$700 for 4).

**Montego Bay Marine Park** (Pier 1, tel. 876/952-5619, mbmptmanager@gmail.com, www.mbmp.org) covers the entire bay from the high-tide mark on land to 100 meters (328 feet) depth from Reading on Mobay's western edge to just east of the airport. The marine park encompasses diverse ecosystems that include mangroves, islands, beaches, estuaries, sea-grass beds, and coral reefs. The best way to see the marine park is with a licensed tour operator for a snorkeling trip or on a glass-bottomed boat tour. Groups of at least 15 can book boat tours (US$20 adults, US$10 students) of the marine park with the park rangers at the Marine Park office.

## GOLF

Montego Bay is the best base for golfing in Jamaica, with the highest concentration of courses on a nice variety of terrains, some with gorgeous rolling hills, others seaside, all within the immediate vicinity.

**White Witch Golf Course** (Rose Hall, tel. 876/632-7444 or 876/632-7445, www.whitewitchgolf.com, 6:30am-9pm daily) is the most spectacular course in Jamaica for its views and rolling greens. The course has a special rate for Hyatt, Iberostar Grand, and Riu guests. The course is also open to nonguests (US$139, US$119 after 10:30am, US$99 after 1:30pm,

White Witch Golf Course

for greens fees, cart, and caddy, not including gratuity). Last tee time is at 4:30pm.

**Cinnamon Hill Golf Course** (Rose Hall, tel. 876/953-2650) is operated by Hilton Rose Hall Resort & Spa and offers special rates to Hilton, Half Moon, and Sandals guests (greens fees, cart, and caddy US$141). After 1:30pm, the club offers a Twilight Special (US$99), in addition to the standard nonguest rate (greens fees, cart, and caddy US$160); club rental (US$40-50) is available. The recommended caddy tip is US$15-20 per player. Cinnamon Hill is the only course in Jamaica that's on the coast. Holes 5 and 6 are directly at the water's edge. A waterfall bubbles at the foot of Cinnamon Hill great house, owned by Johnny Cash until his death.

**Half Moon Golf Course** (Rose Hall, tel. 876/953-2560, www.halfmoongolf.com) is a Robert Trent Jones Jr.-designed course, with reduced rates for Half Moon guests (9 holes US$95 all day, 18 holes US$179 before 11am, US$159 from 11am-2pm, and US$139 after 2pm). Rates for nonguests (9 holes US$20, 18 holes US$40) include green fees, a cart, and caddy, but don't include club rentals. Half Moon is a walkable course.

**Kevyn Cunningham** (cell tel. 876/361-3330, www.kevyngolf.com, office@kevyngolf.com) offers tailored golf-centric concierge services and lessons for all levels.

## HORSEBACK RIDING

**Half Moon Equestrian Centre** (Half Moon Resort, tel. 876/953-2286, r.delisser@cwjamaica.com, www.horsebackridingjamaica.com) has the most impressive public stable in Jamaica, suitable for beginning to experienced riders. The center offers a pony ride for children under age 6 (US$20) and a 40-minute beginner ride (US$60) suitable for children over 6. A beach ride (US$80) includes a horseback swim for riders over age 8, and 30-minute private lessons for any experience level can include basic dressage, jumping, and polo.

**Chukka Caribbean** (www.chukkacaribbean.com) is Jamaica's leading adventure tour operator, taking visitors on horseback for its trademark Ride 'N' Swim at several locations across the island. Chukka has three locations in the vicinity of Montego Bay: at Good Hope Plantation in Trelawny, at Montpelier in St. James, and at Chukka Blue in Hanover. The greatest variety of tours are offered at Good Hope, a citrus plantation crisscrossed by the Martha Brae River, with jitney rides, food and rum tasting, tubing, horseback riding, and ziplines.

## TOURS

**Chukka Caribbean** (U.S. tel. 877/424-8552, tel. 876/656-8026, info@chukka.com, www.chukka.com) offers a host of activities for thrill seekers and adventure lovers, including catamaran cruises, canopy ziplines, cliff jumping, white-water rafting along the upper reaches of the Great River in Lethe, tubing on the White River along the St. Ann-St. Mary border, ziplines, and off-roading on ATVs and dune buggies in several locations across the island, as well as trips to Bob Marley's birthplace at Nine Mile by old country Zion Bus or open-air Land Rover safari vehicles.

**Bamboo Rafting** (US$20) is offered on long bound-bamboo rafts along the lower reaches of the Great River and out onto the tranquil bay where the river meets the sea. Immediately after crossing the Great River, turn inland and back to the river's edge, where several rafts are tied up under the bridge. Ask for Hugh.

**Rocklands Bird Sanctuary and Feeding Station** (just before Anchovy, St. James, tel. 876/952-2009, 11am-5:30pm daily, US$20 pp) was created by the late Lisa Sammons, popularly known as "the bird lady," who died in 2000 at age 96. Sammons had a way with birds, to say the least, summoning them to daily feeding sessions, even after going partially blind later in life. The feeding sessions have continued, and the sanctuary is maintained by Fritz, his wife, Cynthia, and their son Damian. Visitors can sit on the patio and hold hummingbird feeders that entice the birds to perch on their fingers. A nature trail meanders through the property for bird-watching. More than 20 species can be seen on any given day. Fritz offers guided tours through the forest (US$20 pp). To get to Rocklands, head up Long Hill from Reading and turn left off the main road at the big green "Rocklands Bird Sanctuary" sign. Follow one abominable road to the top of the mountain and down the other side, about 100 meters (330 feet), turning right at the first driveway on the descent.

**Barrett Adventures** (contact Carolyn Barrett, cell tel. 876/382-6384, info@barrettadventures.com, www.barrettadventures.com) is a tour company based in Mobay offering tailored itineraries anywhere in Jamaica. Veteran adventurer Carolyn Barrett will ensure anything you could want to do gets done in the allotted time, whether you spend just a few hours or an entire week exploring the island.

**Jamaica Tour Society** (cell tel. 876/357-1225, info@jamaicatoursociety.com, www.jamaicatoursociety.com) is based in Montego Bay and offers all manner of off-the-beaten track tours across Jamaica, with a special expertise on Falmouth and Trelawny, under the guidance of Lynda Lee Burks.

# Entertainment and Events

## BARS AND CLUBS

For an early evening drink, the **Montego Bay Yacht Club** (10am-10pm daily) is a popular spot among the upscale crowd, especially on Friday. The **HouseBoat Bar** is also a popular early evening spot, while **Mobay Proper** has the most consistently happening local scene every night of the week.

**Mobay Proper** (44 fort St. tel. 876/940-1233, 11:30am-1am daily, US$2-15) is a popular local bar with a few billiard tables and gaming machines, with indoor and outdoor seating areas serving local fare like oxtail, stew pork, curry goat, fried chicken, escoveitch, steam fish, and smoked pork. The bar is owned and managed by the congenial Calvin Malcolm.

**Musiq** (72 Gloucester Ave., 4pm-1am daily) opened in July 2009 on the premises of the Pork Pit under the same family ownership. The bar features an in-house DJ Thursday-Sunday playing R&B, hip-hop, reggae, and dancehall. A chic setting with musical motif lends itself to chilling out and watching passersby along the Hip Strip.

**D'Rehab Lounge, Sports Bar & Pool Hall** (32 Gloucester Ave., tel. 876/620-9826, 5pm-2am daily) has a handful of billiard tables (US$0.50 per game) and two bars, and often hosts parties. The lounge only charges a cover when hosting a party.

**Margaritaville** (Gloucester Ave., tel. 876/952-4777, restaurant open 10am-10pm daily, club open until 2am Sun.-Wed., 4am Thurs., and 5am Fri., US$10) is a wildly popular restaurant and bar with a waterslide dropping off into the sea and giant trampoline inner tubes just offshore for patrons' enjoyment. The restaurant serves cheeseburgers, jerk chicken and pork, and lobster (US$10-35). The large open area on the ground level serves as Montego Bay's go-to nightclub, drawing crowds especially on Saturday. Margaritaville has other locations in Ocho Rios, Negril, and the departure terminal at Sangster International Airport.

**Blue Beat** (Gloucester Ave., tel. 876/952-4777, 6pm-2am daily, no cover) is Margaritaville's more sophisticated and upscale cousin, located in an adjacent building under the same ownership. The laid-back club features a resident DJ every night and live jazz (10pm-2am Wed.-Thurs. and Sun.).

**Zinc Shack** (55 Gloucester Ave., 10am-10pm daily, cell tel. 876/383-6089) is a no-frills bar tucked away behind Tease Café that plays mostly dancehall. The bar is run by

Howard Owen and at times draws a decent mix of locals and travelers.

**Hilites Sky Bar and Grill** (19 Queens Dr., tel. 876/775-3152, jamaica_flamingo_ ltd@hotmail.com, 8:30am-6pm daily) has a great view over the harbor and airport from its perch on Top Road and is a good spot for an early evening drink or to watch the planes take off and land at the airport.

**Facebaar** (1139 Morgan Rd., Triangle Mall, Iron Shore, tel. 876/953-0992, 8pm-2am Tues.-Fri., 8pm-4am Sat., US$5, www.facebaarjamaica.com) caters to a wide range of guests with three dance floors and VIP space, with an R&B and hip-hop vibe out front. Latin night is Saturday, and karaoke is Wednesday.

## LIVE MUSIC

Unfortunately, live music in Mobay is hard to find, in sharp contrast to decades past when there was an active music scene. Today, the all-inclusive resorts have house bands to entertain guests, who are often discouraged from leaving the compound. Nevertheless, live jazz is performed at Day-O Plantation, as well as at Blue Beat, and Margaritaville. If you want world-class music, the best time to visit is during Reggae Sumfest in July. Catherine Hall Entertainment Center, the main venue for Sumfest, occasionally hosts other concerts and festivals.

## FESTIVALS AND EVENTS
### ★ Reggae Sumfest

**Reggae Sumfest** (www.reggaesumfest. com) organizers aren't being presumptuous when they claim it's the greatest reggae show on earth. Held over three nights in mid-July, with preceding events starting earlier in the week, the performances kick off on Thursday with Dancehall Night, featuring Jamaica's top acts of the moment and stalwarts of the genre. International Night I and International Night II follow on Friday and Saturday, featuring a dynamic showcase of reggae, dancehall, hip-hop, and R&B legends. The performances typically start around 9pm and run well past daylight the next morning.

### Other Festivals

The Montego Bay Yacht Club (tel. 876/979-8038, mbyc@cwjamaica.com, www.mobayyachtclub.com) has its share of events, including annual and biannual yacht races and a **Marlin Festival.**

**Trelawny Yam Festival** (www.stea.net)

Conscious lyricist Bugle performs at Reggae Sumfest 2015.

is a highlight of the year in Albert Town, Trelawny, a family fun day centered on one of the island's most important staple foods, with tugs-of-war, beauty competitions, and, of course, music.

## THEATER

**Fairfield Theatre** (Fairfield Rd., contact Chairman/Manager Inlen Johnson, cel. tel. 876/781-8792, 876/384-5299 or 876/813-2057, admission US$15, students with ID US$10) is the only venue in the Mobay area for theatrical productions that strive to professional standards. Performances run seasonally, typically on Fridays (8pm), Saturdays (8pm) and Sundays (7pm). The theatre features traditional Jamaican roots plays and other family friendly genres. The Montego Bay Little Theatre Movement, sprung from the Little Theatre Movement in Kingston, which formed by Jamaican cultural icons like them the most renown in theatre, Louise Bennett.

The theatre performs contemporary works from leading Jamaican and Caribbean playwrights, as well as classics like of Shakespeare, Noël Coward, Peter Schaefer, Lorraine Hansberry and Neil Simon. Caribbean writers such as Derek Walcott, Errol Hill and Douglas Archibald have been produced to critical acclaim, but greater audience appeal has been found with the current crop of Jamaican playwrights that includes Basil Dawkins, Trevor Rhone, Patrick Brown and David Heron, and more recently, David Tulloch.

# Shopping

## ARTS AND CRAFTS

**The Gallery of West Indian Art** (Catherine Hall, 11 Fairfield Rd., tel. 876/952-4547, cell tel. 876/871-8103, nikola@cwjamaica.com, www.galleryofwestindianart.com, 10am-5pm Mon.-Fri.) is one of the most diverse galleries in Jamaica, carrying both Jamaican art and pieces from neighboring islands, especially Haiti and Cuba. The gallery is owned and operated by Nicky and Stefan, who make quality pieces accessible with reasonable pricing. Look out for work by Jamaican artists Delores Anglin and Gene Pearson, a sculptor specializing in bronze heads.

**Craft centers** abound in Mobay, including Harbour Street, Kent Avenue, Charles Gordon Market, and Montego Bay Craft Market. A discriminating eye is required at all of these markets to sift out the trinkets from the quality Jamaica-produced crafts.

**Freeport Cruise Ship Terminal** has several shops, most of which carry overpriced souvenirs and mass-produced crafts.

## APPAREL

**Profumo Boutique** (shop 3, The Shops at Bay Harbour, 1-3 Gloucester Ave., tel. 876/979-1842, 10am-7pm Mon.-Sat.) sells Jamaican-made clothing, accessories and jewelry, imported fragrances, sunglasses, bags, and sandals.

**Schatzie** (Fairview, cell tel. 876/383-0992, katrin@schatzie-ltd.com, www.wrightinstyle.com) retails the Wright Style of light cotton resort wear.

Leroy Thompson (cell tel. 876/546-8657) is the head craftsman at **Klass Traders** (Fort St., tel. 876/952-5782) produces attractive handmade leather sandals from a workshop adjacent to Mobay Proper.

**Rastafari Art** (42 Hart St., tel. 876/885-7674 or 876/771-7533) has a variety of red, gold, and green items, including flags, belts, T-shirts, bags, and friendship bands that make inexpensive, authentic, and lightweight gifts and souvenirs.

**Lloyd's** (26 St. James St., tel. 876/952-3172, second location at Shops 24-25 in Fairview Shopping Centre, tel. 876/979-8320) has a great selection of trendy urban and roots wear.

## JEWELRY AND WATCHES

**The Shoppes at Rose Hall** (tel. 876/953-3245, www.theshoppesatrosehall.com) are home to a few dozen duty-free stores selling jewelry and watches as well as boutiques with apparel, cigars, and sunglasses.

**Swiss Stores** (shop 23, tel. 876/922-8050, www.swissstoresjamaica.com) has a long tradition of selling watches and jewelry in Jamaica. It carries international and locally produced jewelry.

**Bijoux Jewelers** (shop 4, tel. 876/953-9530) boasts being the oldest duty-free jewelry store in the island. It carries a few dozen renowned brands of watches and jewelry.

**Jewels in Paradise** (tel. 876/953-9372 or tel. 305/735-3076, www.jewelsinparadise.com, 9am-5pm Mon.-Sat.) carries high-end jewelry and watches.

## BOOKS

**Sangster's Book Stores** sells all kinds of books and magazines and has two locations in Montego Bay: one at 2 St. James Street (tel. 876/952-0319, 8:30am-6pm Mon.-Sat.), the other at 9 King Street (876/979-2134, 8:30am-5:30pm Mon.-Sat.).

## MUSIC

**Tad's International Records** (tel. 876/940-2862, departure lounge at Sangster International Airport) has an extensive catalog of reggae.

**PG's Music Fashion** (Shop 103, Baywest Shopping Centre, Harbour St., contact proprietor Pauline Robinson cell. tel. 876/830-8005, 10am-7pm Mon.-Sat.) sells CDs of classic and contemporary reggae, dancehall, gospel, and R&B, and the odd reggae and gospel 33.

# Food

## BREAKFAST AND CAFÉS

★ **Mocha Café** (shop 13, the Shops at Bay Harbour, Gloucester Ave., next to the Burger King, cell tel. 876/433-8848) serves a selection of hot and cold beverages, breakfast, and sandwiches.

**Café Blue** (www.jamaicacafeblue.com) has two locations in Montego Bay, at Rose Hall (shop 28, Shoppes at Rose Hall, tel. 876/953-4646, cafebluerosehall@coffeetradersjamaica.com, 9am-5pm Mon.-Sat.) and inside Fontana Pharmacy (Fairview), both serving coffee and tea and light savory dishes and pastries. Try the Blue Mountain Fog iced coffee and smoked marlin sandwich.

**Café Tease** (55 Gloucester Ave., tel. 876/618-3644, 9am-7pm Mon.-Tues., 9am-5am Wed.-Sat., 10am-10pm Sun.) serves Blue Mountain Coffee, pizzas, and sandwiches.

## JAMAICAN

**Kaptain Red Hot** (35 Gloucester, cell tel. 876/540-9811, 24 hours daily, US$3-10) is

a greasy spoon serving local dishes at local prices, including fried, jerk, and barbecue chicken, escoveitch fish, curry conch and shrimp, stew pork, jerk pork, oxtail, tripe and beans, cow foot, turkey neck, veggie chunks, and egg and chicken sandwiches. Delivery is free between the airport and Freeport.

**Mobay Proper** (44 Fort St., tel. 876/940-1233, noon-2am daily, US$3.50-14) is the in spot for Mobay's party-hearty youth. The food is excellent and a great value, with dishes like fried or jerk chicken, fish done to order, curry goat, and roast beef as well as steamed, escoveitch, or brown stew fish. This is a good place to get a beer (US$2) and play some billiards (US$1 per game).

**Nyam 'n' Jam** (shop 28, City Centre Bldg., tel. 876/971-1181, cell tel. 876/829-8373, 7am-midnight daily; 17 Harbour St., tel. 876/952-1922, 7am-11pm daily, US$3-4.50) serves Jamaican staples like fried chicken, curry goat, and oxtail buffet-style as well as shrimp, lobster, conch, and veggie chunks to order.

Breakfast items include ackee and saltfish, callaloo and saltfish, brown stew chicken, yam, boiled bananas, and fried dumpling.

**Martina's** (1 Howard Cook Blvd., tel. 876/953-6557, Marcia's cell tel. 876/856-3086, msaunders06@yahoo.com, 8am-midnight daily, US$6-13) serves Jamaican specialties like stew pork, curried goat, oxtail, baked chicken, fresh whole fish, filet fish, conch, and shrimp. Guest DJs spin (Fri.-Sun.). An ice creamery (10am-8pm Mon.-Sat., 10am-10pm Sun.) on the same property sells Devon House ice cream in cones and cups (US$3-4). The property is also home to a nursery, an aviary, and a playground with a swing set, slide, and seesaw, complimentary for patrons.

**Sweet Spice** (shop 3, Westgate Shopping Centre, tel. 876/952-3199, 8:30am-9pm Mon.-Sat., 8:30am-6pm Sun.) serves Jamaican breakfast dishes like callaloo and codfish, ackee and saltfish, kidney and onion, and brown stew chicken. The lunch menu includes items from curry goat to escoveitch fish.

**The Beach Restaurant & Beach Bar** (Doctors Cave Beach, tel. 876/631-4952, ddouglas@thebeachja.com, www.thebeachja.com, 9am-6pm daily, US$10-35) is popular with locals and visitors alike. It serves a wide range of bar food with Jamaican staples including steamed fish, escoveitch fish with bammy, jerk chicken and pork, and curry shrimp and lobster tail. The restaurant's location on Doctors Cave Beach is unbeatable. The restaurant hosts a monthly "We Are Reggae" series on the last Saturday of each month.

**Biggs BBQ Restaurant & Bar** (tel. 876/952-9488, www.biggsbbqmobay.com, 11am-2am daily, US$15-30) specializes in slobbered ribs, pulled pork, and Southern-style barbecue chicken. The bar is set up for sports, with three large flat-screen TVs above the bottle shelves. Outside, a large terrace overlooks the sea.

★ **Pier 1 Restaurant and Marina** (tel. 876/952-2452, 9am-11pm daily, later on weekends) is a popular restaurant and entertainment venue. Seafood all day Sunday offers shrimp specials, discounts on beer, and a retro DJ. Pier 1 hosts the Pier Pressure party on Friday, a fashion and talent show on Wednesday, and occasional large events. Appetizers include crunchy conch (US$5), chicken wings (US$8), and shrimp cocktail (US$10), while entrées include chicken and mushrooms (US$12), bracelet steak (US$25), whole snapper (US$16 per pound), and lobster (US$28).

**The Seahorse Grill** (Montego Bay Yacht Club, Freeport, tel. 876/979-8038, 10am-10pm daily, US$6-25), led by executive chef Robbie Joseph in a pleasant waterfront setting, has a good menu with burgers, sandwiches, salads, and entrées like lobster and shrimp thermidor, snapper, lamb chops, seafood pasta, coconut curry chicken, and zucchini pasta. A popular buffet dinner (US$14) with a rotating menu is served on Friday.

## JERK

★ **Scotchies** (Carol Gardens, tel. 876/953-3301, 11am-11pm daily, US$4-11) consistently prepares the best jerk pork and chicken in Jamaica. It also serves steam roast fish fillets, chicken sausage, pork sausage and a soup of the day. Sides include breadfruit, festival and yam. The legendary jerk pit was founded after Tony Rerrie began occasionally bringing a master jerk chef from Boston Bay in Portland, where locals claim jerk originated. Fans begged him to make the jerk offering a regular thing, and Scotchies was born when Tony pieced together a few cinder blocks, some bamboo poles, and a few sheets of zinc roofing. The minimalist ambiance remained true to its origins as the jerk joint grew with franchises in Ochi and Kingston.

**The Pork Pit** (27 Gloucester Ave., tel. 876/940-3008, 11am-11pm Sun.-Thurs., 11am-midnight Fri.-Sat., US$5-12) is MoBay's original jerk joint and shows no signs of slowing down. The Pork Pit serves mouthwatering jerk chicken, shrimp jerk pork, and ribs, with sides of festival, rice-and-peas, fries, bammy, and sweet potato.

**Jerky's** (29 Alice Eldemire Dr., tel. 876/684-9101, 11am-midnight Sun.-Fri.,

11am-late Sat. for karaoke, US$3-10) has jerk chicken, steamed fish, escoveitch fish, ribs, conch, shrimp, and fried fish. There is a large bar where beer costs US$1.75.

★ **MVP Smokehouse** (Bogue Rd., Reading, tel. 876/622-7198, info@mvpsmokehouse.com, www.mvpsmokehouse.com, noon-9pm Tues.-Thurs., noon-10pm Fri.-Sun., US$5-25) was launched in late 2012 by Michelle and Boris Reid, who developed the Medina Valley Pride line of sauces, now called MVP. The restaurant specializes in smoked meats and seafood with creative twists that go beyond jerk. Weekly specials include curry chicken roti on Wednesday, stew peas and pigs tail on Tuesday, and conch prepared your way on Friday. Oldies are blasted 3pm-close Sunday.

## INTERNATIONAL

**King Palace Chinese Restaurant** (shop 62, City Centre, Alice Eldemire Dr., Bogue, tel. 876/940-2104, 11:30am-9:30pm Mon.-Sat., 1pm-9:30pm Sun., US$9-15) serves some of Montego Bay's best Chinese food and great-value buffet combo lunch specials (US$5).

**Dragon Court** (Fairview Shopping Center, Alice Eldemire Dr., Bogue, tel. 876/979-8822 or 876/979-8824, 11:30am-10pm Mon.-Sat.,

US$5-18) has good dim sum every day. The shrimp dumplings are a favorite.

**China House Restaurant** (32 Gloucester Ave., tel. 876/979-0056, 10am-10pm daily, US$2.25-22.50) serves Chinese, Mongolian, Thai, and Jamaican cuisine, as does its neighbor, **Golden Dynasty Chinese Restaurant** (39 Gloucester Ave., tel. 876/971-0459, 11am-10pm Mon.-Sat., noon-10pm Sun., US$2-20). China House serves dim sum on Sunday.

**Mystic India Restaurant** (Shop 13, Whitter Shopping Village, tel. 876/953-9460 or 876/630-4043, 11am-10pm daily, US$12-25) serves authentic Indian dishes.

**Facebaar Restaurant** (1139 Morgan Rd., Triangle Mall, Iron Shore, tel. 876/953-0992, cell tel. 876/855-8708, 8am-11pm Sun.-Fri., 8am-midnight Sat., US$8-24) serves internationally flavored fare like shrimp linguine, rib-eye, Rasta pasta, and coconut breaded shrimp in a casually elegant atmosphere.

## FINE DINING

★ **The HouseBoat Grill** (Southern Cross Blvd., Freeport, tel. 876/979-8845, houseboat@cwjamaica.com, www.montego-bay-jamaica.com, 6pm-11pm Tues.-Sun., bar from 4:30pm, happy hour 5:30pm-7pm, US$12-26) on Montego Bay's Bogue Lagoon

grilling at The Pork Pit

is an unparalleled setting for a romantic dinner, and the food is excellent. Dishes include chicken, fish, and lobster. Reservations are recommended.

**Marguerite's** (Gloucester Ave., adjacent to Margaritaville, tel. 876/952-4777, 6pm-10:30pm daily, US$20-50) is the fine-dining wing of Mobay's popular Margaritaville, serving dishes ranging from Caribbean-style chicken to seafood penne and sugarcane-seared drunken lobster tail.

**Day-O Plantation** (Fairfield Rd., tel. 876/952-1825, cell tel. 876/877-1884, day-orest@yahoo.com, www.dayorestaurant. com, US$16-35, lunch by reservation, dinner 6pm-11pm Tues.-Sun.) was formerly part of the Fairfield Estate, which at one time encompassed much of Mobay. It is perhaps the most laid-back and classy place to enjoy a delicious dinner. Entrées range from typical chicken dishes (US$25) to grilled spiny lobster (US$40). A beer costs US$5. Day-O is a favorite for weddings and other events that require the finest setting around a gorgeous pool. On a good day owner Paul will bring out his guitar and impress diners with his talent. Other professional musicians who have played at the restaurant's dinner shows include guitar legend Ernest Ranglin, jazz artist Martin Hand, and steel pan artist Othello Molineaux. Etana performed on a recent Mother's Day.

**The Pelican Grill** (Gloucester Ave., tel. 876/952-3171, pelican@cwjamaica.com, www.pelicangrillja.com, 7am-10:30pm daily, US$10-40) is a Mobay institution, founded in 1964 by Jeremy and Clarissa Bennett, who still oversee day-to-day operations while managing a lovely B&B up the hill. The Pelican serves a mix of local and international dishes, including Jamaican favorites like stewed peas (US$10), curry goat (US$15), steamed or brown stew fish (US$15), and lobster (US$45). It's Jamaica's answer to comfort food in the kind of casual, homely environment sitcoms are made of. International staples like cordon bleu (US$20) and hamburgers (US$12) match booths reminiscent of a 1980s diner. The milk shakes are a draw for locals and visitors alike.

Ras Mudada Hamanot sells books in addition to vegetarian meals at Adwa Nutrition for Life.

★ **The Sugar Mill Restaurant** (across the highway from Half Moon Shopping Village, tel. 876/953-2314 or 876/953-2228, 6pm-10pm daily) is one of the area's high-end establishments, specializing in Caribbean fusion cuisine with openers like pumpkin or conch soup (US$7.50), spring rolls, smoked marlin or conch in fritters, salad, or jerked (US$13-15). Entrées range from coconut-crusted or escoveitch fish to lobster tail (US$35-50).

## VEGETARIAN

**Adwa Nutrition for Life** is the best place in town for natural food. It has two locations: a full-service, sit-down restaurant (City Centre Bldg., tel. 876/952-6554, 8am-9pm daily), and a retail store selling nutritional supplements, books, juices, and vegan food (shop 2, West Gate Plaza, tel. 876/952-6554). Dishes (US$4-10) include curried tofu, peppered veggie steak, and red pea soup, with beverages like cane juice, fruit smoothies, and carrot juice.

**Wright Life** (Fairview Town Centre,

cell tel. 876/376-8708, 10am-6pm Mon.-Sat., US$5-15) is a live eatery serving salads, juices, and natural products in an impeccably clean minimalist restaurant beside Fontana pharmacy.

## SWEET SPOTS

**Cream & Crumbs** (shop 1, Shops at Bay Harbour, 1-3 Gloucester Ave., tel. 876/619-1595, 11am-7pm Mon.-Fri., noon-8pm Sat.-Sun.) serves Deja Fruit sorbet, Devon House ice cream, patties, and beverages from its shop facing the sea.

**Sweet Treats** (1 Seaview Plaza, tel. 876/953-2303, cell tel. 876/448-9037, 11am-10pm daily) is a convenient dessert spot located next to Scotchies, serving ice cream, coffee, and chocolates.

**Devon House I Scream** (Bay West Center, tel. 876/940-4060, 11am-11pm daily) has some of the best ice cream around.

**Montego Bay Chocolate Company** (Bay West Center, tel. 876/940-4060, 11am-11pm daily) has some of the best ice cream around.

# Accommodations

Options range widely, with cheap dives, mid-range B&Bs, guesthouses, luxury villas, world-class hotels, and all-inclusive resorts. In the center of town, on Queens Drive (Top Rd.), and to the west in Reading are several low-cost options, while the mid-range hotels are concentrated around the Hip Strip along Gloucester Avenue (Bottom Rd.) and just east of the airport. Rose Hall is the area's most glamorous address, with several resorts in the vicinity of the city's top-notch golf courses. Also on the eastern side of town is Sandals Royal Caribbean, easily the chain's most luxurious property, complete with a private island. Along the Hip Strip several mid-range hotels provide direct access to Mobay's nightlife, a mix of bars and a few clubs. Guesthouses farther afield offer great rates.

Mobay is the principal entry point for most travelers arriving on the island, many of whom stay at one of the many hotels in the immediate vicinity. The old Ironshore and Rose Hall estates, east along the coast, are covered in luxury and mid-range hotels.

## UNDER US$100

**The Bird's Nest** (177 Patterson Ave., Ironshore, cell tel. 876/781-2190, info@thebirdsnestjamaica.com, www.kitesurfvilla.com), aka Kite Surf Villa, has 10 bunk beds in two dormitories with a shared bath, two private rooms with double beds and private baths, and one private room with a single bed and private bath. The manager also manages Kiteboarding Jamaica.

**Palm Bay Guest House** (Reading Rd., Bogue, tel. 876/952-2274, www.palmbayguesthouse.com) has basic, clean rooms (from US$65) with air-conditioning and hot water in private baths. It is not the most glamorous location in town, opposite Mobay's biggest government housing project, Bogue Village, built to formalize the squatters of Canterbury, but Palm Bay is quiet, safe, and removed from the bustle along the Hip Strip. A restaurant (7am-10pm daily) specializes in jerk, and Wi-Fi reaches most of the rooms.

**Hartley House** (contact Sandra Kennedy, tel. 876/956-7101, cell tel. 876/899-5979, sandravkennedy@gmail.com, www.hartleyhousejamaica.com, US$60 s, US$80 d, including breakfast) is a lovely B&B located on a 0.8-hectare (two-acre) property at Tamarind Hill by the Great River, on the border of Hanover and St. James about 20 minutes from the airport. Rooms are appointed in traditional colonial style with four-poster queen beds or two twins, sitting areas, ceiling fans, and private baths. The villa was designed by architect Robert Hartley as a satellite property to Round Hill in 1965. Guests have access to a common area with a library and a TV room. Wi-Fi, tea, and coffee are complimentary all day long. Guests are provided low-calorie, continental, Jamaican, or English breakfast. A round three-meter-deep (10-foot-deep) pool is the centerpiece in the courtyard.

## US$100-250

★ **The Spanish Court Hotel Montego Bay** (7 Gloucester Ave., tel. 876/979-0000, info@spanishcourthotel.com, www.spanishcourthotel.com) is a 125-room boutique hotel offering all-inclusive or room-only lodging, with two pools, two restaurants, a spa, a lounge, and a sky bar. The hotel faces Doctors Cave Beach, the most popular and best-cared-for strip of white sand in Jamaica's second city.

★ **Polkerris Bed & Breakfast** (13 Corniche Rd., tel. 876/877-7784, www.polvista.com, from US$134) has a total of 10 rooms in two villas on opposite sides of the road. Rooms have a king, queen, or two doubles, all with en suite baths, air-conditioning, and flat-screen TVs. Hidden on a quiet residential street, the villas seem far from the bustle of the Hip Strip but are only a five-minute walk away, striking the perfect balance of seclusion and proximity.

**Richmond Hill Inn** (tel. 876/952-3859, www.richmond-hill-inn.com, from US$153) is a bed-and-breakfast at the highest point in the vicinity of downtown Mobay, with easily the best view in town, from a large terraced swimming pool area and the open-air dining room. While the rooms fall short of luxurious, the sheets are clean, the restaurant is excellent, and the pool area's unmatched view and free Wi-Fi make Richmond Hill one of the best values in town.

★ **Wharf House** (Bogue Rd., Reading, contact Nicky, cell tel. 876/839-9001, or Stefan, tel. 876/871-8103, tarah@cwjamaica.com or prohaska@cwjamaica.com, rooms US$150, exclusive rental US$560 for up to 8 people) is an impeccable 300-plus-year-old collection of stone-hewn buildings facing Bogue Lagoon, a protected marine sanctuary. Gun slits in the 45-centimeter (18-inch) walls were once used to protect the sugar and rum warehoused here. The property has been remodeled into a rustic luxury lodging with TVs, sound system, and Wi-Fi. Bedrooms have air-conditioning and common areas have plush, inviting furniture and delightful artwork. Meals can be enjoyed on the large deck overhanging the water or in the formal dining room inside. The master suite in the main house has a king bed and

Wharf House

shares a bath with a second bedroom with two single beds, ideal for families. Two outlying buildings accommodate two guests each with a king bed in each. A tiled pool is set back from the lawn and the beach.

## OVER US$250

★ **Half Moon Resort** (Rose Hall, tel. 876/953-2211, reservations@halfmoonclub. com, www.halfmoon.com, US$250-1,250 low season, US$400-1,800 high season) is one of the most upscale resorts in Jamaica, comprising an assortment of rooms, cottages, and villas. Most of the cottages and all the villas have private pools. Set on a 162-hectare (400-acre) estate, the resort has 33 staffed villas with three to seven bedrooms, 152 suites, and 46 rooms. The cottages are tastefully furnished and cozier than the villas, which can feel cavernous due to their immense size and vary considerably in decor based on the taste of their individual owners.

Half Moon attracts golfers to its championship par-72 Robert Trent Jones Sr. course and tennis players to its 13 lighted courts. A range of water sports includes a dolphin lagoon, operated by Dolphin Cove exclusively for Half Moon guests. Food at the estate's six restaurants is top-notch, with a number of snack bars dotting the property for quick bites. Also on the resort is the recently renovated **Fern Tree Spa,** among the best in the Caribbean. The crescent-shaped Half Moon Beach is one of the finest private beaches in the Mobay area.

**Zoetry Montego Bay** (Rose Hall, tel. 876/953-9150, www.zoetryresorts.com, from US$400) is a 46-room, five-star, all-inclusive boutique property on a private white sand beach 10 minutes east of the airport. The hotel has three seafront à la carte restaurants, a tapas bar, and unlimited top-shelf spirits. Zoetry features 24-hour room service in junior or master suite categories, swim-out pools from ground-level rooms, a wraparound infinity pool, and water sports. The property also features a 230-square-meter (2,500-square-foot) spa with plunge pools.

## ALL-INCLUSIVE RESORTS

**Royal DeCameron Montego Beach** (2 Gloucester Ave., tel. 876/952-4340 or 876/952-4346, ventas.jam@decameron.com, www. decameron.com, US$116 low season, US$240 high season) is a budget-minded all-inclusive resort, the chain's second property in Jamaica. At times it can be hard to get through for a

Half Moon Resort has a private beach.

reservation, but otherwise the property can be a good value compared to other all-inclusives.

**Secrets St. James** and **Secrets Wild Orchid** (tel. 876/953-6600, reservations. sesmb@secretsresorts.com, www.secretsresorts.com, US$188 low season, US$326 high season), located next to one another on the southwestern tip of the Freeport peninsula, opened in 2010. All 700 suites at the two properties have a similar layout, with whirlpool tubs and either a balcony or a patio. The food is above average for all-inclusives, with an excellent breakfast buffet spread and fine dining restaurants specializing in French, Italian, and Japanese cuisine.

**Sunscape Splash Montego Bay** (tel. 876/979-8800, www.sunscaperesorts.com, from US$280 low season, US$365 high season) has a casual, family-friendly atmosphere with tennis courts, a water park, and a private beach. The 430-room resort is located in Freeport, facing west. Rooms are divided between a main building and smaller structures on the opposite side of a large pool area. Rooms either face out to sea or toward central Montego Bay. Unlimited food, along with local and international beverages, is available 24 hours a day in several restaurants and bars across the property. The hotel is about 10 minutes by cab to the Hip Strip or central Montego Bay.

★ **Sandals Royal Caribbean** (Mahoe Bay, Ironshore, tel. 876/953-2231, srjmail@grp.sandals.com, 3-night minimum, from US$473 d) is the most opulent Sandals hotel in Montego Bay, with 197 rooms and suites well deserving of the chain's "Luxury Included" motto. The suites are over-the-top, with wood paneling, large flat-screen TVs, and tiled baths with standing showers and tubs. Balconies look over the courtyard and out to sea, with steps off ground floor suites leading directly into a large pool. The private island at Sandals Royal Caribbean is the trademark feature, where boats shuttle guests out for dinner or to laze on the fine-sand beach. In 2016 Sandals Royal Caribbean inaugurated five over-the-water villas (from US$2938 d) with king size beds, tubs, glass floors, and infinity pools for two on large private balconies.

**Riu Montego Bay** (tel. 876/940-8010, www.riu.com, US$115-160) is a 680-room all-inclusive resort with standard double and suite rooms and an immense swimming pool. Suites have hydro-massage tubs and lounge areas. All rooms have a minibar, satellite TV, air-conditioning, balconies, and en suite baths. The resort offers a host of activities, including water sports and tennis on two hard-surface courts. The gym has a weight room, a sauna, and a whirlpool tub. The resort is located in Ironshore, near the end of the airport runway, next door to Sandals Royal Caribbean.

**Hyatt Ziva Rose Hall** (U.S. tel. 888/763-3901, tel. 876/618-1234, www.rosehall.ziva.hyatt.com, from US$830-970) is a 387-room all-inclusive resort catering to families. The best rooms are located at the ground level with swim-out pools from the balconies. Food options include both buffet and à la carte restaurants: Di Roza, serving pizzas from a wood-fired oven, and Fuzion, an Asian-style restaurant with a chef station as its centerpiece doing noodles in a wok. Calypzo is a beachfront grill, and other options include a deli, a grill, and an English pub. An enormous pool with two hot tubs is in the expansive courtyard of the hotel face the beach.

**Hyatt Zilara** (from US$886-1060, www.rosehall.zilara.hyatt.com) is 234-room resort adjoining the Hyatt Ziva catering to couples only. The hotel also features swim-up pools in select ground floor suites and two lighted tennis courts that are shared with guests of Hyatt Ziva.

**Hilton Rose Hall Resort & Spa** (Rose Hall, tel. 876/953-2650, U.S. tel. 800/445-8667, rosehallroomscontrol@luxuryresorts.com, www.rosehallresort.com, from US$148 pp) is a 489-room, seven-floor property built in 1974. The hotel boasts a sleek South Beach design. Food is excellent, with indoor and outdoor seating in buffet and à la carte formats, and a seaside bar and grill by the Olympic-size pool directly in front of the hotel. The Sugar

Hammerstein Highland House

Mill Falls Water Park on the property boasts an 85-meter (280-foot) water slide for a thrilling ride on tubes, spilling into a freeform pool with a swim-up bar, a lazy river, waterfalls, and hot tubs in a lush garden setting. The beach, located below the main pool and grill area, has fine white sand along a respectable stretch of coast.

**Iberostar** (tel. 876/680-0000, U.S. tel. 305/774-9225, reservations@iberostar-hotel.com, www.iberostar.com) has three all-inclusive hotels in three distinct price categories. Guests staying at the more expensive hotels can use the restaurants and facilities of the lower categories, but guests of the lower-category hotels are not permitted on the more expensive properties. The quality of the food varies considerably by the price point. The **Iberostar Rose Hall Beach** (from US$190 low season, US$309 high season) is a 366-room property that caters to the lower end of the Iberostar spectrum. Standard rooms have either one or two beds and overlook the gardens; junior suites have either ocean or garden views. **Iberostar Rose Hall Suites** (from US$235 low season, US$363 high season) has 319 rooms, two pools with swim-up bars, and a lazy river meandering across the lawn. All rooms are suites with living rooms and minibars and have soaking tubs. **Iberostar Grand Rose Hall** (from US$336 low season, US$472 high season) has 295 suites, all with living areas, verandas with a swing, jetted tubs, rain showers, and minibars. The property has four pools with one swim-up bar. The food is excellent, with buffet and à la carte options, with top-of-the-line dishes like lobster and steak.

## VILLAS

**Hammerstein Highland House** (in Content, up Long Hill from Reading, U.S. tel. 805/258-2767, keressapage@yahoo.com, www.highlandhousejamaica.com, 4-night minimum, weekly from US$7,500 low season, US$9,500 high season) is a stunning six-bedroom villa on a lush seven-hectare (17-acre) property overlooking Montego Bay. Smaller groups can opt to rent a minimum of four bedrooms (US$6,500 low season, US$8,500 high season). There are two king beds, one queen, two rooms with two twins, and a room with a double bed. The two twin rooms can be converted to king beds. Amenities include Wi-Fi, a large pool, and beach club membership at Round Hill. All rooms have air-conditioning and satellite TV. A screened-in yoga pavilion with ceiling fans that accommodates up to 12 adults makes the property a favorite for yoga retreats. The staff includes a housekeeper, a butler, a cook, a laundress, a gardener, and a farmer. The one-hectare (two-acre) organic farm on the property supplies much of the food for the villa and is linked with the Anchovy school breakfast program and an orphanage up the road as part of the villa owner's One Love Learning Foundation.

**Villas by Linda Smith** (U.S. tel. 301/229-4300, linda@jamaicavillas.com, www.jamaicavillas.com) is the leading villa agency in Jamaica, booking a large proportion of the island's most luxurious properties, some beachfront, others at the exclusive Tryall

Club. **SunVillas** (contact Alan Marlor, U.S. tel. 888/625-6007, alan@sunvillas.com, www. sunvillas.com) also rents a nice assortment of villas across Jamaica.

★ **Silent Waters** (tel. 847/304-4700, information@jamaicavillas.net, www.jamaicavillas.net, nightly from US$2,208 low season with 2 night min stay, $2,987 high season with 4 night min stay, for five dbl capacity suites, an extra US$714 nightly for owners villa, all rates exclude 10% tax) is a 16.5-acre property perched at the top of Great River Private, a gated villa development just east of the Great River, which forms the border between the parishes of St. James and Hanover, six miles west of Montego Bay. The property can accommodate up to 20 guests in five split-level hillside villas and the owner's villa.

Silent Waters channels a Balinese temple wired for the material world. From the lotus lined gardens just inside the main entrance to the 180-degree ocean view from the infinity pool facing Montego Bay, no details have been overlooked in the design of this hilltop retreat. Perhaps the most stunning feature is the virgin forest surrounding the property and prominently seen from the villas that face west and southwest up and across the Great River.

Five villas hug the hillside with views of either the coast or the river and hills, or both. Queen or King-size four-poster beds, HD Sony LED flat-panel TVs, iPod docks, A/C, ceiling fans, and wet bars are found in each. All villas have his and hers interior showers and many of the villas have outdoor showers and bathtubs en suite; all have private balconies with lounge chairs. The Owner's Villa, or Master Suite, takes comfort to another level. The suite is beautifully decorated, with sliding walls that reveal lush hills and the Great River beyond a wrap-around infinity pool.

The common areas are the greatest asset of Silent Waters when it comes to gatherings of family and friends. The Main Pavilion, overlooking an 80-foot infinity-edged pool, is packed with plush couches, a state-of-the-art home theatre system, a grand piano, and a detached poolside bar and lounge.

Leave the cooking to the master chef for delicacies like steak and spiny lobster cooked to perfection, or succulent snapper filet topped with sautéed shrimp. At the very top of the property, a helipad awaits Silent Waters' next celebrity guest. Just below, a lighted tennis court with Deco Turf surface and a spectator pavilion is fit for any pro.

Silent Waters

# Information and Services

## BANKS AND MONEY

As elsewhere in Jamaica, the easiest way to get funds is from an ATM with your regular bank card. Nevertheless, you can get slightly better rates at the *cambios,* or currency trading houses, that can be found all over town.

**Global Exchange** is an international currency trader that operates at Sangster International Airport. The rates are not as good as at *cambios* outside the airport, but if you need local currency on arrival and don't exchange a lot, the difference is negligible, and the cost certainly won't amount to more than ATM fees if you're not exchanging more than US$100.

**NCB** has locations at 93 Barnett Street (tel. 876/952-6539), 41 St. James Street (tel. 876/952-6540), and Harbour Street (tel. 876/952-0077), with ATMs at the airport and at the junction of Kent and Gloucester Avenues. **Scotiabank** has an ATM on Bottom Road and branch locations at 6-7 Sam Sharpe Square (tel. 876/952-4440), 51 Barnett Street (tel. 876/952-5539), Westgate Shopping Plaza (tel. 876/952-5545), and Fairview II. **FX Trader** is an exchange house that gives the best rates around, with locations at Hometown FSC (19 Church St.), Medi Mart (shop 1, St. James Place, Gloucester Ave.), and at Hometown Overton (shop 9, Overton Plaza, Union St.).

## GOVERNMENT OFFICES

**Jamaica Tourist Board** (18 Queens Dr., tel. 876/952-4425) has information about attractions in the region. JTB (tel. 876/952-2462) also has an information desk at Sangster International Airport.

## MEDICAL SERVICES

**Hospiten Mobay Medical Center** (across from Half Moon, Rose Hall, tel. 876/953-3981) is considered by many the best private hospital in Jamaica. **Soe-Htwe Medicare** (Gloucester Ave., tel. 876/979-3444) is one of the best private clinics in town centrally located on the Hip Strip next to the Pork Pit. **Fairview Medical and Dental Suite** (shop 5, Fairview Office Park, tel. 876/953-6264) is a welcoming general practice.

## PHARMACIES

**City Centre Pharmacy** (shop 30, City Centre Plaza, tel. 876/632-6918, cell tel. 876/427-2600, 9am-7pm Mon.-Fri.) is conveniently located within easy walking distance of the Hip Strip and downtown Mobay. **Fontana** (Fairview Shopping Centre, tel. 876/952-3866, www.fontanapharmacy.com), the leading pharmacy chain in Jamaica, is a full-service pharmacy selling everything imaginable in addition to prescription drugs.

## PARCEL SERVICES

Both **DHL** (34 Queens Dr., U.S. tel. 888/225-5345) and **FedEx** (Queens Dr., U.S. tel. 888/463-3339) have operations near the airport. Domestic carrier **AirPak Express** (tel. 876/952-8647) is located at the domestic airport terminal.

# Getting There and Around

## AIR

**Sangster International Airport** (MBJ, tel. 876/952-3133, www.mbjairport.com) is the primary point of entry for most travelers visiting Jamaica. The airport is located near the Flankers district a few minutes east of the Hip Strip and about 10 minutes from downtown or from Rose Hall.

Sangster is served by most North American carriers, including American, JetBlue, Delta, United, Air Canada, Southwest, AirTran, WestJet, and Spirit as well as regional operators Copa Airlines, Caribbean Airlines, InselAir, Cayman Airways, InterCaribbean, and Aerogaviota. European airlines with regular service include Virgin Atlantic. A number of charter carriers offer seasonal service from Europe.

InterCaribbean flights for Kingston depart a few times daily from the domestic terminal, reached by taking a left just inside the main entrance to the airport before reaching the gas station.

**InterCaribbean Airways** (U.S. tel. 888/957-3223 or 649/946-4999, res@intercaribbean.com, www.intercaribbean.com), a regional airline from Turks and Caicos, has coveted cabotage rights allowing it to operate domestic flights in Jamaica in addition to flights from Providenciales to destinations in Cuba, Haiti, the Dominican Republic, and the eastern Caribbean.

**AirLink Express** (Sangster International Airport, Domestic Terminal, tel. 876/940-6660, reservation@flyairlink.net, www.intlairlink.net) offers scheduled daily flights between Montego Bay and Negril (US$140 pp) as well as charter service between any two airports or aerodromes on the island.

**TimAir** (Sangster International Airport, Domestic Terminal, tel. 876/952-2516, timair@usa.net, www.timair.net) offers air taxi service to Negril, Treasure Beach, Boscobel (St. Mary), Ken Jones (Portland), and Kingston.

## BUSES AND ROUTE TAXIS

**Knutsford Express** (tel. 876/971-1822, www.knutsfordexpress.com, 8am-10pm daily) offers bus service between Montego Bay and Negril (US$15), Ocho Rios (US$15), Mandeville (US$20), Port Antonio (US$28), and Kingston (US$25), among other routes, with onboard Wi-Fi and a lavatory. Reserve online in advance for discounted fares.

**Buses** and **route taxis** run between Mobay and virtually every other major town in the neighboring parishes, most notably Savanna-la-Mar in Westmoreland, Hopewell in Hanover, Falmouth in Trelawny, and Runaway Bay in St. Ann. The bus terminal on Market Street is a dusty and bustling place where it's important to pay attention to your surroundings. Buses to any point on the island, including Kingston, never exceed US$7. Time schedules are not adhered to, but you can generally count on a bus moving out to the main destinations at least every 45 minutes.

## CAR RENTALS

**Island Car Rentals** (tel. 876/952-7225, icar@cwjamaica.com, 8:30am-10pm daily) is Jamaica's largest and most dependable rental-car agency, aligned with Alamo, Enterprise, and National. It has an outlet in the international terminal at Sangster International Airport and offers Toyota, Mitsubishi, Nissan, and Suzuki vehicles, with sedans, SUVs, and vans at competitive rates.

**Budget** (customerservice@budgetjamaica.com, www.budgetjamaica.com) has an office at the airport (tel. 876/952-3838, 8am-10pm daily) and in Ironshore (tel. 876/953-0534, 8am-5pm Mon.-Fri.) where it offers Suzuki Swift, Mitsubishi Lancer, BMW sedan, Mitsubishi Pajero, and Toyota Hiace vehicles.

Sixt (tel. 876/952-1212, 8am-8pm daily) operates from the airport with Toyota and Mitsubishi compact cars, sedans, SUVs, and vans.

Sunsational Car Rental & Tours (Suite 206, Chatwick Centre, 10 Queens Dr., tel. 876/952-1212, sensational@cwjamaica.com, www.sensationalcarrentals.com) is located across from the airport and has decent rates on a variety of Japanese cars (from US$40 low season, US$55 high season). The company also offers free cell phones with a minimum two-day rental.

# East of Montego Bay

East of Montego Bay, Ironshore and Rose Hall cover the coast with hotels and housing developments that range from middle-class to super-luxury before reaching Greenwood, a small community once part of the Barrett estate that borders the sea and the parish of Trelawny. The Trelawny coast has a smattering of tourism development concentrated in the area just east of Falmouth along the bay, while the inhabited parts of Trelawny's interior are covered in farming country, where yam, sugarcane, and citrus fruit are major crops. The early morning mist rises from dew-covered cane fields, making a trip through the interior from Rock, Trelawny, to St. Ann a magical alternative to the coastal route at this time of day.

Three roads lead off the North Coast Highway into Falmouth: one from the east, where the old highway used to run; another, Market Street, a straight shot to Martha Brae; and the third, Rodney Street or Foreshore Road, to the west toward Mobay.

## GREENWOOD
### Greenwood Great House
Greenwood Great House (tel. 876/953-1077, greenwoodgreathouse@cwjamaica.com, www.greenwoodgreathouse.com, 9am-5pm daily, US$14) is the best example of a great house kept alive by the owners, Bob and Ann Betton, who live on the property and manage the low-key tour operation. Built in the late 1600s by one of the wealthiest families of the British colonial period, the Barretts first landed in Jamaica on Cromwell's voyage of conquest, when the island was captured from the Spanish in 1655. Land grants immediately made the family a major landholder, and its plantations grew over the next 179 years to amass 2,000 slaves on seven estates by the time of emancipation. Greenwood Great House boasted the best stretch of road in Jamaica as its driveway. Little upkeep has been performed over the past four centuries, apparently, and today the 1.5-kilometer (1-mile) road requires slow going, but the panoramic view from the house and grounds are still as good as ever.

Interesting relics like hand-pump fire carts and old wagon wheels adorn the outside of the building. Inside the house is one of the best collections of colonial-era antiques in Jamaica, including obscure musical instruments, Flemish thrones, and desks with secret compartments from the 17th century. An inlaid rosewood piano belonged to King Edward VII, and a portrait of poet Elizabeth Barrett Browning's cousin hangs on the wall. Another historical treasure at the great house is the will of Reverend Thomas Burchell, who was arrested for his alleged role in the Christmas Rebellion. Farther inland from Greenwood are the ruins of Barrett Hall, the family's primary residence.

### Hampden Sugar Estate
Hampden Sugar Estate (Wakefield, tel. 876/482-4632, tours@hampdenrumcompany.com, www.hampdenrumcompany.com, tours 10am and 11am Mon.-Fri.) is a historic sugarcane plantation and rum distillery that offers

tours. The tour lasts approximately two hours, and visitors learn about the distillation process and Jamaica's history with sugar.

## Food

**Chill-Out Hut** (Greenwood, tel. 876/953-1666, noon-11pm daily) is a popular waterfront watering hole and seafood joint also serving meat dishes.

**Far Out Fish Hut & Beer Joint** (Greenwood, tel. 876/954-7155, 9am-10:30 daily) serves seafood a variety of ways, with fish either fried (US$15 per pound) or steamed (US$12 per pound), lobster (US$14 per pound), shrimp (US$16 per pound), conch (US$12 per pound), and octopus (US$15 per pound) with a side of bammy or bread.

# FALMOUTH

Trelawny's capital, Falmouth, is today a run-down shadow of its short-lived former Georgian prime. Nevertheless, noble and much-appreciated efforts are underway to dust off years of neglect and shine favor on the town's glorious past by restoring its architectural gems, especially after Royal Caribbean dredged the harbor and built a private cruise ship pier that went into service in 2011.

Today, with somewhat decent roads and its close proximity to resort areas in Montego Bay, the town is attracting a growing population once more. Thanks to the efforts of a nongovernmental organization known as **Falmouth Heritage Renewal** (www.falmouthjamaica.org), the town has become a laboratory for architectural restoration. The group has been working for several years to revitalize the architectural heritage of Jamaica's most impressive Georgian town by training local youth in restoration work. The organization also offers guided tours of Falmouth Historic District (10am-2pm Mon.-Fri., fhrj@falmouthjamaica.org). The **Georgian Society** (www.georgianjamaica. org) in Kingston has a wealth of information on Falmouth.

**Falmouth Heritage Walks** (cell. tel. 876/407-2245, www.falmouthheritagewalks.

com, min group size 4, max 12) works closely with Falmouth Heritage Renewal and the Georgian Society of Jamaica and offers three tours by reservation: Heritage (US$25 adult/ US$15 under 12), Food (US$45/25), and Jewish Cemetery (US$15/10).

Falmouth is famous for its **Bend Down Market** (8am-8pm) held every Wednesday since the town's founding on Rodney Street, next to Falmouth All-Age School. From the court square, pass Scotiabank and head toward the ocean.

## Sights

**Baptist Manse** (Market St.) was originally constructed as the town's Masonic Temple in 1780. The building was sold in 1832 to the Baptist Missionary Society, which had lost many buildings in raids of terror and reprisal following the slave rebellion of 1831, in response to the Baptists' fiery abolitionist rhetoric. The building was home to several Baptist missionaries before it was destroyed by fire in the 1950s, to be reconstructed as the William Knibb School in 1961. Today the building serves as headquarters for Falmouth Heritage Renewal.

**Trelawny Parish Church of St. Peter the Apostle** (Duke St.) is one of the most impressive Anglican churches in Jamaica, built in typical Georgian style in 1795 on land donated by estate owner Edward Barrett, whose descendent, Elizabeth Barrett Browning, would go on to become a well-recognized poet of the Romantic movement. The parish church is the oldest public building in town and the oldest house of worship in the parish.

Other historic churches in Falmouth include the **Knibb Memorial Baptist Church** (King St. and George St.), named after abolitionist missionary William Knibb, who came to Jamaica in 1825 and established his first chapel on the site of the existing structure, erected in 1926, and the **Falmouth Presbyterian Church** (Rodney St. and Princess St.), built by the Scots in 1832. Knibb's first chapel was destroyed by the nonconformist militia after the Baptist War, also called the Christmas Rebellion of 1831-1832. Later structures were destroyed by hurricanes. A sculpture relief inside Knibb Memorial depicts a scene (repeated at several Baptist churches across the island) of a congregation of enslaved people awaiting the dawn that granted full freedom in 1838.

**Falmouth Courthouse** was built in 1815 in classic Georgian style, destroyed by fire, and rebuilt in 1926. The building stands prominently on a little square facing the water just off the main square at the center of town.

**Falmouth All Age School** sits on the waterfront in a historic building and makes a good destination for a stroll down Queens Street from the square.

## Sports and Recreation

**Roy's Kayak Adventure** (cell tel. 876/430-2827 Roy's Lagoon, Green Side, Falmouth, US$40) takes visitors on an hour-long kayak ecotour of Roy's lagoon to explore mangroves and spot marine life. After kayaking, guests are taken to Blue Waters Beach Club to relax and swim.

**Blue Waters Beach Club** (Cooper's Pen, cell tel. 876/405-2976, bluewatersfalmouth@gmail.com, www.bwbcjamaica.com, by reservation only, US$10) is a private beach club with over 180 meters (600 feet) of beach frontage, offering guests lounge chairs and complimentary Wi-Fi. The restaurant (US$10) serves Jamaican favorites like jerk chicken, festival, and rice-and-peas.

**Jamaica Swamp Safari Village** (Foreshore Rd., Falmouth, next to Better Price Hardware, tel. 876/617-2798, cell tel. 876/775-3111, falmouthzoo@gmail.com, www.jamaicaswampsafari.com, 9am-4pm daily, US$25 adults, US$13 children) offers an 80-minute guided walking tour with basic information on the barn owl, Jamaican iguana, coney, yellow snake, and American crocodiles. Guests can hand-feed the birds in the aviary. Scenes from the film *Live and Let Die* were filmed with Swamp Safari founder Ross "Kananga" Heilman acting as stunt double for Roger Moore.

## Shopping

**Isha Tafara** (cell tel. 876/610-3292 or 876/377-0505) is an artist and craft producer who lives in Wakefield, near Falmouth, farther inland from Martha Brae. Tafara makes sandals as well as red, green, and gold crocheted hats, Egyptian-style crafts, handbags, belts, and jewelry with a lot of crochet and fabric-based items. Tafara works from her home, which

Falmouth Courthouse

can be visited by appointment, and supplies Things Jamaican and Sandals boutiques, among other retailers.

## Food

**Nazz Restaurant** (23 Market St., tel. 876/617-5175, 8am-11:30pm daily, US$5-25) serves good seafood and Jamaican staple oxtail, shrimp, quesadillas, burgers, wings, and sandwiches. Customers can use free Wi-Fi. The food is excellent and a good value.

**Pepper's Jerk Centre** (20 Duke St., tel. 876/617-3427, cell tel. 876/385-7512, clintrennie2014@gmail.com, 10am-10pm Mon.-Sat., US$5-6) serves jerk chicken, pork, fish and lobster with sides like festival, bammy, and rice as well as a rotation of Jamaican favorites like baked, curried, and brown stew chicken, curry goat, oxtail, and roast fish.

**Falmouth Jerk Centre and Ganja Bar** (lot 306, Foreshore Rd., tel. 876/572-2858 or 876/891-6077) serves jerk chicken, pork, fish, conch, lobster, and octopus (US$5-25). The ganja bar at the same location serves every mixed drink imaginable, as well as herb brownies and ganja spread, in a hassle free herb-friendly environment.

**Rock Wharf Restaurant & Bar** (Rock District, Falmouth, tel. 876/617-2074, 11:30am-10pm daily, US$5-10) serves a rotating menu with items like fried chicken, curried beef, stewed peas, barbeque pork, and chop suey. Snapper, escoveitch, and steamed or brown stew is prepared to order (US$15-18).

**Tastee Patties** (25 Market St., tel. 876/617-5150), has a restaurant in the center of Falmouth, on the square.

**Spicy Nice** (Water Square, tel. 876/954-3197) sells patties, breads, pastries, and other baked goods.

## Services

**Scotiabank** has a branch built in replica Georgian style next to the courthouse with an ATM. **FX Trader** (U.S. tel. 888/398-7233) has a branch at Big J's Supermarket on Lower Harbour Street (8:30am-4:30pm Mon.-Wed. and Fri.-Sat., 8:30am-12:30pm Thurs.).

**Trelawny Parish Library** (Rodney St., entrance on Pitt St., tel. 876/954-3306, 9am-6pm Mon.-Fri., 9am-4pm Sat.) offers free Internet access. The **Falmouth Police** (tel. 876/954-3073) are based along the waterfront on Rodney Street.

# MARTHA BRAE

Martha Brae is a literal backwater a short distance south of Falmouth, with little to distract travelers as they pass through on their way to start the rafting trip or to Good Hope Plantation in the Queen of Spain Valley.

**Martha Brae River** is one of Jamaica's longest rivers and is navigable for much of its 32 kilometers (20 miles), extending to the deep interior of Trelawny beyond Chris Blackwell's Pantrepant farm and Good Hope Plantation, where it wells up out of the earth near Windsor Cave. Legends surround the Martha Brae, likely owing to its important role in the early colonial years, when the Spanish used the river to reach the North Coast from their major settlement of Oristan, near present-day Bluefields.

## ★ Martha Brae Rafting

**Martha Brae Rafting** (tel. 876/940-6398 or 876/940-7018, or contact Marie Barrett, cell tel. 876/775-3111, info@jamaicarafting.com, www.jamaicarafting.com, 9am-4pm daily) is the only organized bamboo rafting attraction in western Jamaica, with 80 CPR-trained and licensed raft captains. Rafts hold two passengers in addition to the raft captain, who guides the vessel down the normally lazy Martha Brae. The tour (US$60 for 2 people) includes a welcome drink. Round-trip transportation can be arranged from Mobay (US$15 pp, minimum 4 people) and from Ochi (US$25 pp, minimum 4 people) and Negril (US$35).

To reach the departure point on the Martha Brae River, exit left off the highway ramp after passing the first turnoff for Falmouth heading east. Turn inland (right) through the underpass, continuing into the small village of Martha Brae.

At the intersection in the town, turn left, and then right after the second bridge. The five-kilometer (3-mile) raft ride takes about 90 minutes. The excursion will not get the adrenaline pumping; it's a relaxing and romantic experience.

# GLISTENING WATERS

Glistening Waters, just east of Falmouth, is home to the Luminous Lagoon, one of Jamaica's most interesting natural phenomena.

Nearby is the **Greenfield Stadium,** which was built for hosting the Cricket World Cup in 2007. The stadium is now used for sporting events and entertainment.

## The Luminous Lagoon

**The Luminous Lagoon** is one of Jamaica's most touted natural phenomena thanks to the microscopic unicellular dinoflagellate *Pyridium bahamense,* which glows when the water is agitated. The organism photosynthesizes sunlight using chlorophyll during the day and then emits the energy at night. Four tour operators offer boat tours of the luminous lagoon.

**Glistening Waters Restaurant & Marina** (tel. 876/954-3229, info@glisteningwaters.com, www.glisteningwaters.com) provide tours that last half an hour, with boats leaving the marina every half hour 7pm-9pm daily. **Fisherman's Inn** (tel. 876/954-4078 or 876/954-3427, fishermansinn@cwjamaica.com) organizes virtually identical outings (US$15 pp) at 7pm daily.

**Rock Wharf** (Stratty King, cell tel. 876/399-8686 or 876/617-2074, kingstrats@live.com, US$25) offers a 34- to 45-minute tour starting at nightfall daily until about 9:30pm. The tour includes a boat ride around the lagoon and a brief history of the area.

**Luminous Lagoon Tours** (contact Captain David Muschett, cell tel. 876/276-9885, awahoo2@yahoo.com), based at Fisherman's Inn on the Luminous Lagoon, also has night excursions on the lagoon.

## Sports and Recreation
### FISHING
**Glistening Waters Restaurant & Marina** (tel. 876/954-3229, info@glisteningwaters.com, www.glisteningwaters.com) offers fishing charters (US$600) from the marina on a 46-foot sport fisher with a capacity of eight people. A smaller, 32-foot boat (4 hours, US$400) carries five people. Two complimentary drinks are included on fishing excursions. The marina also welcomes visiting yachts (US$1 per foot per day) and can accommodate boats of up to 86 feet. Boaters should call ahead for special instructions on entering the lagoon. Longer stays can be negotiated.

**Luminous Lagoon Tours** (contact Captain David Muschett, cell tel. 876/276-9885, awahoo2@yahoo.com), based at Fisherman's Inn on the Luminous Lagoon, has excursions on the lagoon, trolling and deep-drop deep-sea fishing, and snorkeling day trips to the private beach at Harmony Hall aboard a 35-foot Cabo with an eight-person capacity. Fishing trips chase marlin, kingfish, barracuda, sailfish, and wahoo. Rates range from US$600 for a half day for up to eight passengers to US$1,100 for a full eight hours, including bait and tackle.

## Food
**Fisherman's Inn** (tel. 876/954-4078, fishermansinn@cwjamaica.com) is a hotel and restaurant (US$13-30) facing the lagoon and serving items like callaloo-stuffed chicken breast, stuffed jerk chicken, lobster, and surf and turf.

**Glistening Waters Restaurant & Marina** (tel. 876/954-3229, info@glisteningwaters.com, www.glisteningwaters.com) has food ranging from bay-oyster seafood chowder (US$4) to the Falmouth Seafood Platter (US$35), which comes with grilled lobster, shrimp, and snapper.

**Aunt Gloria's** (Rock District, cell tel. 876/353-1301, 6am-8:30pm Mon.-Sat., US$3-5) caters mostly to locals with brown stew fish, fried chicken, curry goat, and brown stew pork. Gloria opens her jerk center on Friday and sometimes Saturday for the best jerk pork and chicken in town. Breakfast items include ackee and saltfish, kidney, dumpling, yam, and banana.

## Accommodations

**Fisherman's Inn** (just off the A1, Rock District, Falmouth, tel. 876/954-4078 or 876/954-3427, fishermansinn73@yahoo.com, from US$96 d) is an 11-room hotel and restaurant on the Luminous Lagoon with clean, spacious rooms overlooking the lagoon and a small marina, with private baths and hot water, TVs, and air-conditioning. A one-bedroom apartment (US$75) has a kitchenette and sitting area but no air-conditioning. The inn organizes outings (7pm daily, US$25 pp) on the lagoon to see the phosphorescent microbes light up the water when agitated.

**Glistening Waters Hotel & Marina** (tel. 876/617-4625, glisteningwatersja@hotmail. com, www.glisteningwaters.com, US$156 d, extra people US$50) is a 28-room hotel that opened in mid-2015. It offers a variety of room layouts, some with kings, others with queens, and others with a combination of two singles or a king and a single. Guests get a 50 percent discount on Luminous Lagoon tours. Breakfast and Wi-Fi are included. The pool is exclusively for guests.

## BURWOOD BEACH

Burwood Beach in Bounty Bay is one of the best spots on the north coast for windsurfing and kiteboarding, though Irie Kiteboarding with Water Network Jamaica (cell tel. 876/540-4042, info@waternetworkjamaica. com), which once based its operations here, has moved to Montego Bay. Burwood Beach is also referred to simply as Bounty Bay and is popular with locals. To get here, turn off the highway toward the sea about one kilometer (0.6 miles) east of The Royalton White Sands, next to a sign for Bounty Bay.

## Accommodations

**The Royalton White Sands** (on Burwood Beach, Coopers Pen, Falmouth, U.S. tel. 888/774-0040 or 305/774-0040, reservations2@vacstore.net, www.royaltonwhitesandsresort.com) is a 352-room all-inclusive resort with a variety of layouts. Rooms have rain showerheads, Wi-Fi, minibars, and balconies or terraces. Some rooms can interconnect for larger parties.

**Captain's Cove** (Coopers Pen, U.S. tel. 727/946-7724, info@captainscovejamaica. com, www.captainscovejamaica.com, from US$149) has five comfortably appointed suites with king beds, cable TV, Wi-Fi, air-conditioning, mini fridges, and en suite baths in a no-frills villa on one of Jamaica's top beaches. Water sports activities offered on-site include kayaking and paddleboarding.

## DUNCANS

A small community on a hillside overlooking the sea, Duncans has little to interest visitors in the town itself. Just below the population center, however, the coast is lined with fine white sand split by coral: **Jacob Taylor Public Bathing Beach** and **Silver Sands Beach** (day use US$15 pp) in the gated community of Silver Sands. There's a restaurant, bar, and a small grocery store at the complex. It's necessary to call ahead (tel. 876/954-2518) to gain access to Silver Sands so they expect you at the gate.

About one kilometer (0.6 miles) east of Silver Sands, a private estate house facing a small beach lies in ruins, also with fine white sand and crystal waters. To get here, turn off the main road down to Silver Sands through a green gate and drive along a rough, sandy road pocked with coral through the scrub forest until reaching the coast.

A 20-minute walk farther east along low coral bluffs leads to **Mango Point,** where one of Jamaica's few remaining virgin beaches is found. Known as **Harmony Cove,** the area is to be the site of a massive hotel and casino. Harmony Cove can also be reached by turning off the North Coast Highway next to a cell phone tower when coming from the east; from there, drive toward the coast along a dirt road and turn off along a sandy track that disintegrates at the water's edge. Park and rejoin the road on the other side of the fence, walking the remaining distance. It's about 20 minutes' walk from the east as well. Contact Harmonisation (tel. 876/954-2518) for more information on the status of the resort development.

## Jacob Taylor Bathing Beach

Located on the other side of the compound walls from the gated community at Silver Sands, **Jacob Taylor Bathing Beach** is a local hot spot where low-key craft vendors sell their goods and anglers park their canoes to while away the days playing dominoes in the shade. The beach extends for a few kilometers to the west, and while not immaculately swept and maintained like the beach at Silver Sands, the sand is fine, the water's clear, and there's no entry fee. You can't miss the entrance to Jacob Taylor Bathing Beach, marked by a large sign by the road that leads downhill toward the sea to the left of the gated entrance to Silver Sands.

## Food

**Leroy's** (cell tel. 876/447-2896 or 876/447-5414, US$3-12) is a local bar and restaurant seaside at Jacob Taylor Fisherman's Beach that serves fish and Jamaican staples. Leroy can usually be found in the kitchen while his stepdaughter, Cameika "Chin" Wallace, works the bar. The Silver Lights Band performs live reggae starting at 8pm Saturday until late into the night. The no-frills restaurant and bar is notable for its relaxing atmosphere that draws a healthy mix of locals and tourists, appreciably devoid of hustlers to interrupt the quiet seaside landscape.

## Accommodations
### SILVER SANDS

**Silver Sands** (www.mysilversands.com) is a gated community of 44 rental cottages and villas that range considerably in price and comfort, from rustic to opulent. Even at the higher end, Silver Sands villas are among the best value to be found in Jamaica on what is considered by some to be the island's finest beach.

**Cannon Cottage** (contact Karen Sangster, cell tel. 876/831-2221, U.S. tel. 305/482-6925, ksangster@cwjamaica.com, minimum 3 nights low season, 4 nights high season, 2 bedrooms US$250 low season, US$300 high season, 3 bedrooms US$300 low season, US$360 high season) is a charming three-bedroom located at

Fine sand and clear waters make Silver Sands a favorite beach for family fun.

the top of the flight of stairs leading down to Silver Sands' fine white sand beach in a gated community. The villa has a housekeeper, a cook, and a gardener to do the shopping, cooking, and cleaning. A courtyard has a jetted tub that fits six with a little waterfall and outdoor furniture for dining amid lush foliage. Two rooms have kings, one with an additional single, and the third has a queen. The screened rooms have air-conditioning and ceiling fans, and flat-screen TVs get local cable. A stay of a week or more includes round-trip airport transfers. Cannon Cottage is owned and operated by the widow of Ian Sangster, who created Sangster's Rum Cream, Jamaica's equivalent to Bailey's.

Located directly on the waterfront, **Queen's Cottage** (weekly US$1,925 low season, US$2,275 high season) was named after the modest cottage's most illustrious guest, Queen Elizabeth II, who stayed here on a trip to Jamaica. It is a three-bedroom villa with a king in the master, one queen bed in the second bedroom, and two twins in the third, making it ideal for families or a small group of friends. Bedrooms have ceiling fans, air-conditioning, and private baths. A large wood deck overlooks the sea a few steps off

the beach. The villa boasts a large whirlpool tub and is the closest of any at Silver Sands to the water's edge.

**Windjammer** (tel. 876/929-2378 or 876/926-0931, dianas@cwjamaica.com or bookings@windjammerjamaica.com, www.windjammerjamaica.com, US$457 low season, US$557 high season, weekly US$3,200 low season, US$3,900 high season) is a four-bedroom luxury villa with a private pool, Internet access, a large veranda with a sea view, and a built-in barbecue. Two bedrooms have king beds, one has a queen, and the fourth has two twins.

**Moonshine** (tel. 876/954-7807 or 876/954-7606, www.mysiversands.com, US$7,040 weekly) is at the high end of the villas in Silver Sands, sleeping up to eight and featuring wide verandas and open-air entertainment areas, an infinity pool, flat-screen TVs, Wi-Fi, and excellent staff.

## Other Accommodations

★ **Villa Kelso** (www.villakelso.com, up to 8 people US$4,550 weekly low season, US$5,959 weekly high season) is located at the crest of a hill isolated from its Duncans neighbors and privileged with a 180-degree uninterrupted view of the Caribbean. A wide balcony runs

Villa Kelso

the length of the house, with comfortable dark wicker furniture and a table for outdoor dining. Indoors, fine china and silver fills antique hutches around the formal dining room, and the adjacent living rooms is filled with comfortable sofas. Two of the four bedrooms have kings and two have a pair of doubles. Out back, the whirlpool tub overflows into the pool surrounded by lounge chairs. Guests have beach privileges at Silver Sands Beach Club (30 minutes on foot, 5 minutes by car) and discounts for nearby tours run by the family that owns the villa.

**Sea Rhythm** (Jacob Taylor Bathing Beach, contact caretaker Cardella Gilzine, cell tel. 876/857-0119, US$200) is a three-bedroom cottage a few steps from the shore. The master bedroom has a king bed and air-conditioning, with a double bed and fan in the second room and two twins in the third. Each room has a private bath with hot water, and there's a fully equipped kitchen. Meals are prepared to order.

**Villa Victoria** (370 Duncans Ave., tel. 876/954-9353, www.villavictoriajamaica.com, US$90-120), run by a congenial innkeeper everyone affectionately calls Vickie, has six bedrooms and includes breakfast. Two rooms have king beds, one has a queen, others have doubles and twins. The honeymoon suite has a walk-in closet and large bath with a whirlpool tub. The property has a swimming pool and a well-manicured garden. Other meals can be prepared to order. Wi-Fi reaches throughout the property. James Taylor Beach is a 10-minute walk. The decor and furnishings at Villa Victoria epitomize Jamaican style.

# RIO BUENO

The first community in Trelawny across the border from St. Ann, Rio Bueno is considered by many experts to have been the actual landing point of Christopher Columbus on his second voyage, although that claim is also made for Discovery Bay. The port at Rio Bueno was an important export point, as can still be seen by the dilapidated warehouses and wharves along the waterfront.

Today the small village is undergoing something of a renewal, with the new North Coast Highway bypassing the town entirely, which could ultimately enhance its picturesque appeal.

## Sights
The riverbank along the Rio Bueno is great for a stroll; visitors can see ruins of the **Baptist Theological College,** the first of its kind in the western hemisphere. Other ruins in town include **Fort Dundas,** behind the school. The **Rio Bueno Baptist Church** was originally built in 1832 before being destroyed by the Colonial Church Union, whose mostly Anglican members organized militias to terrorize the abolitionist Baptists, who were upsetting the status quo. The church was quickly rebuilt twice as large in 1834, and the present structure was built in 1901. While the roof is largely missing, services are still held downstairs. The **Rio Bueno Anglican Church** was built at the water's edge in 1833 and remains there today.

The extensive **Gallery Joe James** (tel. 876/954-0048, cell tel. 876/401-0484, 10am-8pm daily), on the grounds of the Lobster Bowl and Rio Bueno Hotel, displays artwork by proprietor, Joe James, among other selected Jamaican artists. The gallery extends throughout the restaurant, bar, and hotel and makes for a surreal waterfront setting.

## Sports and Recreation
**Braco Stables** (tel. 876/954-0185, bracostables@cwjamaica.com, www.bracostables.com, US$60, US$70 with transportation from Mobay or Runaway Bay) offers tame horseback riding tours traversing the Braco estate and the beach.

**Braco Rapids Adventures** (tel. 876/954-0185, info@bracotours.com, www.riverrapidsja.com, 10:30am and 1:45pm daily) offers 105-minute white-water river rafting, tubing, river boarding, kayaking, and waterfall explorer tours at Bengal Falls on the Rio Bueno, which runs down the border of Trelawny and St. Ann.

## Food and Accommodations

**The Lobster Bowl Restaurant** (tel. 876/954-0048, cell tel. 876/401-0484, 9am-8pm daily, US$18-40) serves excellent shrimp, chicken, fish, and lobster dishes. The restaurant was started by Joe James and his wife, Joyce Burke James, in 1966. The restaurant is enormous, with outside seating extending out on a dock along the waterfront, as well as inside a large dining hall.

**Rio Bueno Hotel** (tel. 876/954-0048, galleryjoejames40@hotmail.com, from US$100) is a rustic 20-room place with balconies overlooking the sea, ceiling fans, TVs, and hot water in private baths. The ground floor rooms are larger and geared toward families, with three double beds.

**Meliá Braco Village** (Braco, tel. 876/678-0582 or 888/956-3542, melia.jamaica@melia.com, www.melia.com, from US$225 low season, US$486 high season) is an all-inclusive resort geared toward couples and families located seafront in the Braco area of Rio Bueno. The suites are modern, with flat panel TVs, broadband Internet, and double queen or king beds. Some rooms have balconies with sea views. The hotel has five restaurants, including buffet and à la carte. The hotel offers babysitting services, a fitness and wellness center, basketball courts, a football pitch, and a business center.

# North Cockpit Country

Some of the most remote countryside in Jamaica is in the Trelawny interior known as Cockpit Country, with its cockpit karst topography home to myriad caves, sinkholes, and subterranean springs, stretching from the St. James border in the west to St. Ann at the heart of the island. Hiking and exploring this region can be riveting, but adequate supplies and a good guide are essential. The Queen of Spain Valley, only a few minutes' drive inland, is one of the most picturesque farming areas in Jamaica, where the morning mist lifts to reveal a magical countryside of lush, pitted hills.

Cockpit Country has some of the most unusual landscape on earth, where porous limestone geology created what is known as karst topography, molded by water and the weathering of time. Cockpit Country extends all the way to Accompong, St. Elizabeth, to the south and to Albert Town, Trelawny, to the east. Similar topography continues over the inhospitable interior as far as Cave Valley, St. Ann, even farther east.

Two routes lead into Trelawny's interior from Martha Brae, both requiring a vehicle with high clearance. The first route follows the Martha Brae River through Sherwood Content to Windsor. The second route passes through Good Hope Plantation leading to Chris Blackwell's private estate, Pantrepant. To get to Good Hope Plantation, bypass the town of Martha Brae to the right when heading inland from the highway, and take a left less than 1.5 kilometers (1 mile) past the town, following well-marked signs. Continuing on the road past the turnoff to Good Hope ultimately leads to Wakefield, where the B15 heads back west to Montego Bay.

By taking a left at the stop sign in Martha Brae, and then a right after crossing the river, the road leads inland past Perth, Reserve, and Sherwood Content, and ultimately peters out near Windsor Caves.

## ★ GOOD HOPE PLANTATION

The 810-hectare (2,000-acre) **Good Hope Plantation** (cell tel. 876/469-3443, goodhope1@cwjamaica.com, www.goodhopejamaica.com), located in the Queen of Spain Valley, is one of the most picturesque working estates on the island. Citrus has today replaced the cane of the past, while the plantation's great house and a collection of its historic buildings have been converted into the most luxurious countryside villas.

**Chukka Caribbean** (U.S. tel. 877/424-8552, tel. 876/656-8026, www.chukka.com, US$25-185), offers a number of tours of the estate, with dune buggies and ATVs, ziplines, river tubes and kayaking, a challenge course, a bird aviary, a swimming pool, gem mining, a great house tour, and Appleton Estate rum tasting. Multiple activities are packaged together. Tour package prices include transportation from Falmouth, Montego Bay, Ocho Rios, or Negril.

Located on the estate, **David Pinto's Ceramic Studio** (8 kilometers north of Falmouth, cell tel. 876/886-2866, dpinto@cwjamaica.com, www.jamaicaclay.com, 8am-4pm Mon.-Fri., or by appointment) is run by a Jamaican-born potter who studied ceramics during high school in the United Kingdom and later at Rhode Island School of Design before practicing in New York City. He returned to Jamaica in 1992 to establish this studio on Good Hope Plantation, where he runs retreats led by internationally acclaimed guest master potters. Pinto's work includes both functional and decorative pieces and is on display in the permanent collection at the National Gallery in Kingston.

# WINDSOR GREAT CAVE

**Windsor Great Cave** (http://cockpitcountry.com/windsorcave.html) is one of the top draws in the area. Franklyn (Dango) Taylor is the sanctioned warden for the Jamaica Conservation and Development Trust (JCDT) and the official guide for Windsor Great Caves. The caves are best visited with Dango (US$20), although experienced cavers may prefer to go alone. All visitors should check in with Dango and sign the guestbook, which serves to monitor visits and provide records in emergencies. Dango runs a little shop selling drinks and snacks. The source of the Martha Brae River is located nearby, affording a great spot for a dip to cool off.

The Windsor Caves are rich in both geological history and animal life, with up to 11 bat species emerging to feed in the evenings in large swarms. The geological formations inside the caves should not be touched, and a minimal-impact policy should be observed, which starts with visitors staying on the established path. Shining flashlights on the ceiling disturbs the resting bats. Michael Schwartz, of nearby Windsor Great House, warns of a chronic respiratory ailment afflicting cavers, caused by a fungus that grows on bat dung.

Good Hope Plantation

## SPORTS AND RECREATION
### Hiking and Caving

**South Trelawny Environmental Agency** (STEA) (tel. 876/610-0818, cell tel. 876/393-6584, www.stea.net) is based in Albert Town, a little hamlet at the edge of Cockpit Country. The STEA organizes the annual yam festival and also offers guided excursions with its **Cockpit Country Underground Adventure** tours in the surrounding area for caving and hiking.

For more in-depth spelunking of lesser-known attractions, **Jamaica Caves Organization (JCO)** (info@jamaicancaves.org, www.jamaicancaves.org) is an active and useful group that knows Cockpit Country literally inside and out. It can arrange guides for hiking as well as caving. A good circuit is mapped out on the JCO site for a driving tour of Cockpit Country for those less interested in exercise.

For those with a serious interest in hiking, the **Troy Trail** is one of the most interesting and arduous hikes in western Jamaica, traversing Cockpit Country from Windsor to Troy. Again, the JCO can provide guides and maps for a reasonable fee that goes toward helping maintain the organization.

## ACCOMMODATIONS

**The Last Resort** (Ivor Conolley tel. 876/931-6070, cell tel. 876/700-7128, iscapc@cwjamaica.com) is the most remote option in Cockpit Country. It's the headquarters for Jamaica Caves Organization, led by chairman Stefan Stewart. The facilities were recently renovated but remain rustic with 20 bunk beds (US$15 pp) and a common bath. One private room has a queen bed. Expect intimacy with the surrounding environment—bug repellent is essential.

**Windsor Great House** (cell tel. 876/997-3832, windsor@cwjamaica.com, www.cockpitcountry.com) was built by John Tharp in 1795 to oversee his vast cattle estate, which included most of the land bordering the Martha Brae River. Today the great house is operated by Michael Schwartz and Susan Koenig, who offer rustic lodging and a weekly "Meet the Scientists" dinner (US$40).

At Good Hope Plantation, ★ **Good Hope Carriage House** (contact Tammy Hart, cell tel. 876/881-6869, tammyhart3@me.com, www.goodhopejamaica.com, weekly US$6,325 low season, US$7,700 high season) is a six-bedroom villa offering luxurious accommodations at the center of a working citrus plantation where Chukka Caribbean

Good Hope Carriage House

offers a number of tours. Antique furnishings, flat-screen TVs, Wi-Fi, and top-notch cuisine prepared by attentive staff make this the best option in the area. In the Queen of Spain Valley, Good Hope is one of the most picturesque working estates on the island with the characteristic rolling limestone hills of the Cockpit Country interior. Citrus has today replaced the cane of yesteryear, while the plantation's great house and a collection of historic buildings have been modernized. Good Hope features Old World luxury. The villa is staffed with a chef, housekeepers, and gardeners. This is an ideal base for family retreats, birding, hiking, mountain biking, and horseback riding, still the best means of exploring the surrounding countryside. The inviting swimming pool and a brimming river make relaxation a favorite pastime for guests.

## GETTING THERE

To get to Windsor, head inland from Falmouth to Martha Brae, crossing the bridge to the east and turning right to follow the valley south into the hills. On the way, the road passes through the small farming communities of Perth Town and Reserve. Once the road leaves the river, it heads to Sherwood Content, Coxheath, and finally Windsor. To get to The Last Resort, turn right at Dango's shop, continuing for about 1.6 kilometers (1 mile); a left at Dango's shop leads to Windsor Great House. A vehicle with good clearance is recommended, but the route is traveled frequently by vehicles with low clearance, driven with caution.

# Ocho Rios and the North Central Coast

S t. Ann is chock-full of rivers, waterfalls, and gardens, earning it the well-deserved moniker "the garden parish." Ocho Rios, or "Ochi" as the tourism hub is known,

is the biggest town in St. Ann, its name a derivation of the Spanish name for cascades given to the area, *Las Chorreras*.

River gardens and waterfalls from Dunn's River Falls, the most popular, to Konoko Falls, closer to town, and the White River, running down the border of St. Ann and St. Mary, attract many to the area. Of course, beaches are also a draw in Ocho Rios, with spectacular waterfalls spilling onto the sand at Dunn's River Falls and Laughing Waters, where scenes from the first James Bond film, *Dr. No*, were shot.

Prospect Plantation offers a variety of tours, including a visit to the historic Prospect Great House and camel and buggy rides. Mystic Mountain has zipline canopy tours and a harrowing monorail bobsled run through the forest. At Dolphin Cove, visitors interact and marvel at these singular marine mammals in addition to sharks, stingrays, and exotic birds.

Just west of Ocho Rios is St. Ann's Bay,

where the Spanish established Sevilla la Nueva (New Seville) in the early 1500s. Today Seville is an archeological site and a great house museum where several heritage events are held throughout the year. Farther west along the coast are the communities of Runaway Bay and Discovery Bay, both slow-paced beach towns, the former with a golf course, the latter Jamaica's most exclusive villa enclave—where rentals go for upward of US$10,000 per week.

Neighboring St. Mary has gained a reputation as Jamaica's best-kept secret, a place where hustlers are few and far between and the vast majority carry on with their lives oblivious to the tourism industry. The parish has a beautiful rocky coastline punctuated with beaches, forested hills dropping sharply to the sea, and great birding. It was the preferred corner of Jamaica for the likes of Ian Fleming and Noël Coward, who built their island homes here. Fleming's is now the centerpiece of the island's leading luxury retreat, Goldeneye, and Coward's is a museum.

---

**Previous:** "Ride 'N' Swim" with Chukka Caribbean; Dunn's River Falls. **Above:** the Bob Marley Mausoleum.

Look for ★ to find recommended sights, activities, dining, and lodging.

# Highlights

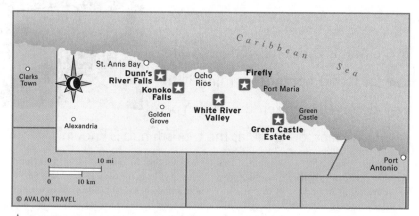

© AVALON TRAVEL

★ **Dunn's River Falls:** The most visited attraction in Jamaica, these falls provide a cool, crisp contrast to the warm water of the Caribbean (page 107).

★ **Konoko Falls:** Visit refreshing waterfalls and beautiful gardens harboring diverse plant and animal life in the heart of Ocho Rios (page 110).

★ **White River Valley:** Explore one of Jamaica's natural gems by tubing down the White River, relaxing at a swimming hole, or enjoying a picnic riverside (page 111).

★ **Firefly:** Tour Noël Coward's estate, which has one of the best views in Jamaica, if not the Caribbean (page 141).

★ **Green Castle Estate:** Immerse yourself in Jamaica's languid country life with an afternoon at this fruit and orchid farm (page 147).

## PLANNING YOUR TIME

Unless your goal is to simply loaf on the beach, or you happen to be staying at a destination resort or villa too comfortable to leave, Ochi is not a place to spend more than a few days. It's the most practical base for a number of key attractions, however, most packaged into organized tours sold at hotel concierge desks or bookable online. If you're driving yourself or chartering a taxi, there's more flexibility to fit in a string of activities in a single day, and there's no reason you can't spend the morning at Dunn's River Falls and go horseback riding or play with dolphins in the afternoon.

Several annual events make a stay in Ocho Rios all the more worthwhile. One of Jamaica's top reggae festivals, Rebel Salute, is held in mid-January. Around Easter, Jamaica's carnival season is in full swing with Bacchanal Beach J'Ouvert, held at James Bond Beach in Oracabessa, and several other beach parties, including SPF and Kampai, are held in and around Ochi. The Ocho Rios Jazz Fest spices things up in June, and Emancipation Jubilee kicks off in Seville at the end of July.

## SAFETY

The Ocho Rios Police Department says that harassment in Ocho Rios is higher than in other places due to the large squatter settlements around town that support thousands from neighboring parishes. St. Ann is a poor parish despite the level of development. Hustlers tend to be more aggressive than in other parishes, and the police recommend greeting advances with a smile, followed by clear communication demonstrating your lack of interest. Ignoring advances is not wise, as it can make hustlers upset. It is not uncommon for people to follow visitors, touting every kind of service, tour, or drug.

Behind the inevitable theatrics used by hustlers to get the attention of visitors, there is a down-to-earth Jamaican sincerity that will often surface by entertaining advances with a "No, thank you" or "I'm all set, thanks."

# Sights

Ocho Rios has many rivers, central to the area's charm and attraction. The most popular, Dunn's River, is a must-see, while others, like the White River, are less popular but every bit as spectacular and refreshing, with several swimming holes and tubing sites along its banks. In the heart of the city, two well-kept gardens with rivers flowing through are worth visiting for a few hours. There are also a few beaches right in town, Turtle Beach and Mahogany Beach, and a few kilometers west, Mystic Mountain offers adrenaline-pumping bobsleds rides and canopy tours.

Dolphin Cove allows visitors to interact with dolphins, sharks, and stingrays. At Prospect Plantation, visitors can ride camels or horses, feed ostriches, and get a glimpse of the colonial era with its 18th-century great house tour. For more activity, an exhilarating off-road experience in mud buggies might be for you.

The central North Coast is within easy reach of Ocho Rios. In Robin's Bay, St. Mary, visitors find a quiet corner of Jamaica where off-roading adventures at Strawberry Fields complement more calming activities like sunbathing or splashing at coral-lined beaches and waterfalls.

## HARMONY HALL

Harmony Hall (Tower Isle, tel. 876/975-4222, www.harmonyhall.com, 10am-5pm Tues.-Sun.) is a stately colonial-era great house with a gallery on the second floor run by Peter Proudlock. It features works by the likes of Cecil Cooper, Susan Shirley, and Graham Davis, among other contemporary painters. A bookshop in the gallery has cookbooks by local authors. Check the

# The Central Coast

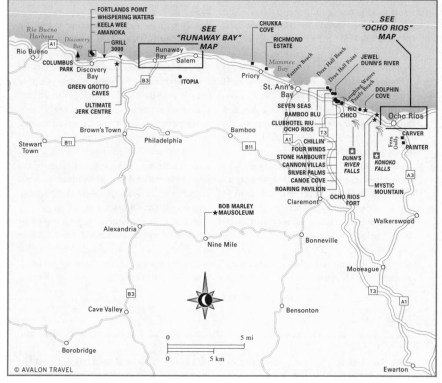

website for temporary exhibitions and craft fairs. Downstairs is Toscanini, the area's best Italian restaurant. The colonial-era building is located five minutes east of Ochi along the main road.

## RIO NUEVO BATTLE SITE

Just east of Harmony Hall, **Rio Nuevo Battle Site** (unmanaged site) is where a decisive battle left Jamaica in English hands in 1658. After three years of guerrilla warfare and harassment of the British, the last Spanish governor, Cristóbal Ysassi, finally received reinforcements from Cuba to help retake the island. The first troops from Spain landed at Ocho Rios, where they were soon discovered by the British and quickly defeated. The

second detail was sent from Cuba and landed at the mouth of the Rio Nuevo, and the battle that ensued left 300 Spanish soldiers dead for Britain's 50. Ysassi miraculously escaped and continued to wage guerrilla attacks with a few remaining loyal bands of Maroons until the treaty of Madrid was signed, officially conceding defeat and leaving Jamaica in British hands. Ysassi finally fled the island in handmade dugout canoes from Don Christopher's Point in Robin's Bay.

## OCHO RIOS FORT

Beside the Reynolds bauxite installation and the helicopter pad for Island Hoppers is **Ocho Rios Fort,** built in the late 17th century. Like many other forts on the island, it was strengthened in 1780 when a French

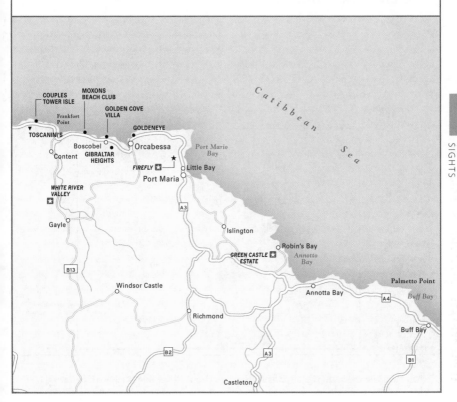

attack was feared. In 1795 a French vessel appeared off Ocho Rios harbor, but fearing the guns there, it made an attack at Mammee Bay. The Ocho Rios Fort was rebuilt by Reynolds Jamaica and contains two of the original guns from Ocho Rios and two of the guns that defended the town of Mammee Bay. The fort is not a managed attraction but is worth a quick stop to have a look around.

## ★ DUNN'S RIVER FALLS

By far the most visited attraction in Jamaica, if not the Caribbean, is **Dunn's River Falls** (tel. 876/974-4767 or 876/974-5944, www.dunnsriverfallsja.com, 8:30am-4pm daily, when cruise ships are in port 7am-4pm daily, US$20 adults, US$12 ages 2-11). The site is owned by the Urban Development Corporation (UDC) and receives over 300,000 visitors a year who come to climb the waterfalls, starting from the mouth of the river where it tumbles down to meet the sea in the middle of a golden-sand beach. The river's cool spring water in the warm Caribbean make an exhilarating swim. The falls themselves are climbable by anyone at least 90 centimeters (36 inches) tall. As long as you're steady on your feet, it's not too much of a challenge, provided the water level isn't too high. Hand rails have been installed at the most challenging stretch just before the underpass beneath the road.

To avoid crowds scrambling up the cascades, Dunn's River is best visited on days

# Ocho Rios and Vicinity

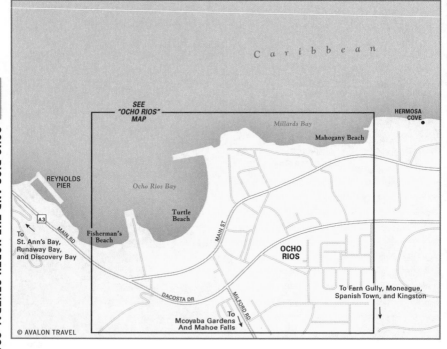

when there's no cruise ship in the port of Ocho Rios, usually Sunday but easy to determine by taking a look at the pier. However, groups are also brought from cruise ships docking in Falmouth and Montego Bay, and every hotel on the island offers tour packages to the falls, so it's hard to avoid the crowds on any day. Arriving as the park opens at 8:30am is the best way to find relative solitude.

The rocks up the falls are slippery, and water booties are recommended. These are rented (US$7) and sold (US$17) on-site. The park also recommends visitors climb the falls accompanied by one of the many guides. You'll likely be corralled and assigned a guide if you're with a group. The guides expect to be tipped; US$5 to US$10 pp is reasonable. Neither guide nor booties are compulsory, but first-timers may find a steady hand and some riverbed knowledge useful for the ascent.

Dunn's River is located two kilometers (1.2 miles) west of Ocho Rios. Route taxis pass the entrance to the falls on their way to St. Ann's Bay and will stop at Dunn's River by request. A private taxi chartered from Ocho Rios shouldn't cost more than US$10, though the hard-hustling Ochi cabbies will likely start much higher. Don't be afraid to haggle, and remind the driver it's only a few kilometers.

On the subject of haggling, for those who enjoy it, the craft market that visitors are subjected to on the way to the park's exit provides ample opportunity to engage with aggressive vendors who lose no time making friends with, "How was it?" "Where're you from?" "Come here, let me show you something." For those who don't enjoy extreme shopping, keep left for the express route through the maze of shops and food concession stands.

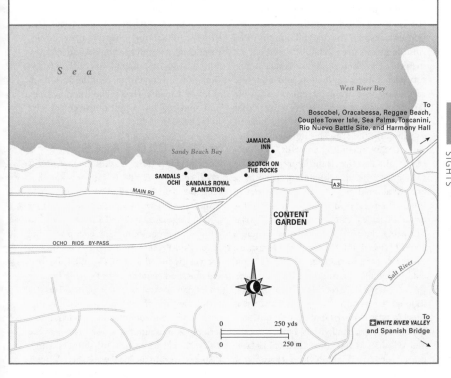

## DOLPHIN COVE

**Dolphin Cove** (on the A1, just before Dunn's River heading west, tel. 876/974-5335, U.S. tel. 974/618-0900, www.dolphincoveja.com, reservations required, 8:30am-5:30pm daily) offers a variety of programs where visitors interact with dolphins with varying degrees of intimacy, depending on the price—starting with the **Encounter Program** (US$99), where you get to touch the dolphins' snout in knee-high water and kiss a dolphin, to the **Swim Adventure** (US$149 adults, US$99 ages 6-12), where you're pulled belly-to-belly with the dolphin through the lagoon, to the **Royal Swim** (US$199 adults, US$99 ages 6-12) with two dolphins, being pulled by dorsal fins and then getting a foot push where the dolphins use their snouts to pushes you into the air. In the **Shark Program** (US$99), guests snorkel with, hold, and feed nurse sharks, 2.5 to 4 meters (8 to 14 feet) in length. Basic admission (US$49 adults, US$30 ages 6-12) includes a jungle trail, a love bird aviary, glass-bottomed kayaking, snorkeling with debarbed stingrays, rides in two-seater mini motor boats, and a 12-meter (40-foot) monster slide that empties into a pool.

For those who can't get enough, Dolphin Cove offers educational half-day (US$440) and full day (US$660) sea keeper programs offering children and adults a more in-depth experience from a caretaker's perspective.

## MYSTIC MOUNTAIN

**Rainforest Bobsled Jamaica at Mystic Mountain** (tel. 876/974-3990, reservations. jam@rfat.com, www.rainforestadventure. com, 9am-3pm daily) is located on 40 hectares (100 acres) of forest west of town, just before Dunn's River Falls and Dolphin Cove.

The tour includes a 15-minute ride up to the peak of Mystic Mountain on the Sky Explorer (US$42 pp), a chairlift similar to what you'd find at ski resorts. The ride and summit afford stunning views over Ocho Rios, and once at the peak, there's an exhibit of Jamaican history and culture, a gift shop, and a bar and restaurant in a wooden replica of an old Jamaican train station. There's a water slide and an infinity pool in front of the building overlooking the sea. The Bobsled Jamaica ride (US$69, including chairlift) is a two-seater tram that travels through the forest on suspended rails, an exhilarating five-minute blast of adrenaline, but only as gut-wrenching as the person in front, controlling the brakes, decides. The canopy tour (US$115, including chairlift) consists of a ride on a series of five ziplines through the forest. All three rides can be packaged for US$137 pp. Additional bobsled runs cost US$22; a family pack (US$44) is five rides. There is no additional charge for use of the pool and water slide. **Mystic Dining** (9pm-5pm daily, US$5-15) offers soups, sandwiches, burgers, pasta, and jerk chicken and pork à la carte in a large dining room overlooking Ocho Rios and the North Coast.

## PROSPECT PLANTATION

**Prospect Plantation** (contact Dolphin Cove, tel. 876/994-1058, 8am-4pm Mon.-Sat.) is a 405-hectare (1,000-acre) working plantation bought by Sir Harold Mitchell in 1936. Mitchell entertained all manner of dignitaries here in the great house and the area's most luxurious villas. A tradition was that his guests would plant a tree on the grounds to mark their visit. The most notable of these tokens of remembrance is the giant mahogany planted by Winston Churchill in 1953. It stands in the driveway behind the great house.

Nestled among the groves of tropical hardwoods below the great house is a beautiful chapel built by Mitchell to mark the passing of his wife, Mary Jane Mitchell Greene, known as Lady Mitchell. The chapel was constructed completely with hardwoods and stone found on the plantation.

**Prospect Outback Adventures** (tel. 876/974-5335, info@prospectoutbackadventures.com, www.prospectoutbackadventures.com, US$39-196) offers tours of the plantation, which range from cooking lessons to rides on camels, horseback, jitney, Segway, and mud buggies. A tour of the great house in included in each.

## ★ KONOKO FALLS

**Konoko Falls** (Shaw Park Rd., tel. 876/622-1712, cell tel. 876/408-0575, www.konoko-falls.com, 8am-5pm daily, US$20 adults, US10 under age 13) was upgraded in December 2015, bringing endangered animal species to a breeding program in partnership with the Hope Zoo Preservation Trust. Visitors can see yellow-billed and black-billed parrots, iguanas, and yellow snakes as well as conies and a pair of American crocodiles. The waterfalls are fit for swimming and climbing, with nearby restroom facilities, a bar, and a jerk pit. A museum features a history of the Taino, Jamaica's earliest inhabitants, and a display covering the local watershed. Ysassi's Lookout Point, named after the last Spanish governor of Jamaica, boasts spectacular views over Ocho Rios and the bay. A Romanesque pavilion above the falls is used for events and weddings.

Konoko Falls is on the Milford River, which flows through the gardens before descending through town and out the storm gulley by Moon Palace Jamaica Grande. Konoko was once a banana walk, or gully, on Shaw Park Estate until the gardens and waterfalls were developed in the early 1990s. To get to Konoko, turn right opposite the Anglican church heading toward Fern Gully on Milford Road (the A3) and follow the signs off Shaw Park Road. Previously known as Coyaba Gardens and Mahoe Falls, the attraction was recently rebranded Konoko, meaning "rainforest" in Arawak, the language of the Taino.

# ★ WHITE RIVER VALLEY

**The White River Valley** runs along the St. Ann-St. Mary border. The waterway was an important topographical feature for the Spaniards, who built the first road from the South Coast to the North Coast along its banks. The oldest **Spanish Bridge** on the island can still be seen at the river's upper reaches, just above the site where Chukka Caribbean's River Tubing Safari begins. Several river parks and gardens dot the banks.

To get to the White River, turn right at the first stoplight heading east from Ocho Rios along the A3, just after the second gas station. Follow the road for four kilometers (2.5 miles) and turn left at the intersection in Lodge, the second community, and then make a right along the rough dirt road adjacent to a JPS substation. Cars with low clearance should not attempt this rough road.

**Calypso River Rafting** (contact Judi Marsh, cell tel. 876/817-8433, yasanadi@ yahoo.com, or Bobby Marsh, cell tel. 876/995-3220, bobmarcon@yahoo.com), offers 40-minute tours down the lower reaches of the White River on bamboo rafts and rubber inner tubes. Rafts (US$55) carry two people; tubes (US$25) carry one.

**Irie River** (cell tel. 876/792-9180, irieriver@ gmail.com, US$15, US$10 under age 13) is well-maintained garden on the banks of the White River east of Ochi, where visitors can cool off, use the rope swing, and enjoy picnics. The river hosts occasional events, and a bar and restaurant serves Jamaican dishes. To get here, follow the White River inland until you reach Bonham Spring, with a white gate and white columns on each side.

**Blue Hole River** features a series of waterfalls and natural pools found along the White River in an area known locally as Breadfruit Walk. Once relatively unvisited by travelers, this section of the river has become a hot spot, and locals who keep the banks clean and guide visitors to the different pools suitable for swimming ask for a US$10 pp contribution. The area is the first set of swimming holes you'll reach after turning right at the JPS substation. You'll see a parking area on the left as you come around the first bend in the rocky road.

**Calby's River Hidden Beauty** (contact Nadani Davis, cell tel. 876/465-6438, nadani_davis@yahoo.com, 9am-5pm daily, US$10, US$5 under age 13) is a riverside park and chill spot along the White River with a rope swing and areas where the limestone riverbed has been formed into smooth slides by

SIGHTS

OCHO RIOS AND THE NORTH CENTRAL COAST

Blue Hole River

gushing water. Tubes, guides, and life jackets are included. A bar and restaurant serve beer, jerk chicken, and pork with rice-and-peas and festival.

**Chukka Caribbean's River Tubing Safari** (tel. 876/972-2506, ochorios@chukka-caribbean.com, www.chukkacaribbean.com, US$65) offers a well-organized and exciting ride down a five-kilometer (3-mile) stretch of the White River starting at a historic Spanish Bridge, an attraction itself built in the 17th century. Tubers float over the limestone riverbed, sometimes lazily, sometimes fast as the banks narrow, creating mild rapids. The tour lasts about two hours.

# Beaches

Most of the resorts in town and along the coast have cordoned off their seafront beach areas. Despite the fact that all beaches in Jamaica fall under public domain, private landowners along the coast can apply for exclusivity permits, a clause in the law most hotels take advantage of. Regardless, all beaches are considered public to the high water mark.

**Ocho Rios Bay Beach** (Main St., US$3), more commonly known as Turtle Beach, dominates the shorefront area in the heart of town. Moon Palace Jamaica Grande has roped off a large piece of the beach on the eastern side of the bay, while Turtle Towers and Fisherman's Point share the western end with the public beach park.

**Fishermen's Beach** (Main St., free) is home to a number of fish shacks and craft vendors. The beach itself is crowded with colorfully painted fishing boats, or canoes, as they're known locally, and swimming is better on the other side of the rocky outcrop at the beach in front of Margaritaville. Fishing boat owners will charter their boats for snorkeling excursions to the reef or for excursions to virgin Pearly Beach and Laughing Waters. Bear in mind that shady characters and hustlers tend to congregate in the area, and arriving at a reasonable price may require some negotiation. A round-trip boat ride to Laughing Waters shouldn't cost more than US$20 pp.

**One Love Trail,** located about one

Ocho Rios Bay Beach, also known as Turtle Beach

# Ocho Rios

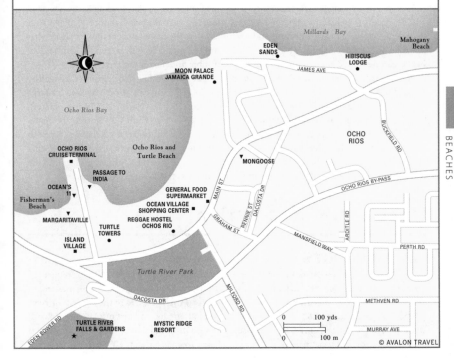

Ocho Rios Bay

Millards Bay

EDEN SANDS
HIBISCUS LODGE
Mahogany Beach
JAMES AVE
MOON PALACE JAMAICA GRANDE
OCHO RIOS
BUCKFIELD RD
Ocho Rios and Turtle Beach
OCHO RIOS CRUISE TERMINAL
PASSAGE TO INDIA
MONGOOSE
OCEAN'S 11
Fisherman's Beach
GENERAL FOOD SUPERMARKET
OCEAN VILLAGE SHOPPING CENTER
MARGARITAVILLE
REGGAE HOSTEL OCHOS RIO
TURTLE TOWERS
ISLAND VILLAGE
MAIN ST
RENNIE ST
DACOSTA DR
OCHO RIOS BY-PASS
GRAHAM ST
MANSFIELD WAY
ARDITLE RD
PERTH RD
Turtle River Park
MILFORD RD
DACOSTA DR
METHVEN RD
EDEN BOWER RD
TURTLE RIVER FALLS & GARDENS
MYSTIC RIDGE RESORT
MURRAY AVE
0    100 yds
0    100 m
© AVALON TRAVEL

kilometer (0.6 miles) west of Island Village Shopping center heading out of town, leads down to a beautiful waterfall spilling onto a small beach protected by a reef just offshore. Caretaker Goshford Dorrington "Histry" Miller (cell tel. 876/893-1867) takes tips for keeping the place clean and sells artwork and natural jewelry.

**Mahogany Beach** (Main St., free) is managed by the operators of Cool Runnings, a catamaran cruise outfit. The beach is east of the town center, just past Bibibip's. It's the best place to soak up the local scene and is also the departure point for the catamaran booze cruises.

**Margaritaville Beach** (free) is a nice beach in front of Margaritaville that can be accessed through Island Village or just past Island Village heading down to the cruise ship terminal.

**Bamboo Beach Club** (east of White River, St. Mary, tel. 876/447-0142, bamboo-beach@live.com, www.bamboobeachclub. com, 8am-6pm Mon.-Thurs., 9am-midnight Fri.-Sun., US$59 adults, US$54 under age 13) is one of the best beaches in the vicinity, previously known as Reggae Beach. It is controlled by Ilan Erlich, who's made it into a private enclave catering mostly to cruise ship passengers with entry sold as part of an all-inclusive food and drink package, in the process pricing out locals.

**Laughing Waters** (contact Janice Chong at St. Ann Development Corporation for bookings, tel. 876/974-5015, chong@udcja. com), located just east of Dunn's River Falls and Pearly Beach, is probably the most stunning beach in Jamaica for the combination of gurgling falls and fine, golden sand. The beach was made famous in the first James

Bond film, *Dr. No,* when Ursula Andress emerges from the sea singing and enchants 007, played by a young Sean Connery.

The beach is privately managed by the St. Ann Development Corporation and isn't open to the public except by rental. The beach can be rented for groups at rates that range according to the number of guests (US$1,000/1,500/2,000/2,500 for up to 75/100/150/250 guests, USD 500 deposit).

Locals however visit the beach and are rarely bothered. They park along the highway on the broad shoulder just west of a JPS substation, step over the barbed wire fence to head down an old paved driveway no longer in use, and then follow a trail that leads off the left side of the mowed field before reaching the bridge across the Roaring River. The trail leads down to the beach about 500 meters west of where the cascades meet the sea. Guards patrol the property with large dogs, but seldom trouble undeterred trespassers.

**Pearly Beach** is also privately managed by the SADCo and can also be booked for large groups (75 guests min, US$10 per person). Also known as Crab Cay Beach, the name used for the fictitious island that was home to Dr. No in Ian Fleming's first 007 novel, this fine stretch of sand is located just around the bend, east from Laughing Waters.

# Sports and Recreation

## WATER SPORTS

From the Marina at Fisherman's Point there are a few boats available for charter for sailing and snorkeling. **Island Dog Water Sports** (Ocho Rios Marina, cell tel. 876/367-8342, shaltonwhyte@hotmail.com) offers deep-sea fishing and snorkeling excursions.

**Cool Runnings Catamarans** (1 Marvins Park, tel. 876/974-2446 or 954/434-5125, www.coolrunningscatamarans.com) has three catamarans and a trimaran. Cruises operate to Dunn's River Falls (12:30pm-4pm Mon.-Sat., US$86 plus transfer) and include an open bar and patties, snorkeling gear, and the entrance fee to the falls. A Taste of Jamaica evening cruise (5pm-8pm Thurs., US $75 pp) offers an open bar and Jamaican food like jerk pork, chicken, rice-and-peas, festival, and bammy. Other cruises offered are by charter, include the clothing-optional Wet and Wild cruise (minimum 15 people, from US$136). The boats depart and return to Mahogany Beach. The open bar serves beer, rum, and soft drinks.

## PARKS

Ocho Rios is known for its lush gardens, though some are far better maintained than others. One of the nicest free waterfalls in Ochi, known as **Nature Falls,** is frequented mostly by locals who come for picnics and to wash off their vehicles in the shade. The river and falls are located just off Shaw Park Road, along a dirt road that branches off the road to Perry Town just past the Y where it splits from Shaw Park Road.

**Turtle River Park** (tel. 876/795-0078, 7am-8pm Mon.-Fri., 8am-9pm Sat.-Sun., free) is located straight ahead as you descend from Fern Gully at the junction of Milford, Main Street, and DaCosta Drive. Ponds have koi, butterfly koi, tilapia, and some turtles inside a picket fence bordering the pond.

**Turtle River Falls & Gardens** (Eden Bower Rd., tel. 876/974-5114 or 876/974-8508, turtleriverfallsandgardens@gmail.com, www.turtleriverfallsandgardens.com, US$20 adults, US$10 under age 12) is a six-hectare (14-acre) river park with 14 cascades and a walk-in aviary.

## TOURS

**Chukka Caribbean** (U.S. tel. 877/424-8552, tel. 876/656-8026, www.chukka.com) offers a host of different activities for thrill seekers and adventure lovers, including catamaran cruises, canopy ziplines, cliff jumping, white-water rafting, river tubing, horseback riding, and off-roading on ATVs and dune buggies as well as trips to Bob Marley's birthplace at Nine Mile.

**Konoko Bike Safari and Blue Mountain Bicycle Tours** (121 Main St., tel. 876/974-7075, www.bmtoursja.com, from US$75) runs a downhill bike tour in the hills above Ocho Rios and in the Blue Mountains above Buff Bay, Portland. The latter tour takes groups of up to 20 riders to Cascade, above Buff Bay in the Blue Mountains, where the route descends for about an hour, with a stop for lunch, before continuing for another hour to the Fish Dunn waterfall above Charles Town. The entire excursion runs 8am-4:30pm.

**Strawberry Fields Adventure Tours** (U.S. tel. 905/481-3138, tel. 876/655-0136, cell tel. 876/999-7169, www.strawberryfieldstogether.com) offers a variety of nature excursions based out of Strawberry Fields Together Beachfront Cottages in Robin's Bay, St. Mary. Guided hikes are offered to a black-sand beach and Kwamen Falls (US$25). Snorkeling trips go to Long Reef (US$50), and Land Rover tours with Everton in one of his many rebuilt classic Rovers can also be arranged. Picnic lunches (US$18 pp) can be added to any of the tours. Transportation can be arranged at an additional cost.

**Single Track Jamaica** (www.singletrackjamaica.com) offers more serious mountain bikers guided tours by the day (US$100), bike rental (US$50), and complete vacation packages (US$240 per day) including accommodations, meals, and guided biking.

## GOLF

**Sandals Golf and Country Club** (tel. 876/975-0119, www.sandals.com, 7am-5pm daily, greens fees US$100) is a *Golf Digest* 3.5-star course in the hills above Ochi, compact and very walkable, but carts (US$40) are also available. Clubs (US$30-45) can be rented, and players are obliged to use a caddy (US$17 plus US$10 pp minimum tip).

A patio restaurant and bar serves burgers, hot dogs, and chicken sandwiches (US$7). The driving range offers baskets of 40 balls (US$4). Sandals guests don't pay greens fees, and special rates apply for guests of several other area lodgings.

# Entertainment

## BARS AND NIGHTCLUBS

**Margaritaville** (Island Village, tel. 876/675-8800, 9am-4am Mon., Wed., and Sat., 9am-10pm on Sun., Tues., and Thurs.-Fri.) is Ochi's most popular club with visitors. It sees a lot of debauchery, and the pool party on Wednesday attracts a large crowd.

**Gen-X Sports Bar & Night Club** (38 Island Plaza, Main St., tel. 876/974-4369, www.genxclub.com) has a large dance floor and separate bar area. The club attracts decent crowds on a good night; otherwise it can be completely empty. Each night features a different theme.

**Amnesia** (70 Main St., tel. 876/974-2633, US$3-7) is Ochi's most authentic Jamaican nightclub. Thursday is "Ladies' Night" and gets quite busy, with a regular after-work jam and occasional DJ performances on Friday.

**Ocean's 11 Watering Hole** (Cruise Ship Pier, tel. 876/974-8444, manbowen@cwjamaica.com, 10am-midnight daily, 8am-midnight daily when ships are in town) is a café, bar, and restaurant serving a full menu of steak, fish, lobster, salmon, conch, and ribs. It's a favorite local hotspot when hours are extended (until 2am) on Tuesday for karaoke, Friday for an after-work jam, and Saturday for the weekly retro party. Live bands play until 1am on Sunday. Coffee is sold by the cup (US$3-6) and by the pound.

## FESTIVALS AND EVENTS

Jamaica can be a tough place when it comes to continuity, and some of the more obscure annual events wane with the passing years, while others regroup and come back stronger. St. Mary hosts a few notable music festivals that are not to be missed.

**Bob Marley's birthday** is celebrated around Jamaica, kicking off **Reggae Month,** which features concerts throughout February. The Marley family's label Tuff Gong International (www.tuffgong.com) has held concerts at Bob's birthplace in Nine Mile, but moved to Montego Bay in 2016 for the inaugural One Love Festival at Rose Hall Great House.

**Ocho Rios Jazz Festival** (U.S. tel. 323/857-5358, tel. 876/927-3544, www.ochoriosjazz.com) is held at various venues in Kingston, Ocho Rios, and Port Antonio over the course of seven days, starting at the end of May or the first week of June. The festival features a few dozen local and international jazz acts.

The **Fat Tyre Festival** (www.singletrackjamaica.com), held each year around the second week in February, was created for mountain biking enthusiasts and showcases much of the talent of the St. Mary Off-Road Bicycling Association. The festival features a Bicycle Bash kickoff at James Bond Beach, with BMX races, stunts, and displays of unusual and pimped-out bikes, followed by several days of competitive and sometimes grueling rides, mostly along single track through the hills of St. Mary.

**Beach J'ouvert** (www.bacchanaljamaica.com) is part of the carnival season's festivities, held at James Bond Beach in Oracabessa in early April, where revelers wine out to soca while showering each other with paint.

**Claremont Kite Festival** is held on Easter weekend in a big field, with a stage show in the evening.

**Kampai** (baycrestlimited@gmail.com, US$50) is one of the best all-inclusive parties, held in Ocho Rios over the Easter Weekend at Enchanted Gardens or a similar exotic venue on Easter Sunday. The party features an assortment of food catered by many of the best Kingston- and Ochi-based restaurants. Bars are plentiful and top-class selectors spin a mix of soca, dancehall, reggae, and hip-hop.

A bit less upscale than Kampai, **Daydreams** (Wright Image Entertainment, US$30) is another popular all-inclusive party held on Easter Sunday at an open-air venue like the beach at Drax Hall.

**Emancipation Jubilee** is held annually on July 31 at Seville Heritage Park.

**St. Mary Mi Come From** is held in Annotto Bay on the first Saturday in August, hosted by conscious reggae icon Capleton, born a short distance from the venue. The event showcases some of Jamaica's most popular reggae artists, many of them inspired Rastas like the King Shango.

# Shopping

**Fern Gully** is a former underground riverbed that was planted with ferns in the 1880s and later paved over to create the main highway (the A3) between Spanish Town and the North Coast. Arts-and-crafts stands line a few of the less precarious curves along the steep, lush, and shady road.

Countless smaller shopping centers vie for the cruise ship dollars in the heart of Ochi, most notably in the Taj Mahal complex. The crafts market on Main Street across from Scotia Bank is definitely worth a visit. There's also another crafts center at Pineapple Place, and a third in Coconut Grove at the eastern junction of Main Street and the Ocho Rios Bypass, across from Royal Plantation, where the best deals can be found.

**Homer Brown** (cell tel. 876/417-8916) is

one of the brilliant artists associated with the defunct Wassi Art collective, which once produced some of Jamaica's most recognized hand painted ceramics.

**Ahead of Time** (77 Main St., tel. 876/974-2358) sells Indonesian furnishings and trinkets like carved chests, moon mirrors, handbags, and ceramics.

**David Simpson's Fine Art Gallery** (11 Old Buckfield Rd., tel. 876/840-1152, by appointment only) sells painting on canvas, woodcarvings, and ceramics.

**Love Chat Mobile** (Shop 10 Island Plaza, tel. 876/795-2775 or 876/974-7035, 9:30am-6:30pm Mon.-Sat.) sells original reggae, dancehall, hip-hop, gospel, and R&B, as well as phones and accessories, jewelry, and handbags.

**The Shoe Works** (shop 6, Ocean Village Plaza, tel. 876/974-5415, 9am-7pm Mon.-Sat.) has the best service in town for reasonably priced name-brand footwear.

**Scent of Incense & Things** (79 Main St., tel. 876/795-0047), run by Janet Gallimore, is a nice shop selling incense, oils, herbs, spiritual products, and a variety of small gift items.

**Island Village Shopping and Entertainment Centre** (www.islandvillageja.com) is a complex owned by Island Records founder Chris Blackwell that houses Margaritaville, Cove Theatre cinema, an ice cream parlor, and a number of shops.

**Bijoux Jewelers** (876/675-5220, bijouxja@cwjamaica.com) claims to be Jamaica's longest standing retailer of jewelry, retailing high quality popular brands of watches, earrings, bracelets and necklaces, including Michael Kors, Fossil and Pandora. **Casa de Oro** (876/675-8999) also sells duty-free jewelry and designer watches from the likes of Cartier, Tissot, Tag Heuer, and Dior, as well as diamonds.

**Tuff Gong Trading** (876/631-8484) retails authentic apparel, most of it depicting the image of reggae legend Bob Marley.

**Hemp Heaven** (876/675-8969) retails hemp apparel, footwear, and arts and crafts.

# Food

## BREAKFAST AND CAFÉS

**Nice-and-Nuff** (shop 8, Simmon's Plaza, 73 Main St., tel. 876/489-2190, 7am-7pm Mon.-Sat., US$3-4) serves typical Jamaican food for breakfast, lunch, and dinner with items like ackee and saltfish, oxtail, curry goat, and fried chicken. Food is served in foam boxes ready for takeout.

★ **Mom's Restaurant** (7 Evenly St., tel. 876/974-2811, 8am-10pm Mon.-Sat., US$5-13), not to be confused with Mother's, is located in a blue building across from the police station, toward the clock tower. It's a local favorite for local dishes, starting the day right with ackee and saltfish, corned pork, mackerel rundown, and liver before moving on to staples like oxtail, brown stew fish and baked or fried chicken on the lunch and dinner menu.

## JERK

**Ocho Rios Jerk Centre** (16 DaCosta Dr., tel. 876/974-2549, 10am-11pm daily, US$5-13) serves pork, whole and half chicken, and ribs and fish by the pound as well as conch, accompanied by breadfruit, sweet potato, bammy, and festival. It's located between Mystic Ridge and the stoplight at the junction of DaCosta and the road to Fern Gulley.

## JAMAICAN

**My Favorite Place Restaurant** (shop 7, Ocean Village, tel. 876/795-0480, 7:30am-7:30pm Mon.-Sat.., US$2-6) serves typical Jamaican dishes like fried chicken, curry goat, escoveitch fish, brown stew, and baked chicken; the menu changes daily.

**Mongoose Jamaica Restaurant & Lounge** (52 Main St., tel. 876/622-6942, www.mongoosejamaica.com, 9:30am-1am Sun.-Thurs., 9:30am-3am Fri./Sat., US$10-35) serves well-prepared and well-presented starters like chicken wings, coconut breaded shrimp, and salads, and main courses that include the signature Mongoose burger with smoked bacon, grilled pineapple, and sautéed onion with ginger wine glaze. Other entrées include local dishes like curry chicken or goat, oxtail, and jerk chicken.

## SEAFOOD

★ **Tropical Vibes Seafood and Bar** (tel. 876/386-0858, 8am-11pm daily, US$8-25) is a breezy two-story bar and restaurant serving fresh escoveitch fish and bammy as well as lobster, conch, and shrimp.

**Fancy Seafood** (3 James Ave., tel. 876/974-4402, 9am-10pm daily, US$6-20) run by the congenial Alicia Archer, serves curry goat, fried chicken, shrimp, steam, escoveitch, brown stew, and fried jerk fish.

## INTERNATIONAL

**Almond Tree Restaurant** (83 Main St., Hibiscus Lodge, tel. 876/974-2676 or 876/947-2813, 7:30am-10:30am, noon-2:30pm, and 6pm-9:30pm daily) serves a mix of Jamaican and international dishes like lobster (US$50),

a variety of chicken (US$35), fish (US$40), lamb chops (US$30), and butterfly shrimp (US$35). A full bar in the restaurant serves beer (US$3), as well as mixed drinks. Indoor and outdoor dining areas overlook the water.

**Evita's** (Eden Bower Rd., tel. 876/974-2333, 11am-11pm daily, US$20-40) is an Italian restaurant serving lobster, steak, and pasta dishes. While Evita's might lack an upscale edge, the view is excellent and worth a trip.

★ **Passage to India Restaurant & Bar** (shop 2, Fisherman's Point Resort, next to Ocho Rios Cruise Ship Pier, 11am-11pm daily, US$11-26) serves authentic north Indian palak paneer, mala kofta, chicken vindaloo, lamb, lobster, and shrimp, as well as south Indian favorites like masala dosa and idli for breakfast. This is the real deal, the best in St. Ann, in a breezy waterfront location at Fisherman's Point overlooking the town's modest marina. It shares the premises with **Bottles & Chimney**, a Jamaican bar and cook shop under the same management.

**Taste of India** (Sonis Plaza, 50 Main St., tel. 876/795-3182, 10am-10pm Tues.-Sun., US$12-22) serves north Indian cuisine with dishes like palak paneer, mala costa, chicken vindaloo, lamb, lobster, and shrimp.

**Hong Kong International Restaurant**

masala dosa and idli at Passage to India Restaurant & Bar

Deano Wynter, owner and chef at Reggae Pot Rastaurant

Broken Rudder is the beachside grill at the same property, offering a more casual dining experience for lunch.

★ **Toscanini Italian Restaurant & Bar** (Harmony Hall, Tower Isle, tel. 876/975-4785, lella.toscananini@gmail.com, www.harmonyhall.com, lunch noon-2pm Tues.-Sun., dinner 6:30pm-9:45pm Tues.-Sun., US$20-50) is the most upscale and best-quality Italian restaurant in town, with tables on the ground floor of a beautifully renovated great house and outside on the patio. Dishes include appetizers like marinated marlin, prosciutto and papaya, and yellow fin tuna tartare, and entrées like homemade fettuccine with lobster versiliese. Bread and pasta are homemade, and fresh local fish and live lobster are delivered daily. The most popular seafood dishes include mahimahi all'acqua pazza, grilled lobster thermidor, and homemade fettucine with bacon, mushroom, and rosé sauce. Vegetarians can try the homemade pasta with roasted fresh vegetables. Toscanini is run by the congenial Lella Ricci, who is always around chatting with customers and ensuring the quality of service.

(3 Champion Plaza, Dacosta Dr., tel. 876/974-0588, 10am-10pm Mon.-Fri., later Sat.-Sun., from US$7) is one of the better places for Chinese food in Ochi, serving chicken, beef, shrimp, seafood, and pork with noodles and rice. It lacks ambience, making takeout a good option.

## FINE DINING

**Spring Garden Seafood & Steakhouse** (Ocho Rios Bypass, tel. 876/795-3149, café. spring@yahoo.com, www.springgardenseafoodsteakhouse.com, 11am-11pm daily) serves well-prepared seafood, steak, and chicken (US$10-40) with indoor and alfresco dining.

**Christopher's Restaurant** (Hermosa Cove, U.S. tel. 855/811-2683, tel. 876/974-3699, 7am-8:30pm daily, US$20-45) serves casual gourmet dishes in an open-air dining area with ocean views, a great way to experience one of the new boutique resorts in the area, with worldly dishes like curried goat ravioli and pimento smoked beef tenderloin. The

## VEGETARIAN

**Healthy Way Vegetarian Kitchen** (Shop 54, Ocean Village, tel. 876/974-9229, 9am-6pm Mon.-Sat., US$1.50-5) serves escoveitch tofu; hominy, peanut, plantain, carrot, and bulgur porridge; steamed cabbage with banana; and fried dumplings.

**Calabash Ital Restaurant** (7 James Ave., 8am-10pm Mon.-Sat., 8am-8pm Sun., US$4-5) serves vegan dishes like ackee, veggie stew, and tofu on a rotating menu and natural juices like beet, cane juice, and june plum (US$2).

★ **Reggae Pot Rastaurant** (86 Main St., cell tel. 876/296-3591, 9am-9pm Mon.-Sat., 10am-8pm Sun., US$3-5) serves vegetarian "ital" food on a rotating menu with dishes like brown stew, curried or stir-fry tofu, and split peas with veggie chunks. Natural seasonal juices are prepared. The shop is owned and operated by chef Deano Wynter.

## BAKERIES

**Golden Loaf Baking Company** (72 Main St., tel. 876/974-2635, pizzeria tel. 876/974-7014, glb@cwjamaica.com, www.golden-loafochorios.com, 8am-8:30pm Mon.-Sat.) makes bread, pastries, pizzas, stewed and jerk chicken and pork, oxtail, curry goat, stewed beef, and turkey neck.

## ICE CREAM

**Scoops Unlimited** (shop 11, Island Village, tel. 876/675-8776, 9am-8:30pm Mon.-Fri., 10am-10pm Sat.-Sun.) sells local ice cream.

# Accommodations

As one of the original resort towns in Jamaica, Ocho Rios has developed a wide array of lodging options. Nevertheless, at the lower end, conditions tend to be consistently shabby, while there are several good mid-range and high-end options.

## UNDER US$100

**Reggae Hostel Ocho Rios** (19 Main St., tel. 876/974-2607, www.ochi.reggaehostel.com, from US$20) has two dormitories with shared baths, one with six bunk beds, the other with eight, and private rooms with en suite baths, one category sleeping two (US$65), the other four (US$100). Located a few steps from the beach, the backpacker-friendly digs offer complimentary Wi-Fi, coffee and tea, parking, a communal kitchen, and a roof bar and lounge. The private rooms have air-conditioning and TVs.

Reasonably priced and with a common balcony overlooking the water, **Carleen's Villa Guest House** (85-A Main St., tel. 876/974-5431) has seven no-frills rooms (US$40) equipped with ceiling fans, two twin beds, TVs, and hot water in private baths. There's no pool and no food, but it's five minutes away Mahogany Beach, Ochi's most popular with locals.

**The Village Hotel** (54-56 Main St., tel. 876/974-9193, villagehtl@cwjamaica.com, www.villagehoteljamaica.com, US$90, includes breakfast) has standard, deluxe, and suite rooms, all with air-conditioning, kitchenettes, cable TV, and ceiling fans. There is a swimming pool on property, and the Village Grill serves a mix of international and Jamaican cuisine (US$10-25).

**Turtle Beach Towers** (tel. 876/954-7807, admin@mysilversands.com, www.turtle-beachtowers.com, from US$75) is one of the original and less-attractive apartment-style options, a cluster of gray towers at the base of Fisherman's Point resembling government housing projects. Do not book here without first seeing the room in person, as individual owners decorate the apartments according to their tastes (or neglect, as the case may be), and the decor and amenities vary greatly from unit to unit. Reduced rates can be negotiated for longer stays.

## US$100-250

**Columbus Heights Apartments** (tel. 876/974-9057 or 876/974-2940, columbush-gts@cwjamaica.com, www.columbusheights.com, US$100-200 low season, US$120-220 high season) is a large condo complex on a hill overlooking Ocho Rios and affording great views. Studios and one- and two-bedroom apartments have air-conditioning and hot water. Longer stays afford reduced rates.

**Fisherman's Point** (Cruise Ship Wharf, contact Charmaine Annikey for bookings, U.S. tel. 877/211-6313, cell tel. 876/798-7647, accounts@selfcateringapartmentsjm.com, www.fishermanspoint.net, US$100 low season, US$125 high season) is run as individual apartment owners pooling their units. These are some of the nicer self-contained units available in Ocho Rios, and while decor and furnishings vary considerably, there is much better oversight of the conditions than at neighboring Turtle Towers. All units are fully furnished, with hot water, living rooms, equipped kitchens, TV, air-conditioning, and phones. There is a nice pool at the center of the complex, with Turtle Beach access two minutes away.

**Rooms on the Beach** (Turtle Beach, Main St., tel. 876/974-6632 U.S. tel. 877/467-8737, info@superclubs.com, www.roomsresort.com, US$105-141) is SuperClubs' answer to the demand for a dependable room-only option in Ochi. Located beachfront in the heart of town, Rooms has a pool and all the fixtures of an all-inclusive without the all-inclusive. The rooms are clean, with TV, air-conditioning, phones, and hot water. The property is a short walk from all the restaurants and nightlife in downtown Ocho Rios.

**Hibiscus Lodge** (83 Main St., tel. 876/974-2676, www.hibiscusjamaica.com) has comfortable rooms with air-conditioning, TVs, and private baths with hot water. Rooms are either garden view (US$135 low season, US$147 high season) or ocean view (US$147 low season, US$159 high season) and have two twins or one queen. Rates include breakfast, and the hotel is within easy walking distance of the heart of Ochi and Mahogany Beach.

**Mystic Ridge Resort** (17 DaCosta Drive, tel. 876/974-9831 or 876/618-1998, info@mysticridgejamaica.com, www.mysticridgejamaica.com, from US$118) is the sister property to the Ocho Rios hilltop theme park, Mystic Mountain, offering guests discounted tour rates and complimentary transport. The stratified complex has standard rooms, loft suites, and one- and two-bedroom apartments. The furnishings and linens are modern and tasteful. Flat panel TVs, Wi-Fi, kitchenettes, private bathrooms, and balconies feature in the apartments. Rates include a complimentary breakfast buffet in the poolside Zedoj Restaurant. A mobile spa offers room service for a variety of treatments.

★ **The Blue House** (White River Estates, St. Mary, tel. 876/994-1367, elise@thebluehousejamaica.com, www.thebluehousejamaica.com, 3-night minimum, US$180-260) is a quaint B&B run by Elise Yapp and her Chinese-Jamaican family, who live on the premises, ensuring attentive service and with home-cooked meals. The property is located in a small subdivision five minutes east of downtown Ocho Rios past the White River and opposite Couples Sans Souci. A well-appointed ground-floor bedroom can accommodate up to five on a king, two twins, and a

Mystic Ridge Resort

queen, with a bath across the hall. Three bedrooms on the second level each have a king and an en suite bath, and there is a cottage around back with a porch surrounded by lush gardens. The property has a small pool, but it doesn't compare to a refreshing dip in the White River, a five-minute walk away. Accessibility is the only drawback, as the innkeepers don't provide guests with a key to the front entrance or gate, but staff is on call into the wee hours to let guests in.

## OVER US$250

One of the classiest hotels on the island, ★ Jamaica Inn (tel. 876/974-2514, U.S. tel. 800/837-4608, reservations@jamaicainn.com) has 60 percent repeat guests, among them Jamaican and foreign dignitaries, including Winston Churchill, who stayed in the signature White Suite, and Marilyn Monroe. Since then the amenities have only improved. You won't find clocks, TVs, or Internet access, seen as distractions from relaxation. There is Wi-Fi in the library and a computer for guest use. What you will find in the rooms is tasteful, soothing decor, with open living rooms just off the bedrooms, literally on one of the nicest private beaches in Jamaica and complete with a foot pan to wash off the sand before stepping inside.

Three room categories vary by beach proximity and size. Second-floor balcony suites (US$290/550 low/high season), deluxe suites (US$340 low season, US$670 high season), and premier suites (US$420 low season, US$825 high season). More exclusive rooms include the White Suite (US$820 low season, US$1,760 high season) and the Cowdray Suite (US$435 low season, US$860 high season). Two spectacular one-bedroom cottages, numbers 3 and 4 (US$820 low season, US$1,760 high season), have private plunge pools, decks, and outside showers.

Hermosa Cove (Hermosa Lane, Pineapple, U.S. tel. 855/811-2683, tel. 876/974-3699, www.hermosacove.com, 1-bedroom from US$451, 3-bedroom US$993) has a total of nine villas with king and twin beds.

Living rooms have air-conditioning and flat-screen TVs with cable, and Wi-Fi is available throughout. A one-bedroom villa (US$715) and a three-bedroom villa (US$1,041) have ocean views from the bedrooms. Two beaches have kayaking and snorkeling, and three infinity pools are found on the eastern end of the property next to the Broken Rudder Beach Bar & Grill (10am-6pm daily). Eight of the villas have private plunge pools. Day passes (US$45 pp) grant access to the infinity pool, kayaks, snorkeling, and the beach bar and grill.

Eden Sands (16 James Ave., cell tel. 876/865-2366, nathanbless@hotmail.com, www.ochoriosbeachvilla.com, US$350) is a quaint two-bedroom house that sleeps up to eight. The house features cable TV, air-conditioning in the bedrooms, a live-in handyman, security, and a housekeeper. The distinguishing feature is a private beach on Ochi's Riviera, the finest stretch of coast around.

## VILLAS

SunVillas (contact Alan Marlor, U.S. tel. 888/625-6007, alan@sunvillas.com, www.sunvillas.com) rents a wide range of villas across Jamaica varying considerably in price and extravagance. Villas by Linda Smith (www.jamaicavillas.com) is the leading luxury villa agent on the island, with an impressive portfolio of properties from St. Mary to Hanover. Prendergast Real Estate and Villa Rentals (7 DaCosta Dr., tel. 876/974-2670, pren@cwjamaica.com), run by Clinece Prendergast and her daughter Jacky, manages and books a large selection of villas, some in the hills overlooking Ochi, others directly on the water in and around town, from Oracabessa to Montego Bay along the North Coast. Indulge (Terry Groves, cell tel. 876/361-4034, tgroves@cwjamaica.com) is a service specializing in providing luxury goods for villa guests staying anywhere between Ocho Rios and Tryall. Email for the complete list of goodies.

★ Scotch on the Rocks (Pineapple Grove, tel. 876/469-4828 or 876/871-1312, scotchontherocksja@gmail.com, www.scotchontherocksja.com, weekly US$6,535 low season, US$8,035 high season) is one of Jamaica's top five villas for its elegance, value, and location, but it's unpretentious and atmospheric. Each bedroom has an en suite bath, air-conditioning, flat-screen TV, and balconies overlooking the sea in the second-floor rooms. The master has a king bed while other rooms have queens. Soft linens invite intimacy, and white linen curtains adorn the breezy windows and French doors. A large pool deck out front overlooks the sea at the top of a staircase leading down to the picturesque dock with a gazebo at the end. Meals can be enjoyed in a large indoor dining room or alfresco. Scotch is on Sandy Bay, Ocho Rios's Riviera; neighbors on either side are the most luxurious hotels in town, Jamaica Inn and Sandals Royal Plantation, each with tennis courts and spa facilities within a few minutes' walk. The staff at Scotch is top-notch.

**Frankfort on the Beach** (U.S. tel. 800/733-5077, tel. 876/994-1373, ian@prospect-villas.com or rory@prospect-villas.com, www.prospect-villas.com) is the crown jewel of Prospect Villas, a collection of five luxurious villas and the Prospect Great House. Part of the Prospect Plantation Estate, formerly owned by Sir Harold Mitchell, Prospect Villas has hosted some of the most important political and entertainment figures of the 20th century, including Charlie Chaplin and Henry Kissinger. The villas are classy, with every amenity imaginable, from Wi-Fi to iPod docks and satellite TV, not to mention a private beach and a full staff.

**Garden House** (Shaw Park, across from Konoko Falls, contact Michelle Garricks, U.S. tel. 345/929-5846, www.gardenhousejamaica.com, US$650 for up to 19 guests) is a hillside villa with a swimming pool located on a 1.8-hectare (4.5-acre) estate, commanding spectacular views of the city and the coast. The main house has eight guest rooms, with a mix of queen and king beds, air-conditioning, en suite baths, balconies, and walk-in closets. Amenities include Wi-Fi and a staff of three.

## ALL-INCLUSIVE RESORTS

**Moon Palace Jamaica Grande** (Main St., tel. 876/974-2200, www.jamaicagrande.com, from US$466 low season, US$652 high season) is the most prominent hotel on Turtle Beach, occupying the prime piece of real estate on the point of the bay. The resort boasts its own Dolphin Cove, a surf pool, a

Scotch on the Rocks

discotheque, and buffet and à la carte dining. Rooms are modern and well-appointed with Wi-Fi throughout.

**Sandals Ochi** (Main St., tel. 876/974-5691, U.S. tel. 305/284-1300, www.sandals.com, US$1,108 low season, US$1,234 high season, 65 percent discount for 3 nights or more) is a 529-room property covering land on both sides of Main Street and the bypass. Sandals properties are exclusively for couples, and Sandals Ochi features two resorts in one amid a 40-hectare (100-acre) seaside estate. High-end villas are nestled among lush foliage and have private pools at The Butler Village & Great House. A small white-sand beach hugged by a wraparound pier dotted with gazebos, dubbed the Grande Promenade, is the prominent feature at The Caribbean Riviera. Amenities include four-poster king beds, flatscreen TVs, stocked fridges, en suite baths, and air-conditioning. Wi-Fi is included in rooms and public areas. Guests can choose from 16 restaurants, 10 bars, 7 pools, and 22 whirlpools, as well as get complimentary access to the Sandals Golf & Country Club.

**Sandals Royal Plantation** (tel. 876/974-5601, U.S. tel. 305/284-1300, www.royal-plantation.com, from US$1,384 low season, US$1,482 high season, 65 percent discount

for 3 nights or more) is an upscale all-butler property with champagne and caviar available at C-Bar. Five restaurants include French and Mediterranean cuisine. Some of the six room categories include whirlpool tubs and French balconies; one-bedroom suites have two walkout balconies with lounge chairs and a huge living room area. Royal Plan guests have greens fees and transportation to the Sandals Golf Course included. All bedrooms have king beds. At Sandals is **Red Lane Spa** (tel. 876/670-9015, www.redlanespa.com), one of the most comprehensive on the island, with 14 full-time employees and 8 full-time therapists. The spa offers a wide variety of services, from hot stone massage to nails and facials. Red Lane Spa is open to nonguests as well.

★ **Couples** (www.couples.com, from US$507 low season, US$551 high season) has two all-inclusive resorts just east of Ochi across the White River into St. Mary: **Couples San Souci** (White River, tel. 876/994-1353) and **Couples Tower Isle** (Tower Isle, tel. 876/975-4271), with a sleek South Beach feel. Couples Resorts are at the top of the all-inclusive ranking for the quality of the food, with a lot of local fruit and produce, a delicious mix of local and international cuisine, details like black pepper

Couples Tower Isle boasts a private island for nudists.

grinders at each table, and premium drinks and liquor. The rooms at Sans Souci, which means "worry-free" in French, are tasteful, with simple decor and balconies overlooking a private beach. Couples Tower Isle boasts a private island within swimming distance of the beach, reserved for nudists.

# Information and Services

The **St. Ann Chamber of Commerce** (tel. 876/974-2629) has tourism booklets that advertise the area's businesses and attractions. **DHL** (shop 3, tel. 876/974-8001, 9am-5pm Mon.-Sat.) is at Ocean Village Plaza.

## BANKS AND MONEY

**NCB Bank** (tel. 876/974-2522) is at 40 Main Street, next to Island Plaza/BK and across from the craft market. **Scotia Bank** (tel. 876/974-2311) also has a branch on Main Street, three buildings west of NCB. **Nancy's Cambio** (Taj Mahal, 4 Main St., tel. 876/974-2414 and 50 Main St., tel. 876/795-4285, both 9am-5pm Mon.-Sat.) offers slightly better exchange rates than the banks. Traveler's checks are accepted with two forms of ID. Money transfers are also possible at the St. Ann's Bay MoneyGram outlet. **FX Trader** has locations at Ocean Village Shopping Centre (Main St., shop 3, 9am-5pm Mon.-Sat.) and at H&L Rapid True Value (105 Main St., Pineapple Place).

## HEALTH CARE AND PHARMACIES

Dr. Pavel Chang at **Medical Care and Surgical Centre** (110 Main St., tel. 876/974-6339, cell. tel. 876/843-8109, 8am-5pm Mon.-Sat.) is a recommended general practitioner and surgeon. Sr. Sonali Thakurani at **Complete Care Medical Centre** (16 Rennie Rd., 876/974-3357 cell. tel. 876/579-5789) is also recommendable.

**St. Ann's Bay Hospital** (Seville Rd., tel. 876/972-2272) is the most important in the region, with people coming from kilometers around. However, better service can be obtained at private health centers in Ocho Rios.

**Fontana Pharmacy** (Eight Rivers Town Centre, tel. 876/974-8889, 9am-8pm Mon.-Thurs., 9am-9pm Fri.-Sat., 10am-6pm Sun.) is the best full service pharmacy chain in the island, similar to the large format stores found in the U.S. **Pinegrove Pharmacy** (shop 5, Ocho Rios Mall, tel. 876/974-5586, 9am-8pm Mon.-Sat., 10am-3pm Sun.) is east of the clock tower on Main Street.

# Transportation

## GETTING THERE

With the completion of the North-South Toll Road in 2016, Ocho Rios is only a little over an hour from Kingston (tolls US$10 each way). The two-land highway descends from the hills to the coast, a few kilometers west of Dunn's River Falls. The drive between Ocho Rios and Montego Bay takes about the same amount of time. Oracabessa can be reached in about 30 minutes and Port Antonio is about an hour-and-a-half further to the east.

**Route taxis** and **buses** leave for Kingston and points east and west along the coast from the lot just south of the clock tower in downtown Ocho Rios. Buses go between Ochi and downtown Kingston (US$5) as well as to Montego Bay (US$5), while route taxis ply every other route imaginable: to Brown's Town (US$4), Moneague (US$2), and east and west along the coast to Oracabessa (US$3) and St. Ann's Bay (US$2). **Knutsford Express** (tel. 876/971-1822, www.knutsfordexpress. com) offers a more comfortable ride with air-conditioning and Wi-Fi from Ocho Rios to Montego Bay (US$16), Kingston (US$16), and Port Antonio (US$17).

**Ian Fleming International Airport** (OCJ, Boscobel, 15 minutes east of Ochi, www.ifia.aero, tel. 876/787-0169 or 876/797-0114) caters to small private aircraft from overseas and domestic charter operators from Kingston, Montego Bay, Negril, or Port Antonio. **TimAir** (tel. 876/952-2516, timair@ usa.net, www.timair.net) offers fixed-wing flights for two passengers from Montego Bay to Boscobel (US$630), to Kingston's Tinson Pen (US$856) and Norman Manley International (US$878), Port Antonio (US$943), and Negril (US$294). TimAir's Cessna 206 aircraft can hold up to four passengers with luggage. **AirLink Express** (tel. 876/940-6660, timair@usa.net, www.timair. net) offers fixed wing service between any two points in Jamaica.

**Captain John's Island Hoppers** (tel. 876/974-1285, helicoptersjamaica@live.com, www.jamaicahelicopterservices.com, 8am-5pm daily) offers helicopter transfers for up to four passengers for (US$1,123 per hour) from virtually any point to any other in Jamaica. The company's Bell Jet Ranger choppers are typically stationed at the airport in Mobay.

## Car Rentals
**Villa Car Rentals** (Shop 7, Coconut Grove Shopping Centre, tel. 876/974-2474, villacar-rentalscoltd@msn.com, 8am-5pm Mon.-Sat., 9am-2pm Sun.) has Toyota Corolla (US$350 per week) and Yaris (US$320 per week) sedans and a couple of Hiace buses (US$700). Insurance and taxes are extra, along with a US$2,000 security deposit.

**Caribbean Car Rentals** (99-A Main St., tel. 876/974-2513, 8:30am-5pm Mon.-Fri., 9am-2pm Sat., 9am-noon Sun., caribcars@ usa.net, www.caribbeancarrentals.net) has Toyota Yaris (US$350), Corolla (US$420), and Suzuki Jimny (US$300) and Vitara (US$500) vehicles as well as a 15-seater Hiace minibus (US$620). Taxes and insurance are extra with a US$1,500-2,000 security deposit.

## GETTING AROUND
Route taxis are the most economical way of getting around if you don't mind squeezing in with several other people. Taxis leave from the rank by the clock tower and can also be flagged down by the roadside if there is any room. Route taxis display their destination and origin in painted letters on the side of the car and are typically white Toyota Corollas. Overcrowding has been somewhat reduced in recent years with increased oversight from the authorities. It is impossible to walk the streets of Ocho Rios without being offered a chartered taxi; bear in mind that these drivers will quote any figure that comes to mind. Haggling is very much a part of hiring a local charter, and be sure not to pay the total in advance if you hope to see your driver stick around.

As you head west from Ocho Rios, the North Coast Highway hugs the waterfront passing Dolphin Cove, Dunn's River Falls, and Laughing Waters before reaching a cluster of villas and resorts in adjacent Old Fort Bay and Mammee Bay.

Continuing west, the next community is St. Ann's Bay, a busy town with one of the few hospitals on the North Coast and a few attractions worth stopping for, including Seville Great House and Heritage Park and a Marcus Garvey Statue at the Parish Library.

Still farther west, the small community of Priory sits along a dusty stretch of highway with few passersby stopping there, except on Sunday when the community's public Fantasy Beach comes alive for family fun days, partying and dancing into the night.

From Priory westward the highway passes Richmond Estate, used as a venue for several annual events; a few subdivisions in various stages of construction; and Chukka Cove, the home base for Chukka Caribbean, the island's leading tour outfit. The next community of any size is Runaway Bay, where several hotels straddle the highway and waterfront. From Runaway Bay the highway continues west to Discovery Bay, the last settlement of any size before the Trelawny border.

Discovery Bay is one of Jamaica's most exclusive villa communities, the eastern side of the bay dotted with luxury villas. In the center of the bay, a bauxite wharf feeds ships from an immense domed storage facility made famous as Dr. No's lair in the film based on Ian Fleming's first James Bond novel.

## OLD FORT BAY AND MAMMEE BAY

Old Fort Bay and Mammee Bay are contiguous to one another a few minutes west of Ocho Rios. Both bays have gated communities where visitors can rent condos and villas. Mammee Bay has two large hotels on its eastern side, ClubHotel Riu Ocho Rios and Jewel Dunn's River Beach Resort, one next to the other. Apart from these two all-inclusive resorts, accommodations in the area tend to the high end, with little in the mid-range.

## Food
**Scallywags Restaurant & Bar** (Mammee Bay, contact Bunny Williams, tel. 876/972-9396, info@bambooblujamaica.com, www.scallywagsjamaica.com, 11am-2am daily, US$12-40) is in an unmistakable boat-shaped building, roadside across from the entrance to Jewel Dunn's River Resort. The restaurant specializes in local Jamaican dishes like curry conch, escoveitch or steamed fish, oxtail, and fried and curry chicken. Scallywags hosts karaoke on Friday and occasional live music and theme parties.

**Bamboo Blu** (Mammee Bay, contact Bunny Williams, tel. 876/974-9983, cell tel. 876/375-0417, info@bambooblujamaica.com, www.bambooblujamaica.com, 10am-10pm daily, by reservation only, US$12-40) is a beachfront bar and restaurant serving soup, breadfruit chips, saltfish bammy bruschetta, crab wontons, spicy shrimp, and heavier dishes like grilled lobster, coconut rundown snapper, and fish and chips. To get there, go through the gate next to Riu.

★ **Scotchies Too** (Drax Hall, beside the Epping gas station, tel. 876/794-9457, 11am-11pm Mon.-Sat., 11am-9pm Sun., US$4-11) is an outpost of Jamaica's most respected jerk center, consistently grilling up the best jerk, with pork, chicken, and roast fish accompanied by breadfruit, yam, and festival.

## Accommodations
### UNDER US$100
**Seacrest Beach Hotel** (Richmond Cove, Priory, tel. 876/972-1594 or 876/972-1547, cell tel. 876/824-0702, seacrestresort@cwjamaica.com, www.seacrestresorts.com, from

US$85 low season, US$91 high season, including breakfast) is a 35-room property with no-frills standard rooms equipped with air-conditioning, private baths with hot water, cable TV, and private balconies with sea views. There's a pool and bar on the property. Honeymoon suites and one- and two-bedroom cottages are more spacious and separate from the main building.

## OVER US$250

**Cannon Villas** (Old Fort Bay, tel. 876/754-1623 or 876/618-5948, cell tel. 876/298-5047, sgms_ltd@hotmail.com, www.cannonvillasja.com, US$560 low season, US$600 high season) is a collection of six four-bedroom cottage-style villas sharing a lawn and a private beach accommodating up to eight guests each. Amenities include air-conditioning, cable TV, and Wi-Fi. A housekeeper is assigned to each villa to prepare meals as needed.

**Chillin'** (Old Fort Bay, tel. 876/754-1623 or 876/618-5948, cell tel. 876/298-5047, sgms_ltd@hotmail.com, www.chillinja.com, US$310-560 low season, US$352-600 high season) is a 12-unit townhouse complex near the beach in Old Fort Bay set on a 0.6-hectare (1.5-acre) property with a pool and a whirlpool. Units have two or four bedrooms each. A housekeeper is assigned to each unit, all of which have cable, Wi-Fi, stereos, air-conditioning, ceiling fans, full kitchens, and balconies.

## VILLAS

**Roaring Pavilion** (www.roaringpavilion.com, US$3,900 low season, US$4,900 high season) is arguably the most well-endowed villa in Jamaica, set 50 meters (165 feet) back from the island's most picturesque virgin beach, Laughing Waters, made famous in the James Bond film *Dr. No* when Ursula Andress confronts Sean Connery. There's nothing lacking at the villa, which sleeps up to 10 with a staff of 10.

**Stone Harbour** (Old Fort Bay, U.S. tel. 925/330-6632, pmumj@aol.com, www.stone-harbourvilla.com, US$5,700 weekly low season, US$6,200 weekly high season) is a four-bedroom villa with a protected private beach, pool, and jetted tub on the western edge of the bay. The villa has Wi-Fi and a staff of four. The main house has three bedrooms; the fourth is in a two-story stand-alone over the pool house. A gazebo stands on one side of the large lawn, and a pergola on the opposite side of the property near the front gate makes a nice spot for reading. A shuffleboard court is a unique feature.

## ALL-INCLUSIVE RESORTS

**Jewel Dunn's River Beach Resort & Spa** (Mammee Bay, U.S. tel. 855/617-2114, tel. 876/972-7400, reservationsdunnsriver@jewelresorts.com, www.jewelresorts.com, from US$309 low season, US$581 high season) has seven room categories, all with four-poster king beds and either inland or sea views. Wi-Fi, available throughout the property, is included. Greens fees at Runaway Bay Golf Club are also included. The resort has two large pools with swim-up bars, a small water park, a nine-hole pitch-and-putt golf course, basketball, volleyball, tennis courts, and nonmotorized water sports.

**ClubHotel Riu Ocho Rios** (Mammee Bay, tel. 876/972-2200, U.S. tel. 888/748-4990, www.riu.com, from US$291 low season, US$346 high season, 3 night min), located in Mammee Bay, is a massive 865-room resort facing the sea. Rooms are clean and well-appointed with replica furniture and either one king, a king and a double, or two doubles. Riu is among the least expensive of the all-inclusive hotels, but it's hard to see the value when obtaining reservations in one of the three "premier dining" restaurants requires standing in a long line 10am-noon to secure a reservation; after all that, the cuisine tends to disappoint. In the buffet dining room, where no reservations are required, the food quality is decent, albeit overwhelmingly imported. There is little inside the purple-painted buildings to remind guests that they are in Jamaica. Internet access, in the café off the lobby, costs a whopping US$18 per hour. Wi-Fi is free in

# Rebel Salute

Bernard Collins of the Abyssinians at Rebel Salute in 2016

The most popular annual music event held in St. Ann Parish is **Rebel Salute** (www.rebelsalutejamaica). It started out commemorating the January 15 birthday of reggae icon Tony "Rebel" Barrett, who shares the birthday with Martin Luther King Jr., as he's quick to point out. The first show was staged in 1994 and moved to Richmond Estate near Piory to capture a wider audience in 2012, when it was extended to two days and nights. The performances tend to stretch well past sunrise each morning.

Rebel demands adherence to a strict no alcohol, no meat, no degrading lyrics policy for the event, but patrons burn herb freely throughout the night, raising lighters in the air when their favorite artists "buss" a big tune. The show typically starts in the evening with the most popular crowd pleasers typically scheduled later in the morning.

The mission, says Rebel, is to preserve the healthy aspects of reggae music and to support community tourism. The annual event, held the Saturday closest to January15, draws thousands of reggae fans from Jamaica and abroad, and typically features the more conscious artists of the genre, often allowing more hard-core artists from the dancehall to reinvent themselves for a night as they reveal their progressive side.

the lobby, available in room for a fee (US$30 for 3 days, US$40 for 7 days).

## ST. ANN'S BAY

The parish capital, St. Ann's Bay, is a small bustling town at the foot of the hills that lead into the interior along rough potholed roads.

### Sights

In a park area a few hundred meters off the highway about 1.5 kilometers (1 mile) before the main junction to turn off to St. Ann's Bay, **Fire River** is named for flammable gas that rises from a pool in the river and can be set ablaze. While locals tell legends of the history and significance of the spot, a large housing subdivision just through the trees raises the question whether the gas is actually methane from the area's septic systems. Still, claims are made that the phenomenon predates the adjacent urbanization. The attraction is not managed, and can be reached by turning off the highway by the easternmost entrance to St. Ann's Bay and taking an immediate left after the dog clinic, off the road along a dirt track leading to the river.

# Marcus Garvey: Black Power Prophet

Marcus Mosiah Garvey was born in St. Ann's Bay in 1887 to humble but educated parents. After completing elementary school, he moved to Kingston, where he worked in a print shop and became increasingly interested and engaged in organized movements aimed at improving conditions for black Jamaicans. While free from the bonds of slavery since 1838, black Jamaicans were far from equal to their white compatriots and denied the right to vote, among other basic rights. In 1907 Garvey was elected vice president of the Kingston Union, which cost him his job at the printer when he got involved in a strike. At age 23 Garvey left the island to work in Central America, as many Jamaicans in search of opportunity did at the time. His travels around the region gave Garvey an awareness of the common plight faced by blacks, seeding in him what would become a lifelong struggle to unite people of African origin of all nations under one common aim. In 1912 Garvey traveled to England, where he became engaged with black Africans and further broadened his vision. In 1914 he returned to Jamaica and founded the first chapter of the United Negro Improvement Association (UNIA), whose motto, "One God! One Aim! One Destiny!" summed up the broad goal of the organization to improve the lives of black people through solidarity and self-determination.

While Garvey's message was well received by his followers in Jamaica, it was in the Harlem Renaissance in New York City that he was first lauded as a prophet. Garvey is credited as the father of the Black Power movement, which would take Harlem and the rest of the United States by storm and eventually lead to the Civil Rights Movement of the 1960s. Garvey sought to enfranchise black people by generating black-owned businesses that would be linked on an international level. To facilitate this project, he established the Black Star Line, an international shipping company.

Garvey's followers numbered four million worldwide in 1920, a movement large enough to get

**Marcus Garvey** is remembered with a statue in front of the St. Ann parish library (tel. 876/972-2660, 9:30am-5:30pm Mon.-Fri., 9:30am-3pm Sat.) just above the center of town. Garvey's bust stands in remembrance of the man whose ideas were suppressed by the powers of his day but whose teachings nonetheless made serious ripples, inspiring black power movements the world over. The library has several computers free to use for half-hour intervals.

Atop a hill commanding a panoramic view of the North Coast, **Seville Great House** (tel. 876/972-2191 or 876/972-0665, seville@anbell. net, 9am-4pm Mon.-Fri., US$15 adults, US$6 under age 13) stands at the center of rolling lawns and contains a museum with a tour highlighting the area's history and a selection of artifacts on display. A large waterwheel along the driveway below the great house stands as a reminder of the old sugar works. Seville hosts the Emancipation Jubilee on July 31 with a stage show, food, and crafts.

## Food

**The Roxborough Restaurant Bar & Grill** (Roxborough Beach, St. Ann's Bay, cell tel. 876/562-6725 or 876/460-9041, 10am-10pm daily), located seaside opposite the turn-off to St. Anne's Bay, specializes in reasonably priced seafood dishes like brown stewed conch, steamed fish, coconut crusted, or grilled lobster (US$16-25) served with sides of festival, rice-and-peas, fries, bammy or creamed potatoes.

**Stush in the Bush** (Free Hill, contact Lisa and Christopher Binns, cell tel. 876/562-9760, www.stushinthebush.com, by reservation only Sun.-Fri., from US$55) offers inspired vegetarian and seafood farm-to-table lunch and dinners, including a tour of the hosts' Zionites Farm and medicinal plants. The couple started a brand of delicious all-natural condiments in 2011, and in 2014 began preparing meals for visitors, creating an opportunity to connect over food. Quarterly moonlight dinners and yoga brunches are held throughout the year.

the attention of both the U.S. and British governments. When Garvey began to sell the notion of a mass return to Africa, however, he met resistance at the highest levels of government. He was convicted of mail fraud in the United States and imprisoned for five years on what his followers considered trumped-up charges. After two years, he was released on an executive pardon and deported back to Jamaica. Local authorities were not happy to see Garvey continue agitating for increased rights by forming the People's Political Party (PPP) in an effort to bring reform to Jamaica's colonial system. Garvey ran for a seat in parliament and lost; later he won a seat on the Kingston and St. Andrew Corporation, the local government, from a jail cell, where he'd been placed for contempt of court. At the time, voting was limited to landowners, a class to which many of Garvey's followers did not belong, and his political support was accordingly stifled. Frustrated by the slow pace of change in Kingston, Garvey returned to London in 1935, where he would remain until his death in 1940. In 1964 Garvey was declared a national hero in Jamaica, and his remains were reinterred at Heroes Memorial in Kingston.

Garvey's legacy has been mixed in Jamaica, to say the least. Perhaps the greatest disservice to his ideas lies in the fact that his pleas for universal education have never been answered at an institutional level. At the same time, there is no doubting the impact he has made in certain circles. Rastafarians claim Garvey repeatedly iterated the call, "Look to the east for the crowning of a black king." It was one of Garvey's followers, Leonard Howell, who first cited the crowning of Ethiopian Emperor Haile Selassie on November 2, 1930, as a fulfillment of that prophecy, leading to the birth of the Rastafarian movement. Even today, it is the Rastafarian community both in Jamaica and abroad that has embraced Garvey's teachings to the greatest extent, often comparing him to John the Baptist.

# PRIORY

Priory is a small community with one stoplight along the main road that is noteworthy only for its popular beach and a few pan chicken vendors.

## Fantasy Beach

**Fantasy Beach,** just east of the stoplight in Priory, is one of the most popular beaches for locals on the North Coast. A beach bar and restaurant serves local dishes and blasts dancehall throughout the day.

## H'Evans Scent

**H'Evans Scent** (Free Hill, cell tel. 876/847-5592 or 876/427-4866, www.hevansscent. com, US$85 pp) is an ecotourism outfit run by Derrick Evans, aka Mr. Motivator, offering ziplines, paintball, nature tours, and an experience where visitors get to mingle with locals 610 meters (2,000 feet) up in the hills of St. Ann. To get to H'Evans Scent, turn inland along the Bamboo Road in Priory for seven kilometers (4 miles) up the hill. The operation offers transportation from nearby lodgings in Ocho Rios, Runaway Bay, and Discovery Bay.

## Food

**LFA Country Store** (Richmond Estate, tel. 876/794-8562, 8am-8pm daily) has groceries, a basic deli, and a pharmacy.

# Runaway Bay

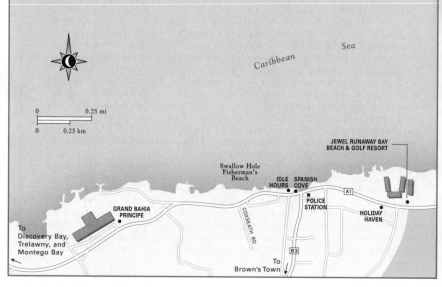

# Runaway Bay

The waterfront along Runaway Bay has several fine sand beaches that are protected by the reefs offshore. A slew of all-inclusive resorts occupy prime property on the waterfront. A few shopping plazas dot a stretch of road near the waterfront, where hole-in-the-wall restaurants, grocery stores, and a multitude of small dive bars decorated with strands of colored lights attract a mix of locals and tourists.

## BEACHES

**Runaway Bay Public Beach** has a grill that serves fried chicken and beer and is a popular hangout that attracts throngs on weekends with loud music. The beach itself has fine clean sand with a reef just offshore.

**Swallow Hole Fisherman's Beach** (tel. 876/870-7331), located about one kilometer (0.6 miles) west of Jewel Runaway Bay, is a nice chill-out spot shaded by sea grapes. In the morning women can be found scaling the

day's catch, which they'll readily sell, as children play in the water. The beach does not have fine sand.

## SPORTS AND RECREATION

**Jamaica Scuba Divers** (Runaway Bay, cell tel. 876/381-1113, www.scuba-jamaica.com, US$55, US$65 with equipment, 2-tank dive US$100) offers a beginners class lasting about three hours with classroom and pool time and one open-water dive. The dive outfit is owned by Christian Rance, who also runs Sun Divers in Negril.

**Resort Divers** (Salem Beach, contact Everett Heron, cell tel. 876/881-5760, heron@resortdivers.com, www.resortdivers.com) is a five-star PADI dive facility operating out of Royal Decameron in Runaway Bay, offering snorkeling, glass-bottomed boat tours, banana boat rides, drop-line and deep-sea

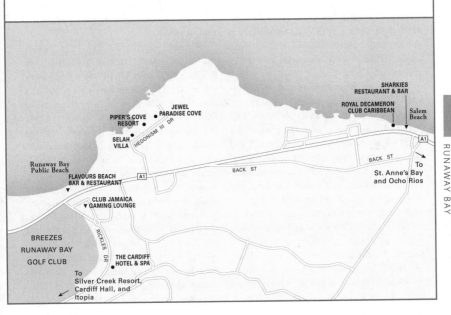

fishing, and parasailing in addition to its core dive services, which include full certification. Runaway Bay dive highlights include canyons, crevices, and flats, with popular sites being Ricky's Reef, Pocket's Reef, a Spanish Anchor, and wreck of a 100-foot freighter, two airplanes, and a car. Resort Divers also operates Sharkies Seafood Restaurant at Salem Beach.

**Runaway Bay Golf Club** (Runaway Bay, tel. 876/973-7319, greens fees US$80, JGA members US$25, caddy US$16, cart US$35, clubs US$20-30, gratuity US$10 or more pp) has an 18-hole championship course with discounts for golfing on consecutive days. Guests at Jewel Resorts have greens fees waived.

## NIGHTLIFE

Runaway Bay is not known as a nightlife haven outside the touristy clubs at the area's all-inclusive resorts.

**Club Jamaica Gaming** (Lot 20B, Cardiff Hall, tel. 876/973-5815 or 876/973-5311, www.clubjamaicagaming.com) is a gaming

lounge that comes to life Friday for Lyming on the Roof.

**Seven Stars,** located on the left when heading west just past the stoplight as you enter Runaway Bay, hosts occasional street parties in the open-air compound.

## FOOD

**The Runaways Sports Bar and Grill** (cell tel. 876/408-2101, 7am-3am daily, US$9-36) is a cool local joint on top of a four-story no-frills hotel in the easternmost of Runaway Bay's little shopping plazas in the Salem district. The roof has a small swimming pool, two billiard tables, and satellite flat-screen TVs for major sports broadcasts. The bar serves domestic beer and mixed drinks, with the kitchen serving breakfast items like ackee and saltfish and for lunch fried chicken and steam fish for dinner.

**Flavours Beach Bar & Restaurant** (tel. 876/973-5457, 10am-10pm daily), located on Runaway Bay's public beach, is a popular local hangout specializing in seafood, burgers, and local dishes (US$5-40).

**Bayside Pastries** (2-A Main St., tel. 876/973-5807, 8am-6pm Mon.-Sat.) sells rum and fruit cake, potato pudding, and Jamaican staples (US$2.50-4.25), soups (US$0.70-2.25), and patties (US$0.80).

**Northern Restaurant** (tel. 876/973-7365, 7:30am-midnight daily), in Northern Shopping complex, next to Northern Bar, has good food and maintains a clean kitchen. Fried and baked chicken, cow foot, oxtail, and fish in addition to jerk (US$4-8) are served. Breakfast is ackee and saltfish, stew chicken and salt mackerel with boiled dumpling, and steam vegetable and kidney (US$4). A pastry shop serves ice cream, cakes, and pastries.

★ **Food Fa Life** (contact Lantie Minto, cell tel. 876/388-5322, 6am-9pm Mon.-Sat.), located in a container near the Devon House ice cream shop, serves veggie dishes like veggie chunks, mince, ackee (US$3-4.50), and natural juices like June plum, cherry, beet, lemonade, and ginger (US$2-3.50).

**Sharkies** (Salem Beach, cell tel. 876/881-5760, 8am-10pm daily) is a seafood restaurant serving fried, roasted, and steamed fish (US$7-10), fritters, stewed, or curried conch (US$5-7), and lobster (US$15).

At **Jamaica Seafood Restaurant** (Main St., tel. 876/398-2838, 8:30am-10pm daily), chef Noel serves typical Jamaican dishes, fish, and conch soup.

**Leaca's Restaurant** (Main St., tel. 876/434-5466, 8am-9pm Mon.-Sat.) serves Jamaican breakfast and lunch and dinner staples like ackee and saltfish, fried chicken, curry goat, and oxtail accompanied by rice-and-peas.

## ACCOMMODATIONS
### Under US$100

**The Runaways Suites Hotel** (Lot 1, Main St., Salem, cell tel. 876/408-2101, camelliab1970@yahoo.com, US$50) has basic one- and two-bedroom suites (US$80) with tiled floors, air-conditioning, cable TV, and en suite baths with hot water. While not the most charming option, rates are reasonable and the hotel is centrally situated along the highway, with food upstairs and the beach five minutes away.

★ **Last Lick** (Black Ants Corner, contact Adina Parchment, villa manager at Jake's, tel. 876/965-3000 or 876/844-9803, US$95 low season, US$115 high season) was a gift of land from the late film director Perry Henzell (*The Harder They Come*) to his wife, Sally. In 1981 her Robinson Crusoe-like two-story cottage was erected amid a garden of flowering shrubs and trees with the sea on two sides. A sand-pit for sunbathing and a shower for washing off separate the cottage from the sea, where a ladder descends to the water, shallow enough to stand in, and good for snorkeling around the coral heads. Other steps lead down to a shallower part of the sea with a clear mineral spring. An upstairs bedroom and bath has French windows opening to a sea view and is accessible using the outside stairs or a ladder from the ground level. Housekeeping is included, with meals prepared for an additional US$25 pp per day.

**Piper's Cove** (tel. 876/973-7156, piperscove@msn.com, www.piperscoveresortjamaica.com) has six studios (US$95) and 14 one-bedroom apartments (US$116) with air-conditioning, cable TV, Wi-Fi, and utilitarian kitchenettes. The dated furnishings can be overlooked given the affordability. Some apartments have sea views. A restaurant and bar on the property serves breakfast, lunch, and dinner.

**Holiday Haven Condo Resort** (tel. 876/973-4893, www.holidayhavenresort.com, from US$100) is a condo complex offering standard rooms as well as one- and two-bedroom suites with kitchen, living, and dining areas. The complex is across the road from the coast, a short walk to the fishermen's beach.

### US$100-250

In close proximity to the golf course, ★ **The Cardiff Hotel and Spa** (tel. 876/973-6671, www.thecardiffhotel.com, US$114 low season,

US$137 high season) is run by Jamaica's HEART training institute with 44 rooms with tiled floors and balconies spread across four two-story blocks. Junior suites (US$137) have kings, ultra-deluxe rooms (US$123) are on the second level, and standard rooms (US$114) are on the ground floor with two double beds. The north-facing rooms overlook the golf course and the bay. Amenities include cable TV, air-conditioning, and private baths with hot water. Wi-Fi covers the property. A pool is just off the lobby, bar, and restaurant. Rates include breakfast.

## Villas

**The Selah Villa** (8 Silver Spray Rd., Salem, tel. 876/978-1771, US$7,500 weekly low season, US$9,500 weekly high season) is a four-bedroom villa with a 12-meter (40-foot) infinity pool and whirlpool tub facing a protected cove a few minutes off the highway in Runaway Bay. The villa is furnished with colonial-era antiques throughout; rooms have en suite baths and air-conditioning. The property has Wi-Fi, a tennis court, and kayaks.

**Spanish Cove** (cell tel. 876/564-4785, spanishcovejamaica@gmail.com, US$5,160 weekly low season, US$6,360 weekly high season) is a four-bedroom villa with a pool and 76 meters (250 feet) of beach in the heart of Runaway Bay. All rooms have air-conditioning and en suite baths, two with tubs. A chef, two housekeepers, and a butler attend to guests. Two bedrooms have kings, the third a queen, and the fourth two twins that can be joined to make a king. The property has Wi-Fi, and guests have use of kayaks.

★ **Idle Hours Villa** (Ingrid Fitt, tel. 876/361-3488, sfittja@hotmail.com, US$3,500 weekly low season, US$3,800 weekly high season) is a three-bedroom, three-bath villa on one of Jamaica's finest strips of private beach in the heart of Runaway Bay. Amenities include a private pool overlooking the beach, a well-manicured lawn, and Wi-Fi, with a full-time housekeeper, a chef, and security. Rooms have king beds, ceiling fans, and air-conditioning.

**Itopia** (Cardiff Hall, tel. 877/526-2428 or 876/965-3000, stay@jameshotel.com, from US$325) is a unique cut-stone country home owned by the Henzell family, whose late patriarch, Perry, brought the world *The Harder They Come,* the film that helped catapult a young Jimmy Cliff to international stardom in the early 1970s. Built in 1660 as the overseer's house at Cardiff Hall estate, the three-bedroom home is cozy and charming in a preserved colonial state enhanced by the design genius of Sally Henzell and appointed with era furnishings and funky family memorabilia. A fourth bedroom is located around back in a separate building. It's located 15 minutes from Runaway Bay on terrible roads, but the serenity found on arrival is thanks to its remote location.

## All-Inclusive Resorts

**Royal DeCameron Club Caribbean** (tel. 876/973-4802, ventas.jam@decameron.com, from US$127 pp) has 183 pleasant rooms, some in the main block; others are either beachfront or garden cottages with king beds, air-conditioning, TVs, and hot water. The property has two pools and a private beach and offers guests bicycles, which can be useful for navigating Runaway Bay's spread-out strip.

**Jewel Resorts** (www.jewelresorts.com) has two properties in Runaway Bay: **Jewel Paradise Cove** (from US$299 low season, US$526 high season), with 210 rooms, 15 junior suites, 6 restaurants and bars, and a single pool; and **Jewel Runaway Bay** (from US$299 low season, US$526 high season), with 266 rooms and 3 swimming pools, including 44 suites with private plunge pools. Rooms are spacious with complete amenities. Staying at either property includes greens fees at Runaway Bay Golf Club.

**Gran Bahia Principe** (Salt Coppers Villa, tel. 876/973-7000, U.S. tel. 866/282-2442, from US$224 low season, US$360 high season) is a monstrous, 680-room resort quite obviously built in a hurry. The hotel features junior suites facing the sea or the pool area, buffet and à la carte dining, and Jamaica's longest lazy river. Rooms have one king or two queens, local cable and satellite TV, and en suite baths. This is one of the least expensive all-inclusive hotels on the island, with the quality of the experience corresponding to the cost.

# Discovery Bay

Originally named Puerto Seco (Dry Harbor) by Christopher Columbus, Discovery Bay was renamed to reflect the debated assertion that this was the first point in Jamaica where the explorer made landfall. Many experts believe that the actual first point of entry was in Rio Bueno, a few kilometers farther west, where Columbus could have sought freshwater. Irrespective of this disputed detail, Discovery Bay has played an important role in Jamaica's recent history, first as a bustling export port where barrels of sugar and rum departed for Europe, and then, from the early 20th century, as a bauxite port. It remains one of the few active bauxite facilities in Jamaica following the global economic downturn of 2009, when half the island's alumina and bauxite operations went idle. The industrious port is the curious backdrop for perhaps Jamaica's staunchest enclave of old Jamaican money, with several of the country's wealthiest families owning beachfront villas facing the bay.

## SIGHTS

**Green Grotto Caves** (tel. 876/973-2841 or 876/973-3217, 9am-4pm daily, US$20 adults, US$10 children) is Jamaica's most commercially successful cave attraction, located on a 26-hectare (64-acre) property between Runaway and Discovery Bays. While tamer than the experiences you can have in Cockpit Country a bit farther west, Green Grotto, also known as Runaway Cave or Hopewell Cave, is nonetheless a well-conceived tour. During the 45-minute tour that descends to an underground lake, well-versed guides give a history of the caves, their formations, and their importance to the Taino and the Spanish. A drink is included. Green Grotto is located on the eastern edge of Discovery Bay.

Columbus Park

Just west of the public beach in Discovery Bay, around the bend from the gas station, is Old Folly, a district covering the narrow valley containing the bauxite plant and terminal, overlooking the stretch of sand on the opposite side of the bay that is home to some of Jamaica's most luxurious villas. **Quadrant Wharf** is the old sugar terminal where an old winch lies rusting. A plaque on the wall facing the road tells of the importance of the location, from Columbus's landing to the export of sugar, arms, and bauxite.

Just around the bend from the bauxite terminal in Old Folly, **Columbus Park** (free) hugs the steep slope rising from the western side of the bay. The park consists of an open-air museum wedged between the highway and the slope descending to the water, with a mural depicting the arrival of Christopher Columbus and several relics from the colonial period scattered around.

## BEACHES

**Puerto Seco Beach** (9am-5pm daily), pronounced "SEE-ko," is located in the heart of Discovery Bay opposite the police station. The beach has some of the cleanest restrooms at any public beach in Jamaica as well as Jupsy's Snack Bar and Puerto Seco Beach Bar.

## FOOD

★ **Ultimate Jerk Centre** (10 minutes west of Breezes, approaching Discovery Bay, tel. 876/973-2054, 10am-10pm daily, US$1-5) does stewed chicken and pork, curry goat, stewed conch, potato, festival, bammy, fritters, rice-and-peas, and French fries. The bar serves a variety of liquor, and an oldies party is held the last Saturday of the month. Ultimate is a popular spot for locals to congregate to take in a cricket match, eat jerk, and vibe out. The jerk is the best in the area and doesn't linger on the grill thanks to a steady flow of traffic.

★ **Grill 3000** (Main St., 400 meters/0.25 miles west of Green Grotto Cave, by Auto Towing and Repossession, tel. 876/973-3000, cell tel. 876/477-3000, 9am-11pm daily, US$5-15) serves steamed fish and fish soup accompanied by cornmeal dumplings as well as cappuccino to wash it down. Grill 3000 is little more than a roadside barbecue pit, but the bargain-priced steamed fish is some of the best on the island, incredibly prepared by a man who spends most of the day towing vehicles.

**Coconut Tree Restaurant & Bar** (Dairy Pen, tel. 876/973-9781, 8am-8pm daily) serves typical Jamaican fare, jerk, and patties.

**Baywatch Bar & Restaurant** (Old Folly, across from bauxite terminal, tel. 876/578-7706, noon-11pm Mon.-Sat., US$3-4.50) serves typical Jamaican fare in local atmosphere overlooking the bay.

**Hot & Spicy Tavern** is a cook shop run by Morton "Beaks" Willis (tel. 876/853-0103), located inside the ruins of the old warehouse at Quadrant Wharf. Beaks also runs the bar on the property.

**Coconut Lagoon Bar and Restaurant** (Queen's Hwy., tel. 876/899-1245, 8am-9:30pm daily, US$5-12), located on the sea side of the road as you round a bend approaching Rio Bueno from Discovery Bay, opposite the derelict Bay Vista Resort, is a popular pit stop serving typical Jamaican fare and fish dishes.

## ACCOMMODATIONS
### Under US$100

Many of Jamaica's wealthiest families have weekend homes on Discovery Bay, making it one of the island's most exclusive villa enclaves. Many of these homes rent through agents, while some rent directly through the owners, but usually the pricing is the same, and renting through an agent provides some recourse should you have any problems. A dependable agent for villas throughout Jamaica, including in Discovery Bay is **SunVillas** (contact Alan, U.S. tel. 888/625-6007, or Latoya, tel. 876/544-9497, info@sunvillas.com, www.sunvillas.com). **Villas by Linda Smith** (www.jamaicavillas.com) is the leading luxury villa agent on the island, with an impressive portfolio of properties from St. Mary to Hanover.

**Paradise Place** (54 Bridgewater Garden,

Poinciana Dr., corner of Sunflower Dr., contact owner Paul Shaw, tel. 876/973-9495, cell tel. 876/862-2095, shawtop@aol.com, www.paradiseplace54.com) is set back from the highway in a quiet subdivision, run by a returning resident who offers two-bedroom apartments (US$100) and two stand-alone rooms (US$60), all with pine furniture, air-conditioning, microwaves, and fridges. There's a front and back veranda accessible to guests with sea views from the back, and a hot tub in a gazebo in the yard also for guest use.

## Villas

**Sea Grapes** (Discovery Bay, tel. 876/979-8080, cell tel. 876/550-8977, reservations@highhopeestate.com, www.seagrapesjamaica.com, US$7,600 low season, US$10,100 high season) is a lovely six-bedroom property with a pool and private beach frontage.

**Sugar Bay** (Peter McConnell, tel. 876/903-6125, pmcconnell@worthyparkestate.com, www.jamaicavillas.com, US$11,900 weekly low season, US$14,400 weekly high season) is a deluxe five-bedroom, 5.5-bath villa, with a private beach and exquisite decor.

**Amanoka** (contact Denise McConnell, cell tel. 876/361-4008, tel. 876/973-2626 or 347/329-2752, amanokavilla@gmail.com, www.amanoka.com, up to 14 people, US$18,000 weekly low season, US$21,000 weekly high season) is one of the most luxurious villas in Jamaica, if not the most over-the-top, catering to the pinnacle of the high-end market. Amenities include a spa, tennis courts, a private beach, an infinity pool, and a large hot tub.

★ **Whispering Waters** (Fortlands Rd., contact Heather Wates, cell tel. 876/399-2766, heatherwates@gmail.com, US$17,500 weekly low season, US$19,000 weekly high season) is a 840-square-meter (9,000-square-foot) ultra-luxurious villa with seven bedrooms, each with en suite baths, air-conditioning, and flat-screen TVs with cable and DVD players. Other features include a business center, a private beach with kayaks, a large pool and a whirlpool tub, lighted tennis courts, and a state-of-the-art gym. The wide veranda has teak furniture and a bar overlooking magical grounds.

**Makana** (contact Heather Wates, cell tel. 876/399-2766, heatherwates@gmail.com, weekly US$16,500 low season, US$18,500 high season) is a six-bedroom, 6.5-bath luxury villa with a private beach, manicured lawns, an infinity pool, and a charming gazebo. Wicker, bamboo, and teak furnishings, soft colors, and original artwork create the most relaxing ambiance. Creature comforts include eight flat-screen TVs, Wi-Fi, a tennis court, a weight room, and a whirlpool tub.

**Fortlands Point** (contact Nora May Desnoes cell tel. 876/564-2020, nmdesnoes@gmail.com, weekly US$18,000 low season, US$21,000 high season) is a super-luxurious seven-bedroom villa with three private beaches, affectionately known as The Fort. Amenities include a squash court and a full gymnasium. The living and entertainment areas are on the north side of the property, with a 180-degree view and absolute privacy.

**Indulge** (Terry Groves cell tel. 876/361-4034, tgroves@cwjamaica.com) is a service specializing in providing luxury goods for villa guests staying anywhere between Ocho Rios and Tryall. Email for the complete list of goodies.

# Inland from Ocho Rios

## BROWN'S TOWN

Brown's Town is the closest town of any size to the Bob Marley Mausoleum in Nine Mile and is famous for its bustling market. The market takes places on Wednesday, Friday, and Saturday. If you're heading to Nine Mile via route taxi, Brown's Town is the connection point from St. Ann's Bay.

## MONEAGUE

Moneague is a small community along the main road between Spanish Town and the North Coast notable for the Moneague Teacher Training College, the Jamaica Defense Force Training Camp, and the mysterious rising lake.

### Faith's Pen

A few kilometers south of Moneague, **Faith's Pen** has a famous rest stop lined with shacks dishing out jerk and conch soup at the best local prices. Fruit stands also appear sporadically along the road north and south of Faith's Pen. The fate of these stalwarts may be up in the air following the inauguration of the toll road, which reroutes most of the traffic between the south and north coasts.

## NINE MILE
### Bob Marley Mausoleum

The **Bob Marley Mausoleum** (contact Harry Shivnani, cell. tel 876/843-0498, harry. reggaeking@yahoo.com, 9am-5pm daily, adults US$19, children 5-11 US$10) was built next to the humble country house where the world's foremost reggae superstar was born. Today it's part of a complex that draws fans from around the world to experience the humble beginnings of a man many consider prophetic. Arriving at the hillside hamlet of Nine Mile, the Cedella Marley basic school looms in red, gold, and green splendor just before the Marley family home. In a large parking area, countless Rastas offer guide services and other paraphernalia, all of which will require compensation at the end of the tour.

The tour starts at the gift shop, where visitors pay an entry fee and from there are led up to the mausoleum and Bob's small house. In and around the house are countless details the Rasta guides make note of as inspiration for a multitude of songs from Marley's discography, including the single bed and the rock pillow from "Talkin' Blues." Below the mausoleum, a clubhouse-style building with contemporary Rasta styling has a restaurant and lounge on the second floor and great views from the balcony over the quiet hills of the St. Ann interior.

## FOOD AND ACCOMMODATIONS

**Lyming at Walkerswood** (tel. 876/917-2812 or cell tel. 876/364-3407, US$5-10) makes a great pit stop for authentic jerk chicken, pork, and sausage, accompanied by breadfruit and festival.

**Bromley** (contact Johnathan or Alex Edwards, cell tel. 876/857-2960, alexandra. sale@gmail.com, www.bromleyjamaica.com, US$80) is a stately great house that operates as a bed-and-breakfast. Bromley is set in the cool hills of Walkerswood, a 15-minute drive above Ocho Rios. Miss Mineta, the caretaker, cooks breakfasts of fresh fruits, homemade granola, eggs, and Blue Mountain coffee, with other meals prepared to order (US$25 per day plus the cost of food). Views of the St. Ann interior are remarkable, and a host of birds thrive in the lush gardens. The property is suitable for retreats, with a yoga deck and small immersion pool in the yard. Wi-Fi is included.

## GETTING THERE AND AROUND

From Ocho Rios, Milford Road (the A3) heads south from the main intersection by Turtle Park and uphill along the steep, winding route

## Bob Marley: King of Reggae

If you mention reggae, Jamaica, Rastafari, or marijuana, chances are the first thought that comes to most peoples' minds is Bob Marley. The man has become synonymous with all things good about Jamaica and its people, carrying the country's cultural torch decades after his death in 1981. There's no way to measure the goodwill this man has brought the country. Even in times of global economic crisis, Jamaica is among the top tourism destinations in the Americas, ranked 10th in the western hemisphere in terms of visitor volume and third in the Caribbean after Barbados and Puerto Rico. The good will Bob Marley brought the world through his intoxicating music, full of uplifting messages, is also hard to quantify.

Born Robert Nesta Marley on February 6, 1945, in Nine Mile, St. Ann, to Cedella Malcolm Marley Booker and Norval Sinclair Marley, Bob grew up a country boy in the small agricultural community before moving with his mother to Trench Town, a ghetto in central Kingston. His father, a white English naval officer and plantation overseer, was a scarce presence throughout Bob's childhood, and died in 1955 at the age of 60. Bob's racial mix set him apart from his peers and often made him the target of name-calling, but this same heritage afforded him a perspective to approach issues of race and justice, and infused his music with universal appeal.

While his late mother said in documentaries that Bob could frequently be heard singing as a youth, it wasn't until he reached Trench Town that he teamed up with Peter McIntosh and Bunny Livingston to form the Wailin' Wailers. Trench Town in the 1960s was the creative epicenter of Jamaican music, where fledgling composers and musicians listened attentively to radio broadcasts of American music and reinterpreted classics on their ramshackle instruments, sparking a swing

through Fern Gully. A few roadside vendors sell crafts in the shade of the wider corners. The road exits Fern Gully in Colgate and continues on to Bromley, Walkerswood, and then Moneague before reaching Faith Pen just before the border with St. Catherine. From the main intersection in Moneague, the A1 heads to St. Ann's Bay, passing through Claremont. A left at the intersection in Claremont leads to Nine Mile.

Staying on the A1 past Claremont will take you through Green Park, where the road splits. Taking a left at the Y intersection, you reach Brown's Town, where the road meets the B3, which runs from May Pen through Cave Valley, Alexandria, and from Brown's Town to Runaway Bay on the North Coast. The region is known as the Dry Harbour Mountains.

# East of Ocho Rios

One of the least visited corners of Jamaica, St. Mary is considered by many to be the most attractive parish for its proximity to Kingston, Ocho Rios, and Portland; for its vast wilderness areas; and for its people, who don't exhibit the same hustler mentality rampant in more touristed areas. St. Mary is one of the best places in Jamaica for birding and farm tours, with Green Castle Estate standing out clearly among the large plantations of the area that are still active in agricultural production.

## ORACABESSA

Oracabessa is derived from yet another Spanish name, Oro Cabeza, which translates as "gold head." A half hour's drive east of Ocho Rios, Oracabessa is a secluded enclave of high-end tourism where Ian Fleming's Goldeneye has become the benchmark for sophisticated, hip luxury tourism in Jamaica. Oracabessa has fostered a number of artists whose crafts are more original and far less expensive than in the markets of Ochi, away from traditional Jamaican music like mento that led to the birth of ska, rocksteady, and reggae. Bob's early career spanned the development and evolution of these genres, but it was reggae that became the vehicle for his message at the international level.

While Bob's talent was clearly apparent in the early days of the Wailers to producers like Leslie Kong, who recorded his first two singles "Judge Not" and "One Cup of Coffee," and Clement Dodd, who later produced "It Hurts to Be Alone" and "I'm Still Waiting," it wasn't until Bob traveled to London and recorded his first full album, *Catch a Fire*, on Chris Blackwell's fledgling Island Records label that he gained international recognition. Blackwell nurtured the Wailers and helped create a sound that had wide international appeal without watering down the message.

After recording several albums on Island Records, Bob established his own label, Tuff Gong, using his street name. Tuff Gong remains a symbol of artistic independence, a departure from the days when musicians were paid measly sums to play on studio recordings while the producers reaped the rewards. Bob's larger-than-life persona outgrew the Wailin' Wailers, creating resentment among fellow founders Bunny Livingston, known as Bunny Wailer, and Peter McIntosh, or Peter Tosh, both of whom left the group to pursue successful solo careers. Following the departure of his bandmates, he renamed his band Bob Marley and the Wailers and went on to tour the world, filling stadiums and concert halls until his untimely death at age 36 from cancer. Bob's popularity has only grown since his passing, with his posthumous *Legend* album going platinum several times over. Countless up-and-coming artists aspire to carry on his work, crowning him with immortality.

Montego Bay, or Negril. The small community offers some decent beaches and picturesque countryside for those looking to get off the beaten track.

Oracabessa experienced a brief boom as an important banana port in the early 1900s. Today the community is experiencing a different kind of boom, due to entrepreneur Chris Blackwell's luxury villa development at Goldeneye, which will cement the area's reputation for exclusivity.

The area from Oracabessa to Port Maria has one of the nicest stretches of coast in Jamaica, where cliff-side villas were built by the likes of Ian Fleming, Noël Coward, and in more recent times, record magnate Chris Blackwell. The districts of Race Course, Galina, and Little Bay have small quiet communities where discreet tourism accommodations blend so well with the landscape that they're easy to miss.

## James Bond Beach

**James Bond Beach** (cell tel. 876/371-1528, marshall.bailey@jamesbondbeach.com, www.jamesbondbeach.com, 9am-5pm daily, US$5)

has two private beaches along with a bar and restaurant serving fish, lobster, shrimp, burgers, and chicken. The beach park occasionally hosts events and live performances, including **Beach J'ouvert,** held on Easter weekend when Bacchanal, Jamaica's carnival, is nearing climax.

## ★ Firefly

**Firefly** (Island Outpost, tel. 876/975-3677, or caretaker Victor Taylor, cell tel. 876/420-5544, or tour guide Annette Tracy, tel. 876/424-5359, 9am-4pm daily, US$10 includes guided tour and refreshment) is easily one of Jamaica's most beautiful properties, with the most magnificent view of the St. Mary and Portland coast. The property has had a glamorous past, first as the home of the pirate Henry Morgan, and centuries later as a playground for playwright Noël Coward, both of whom were captivated by the stunning view that graces the small plateau. Henry Morgan's house, which dates from the 17th century, has been rebuilt and is now used as the visitors center. It has a small bar and several tables.

Across the lawn, Coward's house remains

preserved as a museum essentially as he left it. Downstairs in his studio, an incomplete painting stands on the easel as if he had been interrupted mid-stroke. His famous "room with a view" was inspiration for several works completed in it, and the piano where he entertained his famous Hollywood guests remains the centerpiece in the study. On the lawn outside, a statue of Coward immortalizes his fascination with the view as he holds his cigarette and ponders the northeast coastline. Coward's tomb is at a corner of the lawn.

At the time of Coward's death, the property was left to Graham Payne, who in turn gave it to the Jamaican government, which today leases it to Chris Blackwell, whose Island Outpost manages the attraction. Up to 120 people visit Firefly daily in the high season, while the visits can drop to a trickle during the slower months of the summer and fall.

## Other Sights

**Sun Valley Plantation** (cell tel. 876/995-3075 or 876/446-2026, sunvalleyjamaica@yahoo.com, 9am-2pm daily, US$15) offers an excellent guided farm tour that includes a welcome drink and a drink and snack at the end of the tour. The educational stroll around the farm familiarizes visitors with native crops

like sugarcane and banana that have played important roles in Jamaica's economy and the history of the area. Sun Valley's owners live on the property. Today the farm produces mainly coconuts for the local market. To get to Sun Valley, head inland at the main junction in Oracabessa, passing through Jack's River. After the primary school, continue straight through the junction for about 1.5 kilometers (1 mile).

**Brimmer Hall** (tel. 876/994-2309, 9am-4pm Mon.-Fri., US$25 adults, US$10 children) offers tractor-drawn jitney tours around the plantation and great house. Guests can swim in the pool and bring lunch to enjoy in the picnic area or on the great house veranda. Guides teach visitors about the fruit trees and give a bit of history of the estate, which dates to the 1700s. The house is full of period furnishings and antiques. To get to Brimmer Hall, head east from Port Maria and turn right three kilometers (2 miles) past Trinity on the road toward Bailey Town, continuing about 1.5 kilometers (1 mile) farther.

## Shopping

**Exotic Jewelry by Jasazii** (Jasazii and Maji McKenzie, cell tel. 876/909-8403, jasazii@

English playwright Noël Coward is immortalized in bronze at Firefly.

# Chris Blackwell and Island Records

One of the world's foremost music producers and founder of Island Records, London-born Chris Blackwell is credited with having introduced reggae music to the world. He built his early career first by selling record imports to the Jamaican market and then by bringing international attention to the budding careers of artists like Millie Small, whose "My Boy Lollipop" topped the charts in England in 1964, giving Island its first hit. Blackwell signed a slew of early English rock artists like Jethro Tull, King Crimson, Robert Palmer, and Cat Stevens. Then came Bob Marley, whose 1973 *Catch a Fire* album would be the first of many for Bob on the Island label. The deal was a huge hit and brought world recognition to a genre that was gaining popularity in Jamaica but unheard of elsewhere.

Blackwell bought some of the Jamaica's most beautiful properties, including Strawberry Hill and Goldeneye, eventually forming Island Outpost to market them to luxury travelers without hype. His grand vision has set in motion a transformation in Oracabessa with the new villa development on a private island next to Ian Fleming's Goldeneye.

Blackwell was inducted into the Rock and Roll Hall of Fame in 2001 for his contributions to the music industry. He sold Island Records in 1989 and left the company in 1997, going on to establish Palm Pictures, a film production and distribution company based in New York. Blackwell's first foray into film was by backing Perry Henzell's cult hit *The Harder They Come* in 1971, which brought fame to Jimmy Cliff, before going on to produce other Jamaican classics like *Country Man* as well as successful Hollywood films. Blackwell's eye for talent and opportunity has made him one of the world's most creative and successful businessmen.

gmail.com) is based in Gibraltar Heights at the Sacred Healing Artz Sanctuary.

**Wilderness House of Art** (Idlewhile Rd., between Galina and Race Course districts, across from a yellow house, cell tel. 876/462-8849 or 876/994-0578, babaireko@yahoo.com) is the home and studio of Ireko "Baba" Baker, a member of the A Yard We Deh artist collective together with Tukula N'Tama and Orah El. Ireko does excellent screen-printing work and gourd art. His work can be seen displayed in the foyer and rooms at Couples Negril.

## Food

**Chris Café** (Main St., Oracabessa, cell tel. 876/861-1611, 7:30am-11:30pm Mon.-Sat., 7:30am-8:30pm Sun., US$8-25) serves local dishes like ackee and saltfish, mackerel rundown, liver and kidney and curried chicken on a dining deck overlooking the sea. Reservations are recommended.

**Susie's** (Main St., Oracabessa, cell tel. 876/844-1621, 8:30am-6pm Mon.-Sat., US$3-5) serves local dishes like stew peas,

curry goat, sweet and sour chicken, on a rotating menu.

★ **Dor's Fish Pot** (Race Course, cell tel. 876/372-4975, tel. 876/849-3534, US$4.50-8.50) is a local favorite for all manner of fish, lobster, octopus, crab, and shrimp. The informal open-air dining area overlooks the sea, and a round bar at the entrance serves drinks.

Fresh seafood is prepared at **Conscious Corner Bar** (cell tel. 876/458-1430 or 876/399-2366, by reservation only, 9am-8pm daily), located in Rio Nuevo on the fisherman's beach, is a popular hangout for locals and cyclists associated with the St. Mary Off-Road Biking Association.

## Accommodations
### UNDER US$100
★ **High View Cottages** (Gibraltar Heights, tel. 876/975-3210, cell tel. 876/831-1975, U.S. tel. 718/878-5351, monica.hucey@hotmail.com, US$60, includes breakfast) is owned by the amiable Colleen Pottinger, who lives in the main house on the property. There are two one-bedroom self-contained cottages with kitchens, private baths with hot water, access

to the swimming pool, and Wi-Fi. One cottage has a queen bed and one has two twin beds. An inflatable mattress is available for extra guests (US$30). Additional meals can be prepared on request. The personal attention of its owner and the quiet location on the lush Gibraltar hillside make High View a favorite home away from home for budget-minded travelers. Guests can access the private beach for residents of Gibraltar.

**Tamarind Great House** (cell tel. 876/995-3252, tamarindgreathouse@yahoo.com, US$75-105 d) on Crescent Estate was destroyed by fire in 1987, and then rebuilt and restored as a 10-bedroom colonial-style great house by English couple Gillian and Barry Chambers, who live on the property with their son Gary. Nine attractive rooms have fans and private baths with hot water. Some rooms have private balconies. Furnishings and decor reflect the colonial period. To get to Tamarind House, head inland at the roundabout in Oracabessa along Jack's River Road, keeping straight ahead at the Epping gas station. Continue for about 0.8 kilometers (0.5 miles) past Sun Valley Plantation, keeping left at the broken bridge and continuing up the hill.

## US$100-250

★ **Moxons Beach Club** (Stewart Town, moxons_beach_club@flowja.com, www.moxonsbeach.club, tel. 876/620-7071, from US$136) is a top-notch boutique hotel perched on a cliff overlooking the sea. Steps lead down to a pier where kayaks are available for exploring the coast and reefs offshore. Rooms have kings or queens, some with kitchenettes, and fine linens, comfortable mattresses, and Wi-Fi. The restaurant on the property serves a mix of Jamaican and international fare with indoor and outdoor dining areas overlooking the water. The pool deck is found a few steps from the dining area.

A modest three-bedroom property with a wide veranda for enjoying the panoramic view of the coast, Oracabessa, and Ian Fleming's Goldeneye is **Loveland Villa** (Lot 1, Gibraltar Heights, cell tel. 876/833-9142 or 876/564-5114, dpalmer7@gmail.com, US$175 low season, US$200 high season). The master suite has a king bed and en suite bath. Two other rooms each have two single beds that can be joined to make king beds and share a bath between them. The kitchen is fully equipped, and the housekeeper comes daily to cook and tidy up. The villa holds six comfortably and up to eight (US$20 pp after 6 guests). Wi-Fi covers the house; a flat-screen TV in the living room has a DVD player.

## VILLAS

**Golden Cove** (Gibraltar, contact Nadia McKitty, nmckitty@yahoo.com, U.S. tel. 301/326-3201, from US$500) is one of the more luxurious options in the area, with four bedrooms, lush gardens dotted with palms, and a panoramic view of the coast. The villa has a deck with a large pool and a hot tub overlooking the sea. The villa has staff, including a butler, a gardener, a housekeeper, and a cook, with meals prepared à la carte. Wi-Fi extends throughout the villa. Rooms have en suite baths and either kings or queens. The owner lives on property.

**Bolt House Estate** (bookings@bolthousejamaica.com, www.bolthousejamaica.com, four-day minimum, US$2,400) is a spectacular 20-hectare (50-acre) hilltop property owned by the family that founded Fila sportswear. A stunning infinity pool overlooks the northeast coastline beyond Port Maria towards Port Antonio and the Blue Mountains. The villa boasts an impeccable mix of modern and colonial styling together with unparalleled views and grounds. The master bedroom has a king, as does the second bedroom, with two double beds in the third. An annex has two additional cozy bedrooms appointed with rustic touches. The house is fully equipped with streaming TV, Wi-Fi, and a surround-sound system. A yoga deck, wet and dry saunas, and a hot tub round out the luxurious amenities. The property has a rich history, having hosted many a soirée with luminaries such as Sean Connery, Audrey Hepburn, Elizabeth Taylor,

Charlie Chaplin, Noël Coward, Ian Fleming, and Queen Elizabeth II. Food costs US$80 pp per day, not including alcohol.

## GOLDENEYE

★ **Goldeneye** (tel. 876/622-9007, U.S. tel. 800/6887678, info@goldeneye.com, www.islandoutpost.com, from US$620 low season, US$1,150 high season) is a seaside estate formerly owned by 007 creator Ian Fleming and is where he penned all 14 of the famous spy thrillers. Today it is Jamaica's most exclusive boutique resort. The one- and two-bedroom lagoon and beachfront villas have full kitchens, and the lagoon cottages don't. All units have flat-screens with streaming TV and international cable, music players, and Wi-Fi.

The 26 one- and two-bedroom **Goldeneye Beach Huts** (from US$400 low season, US$685 high season) were completed in early 2016. They are raised off the sand, some with lounges and outdoor garden showers and bathtubs. Rooms have custom kings, flatscreen TVs, balconies, and baths with double rain showerheads.

The crown jewel of the property is the five-bedroom **Fleming Villa** (www.theflemingvilla.com, US$6,600 low season, US$8,500 high season), boasting enormous bamboo-framed canopy beds, original furnishings, and indoor and outdoor master baths. Large windows open to the sea breeze and steps lead down from the spacious living room to an outdoor dining area high above the private beach for villa guests. A poolside lounge features a projection screen and bar.

Meals at Goldeneye are offered à la carte in a casual setting at **Bizot Bar** on Low Cay and at **Gazebo,** overhanging the lagoon. The food is a mix of international comfort dishes and creative embellishments of local Jamaican cuisine. Meals can also be served in the villas. Nonguests may dine on property by reservation at least 24 hours in advance.

Water sports activities offered at Goldeneye include kayaking, paddleboarding, snorkeling, fishing, and glass-bottomed boat tours. Goldeneye has evolved in recent years into Jamaica's most exclusive resort community, with several villas owned independently.

## PORT MARIA

One of the most picturesque towns in Jamaica, Port Maria has a large protected harbor with the small Cabarita Island, also known as Treasure Island, in the center. Originally inhabited by the Taino and later by the Spanish, the island was vulnerable to pirate attacks and

Goldeneye

# Tacky's War

On the morning after Easter Sunday in 1760, an enslaved man known as Tacky led a revolt in St. Mary that would reverberate around northeastern Jamaica until September of that year. The uprising became known as Tacky's Rebellion or Tacky's War.

Tacky was an overseer on Frontier Plantation outside Port Maria, giving him the limited freedom necessary to strategize and organize the rebellion at both Frontier and bordering Trinity Plantations. A former chief in his homeland of Ghana, Tacky had the confidence and clout to amass wide support for what was meant to be an island-wide overthrow of the British colonial masters.

Tacky and about 50 of his followers awoke before dawn that morning and easily killed the master of Frontier Plantation before raiding the armory at nearby Fort Haldane, where they killed the storekeeper and took guns and ammunition. The owner of Trinity Plantation escaped on horseback to warn the surrounding estates. But with newfound artillery, the ranks of the rebel army began to swell, and they quickly took nearby Haywood and Esher Plantations and began to celebrate their early success. A slave from Esher plantation, however, slipped away to call in the authorities, and before long a militia of soldiers from Spanish Town and Maroons from Scott's Hall were sent to quell the uprising.

fell into the hands of the pirate Henry Morgan until he lost it gambling. In the late 1700s a village began to take shape on the harbor shores, and by 1821 public buildings, including the parish council offices and the courthouse, were built. Port Maria boomed with exports of sugar, rum, indigo, pimento, tropical hardwoods, and coffee, but the town has long since passed its prime. Nevertheless, it still has a strong fishing community and is a commercial center for the surrounding rural districts. Several infrastructure improvements associated with the North Coast Highway project have recently given the town a bit of a face-lift. The Outram River forms the eastern border of town, beyond which begins a vast wilderness area wrapping around the hilly coastline all the way to Robin's Bay.

## Sights

**Fort Haldane** (unmanaged), or the sparse and scattered remains of it, is located on a road that cuts across the point jutting into the sea, forming the western flank of Port Maria's harbor. The road runs between the Anglican Church and the middle of the bend on the other side of the hill on Little Bay. Two cannons overgrown with bush aim out to sea just past the oldest structure on the premises, a low brick building alongside discarded car parts. The Fort was built in 1759 for coastal defense during the Seven Years' War and named after then-governor George Haldane. The property was later a home for the elderly but has since fallen into disuse. The gates to this seldom-visited historical site are typically left ajar and unlocked.

The building that housed the old **courthouse** and **police station** (across from the Anglican church, on east side of town), originally built in 1821, is one of the best examples of Georgian architecture in Port Maria. Much of the original building was destroyed by fire in 1988 but completely restored in 2002 with funds from the Jamaican and Venezuelan governments. The building is now in use as the Port Maria Civic Center. A plaque by the main entrance dedicates the premises to labor leader and politician Alexander Bustamante.

**St. Mary Parish Church** was built in 1861 and has an adjoining cemetery with an epitaph dedicated to the Jamaicans who fought in World War I. The **Tacky Memorial** is also located in the church cemetery.

## Beaches

Port Maria's anglers keep their boats and bring in their catch at **Pagee Beach**. Outings to Cabarita Island, a great place to

The rebels' confidence had been bolstered by Obeah men (shamans) among their ranks who spread incantations and claimed the army would be protected and that Obeah men could not be killed. This confidence took a blow when the militia, learning of these claims, captured and killed one of the Obeah men. Nonetheless, the fighting would last months and take the lives of some 60 whites and 300 rebels before it was defused. Tacky himself was captured and beheaded by the Maroons from Scott's Hall, who took his head to Spanish Town on a pole to be displayed to dissuade any further resistance.

The legend of Tacky spread across the island, giving inspiration to other resistance movements that would come in the later years of slavery and after emancipation. Many of Tacky's followers committed suicide rather than surrendering, while those who were captured were either executed or sold and shipped off the island. Ringleaders were either burned alive or starved in cages in the Parade in Kingston. It was during Tacky's War that the British authorities first learned of the role African religion played behind the scenes in these uprisings, and Obeah thus became part of the official record with a 1770 law passed to punish its practitioners by death or transportation, at the court's discretion.

explore in true Robinson Crusoe fashion, can be arranged from here by negotiating with the fisherfolk; US$10 pp is a reasonable round-trip fare. Pagee is not a good spot for swimming.

## Shopping

**St. Mary Craft Market** (Port Maria Civic Center, by appointment, cell tel. 876/373-7575) features work of artists residing in the parish. If you're planning a stop to check out the old courthouse and Anglican Church, call ahead to see the crafts.

## Food

★ **Romney's Restaurant Bar & Grill** (Llanrumney Square, 5 kilometers/3 miles east of Port Maria, cell tel. 876/849-9106, naturefeelltd@yahoo.com, 8am-10pm daily, US$5-12) serves chicken and pork hot off the jerk pit as well as dishes like fried chicken, cow foot, and steamed or roast fish, along with fresh juice smoothies and juice blends.

**Pirates Treats** (Llanrumney Square, 5 kilometers/3 miles east of Port Maria, tel. 876/772-3282, 8:30am-9pm Sun.-Thurs., 1pm-9pm Fri.-Sat.) serves Devon House ice cream and pastries between the jerk grill and bar.

# ROBIN'S BAY

One of the most laid-back and picturesque corners of Jamaica, Robin's Bay is entirely different than what's marketed on posters. Robin's Bay is the Treasure Beach of the North Coast, remaining a quiet fishing and subsistence agricultural community with a few lodging options for an easygoing retreat and intimacy with nature. Beginning with Green Castle Estate, a working farm that commands a large swath of land fronting the bay, the area is a small, tight-knit community and has a slow pace that's easy to get used to.

## ★ Green Castle Estate

**Green Castle Estate** (cell tel. 876/881-6279, info@gcjamaica.com, www.gcjamaica.com) is a 650-hectare (1,600-acre) farm producing a mix of fruit, vegetables, and flowers. Named after the Irish holdings of one of its earlier owners, several archaeological finds on the property indicate it has been continuously occupied since the time of the Taino. Early English settlement at Green Castle left the iconic windmill that still stands today. Land use has changed from cassava cultivation under the Taino and Spanish to orange, cotton, pimento, cacao, indigo, sugarcane, and then bananas. For centuries the estate was connected with the rest of Jamaica only by sea. Since the 1950s the farm has grown an increasingly diverse mix of fruit crops and more recently organic fruit and orchids. Current ownership has turned the estate into an ecotourism paradise, especially popular for **birding,** and 20 of the country's 28 endemic species can be seen.

Historical sites on the expansive estate include excavated Taino middens dating to 1300, a militia barracks (1834), and the signature coral stone windmill tower (1700). **Estate Tours** (adults US$30, children U$10) introduce visitors to some of the 120 hectares (300 acres) of certified-organic tree crops, and focuses on organic coconut oil production and the roughly 2,000 pimento (allspice) trees and cocoa trees. Beef production is also a major activity, with hundreds of cattle roaming the rolling grassy hills. The tour concludes with a visit to the orchid houses, where visitors are dazzled with 50,000 orchid plants in several varieties.

Day passes (US$30) allow visitors to roam free, or contract the services of a guide (US$40 per hour, half day US$120, full day US$180). Guests are offered Jamaican lunch (US$15 adults, US$7.50 children).

## Sunrise on the Cliff

Sunrise on the Cliff (cell tel. 876/436-1223, from noon daily) has a fenced-in lawn overlooking Robin's Bay with benches for enjoying the view and a cook shop preparing steamed and fried fish and occasionally conch soup (US$5-15). The bar serves rum and beer, with stacks of speakers perpetually warming up for the next session.

## Shopping

**Clonmel Potters** (Arthur's Ridge, east of Highgate on the B2, tel. 876/992-4495, clonmelpotters@hotmail.com, www.clonmelpotters.tripod.com, call to arrange a visit 9am-5pm Mon.-Sat., US$20-300) are Donald and Belva Johnson, who work in a variety of local media, from porcelain to terra cotta. Donald's favorite subject is the female nude, countered by his wife's concentration on organic forms. Both are graduates of Kingston's Edna Manley School of Visual Arts, Jamaica's foremost art college.

## Accommodations

★ **Strawberry Fields Together Beachfront Cottages and Adventure Tours** (tel. 876/655-0136, U.S. tel. 718/618-9885 or 905/481-3138, kim@

the view from Green Castle Estate

strawberryfieldstogether.com, www.straw-berryfieldstogether.com, US$70-280) sits on a seven-hectare (18-acre) seafront property with a range of cottages. Two small private beaches with fine white sand line idyllic crystalline coves protected by coral reefs. An outdoors dining area has a wood deck, a bar, a pizza oven, and a jerk center. Wi-Fi covers the property. One-week adventure packages are offered that include airport transfers, meals, and three excursions.

**River Lodge** (tel. 876/995-3003, river-lodge@cwjamaica.com, www.river-lodge.com, US$32-50 pp, includes breakfast and dinner) is located in a refurbished 400-year-old Spanish fort. Rooms inside the fort complement a pair of cottages. From River Lodge, vast unspoiled wilderness stretches along the coast almost to Port Maria, where waterfalls and black-sand beaches are best reached by boat with the local fisherfolk.

★ **Green Castle Estate Great House** (B&B from US$240, 4-bedroom villa US$5,990 weekly) is the most luxurious option in the area. There are colonial furnishings in four spacious bedrooms with private baths. An outlying cottage (B&B from US$150, US$4,750 weekly) has an additional four bedrooms, three with their own

baths. The swimming pool overlooks the gardens. There is a view of the coast and the Blue Mountains from almost every window and veranda. You're guaranteed to see several species of hummingbird, including the red-billed streamertail, the national bird. Tennis courts are well maintained. All estate tours are included with house rental. Opportunities for farm volunteer work and outreach in the neighboring community of Robin's Bay are sometimes available by request. The estate can accommodate up to 21 guests.

**Robin's Bay Oasis** (just before Strawberry Fields, contact Cheryl Russell, U.S. tel. 860/231-0041, russell_realtors@yahoo.com) offers five rooms on a per-unit basis (US$80-90), each with private bath. The entire property can also be rented (US$500). There is Wi-Fi and a fully equipped kitchen. A cook and housekeeper can be hired.

## Getting There and Around

The best way to reach Robin's Bay is by **route taxi** (US$1) or **private taxi charter** (US$10) from Annotto Bay. Getting around in Robin's Bay often requires long waits before a car passes, but the road is only a few kilometers long before it becomes a dirt track and disappears into the wilderness to the west.

Strawberry Fields Together has a sandy cove protected by reef.

# Port Antonio and the East Coast

# Jamaica's easternmost region contains the island's least exploited natural treasures. Port Antonio, or "Portie," is a quiet town in the center of Portland's coast, boasting some

of Jamaica's most secluded beaches and a handful of other natural wonders.

The world-famous Blue Hole, or Blue Lagoon, where ice-cold spring water mixes with the warm sea, is surreal beyond measure and reason enough to visit the region. Navy Island, an abandoned little paradise in the middle of Port Antonio's twin harbors, is surrounded by coral reefs and sandbars. Steep, lush hills rise form a coastline dotted with beaches, inlets, and mangroves. Reach Falls is a nature-lover's paradise, where local guides take visitors by the hand along trails that only they can see through the middle of the river. In Bath, natural hot springs are reputed to cure almost any ailment.

When one of these destinations occupies top priority on your daily agenda, life seems to flow at the right speed. Perhaps the languid pace of this side of the island is just meant to be, and as a visitor, you won't mind the lack of crowds.

## PLANNING YOUR TIME

Some say Port Antonio is a place time forgot. It's definitely an easy place to fall in love with, and despite the languid pace, it's hard to be bored. You'll want no less than three days for all the main sights without feeling rushed, but if you go at the beginning of a trip to Jamaica, it's possible you won't want to see anything else.

Port Antonio is small enough to fit in two main activities in a day. Folly Mansion makes a good morning jaunt, when the sun lights up the side facing the sea, and is nicely complemented with an afternoon at the beach. The dusk hours are best spent on a bench at Errol Flynn Marina with a Devon House ice cream cone in hand.

If you're planning to head into the higher reaches of the Rio Grande Valley, it will take at least a day there and back with a hike to the falls, and at least three days round-trip to hike with Maroon guides to the site of Nanny Town, higher up in the Blue Mountains.

**Previous:** Port Antonio; Long Bay Beach. **Above:** Hotel Mockingbird Hill.

Look for ★ to find recommended sights, activities, dining, and lodging.

# Highlights

★ **Rafting the Rio Grande:** This wide river valley has a rich history and some of the island's most unspoiled wilderness. Enjoy it by cruising gently downstream on a bamboo raft (page 169).

★ **Blue Hole:** Also known as the Blue Lagoon, this freshwater spring wells up in a protected cove and mixes with the warm, salty sea, creating a blurring effect that enhances the magical hue (page 172).

★ **Winnifred Beach:** One of Portland's finest beaches is a popular gathering place for locals. It also has great seafood at Cynthia's (page 174).

★ **Boston Beach:** Some of the best waves for surfing in the northeast are here, a stone's throw from Portland's famed jerk pits (page 175).

★ **Long Bay Beach:** Palm trees are likely to be your only company on this two-kilometer stretch of white sand and strong surf (page 176).

★ **Reach Falls:** Dotted with caves and crystal-clear pools, the island's most exciting waterfalls carve through a lush valley (page 177).

★ **Bath Hot Springs:** Purported to cure all

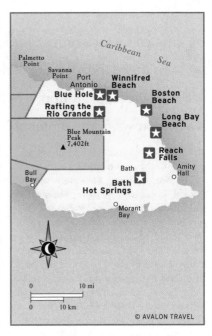

© AVALON TRAVEL

manner of diseases, the hot springs at Bath provide rejuvenating relaxation (page 179).

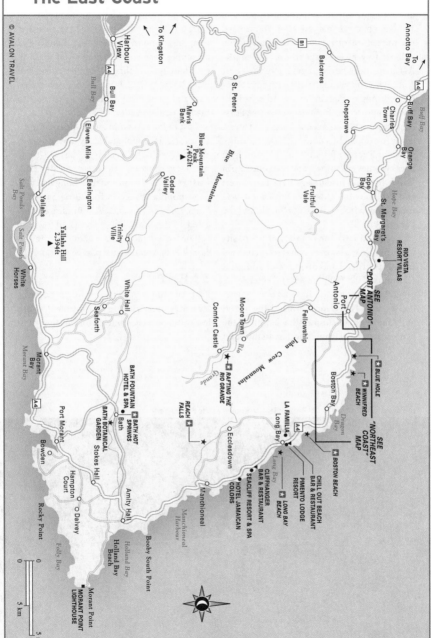

**153**

# The East Coast

© AVALON TRAVEL

PORT ANTONIO AND THE EAST COAST

Annotto Bay
To
Buff Bay
Harbour View
To Kingston
Balcarres
B1
A4
Bull Bay
Charles Town
Orange Bay
Buff Bay
Bull Bay
St. Peters
Chepstowe
Hope Bay
Eleven Mile
Mavis Bank
Blue Mountain Peak 7,402ft
Blue Mountains
Hope Bay
St. Margaret's Bay
Easington
Cedar Valley
Fruitful Vale
RIO VISTA RESORT VILLAS
Yallahs
Trinity Ville
Yallahs Hill 2,394ft
SEE "PORT ANTONIO" MAP
Salt Ponds Bay
Salt Pond
White Horses
Seaforth
White Hall
Moore Town
John Crow Mountains
Port Antonio
Fellowship
SEE "NORTHEAST COAST" MAP
Comfort Castle
Rio
Boston Bay
BLUE HOLE
WINNIFRED BEACH
Morant Bay
Morant Bay
RAFTING THE RIO GRANDE
Rio Grande
Dragon Bay
BOSTON BEACH
A4
BATH FOUNTAIN HOTEL & SPA
REACH FALLS
LA FAMILIA
Long Bay
A4
Port Morant
BATH HOT SPRINGS
Bath
BATH BOTANICAL GARDEN
Ecclesdown
Long Bay
LONG BAY BEACH
CHILL OUT BEACH BAR & RESTAURANT
PIMENTO LODGE RESORT
Stokes Hall
CLIFFHANGER BAR & RESTAURANT
SEACLIFF RESORT & SPA
HOTEL JAMAICAN COLORS
Bowden
Hampton Court
Dalvey
Amity Hall
Manchioneal
Manchioneal Harbour
Rocky Point
Booby
South Point
Folly Bay
Holland Bay Beach
Holland Bay
MORANT POINT LIGHTHOUSE
Morant Point

0
5 km
0
5 mi

# ORIENTATION

The town of Port Antonio is easy to get around on foot or on bicycle, with the farthest-flung sights no more than a few kilometers apart. For the natural attractions east of town, you will need a vehicle. While the main road (the A4) along the north coast passes through Port Antonio, it follows many different streets before coming out again on the other side of town. Approaching from the west, the A4 first becomes West Palm Avenue, then West Street going through the center of town, joining Harbour Street in front of Royal Mall, which later becomes Folly Road, and then once again simply the main road (the A4). Harbour Street and William Street together form a one-way roundabout circling the Courthouse and the Parish Council.

Titchfield Hill, the old part of town, sits on a peninsula across a narrow channel from Navy Island and divides East and West Harbours. Titchfield has several interesting gingerbread-style buildings and a few guesthouses, with Fort George Street, King Street, and Queen Street running the length of the peninsula parallel to one another. In the heart of town, most of the action is on Harbour and West Streets, where the banks, a few restaurants, and Musgrave Market are located. From Harbour Street, West Avenue starts again, wrapping around a residential district and becoming East Avenue before reuniting with the Main Road, at this point called Allen. Red Hassell Road, which is the delineator between East and West Palm Avenues, is the route to the Rio Grande Valley.

East of Port Antonio along the coast are a series of hills dropping sharply down to coves and bays, which help delineate the districts of Anchovy, Drapers, San San, and Fairy Hill. Farther east is Boston and then Long Bay. The most popular beaches, including San San, Frenchman's Cove, and Winnifred, are all located on this stretch of coast east of town, as is Blue Hole. Reach Falls is about 40 minutes east of Port Antonio, just past Manchioneel.

# SAFETY

Port Antonio is not as sprawling as some of Jamaica's other cities, and thus hustlers are less commonly encountered for the most part.

the deep turquoise waters at Blue Hole, also known as the Blue Lagoon

# Port Antonio

Port Antonio is the capital of Portland, a parish of spectacular natural beauty, Old World charm, and one-of-a-kind beaches. Most visitors never see this side of the island, unaware of the town's illustrious history as a playground for the rich and famous. Hollywood actors and industrial barons were on to something when they built their vacation villas in San San, the area's most auspicious address, and their heirs, alongside Kingston's elite, who have weekend homes here, are apparently content not to advertise.

The area's primary draws are the beaches. Two marinas offer safe harbor to boaters, where a scuba outfit and a sailboat charter operator can be hired for excursions off shore. Rafting on the Rio Grande, snorkeling around and exploring Pellew and Navy Islands, and splashing around in the rivers and at Blue Hole are all great affordable ways to spend the day.

## SIGHTS
### Titchfield Hill

The heart of historic Port Antonio, known as **Titchfield Hill,** is best visited by strolling around the peninsula, taking an hour at a leisurely pace. Titchfield Hill today is a run-down neighborhood dotted with several buildings that hint at more prosperous times with decorative latticework and wide front steps leading up to wraparound verandas. The **Demontevin Lodge** (21 Fort George St., tel. 876/993-2604) is a case in point. It was once the private home of David Gideon, who became Custos of Port Antonio in 1923. Today it is a tired hotel operated under unenthusiastic management and not recommended for lodging, but its decorative gingerbread house ironwork, reminiscent of old sea captains' homes on the Massachusetts coast, is striking and worth a look.

The foundation and scattered ruins of the **Titchfield Hotel,** built by banana boat captain Lorenzo Dow Baker of the Boston Fruit Company, stand across Queen Street from Ocean Crest Guest House and are now occupied by the Jamaica Defense Force, which patrols Navy Island across the water. At its peak the hotel was a favored watering hole for luminaries like Bette Davis, J. P. Morgan, and Errol Flynn, who ended up buying the place in addition to Navy Island and the Bonnie View Hotel, overlooking the town from the best perch around. The Titchfield was destroyed and rebuilt several times before it was gutted and abandoned after Flynn's death.

At the tip of the Titchfield peninsula stands **Titchfield School,** constructed on the ruins of **Fort George.** Built by the English to defend against Spanish reprisals that never came, Fort George never really saw any action but operated until World War I. It had walls three meters (10 feet) thick and embrasures for 22 cannons, a few of which are still present. Nobody manages this historic site, making it free and accessible anytime.

### Bonnie View

Another dilapidated former Errol Flynn property is the **Bonnie View Hotel** (Bonnie View Rd.), no longer in operation as a hotel. The view is the best in town. To get here, take the washed-out Richmond Hill Road directly across from the Anglican Church on the corner of West Palm and Bridge Streets. Bonnie View is not an organized attraction and there is no cost to have a look, as long as no one is around to make reference to the sign on property that states all sightseers must pay US$3 (J$150), which doesn't compute for today's exchange rate and dates the effort. Bonnie View makes a good early-morning walk from town for some aerobic exercise, and if someone asks for money to look at the view, perhaps offering to buy a drink from the nonexistent bar would provide adequate incentive for someone to establish a legitimate business there once again.

# Port Antonio

To Hope Bay, Buff Bay, Antonio Bay, and St. Mary

FIRST AND LAST BAR & RESTAURANT

DICKIE'S BANANA (BEST KEPT SECRET)

A4

Shan Shy Beach

Crab Point

Caribbean Sea

WEST PALM AVE

Bryan's Bay

MUSGRAVE MARKET

POLICE STATION

WEST ST

HARBOUR ST

THE ITALIAN JOB

GIDEON AVE

BUS STATION

RICE PIECE RD

HALLS AVE

Annotto River

BOUNDBROOK MARINA

BOUNDBROOK WHARF

West Harbour

Navy Island Beach

Navy Island

Port Antonio

Old Marina

0
0.25 km
0
0.25 mi

ERROL FLYNN MARINA

SEE DETAIL

WEST ST

TITCHFIELD HOTEL RUINS

QUEEN ST

KING ST

GIDEON AVE

DEMONTEVIN LODGE

IVANHOES

Titchfield Hill

WEST PALM AVE

PARISH CHURCH

To Mupper Rio Grande Valley, Rafting, And Moore Town

East Harbour

THE VILLAGE CRAFTS CENTER

ALLAN AVE

Garden Park

West Town River

A4

To San San, Boston, Long Bay and St. Thomas

ANNA BANANNA

YVAAD

RAMATULLAH'S

FOLLY LIGHTHOUSE

Folly Point

Woods Island

FOLLY RUINS

Folly Beach

The hill is passable by car if you drive at a snail's pace up the steep, potholed road.

## Marinas

**Errol Flynn Marina** (tel. 876/993-3209 or 876/715-6044, www.errolflynnmarina.com, 8am-5pm daily) has 32 births. Transient vessels under 50 feet are charged US$0.95 per foot per night, over 50 feet US$1.75 per foot per night; metered electricity and water are available. A well-laid-out and planted promenade along the waterfront has benches. A swimming pool and Wi-Fi are available for marina guests, and an Internet café (US$4 per hour) is open to nonguests. A Devon House ice cream parlor and two bars serving food are found within the gated complex, and the scenic waterfront makes a romantic spot for an evening stroll. A private beach faces Navy Island. The park along the waterfront (7am-11pm Mon.-Fri., 7am-midnight Sat.-Sun.) is open to nonguests, as is the beach, marina, and bars; the docks and pool are reserved for marina guests.

**Port Antonio Marina** (8:30am-5pm daily) also offers docking at lower rates with metered water, electricity, and showers, but no security after 4pm. It is down the road next to the old train station, now home to the Portland Art Gallery, across from CC Bakery.

The difference between them comes down to security, proximity to the bar and restaurant, and wireless Internet access. Marina guests have access to showers and laundry 24 hours a day with an access card. The Marina has 24-hour security and a gate to the dock opens with the guest access card as well.

## Folly Mansion

Just east of Port Antonio along Alan Avenue, a left onto a dirt road before the cricket pitch follows the edge of East Harbour out to Folly Point Lighthouse. A right turn after the cricket pitch along a grassy vehicle track through a low scrub forest leads to **Folly Mansion** (unmanaged), a free and always accessible attraction on government-owned land. Built by Connecticut millionaire Alfred Mitchell in 1905, the 60-room mansion was once the most ostentatious building in Jamaica. Apparently the cement used in the construction was mixed with saltwater, which weakened the structure and eroded the steel framework, causing almost immediate deterioration. Nonetheless, Mitchell lived part-time in the mansion with his family until his death in 1912, and the house was abandoned in 1936.

On the waterfront in front of the pillared mansion is the humble little **Folly Beach,**

Folly Mansion

which faces small Wood Island, where Mitchell is said to have kept monkeys and other exotic animals. The beach is swimmable but care should be taken as the sea floor is not even and parts are covered with sharp coral. The area is known to have a strong current at times.

The name Folly predates the ill-fated mansion in **Folly Point Lighthouse,** built in 1888. Apparently the name refers to the one-time landowner and Baptist minister James Service and his frugal ways. The lighthouse stands on a point extending along the windward shore of East Harbour and is not generally open to the public, but the property manager is known to let visitors in on occasion. A track usually too rutted and muddy for a vehicle runs along the water's edge between the lighthouse and the mansion.

## Navy Island

Originally called Lynch's Island, Navy Island is a landmass slightly larger than Titchfield Hill, about 0.75 kilometers (0.5 miles) long with an area of about two hectares (5 acres). It protects Port Antonio's West Harbour with a large sandbar extending off its western side. The island was once to be the site of the town, but the British Navy acquired it instead as a

place to beach ships for cleaning and repairs. A naval station was eventually built, and later Errol Flynn bought the island and turned it into an exclusive resort. Today Navy Island is owned by the Port Authority and will be developed at some undetermined future time. A private bid for the land put together by a consortium of local landowners was blocked by the authority, which seems wary of ceding control in spite of doing nothing with the land, to the dismay of many local residents.

The island has no services, but it's a great place to tromp around and explore, and the Jamaica Defense Force Officers on patrol there are friendly enough to visitors. **Dennis Butler** (cell tel. 876/809-6276) will take visitors to the island (US$10 pp, US$20 with lunch) from Shan Shy Beach just west of Port Antonio, adjacent to his father's restaurant, Dickie's Banana.

## Other Sights

**Boundbrook Wharf** is the old banana-loading wharf just west of town, facing Titchfield on the opposite side of West Harbour. While not as busy as in the banana-boom days, the wharf continues to be used on occasion. The wharf is a good 20-minute walk from town. Just north from the entrance to the wharf,

Navy Island

# Portland's Banana Boom

The global banana trade, multibillion dollar industry, has its roots in Portland and St. Thomas. American sea captains George Busch and later Lorenzo Dow Baker of the 85-ton *Telegraph*, who arrived in 1870, established a lucrative two-way trade, bringing saltfish (cod), shoes, and textiles from New England, where the bananas sold at a handsome profit. Baker was the most successful of the early banana shippers, forming the Boston Fruit Company in 1899, which later became the United Fruit Company of New Jersey, which went on to control much of the fruit's production in the Americas. As refrigerated ships came into operation in the early 1900s, England slowly took over from the United States as the primary destination, thanks to tariff protection that was only recently phased out.

With the establishment of the Jamaica Banana Producers Association in 1929, smallholder production was organized, a cooperative shipping line established, and the virtual monopoly held by United Fruit was somewhat broken. In 1936 the association became a shareholder-based company rather than a cooperative due to near bankruptcy and pressure from United Fruit. It was perhaps this example of organized labor that gave Marcus Garvey the inspiration for a shipping line to serve the African diaspora and bring commerce into its hands. In the 1930s, Panama disease virtually wiped out the Jamaican banana crop, hitting small producers especially hard. Banana carriers and dockworkers were at the fore of the labor movements of 1937-1938 that led to trade unions and eventually the establishment of Jamaica's political parties.

a sandy lane leads off the main road to the beach, where fishing boats are tethered in front of the small fishing community.

## BEACHES

**Shan Shy Beach** on Bryan's Bay charges no entry fee and is home to a beach complex run by Donovan "Atto" Tracey (tel. 876/394-1312). An open building has a billiards room with two tables. One of the less frequented beaches in Port Antonio, Shan Shy is a good place to take off on snorkeling or fishing excursions, which can be arranged through Atto or **Dennis Butler** (cell tel. 876/854-4763 or 876/869-4391, US$20-50) of Dickie's Banana. The beach is located five minutes west of town at a sharp curve in the main road.

Around the bend in **White River,** Lucky Star Cookshop and Bar overlooks another angler's beach. It's a favorite cool-out spot for local men, who are often found in the evenings playing poker and dominos.

**Errol Flynn Marina** has a well-maintained private beach for guests of the marina and patrons of Bikini Bar.

## SPORTS AND RECREATION
### Water Sports
**Pellew Island** is a private island, given, as the legend has it, by industrial magnate and famed art collector Hans Heinrich Thyssen-Bornemisza to supermodel Nina Sheila Dyer, one of his many brides, as a wedding gift in 1957. Dyer committed suicide five years later, and Thyssen-Bornemisza himself died in 2002. There are no organized tours of the private island, but fishers and seafaring entrepreneurs from the small beach adjacent to Blue Hole can take visitors over for snorkeling along the reefs for about US$10 pp round-trip.

**Lady G'Diver** (Errol Flynn Marina, contact Steve or Jan Lee Widener, tel. 876/715-5957, cell tel. 876/995-0246 or 876/289-3023, www.ladygdiver.com) runs diving excursions from the marina. Port Antonio's waters are quieter than those off Ocho Rios or Montego Bay and are less overfished. Wall diving is especially popular. Lady G'Diver offers a wide range of packages and programs, from basic PADI certification to master courses. The most basic is the two-dive package (US$100, including equipment), followed by a four-dive package (US$180).

The Lark Cruises (contact Captain Carolyn Barrett, cell tel. 876/382-6384, www.barrettadventures.com) offers seven-day (US$3,500 for up to 4 people) cruises out of Port Antonio on *The Lark*, a 40-foot Jeanneau Sloop. Provisioning is at the guests' expense, while the captain and cook are included.

## Cycling

**Blue Mountain Bicycle Tours** (121 Main St., Ocho Rios, tel. 876/974-7075, www.bm-toursja.com) runs a popular downhill biking tour. The office is in Ocho Rios, but those staying in Portland can catch the bus in Buff Bay before it leaves the coast to ascend the B1 into the Blue Mountains to the starting point of the downhill ride.

## Tennis

**Goblin Hill** (San San, tel. 876/993-7537) allows nonguests to use the hotel's hardtop tennis courts (US$15 per hour, US$12 for 2 rackets).

# ENTERTAINMENT AND EVENTS

Port Antonio is by no means a haven for club-goers, but there are a few good venues that hold regular theme nights throughout the week, as well as occasional live performances. Several times a year, stage shows are set up around the area, Somerset Falls being a favorite venue for concerts; Boston and Long Bay also host occasional events. Many of the area's upscale villa owners and visitors prefer to entertain with dinner parties, which can be quite lavish.

## Nightclubs

**Cristal Night Club** (19 W. Palm Ave., contact Peter Hall, cell tel. 876/288-7657, cristal-niteclub@yahoo.com, ppeter13@yahoo.com, 5pm-4am Thurs.-Sat.) is Port Antonio's top nightclub, with Roadblock bringing a street dance vibe 5pm-midnight Thursday with a sound system outside; then the party moves indoors until 4am. Portland Day Rave is held 9pm-4am the last Saturday of the month, featuring up-and-coming selectors (DJs) and dancers.

## Bars

**Marybelle's Pub on the Pier** (Errol Flynn Marina, tel. 876/413-9731, bellmar_bell92@ yahoo.com, noon-11pm daily, US$4-16) serves drinks and finger food like burgers, pizza, salads, and fruit by the pool. The bar offers customers complimentary Wi-Fi.

**Bikini Beach** (Errol Flynn Marina, contact Basel, cell tel. 876/403-0501) is a beach bar and grill.

**Irie Vibes** (shop 10, West Harbour Plaza, by KFC, contact William Saunders, cell tel. 876/375-4495, noon-close Mon.-Sat., 4:30pm-close Sun. and holidays) is a popular bar with two pool tables overlooking the West Harbour; drinks run US$1-5.

**Club La Best** (5 West St., contact Naldo, cell tel. 876/432-0798) is a sports bar located in what was once a nightclub.

## Festivals and Events

**Marbana** (www.m7events.com, US$85) is an exclusive all-inclusive party held at Frenchman's Cove on Easter Sunday, the weekend before the carnival season finale. The event features top soca selectors, carnival dancers in full regalia, and fire jugglers, all contributing to "Jamaica's Ultimate Beach Club Experience."

**Portland Jerk Festival** (cell tel. 876/543-1242, US$10) is held on the first Sunday of July, rain or shine. Local arts and crafts and a stage show with leading reggae acts, contemporary and retro, complement every kind of jerk meat imaginable. The festival was relocated from its original home in Boston to Folly Oval in 2007 to accommodate growing crowds, and the festival's popularity has continued to grow.

The **International Blue Marlin Tournament** (contact Ron DuQuesnay, chair of the Sir Henry Morgan Angling Association, cell tel. 876/909-8818, rondq@

mail.infochan.com, registration US$170) is run from Boundbrook Marina, opposite Errol Flynn, each October. The event draws anglers from far and wide and runs a concurrent 35-canoe folk fishing tournament for local anglers who fight the billfish with handheld lines and usually bring in a better catch than the expensive big boats.

**Flynn Flim Festival** (Errol Flynn marina, cell tel. 876/715-6044)—no, that's not a typo, it's a play on words—is one of the highlights of the sparse annual event calendar in Port Antonio. The quaint festival is held the third week of June and features Errol Flynn movie screenings, a rafting race down the Rio Grande, a Flynn lookalike contest where patrons dress as Errol or one of his female costars in their favorite Flynn movie. Jazz on the pier each evening extends the sounds of the preceding Ocho Rios Jazz Festival.

## SHOPPING

**Musgrave Market** (6am-6pm Mon.-Sat.) is located across from the square in the heart of Port Antonio. The market sells fresh produce toward the front and down a lane on one side. The deeper you go toward the waterfront, the more the market tends toward crafts, T-shirts, and souvenirs. For jewelry, clothing, and other Rasta-inspired crafts, check out Sister Dawn's (shop 21, cell tel. 876/486-7516, portlandcraftproducers@yahoo.com).

### Art and Crafts

**Rock Bottom** (cell. tel. 876/844-9946), a veteran woodcarver with decades in the business, was once based at Musgrave market but has since relocated fittingly to The Craft Village at 1 Allan Avenue, where he hawks his own artistry and that of select peers alongside a handful of other vendors.

Located inside the old railroad station by the Port Antonio Marina on West Street, about 10 minutes' walk from the Main Square, is **Portland Art Gallery** (9am-6pm Mon.-Sat.). Hopeton Cargill (cell tel. 876/882-7732 or 876/913-3418), whose work includes landscape paintings, portraits, and commercial signs, is the gallery director. **Philip Henry** (tel. 876/993-3162, philartambokle@hotmail.com) is a talented artist who has prints, portraits, and sculpture for sale in his small home studio. Call or email to set up an appointment.

**Michael Layne** (19 Sommers Town Rd., tel. 876/993-3813, cell tel. 876/784-0288, miclayne@cw.jamaica.com) is considered by many the top ceramist in the parish and has exhibited at galleries in Kingston countless times. Today Layne teaches art at Titchfield High School and works out of his home studio (open by appointment), where he creates works that include large bottles, bowls, and vases assembled with clay slabs, decorated with oxides, and single-fired.

**Marcia Henry** (lot 5, Red Hassell Lane, tel. 876/993-3162) is a talented local artist with a home studio.

**Carriacou Gallery** (Hotel Mockingbird Hill, tel. 876/993-7134, 9am-5pm daily) features work of co-owner Barbara Walker in addition to many other local artists.

### Books

**Hamilton's Bookstore** (24 West St., contact Avarine Moore, tel. 876/993-3792, 9am-7pm Mon.-Sat.) has a small but decent selection of Jamaican folk books and cookbooks.

### Music

**A&G Record Mart** (4 Blake St., contact Janet, cell tel. 876/488-1593 or 876/427-8766, 10am-9pm Mon.-Sat.) has a great selection of CDs, DVDs, LP singles and complete albums, 45s, and 33s. Gospel, R&B, dancehall, reggae, soul, soca, and calypso are well represented.

## FOOD
### Breakfast and Cafés

**Yosch Cafe** (The Craft Village, 1 Allan Ave., East Harbour, tel. 876/993-3053, majumidb@yahoo.com, 9am-11pm Mon.-Sat., 1pm-10pm Sun.) offers great breakfast and sandwiches on a wooden deck on the waterfront.

**Yellow Canary** (1 Harbour St., contact Crissie, cell tel. 876/404-8161, 8am-5pm daily, US$2-4.50), also known as Bramwell's

Restaurant, serves typical Jamaican fare for breakfast and lunch: ackee and saltfish, liver, corned beef, stew peas, and fried chicken.

**Devon House I Scream** (Errol Flynn Marina, tel. 876/993-3825) serves the best ice cream for kilometers around, but avoid the tubs that have thawed and refrozen.

## Jamaican

**Dickie's Banana** (Bryan's Bay, about 1.5 kilometers/1 mile west of town center, cell tel. 876/809-6276, hours vary, reservations required, US$25 pp) is also known as a best-kept secret since it was the winner of the *Jamaica Observer*'s Best Kept Secret award. It has wonderful food at great value and even better service. Five courses are served based on Dickie's inventive culinary magic, with no ordering necessary. For the main course there's a choice of fish, chicken, goat, lobster, or vegetarian.

**First and Last Bar & Restaurant** serves up authentic Jamaican dishes including curry goat, oxtail, brown stew fish, and callaloo. Howard "Howie" Cover (cell tel. 876/367-7700) owns the bar, and Clement Chambers (cell tel. 876/450-5143) runs the restaurant.

**Sir P's Cook Shop** (cell tel. 876/787-5514) serves up local dishes like jerk chicken, roast fish and bammy, conch, and natural juices.

Peanut porridge and pastries are served in the morning.

**Bikini Beach Bar & Grill** (Errol Flynn Marina, tel. 876/946-0005, bikinibeachjamaica@gmail.com, noon-10pm daily, US$5-25) serves jerk chicken, burgers, pasta Alfredo dishes, and lobster on the beach that faces West Harbour and Navy Island.

**Nix Nax Centre** (16 Harbour St., across from Texaco, tel. 876/993-2081, cell tel. 876/329-4414, 8am-7pm Mon.-Thurs., 8am-8pm Fri.-Sat., 2pm-8pm Sun., US$3-5) serves Jamaican favorites like fried chicken, curry goat, and stewed pork. Ackee with saltfish and stewed chicken are served for breakfast daily.

**Wi Yard Anna Banana Restaurant** (7 Folly Rd., tel. 876/715-6533, cell tel. 876/542-1497, 11am-11pm daily) serves seafood and meat items. Fish costs about US$12 per pound, and pepper shrimp (highly recommended) is US$16 per pound. There's a happy hour 6pm-7pm Friday and a selector playing music to keep patrons entertained.

★ **Woody's Low Bridge Place** (Drapers, tel. 876/993-7888, 10am-10pm daily), run by Charles "Woody" Cousins and his charismatic wife, Cherry, is definitively the coolest snack bar and restaurant in Port Antonio; it

Tasty lobster is being cooked up at Cynthia's.

serves what is quite possibly the best burger (US$2.50) in Jamaica.

★ **Cynthia's** (Winnifred Beach, tel. 876/347-7085 or 876/562-4860, 9am-6pm daily), run by Cynthia Miller, serves the best fish, lobster, and chicken accompanied by vegetables, rice-and-peas, and festival at the best value (US$7-15).

★ **Soldier's Camp** (83 Red Hassell Rd., tel. 876/715-2083, cell tel. 876/351-4821, from 6pm daily), better known as Soldji's, draws a healthy cross-section of locals on Wednesday and especially Friday nights for deliciously seasoned janga (crayfish) as well as jerk chicken, pork, and curry goat. Special order can be arranged on any other night. The bar is open 10am-9pm daily.

## International

**Golden Happiness** (2 West St., tel. 876/993-2329, 10:30am-10pm Mon.-Sat., 2pm-9pm Sun., US$4-7) is the best Chinese food in town, but the place lacks ambience and is best for takeout. The food is good value. **Wonderful Palace Fast Food** (9 Harbour St., tel. 876/993-2169, 9am-9pm Mon.-Sat., 3pm-9pm Sun., US$3-8) has decent Chinese and Jamaican staples.

**Chenel's Pizza** (28-A West St., tel.

876/440-0968, 9am-7am Mon.-Thurs., 11am-11pm Fri.-Sat., US$5-20), run by Michael "Mikey" Badarie, serves pizza made to order with 15 different toppings baked in a gas oven.

**The Italian Job** (29 Harbour St., cell tel. 876/573-8603, theitalianjobjamaica@gmail.com, noon-10pm Tues.-Sat., US$7-20), was launched by Gianmaria Pedroli, a native of northern Italy who came to vacation in Portland in 2010 and fell in love with the area. In addition to pizza, the cozy restaurant serves salads, calzones, lasagna, carbonara, and seafood spaghetti.

## Fine Dining

At ★ **Mille Fleurs** (Hotel Mockingbird Hill, tel. 876/993-7134 or 876/993-7267, breakfast 8am-10:30am daily, lunch noon-2:30pm daily, dinner 7pm-9:30pm daily, entrées US$25-40), the menu changes daily, serving creative Asian, European, and Jamaican dishes that emphasize local fresh ingredients, like jerk meat with papaya salsa or a pimento-roasted steak with rum-honey glaze alongside grilled banana or pineapple. Reservations are strongly advised.

**The Veranda** (Trident Hotel, reservations required for non-guests, tel. 876/633-7100, 7am-10am breakfast, 12pm-4pm lunch,

Soldier's Camp serves delicious steamed fish.

7pm-9:30pm dinner, daily, US$15-45), offers creative dishes with area's fresh seafood. On Saturdays, the semi-formal **Mike's Supper Club** has live music and special dishes with items like whole lion fish, jerk pork, curry goat, and a Portland seafood platter. Regular entrees include grilled rack of lamb, braised oxtail, chicken masala, herb crusted beef tenderloin, vegetable casserole, and fresh fish fillets—grilled, steamed, or jerked, served with herb garlic butter and grilled polenta.

### Vegetarian

**Survival Beach Restaurant** (Allan Ave., Oliver Weir, cell tel. 876/384-4730 or 876/442-5181) is an ital shack on the beachfront marked by a yellow picket fence on East Harbour. Vegetarian food, jelly coconut, and ital juices are served at reasonable prices (US$5-10).

**Dixon's Corner Store** (12 Bridge St., tel. 876/993-3840, 8:30am-6:30pm Mon.-Fri.) is an ital restaurant serving excellent vegetarian dishes (US$3) like veggie chunks, veggie steak, fried whole-wheat dumplings, steamed cabbage, and saltfish. Delicious fresh juices (US$1) like sorrel and ginger are also served.

## ACCOMMODATIONS
### Under US$100

**Mango Ridge** (Somers Lane, tel. 876/275-7222, mikeodonnell39@yahoo.com, www.mangoridge.com, from US$50 d) has four rustic self-contained cottages with private cold-water baths with foam double beds or a real mattress (US$70, US$25 extra guests). The property is a thin 0.4 hectares (1 acre) stretching up the hill in the Somers Town area. Each cottage has its own Wi-Fi modem. Chickens roam the property and provide fresh eggs for guests.

**Drapers San Guest House** (Drapers, tel. 876/993-7118, carla-51@cwjamaica.com) is ocean-side toward the easternmost end of Drapers district; it's an excellent budget option. A few rooms have shared baths (US$50, including breakfast) and a few have private baths (US$60). Two newer rooms offer a step

up: Rasta Cottage (US$70) is self-contained with a private bath and a veranda; the other "high-end" room is in the main building, with its own bath and a shared veranda (US$60). Drapers San owner Carla Gullotta is an avid reggae fan and can help arrange trips to stage shows and cultural heritage sights and events. She is also a good contact for travelers interested in visiting Culture Yard in Trench Town, Kingston.

**Search Me Heart** (Drapers, cell tel. 876/453-7779, www.searchmeheart.com, US$70-80, including breakfast) is a comfortable and clean four-bedroom cottage run as a guesthouse by Roseanna Trifogli. Amenities include hot water in en suite baths and ceiling fans. The cottage is about a 10-minute walk to Frenchman's Cove, one of Port Antonio's best beaches.

### US$100-250

**Bay View Villas** (Anchovy, tel. 876/993-3118, www.bayviewvillas-ja.com, US$90) is a large building with 21 rooms in a variety of configurations. The hotel sits above Turtle Crawle Bay, just east of Trident Castle. B&B (US$102) as well as all-inclusive (US$126) packages are offered. Rooms are comfortable and airy, with TVs, air-conditioning, balconies, and private baths with hot water.

**The Fan** (contact Nino Sciuto, tel. 876/993-7259, cell tel. 876/390-0118, nino@villaswithclass.com, www.villaswithclass.com, US$160-180) is a private villa in the hills above Drapers with a breathtaking view of Dolphin Bay, Trident Castle, and Blue Mountain Peak. The villa rents two guest apartments. The grand suite, located on the top level, has a king bed, a large living room, a kitchen, and a balcony. The junior suite, on the ground level, has a double bed and a couch that can be turned into an extra bed if needed. Meals are prepared to order at additional cost by the housekeeper, who should be tipped the customary 10 percent of the rental cost for your stay. The Fan's owner, Gloria Palomino, also runs The Gap Café, a small bed-and-breakfast near Hardwar Gap in the Blue Mountains, and offers mountain and seaside packages for guests interested in experiencing both Port Antonio and the Blue Mountains.

★ **Goblin Hill** (tel. 876/993-7537, reservations tel. 876/925-8108, reservations@ goblinhill.com, www.goblinhillvillas.com), farther up the hill in the San San district, is an excellent option for families or couples. The spacious rooms and self-contained duplex suites (US$115-195 low season, US$125-265 high season) are a great value, especially for a family. The two-bedroom duplex suites have large master rooms with a second bedroom upstairs, and a living area and kitchen downstairs. Sliding doors open onto a beautiful lawn rolling down to San San Bay, also visible from the master bedroom. Interiors are less extravagant than some neighboring villa properties, but Goblin Hill boasts a large swimming pool, tennis courts, and easy walking distance to San San Beach and the Blue Lagoon. Guests get complimentary use of the beach at Frenchman's Cove. Goblin Hill was recently wired with state-of-the art Wi-Fi, affording the most reliable and fastest service in Port Antonio.

## Over US$250

**The Trident Hotel** (U.S. tel. 800/300-6220, www.thetridenthotel.com, from US$500) is Port Antonio's most luxurious boutique hotel, featuring 13 oceanfront villas with a modern design and retro artwork and fixtures. The villas have private pools and the latest technology.

★ **Hotel Mockingbird Hill** (Drapers, tel. 876/993-7134 or 876/993-7267, www. hotelmockingbirdhill.com, Oct.-Aug.) has pleasantly decorated garden view (US$195 low season, US$255 high season) and sea view (US$235 low season, US$295 high season) rooms with ceiling fans and mosquito nets. Wi-Fi is available in the lounge, where a computer is set up for guest use. Solar hot-water systems, locally minded purchasing practices, and minimal-waste policies have earned Mockingbird Hill an ecofriendly reputation. With stunning views of both the Blue

Mountains and Portland's coast, it's hard not to love the place. Several large dogs can often be seen tagging along behind the innkeepers. To get to the hotel, take a right immediately after Jamaica Palace and climb for about 200 meters (650 feet). The entrance in on the left.

**Geejam** (San San, tel. 876/993-7000 or 876/618-8000, www.geejam.com, US$595-705 low season, US$2,035-2,125 high season) is a recording artists' paradise, where Les Nubians, No Doubt, India Arie, Amy Winehouse, and Tom Cruise have taken working vacations. Sitting on a low hill overlooking San San Bay, the property consists of the main house with three bedrooms, three cabins dispersed across the property, and a one-bedroom suite below the recording studio. Inside the huts, are TVs, home theater systems with DVD players, and minibars. Wi-Fi covers the entire property. Mattresses are comfortable, linens are soft and clean, and there's hot water. Two cabins and the suite have steam rooms as well. The main house, a bona-fide villa, has a stylish pool out front. The recording studio is located at the lower reaches of the property, a deck with whirlpool tub crowning its roof. The studio has all the latest gear and oversize windows overlooking the water. While the property is specifically designed as a recording retreat for a band-sized group renting the whole place (US$5,795 low season, US$6,500 high season), it is also ideal for couples and other kinds of retreats. The property is a 10-minute walk from San San Beach, with the Blue Lagoon also a stone's throw away. Rates include a full staff.

**Kanopi House** (tel. 876/632-3213, U.S. tel. 800/790-7971 www.kanopihouse.com, US$300-600) is an assortment of six tree houses in the dense forest hugging the eastern banks of Blue Hole. The cottages stand on stilts with French doors leading to wide balconies, louvered windows, and exposed wood interiors. Spacious sitting areas have bamboo and wicker furniture; bedrooms have kings. The cottages are naturally cool in the shade of the forest, with ceiling fans rather than air-conditioning, and do not have TVs. Each cottage has an outdoor grill. Meals are prepared to order, but there's no restaurant on the property. To get here, take a left off the driveway leading into Dragon Bay. Guests have use of snorkeling gear and kayaks and unfettered access to the Blue Lagoon.

**Wilk's Bay** (contact owners Jim and Mary Lowe, tel. 876/993-7400, cell tel. 876/471-9622, www.wilksbay.com, US$225-450 low season, US$275-600 high season) has one- to three-bedroom villas, each staffed with its own cook-housekeeper. The recently refurbished property, situated on Wilk's Bay between Frenchman's Cove and Alligator Head, boasts a white-sand private beach, a dock, and a swimming pool. Bedrooms have air-conditioning, high ceilings, mahogany woodwork, and louvered windows. Last minute bookings can stay on a B&B plan with no minimum time, based on availability. Plans are afoot to add six stand-alone units and a reception area.

## Villas

Port Antonio's villas are definitely some of the nicest in Jamaica, and far less pricey than those in Ocho Rios and Montego Bay. Typically they have either breathtaking hilltop views over mountains and out to sea or are directly on the water, like the famous Blue Lagoon Villas (a collection of independently owned villas)—the most coveted real estate in Jamaica, perfectly placed between San San Bay and the Blue Lagoon.

**Island Villas** (2 West St., cell tel. 876/276-7019, www.islandvillasjamaica.com) is run by Yvonne Blakey, who represents owners of many of Port Antonio's finest villas and can perfectly tailor your interests with a villa. **Villas with Class** (www.villaswithclass.com), run by Nino Sciuto, offers booking services for many of the area's villas and runs a community-oriented site featuring the area's attractions and services.

★ **San Bar** (tel. 876/929-2378 or 876/926-0931, dianas@cwjamaica.com, www.sanbarjamaica.com, US$10,500 weekly low season, US$12,000 weekly high season) is a six-bedroom villa sleeping up to eight adults and six children, ideally situated among the Blue Lagoon Villas with a clear view of Pellew Island and Alligator Head. Easily one of the best villas around, San Bar boasts an oversize hot tub on the deck, impeccable furnishings, and more balconies than you'll want to count. Cable TV, broadband Internet, and a stereo keep guests plugged in.

★ **Norse Hill** (www.norsevillas.com, US$4,800 weekly low season, US$6,300

Birdie'ill

weekly high season) is a steadfast, gorgeous, stately structure, with an industrial-size kitchen, three bedrooms, and a loving and dedicated staff. The master bedroom and the slightly less opulent room on the other end of the chateau both have large tiled baths and oversized mirrors. Verandas look out over the pool and gardens and, beyond that, the sea. All amenities are here, including Internet access. The property is arguably the best endowed in Port Antonio. Hectares of botanical gardens sit on top of a hill looking over San San Bay. An enormous ficus tree shades the best seat in town, and the gardens have extensive pathways through lush flowerbeds.

**Birdie'ill** (San San, cell tel. 876/276-7019, www.islandvillasjamaica.com, US$4,000 weekly low season, US$5,000 weekly high season) is a four-bedroom hilltop villa ideal for families or small groups overlooking San San Beach and Alligator Head. Amenities include a large living room with a marble floor and a dining room. A crescent-shaped three-meter-deep (9-foot) pool with arched nooks on either side have sofas for relaxing in the shade to escape the heat. Balconies are found throughout the villa, some for sunning, others for dining. An excellent library provides companions for the beach or amid the two-hectare (5-acre) gardens surrounding the villa. It's comfortable by any measure, but the kitchen, baths, and entertainment system are outdated.

**Norse Point** (cell tel. 876/383-5571, adougall.parquet@cwjamaica.com, www.norse-point.com, US$400 low season, US$425 high season) is the only one-bedroom villa in Port Antonio, a quaint cottage directly across a short stretch of water from Pellew Island, between San San Beach and Blue Hole.

**Alligator Head** (contact manager David Lee, cell tel. 876/298-5675, info@alligator-head.net, US$2,500 nightly for up to 8 guests) is one of the most exclusive and luxurious estates in Jamaica. It rents two villas, one three-bedroom and one four-bedroom, sleeping six and eight, respectively, with two beaches, several pools, Wi-Fi across the property, and 17 staff members attending to the peninsular

estate. A new villa was recently added, designed by Caribbean architect Vidal Dowding. There is a Boston Whaler available for rent (US$350/day) and three Sea-Doo watercrafts (US$150 each/day). 15% gratuity for the staff is customary to add to the overall bill.

## INFORMATION AND SERVICES

**Portland Parish Library** (1 Fort George St., tel. 876/993-2793) offers free Internet access on a set of computers. **Don J's Computer Centre** (shop 10, Royal Mall, tel. 876/715-5559, 9am-7pm Mon.-Sat.) offers Internet access (US$1 per hour), faxing, and VoIP calling.

### Banks
**Scotiabank** (tel. 876/993-2523) is located at 3 Harbour Street. **Firstcaribbean** has a branch on Harbour Street (tel. 876/993-2708). For currency exchange, try **Kamal's** (12 West St., tel. 876/993-4292, 8:30am-9pm Mon.-Thurs., 8:30am-10:30pm Fri., 8:30-11pm on Sat., 9am-6pm Sun.) and **Kamlyn's Supermarket and Cambio** (19 Harbour St., tel. 876/993-2140; 12 West St., tel. 876/993-4292; 8:30am-5pm Mon.-Thurs., 8:30am-6pm Fri., 8:30am-5pm Sat.).

### Postal Services
For shipping services, **DHL** operates through local agent **True Venture Western Union** (shop 6A West Harbour Plaza, 22 West St., 876/993-3441, 9am-5pm Mon.-Sat.).

### Police and Medical Emergencies
**Port Antonio Police** (tel. 876/993-2546) are located at 10 Harbor Street, whereas **San San Police** (tel. 876/993-7315) are at the base of San San Hill.

**Port Antonio Hospital** (Naylor's Hill, tel. 876/993-2426) is run by doctors Terry Hall and Jeremy Knight, who have a very good reputation. **Dr. Lynvale Bloomfield** (32 Harbour St., tel. 876/993-2338, cell tel. 876/417-7139) has a private general practice in town. **Dr. Tracey Lumley** (tel. 876/993-2224, cell. tel. 876/874-7583 or 876/339-0024) is also a well-regarded local physician.

Eric Hudecek at **Modern Dentistry** (9 West Harbour St., tel. 876/715-5896, cell tel. 876/860-3860, info@modern-dentistry.de) is a highly regarded dentist with a smart, well-equipped office overlooking Navy Island. Patients travel from across Jamaica and even abroad.

## GETTING THERE

Port Antonio is served by **route taxis** from Buff Bay (US$3) from the west and Boston (US$2) and Morant Bay (US$5) from the east. **Minibuses** leave twice daily for these areas from Market Square. **Taxis** gather in Market Square and in front of the Texaco station on Harbour Street. Most guesthouses and hotels arrange transportation from Kingston or Montego Bay airports, Kingston being the closer international airport, about 2.5 hours away.

The quickest route from Kingston (the A3) passes over Stony Hill and then through Castleton, St. Mary, and Junction before hitting the north coast just west of Annotto Bay at a roundabout. The A4 begins at the roundabout, running east through Port Antonio and then following the northeast coast, turning south near the eastern tip of Jamaica and then back west to Kingston. The latter route is every bit as scenic, but the time and distance are greater. Count on dodging potholes for at least three hours from Port Antonio to Kingston along the coast. It's about two hours from Kingston to Port Antonio through Stony Hill, most of the time following a winding road that hugs the banks of the Wag River. An even more scenic route (the B1) passes over Hardwar Gap in the Blue Mountains before descending to the coast in Buff Bay. The descent from Hardwar Gap to Buff Bay is on a very narrow road, in most places hardly wide enough for one car, let alone two. Make liberal use of the horn going around the sharp corners.

**Knutsford Express** (tel. 876/971-1822, www.knutsfordexpress.com) offers coach service from Port Antonio to points throughout Jamaica, connecting in Ocho Rios. **The Ken Jones Aerodrome,** 10 minutes west of Port Antonio, has flights from Kingston, Oracabessa, Montego Bay, and Negril with charter operator **Timair** (tel. 876/940-6660, www.intlairlink.com).

## GETTING AROUND

The town of Port Antonio is compact enough to get around comfortably on foot. For any of the attractions east, west, and south of town, however, it is necessary to jump in a route taxi or hire a private charter. If you're feeling energetic, traveling along the coast between town and Winnifred Beach or even Boston by bicycle is feasible.

Route taxis congregate by the Texaco station on Harbour Street for points east, and in Market Square for points west and south. It's easy to flag down route taxis along the main road. Expect to pay around US$1.50 for a ride a few kilometers down the coast as far as Boston.

**Fisher Tours** (cell tel. 876/488-0319) can give you a lift around for reasonable rates. Driver Andre Thomson will take you from Kingston airport to Port Antonio for US$120, or on excursions to places like Reach Falls from Port Antonio for US$20 pp. Andre's van has a capacity of eight.

**Eastern Rent-A-Car** (16 West St., manager Kevin Sudeall, tel. 876/993-4364, cell tel. 876/850-2449, eastcar@cwjamaica.com, www.lugan.com) has a Toyota Yaris (US$85 per day) or Corolla (US$75), Honda Accord (US$120), Toyota RAV4 (US$120), and Mitsubishi Gallant (US$120), Lancer (US$90), or Space Wagon (US$120). Longer-term rentals are discounted.

# Upper Rio Grande Valley

Nestled between the Blue Mountains and the John Crow Mountains are the culturally rich communities of the Upper Rio Grande Valley. These include the farming communities of Millbank and Bowden Pen and the Maroon community of Moore Town. Trails, including Cunha Cunha Pass, lead into the lush rainforest of the park and provide an opportunity to see the endangered giant swallowtail, the largest butterfly in the western hemisphere. The best way to get to know this area is by contacting the Maroon Council to learn from the people who have staked out this land as their own for centuries.

## ★ RAFTING THE RIO GRANDE

**Rio Grande Rafting** (tel. 876/993-5778, 9am-4pm daily, US$72 per raft) is a much-touted attraction operating along the banks of the wide and gentle Rio Grande. Eighty-three raft captains compete fiercely for clients, who enjoy the sedate relaxation of a 2.5-hour ride down the river on long bamboo rafts. To reach the start of the ride, take Breastworks Road from Port Antonio, keep right on Wayne Road in Breastworks past Fellowship, and keep right following the signs to Berridale. The raft ride ends in St. Margaret's Bay by the mouth of the river at Rafter's Rest. Transportation is not included in the cost of rafting. For Moore Town, take a left over the bridge at Fellowship Crossing.

Raft captains typically stop at Belinda's cook shop (US$5-10), which serves Jamaican staples such as fried chicken with rice n peas, curried *janga* (crayfish), and *bussu* (snail soup); you can order in advance when you book a trip.

## MOORE TOWN

The stronghold of Jamaica's Windward Maroons, led by Colonel Wallace Sterling since 1995, Moore Town is a quiet community located along the banks of the Rio Grande, about an hour's drive south of Port Antonio. Prior to the election of Colonel Sterling, the Moore Town Maroons were led by Colonel C. L. G. Harris from 1964, and before him Colonel Ernest Downer from 1952.

**Colonel Wallace Sterling** (cell tel. 876/898-5714, US$30 pp) can organize B&B-style homestays in the community, as well as hikes to Nanny Town (US$100 pp for guides, food, and shelter) farther up into the mountains, a two- to three-day hike round-trip. If you don't bring your own tent, guides will use materials from the bush to make shelter at night. Along the way you're likely to pick up a few basic Maroon words like *medysie* (thank you). If you are unable to reach Colonel Sterling, Moore Town Maroon **Council Secretary Charmaine Shackleford** (cell tel. 876/421-5919) can also help arrange homestay visits and guides.

The Maroons have maintained their customs throughout the years, as well as their language, a mix of West African tongues brought by enslaved people who belonged to the Ahanti, Fanti, Akan, Ibo, Yoruba, and Congo groups, among others.

### Sights

**Bump Grave** (donation) is the final resting place of Nanny, the legendary Maroon leader and Jamaica's first national heroine. It's the principal attraction in Moore Town; a plaque and monument recall her glorious leadership and victory over British forces that tried unsuccessfully to conquer the Maroons. Bump Grave is fenced off, but the gate can be opened by the caretaker of the school located across the road. Call to alert the Colonel (cell tel. 876/898-5714) or Maroon Council Secretary Charmaine Shackleford (cell tel. 876/421-5919) of your arrival to ensure someone is around to open the gate.

**Nanny Falls** is a small waterfall within an easy hour's walk from Moore Town. Ask any local to indicate where the trail starts, just above Nanny's grave. There is also an alternate longer route, about three hours round-trip, if you're looking for more of a workout. The Colonel can help arrange a guide (US$10).

At time of writing, the **Moore Town Maroon Cultural Center** is still in the conceptual stages, but there is adequate momentum from the Maroon Council and the Institute of Jamaica for the project to develop over the coming years. The concept is to establish a museum and cultural center for the exhibition and preservation of Maroon heritage. Young people will be taught to make and play drums and the *abeng,* a traditional Maroon horn used to communicate over great distances. The *abeng* is said to have struck fear into the hearts of the British, who were never able to conquer the Maroons. Craft items, toys, and a whole range of items considered the basis of the Maroon culture are also to be produced, and the center will have an adjoining gift shop and restaurant to accommodate visitors. "We are looking at a living thing rather than strictly an exhibition of the past," Colonel Sterling said about the project. The Maroon Council is currently working with UNESCO and the Institute of Jamaica in developing the plans and securing funding.

## Accommodations

**Ambassabeth Cabins** (Bowden Pen, contact Neresia "Collette" Hill, cell tel. 876/484-4406 or 876/462-8163, bpfa_ecotourism@yahoo.com, www.bpfaambassabeth.com, from US$70-90 for 2, US$25 for a tent that can sleep 8), owned and operated by the Bowden Pen Farmers Association, is the most remote option in the Rio Grande Valley, located above Millbank. The famous Cunha Cunha Pass Trail leaves from Ambassabeth, as does a trail leading to Bernard Spring Falls. The White River Trail, begins in nearby Millbank, leading to a series of cascades. An unmanned ranger station is maintained by Ambassabeth caretaker Lennette Wilks in Millbank, just over the border in St. Thomas, two miles before reaching Bowden Pen. The Quaco River sacred site and White River Falls are both nearby.

Ms. Wilks can arrange trail guides and meals as well as cultural entertainment. There are a total of nine cabins that can house up to 30 people. Cabins have bunk beds, single beds, and double beds with sheets, blankets, and towels. Insect repellent should be brought along. Most cabins have their own baths with hot water; for the cabin that doesn't, there's a communal bath outside, also with hot water. An indoor dining and recreation area offers traditional Jamaican breakfast with rundown, ackee, or vegetables (US$5-20).

Millbank is nestled between the Blue and John Crow Mountains, 27 kilometers (17 miles) up the river valley from Port Antonio; as an alternative to the route from the Rio Grande Valley, there is a well-established nine-kilometer (5.5-mile) trail from Hayfield, St. Thomas. Trained guides at Ambassabeth are knowledgeable about the local biodiversity and cultural history. The Cunha Cunha Pass Trail is over 500 years old and connects Portland and St. Thomas over the Blue Mountains, where a lookout point at Cunha Cunha offers spectacular views.

## Getting There and Around

**Barrett Adventures** (contact Carolyn Barrett, cell tel. 876/382-6384, www.barrettadventures.com) offers transportation to and from the Blue and John Crow Mountains, as well as a hiking expedition from the Portland side or from Kingston.

**Fisher Tours** (cell tel. 876/488-0319) is a local operator in Port Antonio led by Andre Thompson, who takes visitors on excursions throughout the parish and provides transfers across the island.

# West of Port Antonio

The road west of Port Antonio runs along the coast, cutting inland occasionally through several small towns, including St. Margaret's Bay, Hope Bay, and Buff Bay, before reaching the border with St. Mary just east of Annotto Bay. The region is characteristically lush with fruit vendors and intermittent roadside shops. Apart from Somerset Falls on the eastern edge of Hope Bay, the area is devoid of developed attractions, but the sparsely populated coastline itself is enticing; for the adventurous looking for secluded beaches, there are great opportunities for exploring around Orange Bay.

From Buff Bay, the B1 heads inland, climbing past Charles Town into the Blue Mountains, affording great views. This is the route on which Blue Mountain Bicycle Tours operates.

## ST. MARGARET'S BAY AND HOPE BAY

The quiet seaside village of St. Margaret's Bay is notable principally as the end point for the rafts coming down the Rio Grande. Hope's Bay is a short distance away.

**Likkle Porti** (contact manager Rose Stephens, cell tel. 876/403-7147, 10am-6pm daily, US$5-20), located across the street by the mouth of the Danny River, has a seafood grill serving roast, steamed, and fried fish, accompanied by bammy and festival in the style of Little Ochie, a South Coast favorite. There's bathing access to the river and sea, with rafting and boat rides offered (US$3).

Pauline Petinaud, aka **Sista P** (cell tel. 876/426-1957), recently moved her African-Jamaican **crafts shop** and guest house from Port Antonio to Hope Bay, where she rents two basic rooms with a common kitchen and bath for budget-minded travelers (US$30-40). Not to be confused with the politician with the same pet name, Sista P is an important figure behind the movement to celebrate the

African heritage inherent in Jamaican culture. Her craft shop sells African-inspired Jamaican items as well as a variety of African imports. She is best known for her founding role in the annual African heritage festival, Fi Wi Sinting, which translates as "something for us."

## Accommodations

★ **Rio Vista Resort Villas** (eastern bank of the Rio Grande, tel. 876/993-5444, riovistavillaja@jamweb.net, www.riovistajamaica.com, US$75-250) has two-bedroom cottages, a one-bedroom honeymoon cottage with a spectacular view up the Rio Grande (US$155), and four single rooms. To get here, turn right up the hill just around the corner after crossing the Rio Grande heading east. The Room with a View is perhaps the nicest cottage, with a private balcony overlooking the river and an inviting king bed. The property is run by Sharon, her son Chris, and his wife, Cyndi, who live on the property.

## CHARLES TOWN

Some five kilometers (3 miles) above Buff Bay along what used to be an old Maroon bridle path up the Buff Bay River (now known as the B1) is the Maroon community of Charles Town.

The **Maroon Museum** (free) located at **Asafu Yard** has artifacts and crafts of Maroon heritage. There's an adjoining commercial kitchen producing Jamaican cassava cakes, a gluten-free staple starch dating to the Taino and known locally as bammy.

The late Charles Town Maroon Colonel Frank Lumsden is succeeded by the **Maroon Council** (cell tel. 876/445-2861, www.maroons-jamaica.com), which welcomes visitors and leads community tours and hikes (US$20 pp) to Sambo Hill, the ruins of an 18th-century coffee plantation, Grandy Hole Cave, or Old Crawford Town, an old Maroon Village where Quao settled his people after the first Maroon War in 1739. The late colonel formed a group of drummers who perform Koromanti drumming and dance.

A country-style lunch (US$12 pp) of traditional dishes like crayfish rundown (not to be missed) and saltfish rundown accompanied by boiled green banana and ground provisions (yam, coco, dasheen, pumpkin) can be arranged at **Quao's Village,** a bit farther upstream, where Keith Lumsden (cell tel. 876/440-2200) manages a swimming hole and rustic restaurant attraction. The spot is named after Maroon warrior Captain Quao, the Invisible Hunter, who, alongside Jamaica's first national hero, Nanny of the Maroons, fought off the British to assert his people's autonomy from the colonists.

**Buff Bay police station** (9 1st Ave., tel. 876/996-1497) is located opposite the Adventist Church.

## Food

**G&B Jerk Centre** (contact Glen Ford or Kenroy Ford, cell tel. 876/859-5107, 10am-midnight daily) on the east side of town is the best spot for a roadside bite of jerk pork (US$14 per pound) or chicken (US$4 per quarter pound).

## Getting There and Around

Points between Port Antonio and Annotto Bay can be reached via **route taxi or microbus** for under US$5. Route taxis typically run between the closest population centers, and you will have to string together several legs for longer distances. Most route taxis also offer charter service, where rates are not regulated and have to be negotiated. A chartered car between Port Antonio and Hope Bay shouldn't cost more than US$20, with a chartered trip from Port Antonio to Buff Bay or Charles Town costing around US$50 for two people.

# East of Port Antonio

The region east of Port Antonio is dominated by the eastern ridges of the Blue and John Crow Mountains, which run northwest to southeast and taper down to the coast near Hector's River. The John Crow Mountains are some of the least visited territory on the island, and even the coast in the area, which varies from fine sandy beaches to windswept bluffs, sees few visitors. A few minutes' drive east of Port Antonio, Boston is a quiet community said to be the original home of jerk. Long Bay is the area most sought after by visitors, although it has only a handful of budget and mid-range accommodations serving the trickle of backpackers and adventurous travelers who come to enjoy the undeveloped Long Bay Beach, nearby Reach Falls, and a quieter side of Jamaica.

## FRENCHMAN'S COVE

**Frenchman's Cove** (US$10) has a meandering river emptying into a wide beach with formidable surf. The beach is well protected and drops off steeply after the first 20 meters (65 feet).

## SAN SAN BEACH

**San San Beach** (10am-4pm daily, US$10) is located at the base of San San Hill, where many of the area's most luxurious villas are found. The fine-sand beach hugs a cove next to Alligator Head and facing Pellew Island. The reef around Pellew Island is in decent shape, with plentiful small fish, brain coral, and fan coral, and extends eastward to the mouth of Blue Hole.

## ★ BLUE HOLE

**Blue Hole** is also commonly known as the **Blue Lagoon** thanks to a 1980 Randal Kleiser film of that name starring Brooke Shields. This Blue Lagoon has no relation to the film, though locals erroneously make the connection. Portland's Blue Hole is Jamaica's largest

# East of Port Antonio

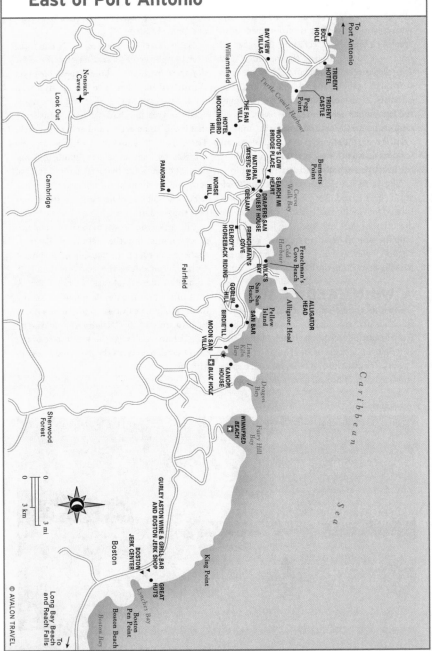

© AVALON TRAVEL

underground spring-fed lagoon. The Blue Lagoon is in a 55-meter-deep protected cove along the coast, where warm tidal waters mix with freshwater welling up from the depths, creating a blurring effect as the two meet. At one time, Robin Moore, the author of *The French Connection,* owned much of the land surrounding the lagoon; today his cottages lie in ruins. A restaurant and bar overhanging the lagoon has been closed for several years. Unfortunately the natural gem is still unmanaged, leaving the environs to a handful of craft vendors insistently hawking their goods along the beach to anybody who arrives for a dip.

Blue Hole is located east of San San Beach and Pellew Island, just past the well-marked turnoff for Goblin Hill heading east. From the direction of Port Antonio, stay left and turn onto the lane off the main road along the Blue Lagoon Villas, and continue down to a small parking area along the beach.

## ★ WINNIFRED BEACH

Known as the people's beach, **Winnifred Beach** is in a wide, shallow, white-sand cove. It is a beautiful, free public beach in the Fairy Hill district just east of San San and the Blue Lagoon. It's also the best place for conch soup and fried fish. Food and beverages are sold by a slew of vendors, and there's a nice restaurant, **Cynthia's,** on the western end of the beach, serving excellent fried fish with rice-and-peas (US$10).

Named after the daughter of Quaker minister F. B. Brown as a resting place for missionaries, teachers, and the respectable poor, Winnifred has remained decidedly local, thanks perhaps to the trust that once managed the area that had provisions ensuring that locals could access and enjoy the beach. The Urban Development Corporation now controls the land, but local resistance to development has ensured that it remains a local hot spot. Inevitably someone will ask for a "contribution," but it's not necessary. Instead, support the vendors.

The rocky road down to the beach has two access points from the main road. The best route goes through the housing development on the ocean side of the road less than 0.75 kilometers (0.5 miles) east of Dragon Bay. A turn into a housing development across the road from Jamaica Crest, followed by a quick right in front of the "Neighborhood Watch" sign, allows you avoid the worst part of the road that descends off the main road next to Mikuzi.

Winnifred Beach

# BOSTON

Boston was bustling in the early years of the banana trade, when it took the name of the North American city that made it prosperous for a brief period. Boston is the alleged origin of jerk seasoning, but the **Boston Jerk Center** that claims this fame has become overrun with hustlers unmindful of the fact that their harassment has damaged the area's reputation. The jerk center is easily recognizable on the western edge of the community of Boston Bay, just before crossing a bridge and going over a rise in the road heading toward Port Antonio. **Max** (cell tel. 876/435-3013) operates one of the newer stalls and is a good bet where integrity is concerned. Many vendors will insist you buy their "noni juice," said to have aphrodisiacal properties and to improve overall performance; others will simply beg for money.

Beyond the annoyance, there are also serious inconsistencies in the quality and pricing of food at Boston Jerk Center. Weekends, when it gets busier, are the best time to go if you must eat here, as during the week the meat can sit on the grill until it goes cold. Fish is also served, but this is not the best place for it. If you do order fish, size it and understand what you will pay before it gets cooked.

The best time to eat jerk is during the annual Portland Jerk Festival (July) when the multitudes don't let the meat sit around for long. Based in Boston in years past, the festival relocated recently to Port Antonio's Folly Oval.

## ★ Boston Beach

**Boston Beach** (free) is on a picturesque cove with turquoise waters that sees more local than foreign visitors, especially on weekends. Boston Bay can have a decent swell suitable for surfing and is the only place around where you can rent boogie boards and surfboards.

## Food and Accommodations

★ **Gurley Aston Wine & Grill Bar and Boston Jerk Stop** (Boston Bay, cell tel. 876/849-7853 or 876/778-4265, be.rhone@ yahoo.com, 10am-10pm Sun.-Thurs., 10am-midnight Fri.-Sat.) serves savory jerk chicken and pork and fresh seafood in a hassle-free environment.

**Great Huts** (8-10 Boston Bay, at the end of the lane that begins at the Jerk Center, cell tel. 876/353-3388 or 876/993-8888, www. greathuts.com, US$60-400 d) is a stylishly rustic option in the heart of Boston, offering Bedouin-style tents, breezy cottages, and tree houses made of wood, bamboo, zinc, and

Boards rent by the day at Boston Beach.

canvas, recreating an African-Amerindian village vibe. Fabrics and masks cover doorways and walls. Modern amenities like fans, mosquito nets, mini-fridges and plumbing accent the open-air environment. Owner Paul Rhodes has been known to kick off the weekly cultural show on Saturday evening by serenading guests with the Israeli national anthem and lounge classics from the 1950s, before Kumino-inspired drummers and dancers recount Jamaican history from the plantation to the dance hall with energetic rhythms and sensual movements. Royal Hut is the best room, with a stunning view of Boston Bay from the queen bed and bathtub. African Sunrise has panoramic views out to sea in cozy quarters up two flights of ladders. Sea Grape is roomy and has a private cliff-top bathtub. The property is not for the physically challenged; loose stone pathways and stairs abound. Wi-Fi is available in the central building, where basic meals are served. A simple breakfast is included.

## LONG BAY

Long Bay is a sleepy fishing village. A few low-key lodgings have sprung up over the past decade, serving a trickle of off-the-beaten-track travelers.

## ★ Long Bay Beach

Long Bay Beach is one of the most picturesque and unspoiled beaches in Jamaica. The beach is also known for its occasional swell and draws surfers from nearby Boston Bay as well as the die-hard Mystic crew from Jamnesia in Bull Bay, St. Andrew. It's also known to have dangerous riptides; caution is always advised.

### Food

★ **La Familia Restaurant** (Pen Lane, tel. 876/913-7843, cell tel. 876/892-2195, lafamiliajamaica@gmail.com, by reservation only, US$10-25), run by Enrico Vicari and Suna Gatti, transplants from Bologna, serves the best lasagna, tagliatelle, and ceviche. Pizza and bread are baked in a conventional gas oven.

**Chill Out Bar & Restaurant** (contact Maxine, cell tel. 876/452-1812, ptomptom@yahoo.com, 10am-10pm daily, US$5-30) is a popular spot on Long Bay Beach for a bite or a drink. Chill Out hosts dances on special occasions. Local dishes include stewed or baked chicken, and there are vegetarian meals like steam cabbage, seafood, hamburgers, and pizzas. Jamaican breakfast of ackee and saltfish as well as omelets are served.

**Cliffhanger Restaurant & Lounge**

The accommodations at Great Huts are rustic and close to nature.

(Ross Craig, Kensington District, Portland, cell tel. 876/869-5931, cliffhanger.seacliff@gmail.com, 5 kilometers/3 miles southeast of Long Bay, noon-9pm Mon.-Thurs., noon-10pm Fri.-Sun., US$11-50) serves seafood, specializing in lionfish five different ways, with wine and beer, escoveitch, coconut sauce, curried, and jerk. Oxtail, curried goat, fried and stewed chicken, and vegan fare are served.

## Accommodations

**La Familia Resort and Restaurant** (Pen Lane, tel. 876/913-7843, cell tel. 876/892-2195, lafamiliajamaica@gmail.com) has six basic rooms, three with a shared bath (US$30), three with private baths (US$40), and a small apartment (US$60) with a private bath. Enrico is a promoter and selector of Vinyl Club Jamaica and hosts Vinyl Sunday in front of Natural Mystic Bar in Drapers.

**Seadream Villa** (contact David Escoe, tel. 876/890-7661, vwaterhous@aol.com, www.jamaican-escape.com, US$60-100) offers basic accommodations right in the middle of Long Bay Beach. The villa has three bedrooms, two downstairs and one upstairs, accommodating up to eight people in total. Three full baths have hot water. There's cable TV and a CD player in the living room, and Wi-Fi covers the whole house.

★ **Pimento Lodge Hideaway Resort** (tel. 876/913-7982, cell tel. 876/533-5860 or 876/882-5068, www.pimentolodge.com, from US$155) has three room categories with four-poster king and bamboo frame beds, louvered windows, and breezy verandas. Lloyd Edwards returned from an engineering career in England to launch Pimento Lodge in 2012. Nonguests can make reservations to dine at the property.

**Seacliff Resort & Spa** (Ross Craig, Kensington District, Portland, cell tel. 876/860-1395, pscresort@gmail.com, from US$160, includes breakfast) is a three-story boutique hotel about five minutes east of Long Bay. The property sits at the top of a cliff overlooking the sea 24 meters (80 feet) above the crashing waves. The rooms all have private baths, hot water, cable TV, Wi-Fi, and ocean views.

## ★ REACH FALLS

**Reach Falls** (tel. 876/993-6606 or 876/993-6683, www.reachfalls.com, 8:30am-4:30pm Wed.-Sun., US$10 adults, US$5 under age 12), or Reich Falls, as it's sometimes spelled, is located in a beautiful river valley

Reach Falls

in the lower northeast foothills of the John Crow Mountains. The river cascades down a long series of falls that can be climbed from the base far below the main pool where the developed attraction is based. Start at the bottom and continue far above the main pool to get the full exhilarating experience. To climb the full length requires about two hours, but if you stop to enjoy each little pool, it could easily consume all day. A dirt road about one kilometer (0.6 miles) before the parking area leads down to the base of the falls.

To get to Reach Falls, head inland by a set of shacks just east of Manchioneel, up a picturesque winding road. A large sign for "Reach Falls" marks the turnoff. Unofficial guides often congregate at a fork in the road, where you stay left to get to the falls. The guides are in fact indispensable when it comes to climbing the falls, as they know every rock along the riverbed, which is quite slippery in places. As always, get a sense of what your guide will expect for the service up front: US$10 pp is the going rate. Leonard "Sendon" Welsh (cell tel. 876/488-0661) is a recommended seasoned guide and great company.

The government's lease on the property extends from a little below the main pool to a little above it, and unofficial guides will be turned away from the main waterfalls area on either side of the leased land. **Mandingo Cave,** which is found farther up the river, is not currently part of the official tour offered but can visited with local guides.

# Morant Bay

St. Thomas parish holds an important place in Jamaican history. In the early colonial period, its mountainous terrain provided sanctuary to the enslaved people who escaped and formed the Maroon settlements of eastern Jamaica. Later, it became an important sugar- and banana-producing region under British rule. When slavery was abolished but the formerly enslaved were not permitted advancement in society, the parish erupted in a rebellion that gave birth to Jamaica's labor rights movement.

At the center of what was once some of Jamaica's prime sugarcane land, Morant Bay is a laid-back town with little action beyond the central market. Between Morant Bay and Port Morant, 11 kilometers (7 miles) to the east, there are a couple of basic lodging options that make a convenient base for exploring the seldom visited rivers and valleys that cut across the southern slopes of the Blue Mountains, as well as the isolated beaches and Great Morass on Jamaica's easternmost tip.

## REACH FALLS TO PORT MORANT

**Holland Bay** is an isolated cove tucked into the northeast corner of Duckenfield, an active sugarcane plantation that occupies the easternmost land in Jamaica. The desolate beach is heavily littered but beautiful nonetheless with fine white sand and crashing waves. To get here, head straight east from the village of Golden Grove through the Duckenfield Sugar Plantation. A 4WD vehicle is essential in the rainy season, but otherwise not needed.

**Morant Point Lighthouse** can be reached by continuing past Holland Beach. It stands at Jamaica's easternmost point. Cast of iron in London, the 30-meter-tall (100-foot) lighthouse was erected in 1841 by Kru people, indentured African workers brought to Jamaica in the post-emancipation period.

Built by Luke Stokes, a former governor of the island of Nevis, **Stokes Hall Great House** is located near Golden Grove. Stokes came to Jamaica shortly after the conquest of the island by the British. Like many of the early houses, it was built in a strategic location and was securely fortified. The great house was destroyed in the 1907 earthquake and today stands in ruin. It is currently owned by the Jamaica National Heritage Trust but is not managed. Turn south at the main intersection in Golden Grove and follow the main road past a high school until you reach an overgrown access road to Stokes Hall on the right. It is unmarked, so you may have to ask a local if you get lost.

Overgrown and forgotten, **Port Morant** once busily exported barrels of sugar, rum, and bananas. Today there is an oyster operation on the eastern side of the harbor bordering the mangroves. The oyster-growing zone, which reaches down to Bowden across the bay, is protected from fishing and serves as a spawning area. Several people keep their fishing boats on the waterfront and can be contracted to tour the mangroves and visit the lighthouse on Point Morant.

# BATH

The town of Bath was erected using government resources and had a brief glamorous history as a fashionable second-home community for the island's elite. The splendor was short-lived, however, and the town quickly declined to become a backwater—as it remains today.

## ★ Bath Hot Springs

The hot springs are located 50 meters (165 feet) north of the **Bath Hotel and Spa** (tel. 876/703-4345, US$50-70, including private bath sessions twice a day), which is about three kilometers (2 miles) up a precariously narrow, winding road north of the town of Bath. An easy-to-follow path leads to the springs, where water comes out from the rocks piping hot on one side and cold on the other. There are massage therapists on hand who use wet towels to give an exhilarating albeit exorbitantly priced treatment (typically around US$14). These masseurs are either lauded or despised by visitors and can be quite aggressive in offering their services from below the gate of the hotel. Their technique involves slopping hot towels over the backs of their subjects.

**Bath Mineral Spring,** formally called The Bath of St. Thomas the Apostle, was discovered by the runaway slave Jacob in 1695 on the estate of his master, Colonel Stanton. Jacob found that the warm waters of the spring healed leg ulcers that had plagued him for years; he braved possible punishment to return to the plantation to relate his discovery to Stanton. In 1699 the spring and surrounding land were sold to the government, and in 1731 the area was developed and a small town was built.

The Bath Hotel and Spa has traditional Turkish-style tiled tubs, as well as more modern whirlpool tubs. There are three rates for nonguests, depending on how many are enjoying the tub: US$5 for one person, US$8 for two, or US$12 for three. All rates are for 20-minute intervals.

The hotel has an on-site restaurant open from 8:30am-5:30pm. Meals (US$8.50-10) are served throughout the day and range from rotisserie chicken to curried shrimp.

## Bath Botanical Garden

**Bath Botanical Garden** was established by the government in 1779 and is the second-oldest garden of its kind in the western hemisphere (one in St. Vincent dates from 1765). The garden retains little of its former glory as a propagation site for many of Jamaica's most important introduced plants, including jackfruit, breadfruit, cinnamon, bougainvillea, and croton. A stand of royal palms lines the road by the entrance, and a two-century-old *Barringtonia* graces the derelict grounds.

From the western side of Bath, a road runs north to Hayfield, where a well-maintained 8.8-kilometer (5.5-mile) trail provides an alternate route over the John Crow to the Rio Grande Valley. If you're heading to Portland, head east along the Plantain Garden River to where the main road east of Bath hits the A4, a few kilometers west of Amity Hall.

## Food and Accommodations

★ **Longboarder Bar & Grill** (Roselle, cell tel. 876/427-0408, thelongboarderja@gmail.

# Paul Bogle and the Morant Bay Rebellion

In 1864, Paul Bogle was the founding deacon at the Native Baptist Church in Stony Gut, St. Thomas, a village at the base of the Blue Mountains about eight kilometers (5 miles) inland from Morant Bay. African elements similar to those found in Revival were strong, and a black pride ethos was a central doctrine. Baptist churches throughout Jamaica provided an alternate philosophy to the Anglican Church, descended from the Church of England and for the most part representative of the suppressive mandate of the white planter class and government. Bogle used the church as a base to gather support for a militant resistance movement, similar to that envisioned by Sam Sharpe in the Christmas rebellion 34 years earlier, in that violence was not the intended means.

Bogle lived in the post-emancipation period, when most people were denied voting rights, justice, and civil rights. As a landowner of mixed race, he was one of 106 people in the parish allowed a vote. The years leading up to the Morant Bay Rebellion coincided with the U.S. Civil War (1861-1865), which complicated the economy of Jamaica. Local food shortages owing to floods and drought, combined with a slump in imports from the fragmented United States, created a mood in Jamaica rife with discontent. While the white ruling class controlled both the legislature and the economy, the poor felt subjugated and left to fend for themselves. Petty crime rooted in widespread poverty and social decay was severely punished by local authorities representing the landowners.

Governor Edward Eyre blamed the condition of the poor on laziness and apathy, while Baptist Missionary Society secretary Edward Underhill sent a letter to the British Secretary of State for the Colonies outlining concerns about poverty and distress among the poor black population. The so-called Underhill Letter spurred a series of civic meetings known as the Underhill Meetings, which provided a public forum for the poor to voice their discontent. Legislator George William Gordon, also of mixed race and Bogle's comrade both in the church and in politics, led several such well-attended meetings in Kingston and elsewhere, in which he criticized the colonial government.

On October 7, 1865, Bogle and some followers staged a protest at the Morant Bay courthouse, disputing severe judgments made on that particular day. When a standoff with the police came to blows, arrest warrants were issued against 28 of the protesters, including Bogle. After the police were deterred from arresting Bogle by a large crowd of his followers in Stony Gut, they returned to Morant Bay and told the *custos rotulorum* (chief magistrate) of Bogle's plans to disrupt a meet-

com, www.makkasurf.com, kitchen noon-8pm Tues.-Thurs., noon-9pm Fri.-Sun., US$8-25) serves fresh snapper, lobster, and burgers beachfront on a quiet surfing beach in Roselle, St. Thomas, between White Horses and Morant Bay. A couple of surfboards (US$25 per day) are available to rent.

**Whispering Bamboo Cove Resort** (105 Crystal Drive Retreat, 7 minutes east of Morant Bay, tel. 876/982-2912 or 876/982-1788, whispering@cwjamaica.com, US$55-100 d) is a decent option with 15 rooms, run by Marcia Bennett. Rooms have cable TV, private baths with hot water, and air-conditioning. Wi-Fi covers the property. Food is prepared to order and served in the dining room.

## WEST OF MORANT BAY

The road west of Morant Bay toward Kingston hugs the coast, passing through dusty communities where jerk vendors and a few shops mark the centers of the action. This is an area most people just pass through. There are a few notable stops, however, but few lodging options before reaching Bull Bay in St. Andrew.

### White Horses

Just east of White Horses is **Roselle Falls,** where locals often congregate to wash or cool off. The small cascade is right next to the main road (the A4). **Reggae Falls,** formed by a reservoir along the Morant River, is an unmanaged attraction with a deep pool at the bottom of the dam where you can swim ing of the Vestry on October 11. The *custos* asked the governor for assistance and called out the local volunteer militia. The next day, Bogle and 400 followers confronted the militia in Morant Bay; during the ensuing violence, the courthouse was burned and the *custos* was killed, along with 18 deputies and militiamen. Seven of Bogle's men were also killed in the fighting, which quickly spread through the parish. Several white planters were killed, kidnapped, or injured. As the news spread through the island, fear of a general uprising grew, prompting Governor Eyre to declare martial law and dispatch soldiers from Kingston and Newcastle. The Windward Maroons were also armed after offering their services, and they ultimately captured Bogle, bringing him to a swift trial and death sentence in Morant Bay. Gordon was also implicated in the rebellion, taken to Morant Bay, and hanged. Martial law lasted over a month, during which time hundreds were killed by soldiers or executed by court martial, and over 1,000 houses were burned by government forces. Little regard was given to differentiating innocent from guilty, augmenting a general sense of fear in St. Thomas and around the island.

The Morant Bay Rebellion pushed Britain to discuss the blatant injustices in its colony. Governor Eyre was ultimately removed from his post for excessive use of force, while the British Parliament debated whether he was a murderer or a hero. Many sought to indict him on murder charges for the execution of Gordon, but others, including the Anglican clergy, supported his actions as a necessary means to uphold the control of the Crown. Meanwhile, the Jamaica House of Assembly, which had operated as an independent legislative body since 1655, was dissolved, and Jamaica became a crown colony under the direct rule of England. In the following years, the colonial rulers ushered in more egalitarian measures that lessened the power exerted by the landed elite for centuries.

Paul Bogle and George William Gordon were considered troublemakers and virtually expelled from the national psyche through the remainder of the colonial period. At independence their memory was rekindled as Jamaica began to come to terms with its past and contemplate its identity. At the 100th anniversary of the Morant Bay Rebellion, Bogle and Gordon were featured prominently, and were declared national heroes in 1969. Today the rebellion is remembered during National Heritage Week and Heroes Weekend, which coincides with the anniversary of the uprising, the second week in October.

behind the waterfalls and are likely to have the place to yourself.

To get to Reggae Falls, turn left at the roundabout immediately after crossing the Morant River heading east. Head north inland passing Bogle High School until reaching the community of Hillside, where you can park and walk approximately two kilometers to the base of the dam.

The **Ethiopian Zion Coptic Church** (services Sat.) has its headquarters at Crighton Hall in White Horses just before reaching Yallahs, where it sits on more than 600 hectares (1,480 acres) of land. To get here, turn inland off the main road (the A4) by a set of fruit vendors in the middle of White Horses. Coptic Road is on the left, marked with a sign. Said to have 20 million members, the church

originated in Ethiopia, where it was the state church for ages. A large tablet that dates from 1738, written in Old English, was found during excavations and is on display. Many of Jamaica's roots reggae artists have attended the Ethiopian Zion Coptic Church. The White Horses Kumina Group, Upliftment, hosts cultural and sports events in the community on a regular basis.

## Yallahs

Sixteen kilometers (10 miles) west of Morant Bay, large **salt ponds** can be seen along the coast marking the approach to Yallahs. These ponds were once used as a source for salt and are home to brine shrimp and yellow butterflies. The name Yallahs is derived from the surname of a Spanish family that settled here

PORT ANTONIO AND THE EAST COAST
MORANT BAY

to raise cattle on a ranch known as Hato de Ayala. The road inland from the center of Yallahs leads up along the river to Bethel Gap, and from there deeper into the mountains, ultimately reaching Hagley Gap on a poor road traversable only by 4WD vehicle.

Eleven kilometers (7 miles) north of Yallahs across the river from Easington is **Judgment Cliff,** which collapsed during the 1692 earthquake—burying an entire valley, it is said, in judgment of the Dutchman who mistreated the enslaved people on his plantation. In any case, judgment was not justice, and most of the slaves died alongside him under the weight of a small mountain.

About 1.5 kilometers (1 mile) west of Yallahs, the broad, washed-out **Yallahs River** overflows during periods of heavy rain and dries completely for much of the year near its mouth due to the dry gravelly soil along its bed. At 37 kilometers (23 miles) from its source to the sea, it's one of Jamaica's longest rivers, starting at 1,371 meters (4,498 feet) elevation and running down the southern slopes of the Blue Mountains. Bridges built across the Yallahs have a tendency to disappear during hurricanes and are routinely replaced. For most of the year the riverbed near its mouth can be forded with no sign of water. The Yallahs River feeds the Mona Reservoir next to the University of the West Indies via an aboveground pipe. Along with the Hope River, it is a major water source for the Kingston metropolitan area. There are decent beaches around Yallahs: Bailey's Beach to the east and Flemarie Beach just west of town.

West of Yallahs, just shy of the St. Andrew border, Eleven Mile is a small community known as the old stomping ground of legendary Jack Mansong, aka "Three-Finger Jack." A runaway slave, Three-Finger Jack became a bandit who took justice into his own hands in the vein of a Jamaican Robin Hood. He wreaked terror on the plantocracy and tried to kill a slave trader before ultimately being captured by Maroon leader Quashie, who carried his head to Spanish Town to collect the reward.

## Getting There and Around

Points between Kingston and Morant Bay along the coast are served by JUTC buses departing from the Transport Centre in Half Way Tree for around US$1. For points farther east or around the coast, a private driver or route taxis are necessary. Taxis and small buses depart from the square in Morant Bay for Bath and Manchioneel as they fill up, costing less than US$5.

# Kingston and the Blue Mountains

Look for ★ to find recommended
sights, activities, dining, and lodging.

# Highlights

★ **Tuff Gong Recording Studio:** Bob
Marley's production base offers a tour that
includes a visit to the studio, record-printing
shop, gallery, and herb garden (page 190).

★ **National Gallery:** At the crown jewel
of the Institute of Jamaica, visitors can view
Jamaican art from its roots to the present day
(page 193).

★ **Devon House:** Take a tour of George
Stiebel's former home, one of the finest estates in
Kingston. The home fronts an array of boutique
shops and restaurants (page 198).

★ **Bob Marley Museum:** The spirit of
Jamaica's most revered son has been preserved
at 56 Hope Road, his former residence (page
198).

★ **Hope Gardens and Zoo:** Kingston's
largest green space contains a meticulously
maintained Chinese garden and recently renovated zoo (page 199).

★ **Lime Cay:** Once a haven for buccaneers,
this idyllic beach comes alive on weekends
with locals, sound systems, and fried fish (page
233).

★ **Hellshire:** An assortment of fried fish and
lobster shacks crowd this popular weekend spot.
Spend an afternoon swimming and relishing
the rustic chic scenery with Kingstonians (page
240).

★ **Old Tavern Coffee Estate:** It stands out
as one of the most spectacular coffee estates
in Jamaica for its location and the quality of its
beans (page 244).

★ **Blue Mountain Peak:** Hikers typically set
out early to be at the top for sunrise, and they're
rewarded with Jamaica's best view (page 252).

# Kingston is the heartbeat of Jamaica, a city teeming with excitement, driving the island's culture and economy.

Arts and entertainment play an important role in everyday life, with more recording studios and self-proclaimed artistes per capita than in any other city on earth. Art galleries abound, and theaters fill to capacity for Jamaica's unique brand of outrageous slapstick comedy. Hardly a week goes by without an internationally acclaimed reggae singer hosting a concert to celebrate a birthday or album launch. Bars and nightclubs throb with pounding bass, and dances routinely take to the street; a car wash, parking lot, or tenement yard turns into a dance hall somewhere in the city on any given night.

Only a small fraction of leisure travelers visit Kingston, and the populace goes about its business refreshingly indifferent to tourism. Those who do visit tend to be devotees of Bob Marley, drawn to the museum and other sights. Through the year, the capital city celebrates food, visual and performing arts, carnival, and national pride, with events spanning days, weeks, or entire months. There's plenty to do in Kingston even when there's no major event on the calendar.

While much of Kingston is crowded with uninspiring architecture, Georgian gems dot the urban sprawl, and greenery is everywhere. The foothills of the Blue Mountains hold the city in a semicircular embrace, and nothing beats the higher elevations for respite from the heat and bustle. The serene vistas and the diverse wild- and plantlife are good reasons to take on the winding, potholed roads. Looking out over the city at sunset, it's easy to be overcome with the same vibes that led Buju Banton to sing, "magic city, magic lights, magic moments, magical heights."

## PLANNING YOUR TIME

All the important historical and cultural sites can be seen in a rush with two days in Kingston. A longer stay is in order if you want to adopt the local pace and fully enjoy all the sights, food, and nightlife the city has to offer.

Most of the historical sights downtown can be seen in one day. Attractions uptown are conveniently concentrated in New Kingston, Half Way Tree, and along Hope Road, and will consume another day if you wish to fit in **Devon House, Bob Marley Museum,** and **Hope Gardens,** with a little shopping

**Previous:** sunrise from Blue Mountain Peak; jamming at Chinna Smith's home. **Above:** walking the runway at Caribbean Fashion Week.

# Kingston and Vicinity

© AVALON TRAVEL

To Colbeck Castle

Old Harbour

Gutters

Hartlands

Gallion Harbour

Salt Island Lagoon

Old House Point

Two Sisters Cave

HELLSHIRE

Hellshire Beach

SHORTY'S

PRENDY'S ON THE BEACH

THE BOARDWALK

Fort Clarence Beach

Waves Beach

Drunken Man's Cay

Great Salt Pond

GRAND PORT ROYAL HOTEL MARINA & SPA

OLD NAVAL HOSPITAL

FORT CHARLES

GLORIA'S (BOTTOM)

Pebble Beach

Port Royal

GLORIA'S (TOP)

XKNOT

The Palisadoes

Lime Cay

South Cay

Maiden Cay

LIME CAY

Caribbean Sea

LITTLE COPA

JAMNESIA

Bull Bay

Cane River Falls

To Bobo Hill and St. Thomas

BOBO HILL

John Crow Peak 5,750ft

SEE "THE BLUE AND JOHN CROW MOUNTAINS" MAP

OLD TAVERN COFFEE ESTATE

Newcastle

B1

Stony Hill

MAJESTIC SUSHI & GRILL

NETTA'S NEST

BOB MARLEY MUSEUM

DEVON HOUSE

HOPE GARDENS AND ZOO

SEE "METROPOLITAN KINGSTON" MAP

NATIONAL GALLERY

KINGSTON

Kingston Harbour

ROYAL JAMAICA YACHT CLUB

Hunts Bay

PORTMORE

Central Village

MUNICIPAL BLVD

Caymanas Park

TUFF GONG RECORDING STUDIO

MANDELA HWY

WASHINGTON BLVD

DYKE RD

WINDWARD RD

A4

A1

A3

A2

A2

B2

Linstead

T3

A1

Rock Hall

Sligoville

Bog Walk

ST. JOHNS RD

Spanish Town

T3

SEE "SPANISH TOWN" MAP

CAYMANAS GOLF & COUNTRY CLUB

KINGSTON POLO CLUB

RED HILLS RD

ST. JOHN'S ANGLICAN CHURCH

MOUNTAIN RIVER CAVE

N

0       5 km
0       5 mi

Bull Bay

and eating in between. The noteworthy attractions in Spanish Town can all be seen in a few hours and combine well with an afternoon at the beach in Hellshire or Fort Clarence.

Kingston's nightlife heats up on the weekends, with stage shows and parties held almost weekly at one venue or another, but there are worthwhile "sessions" almost every night of the week, and the most popular street dances are held on weeknights. Theater performances are held several nights a week. It's worth calling ahead when planning a visit if you want to catch a theater or dance performance.

A few days in Kingston sets the stage for a nice break in the Blue Mountains. All the accommodations in the Blue Mountains can help arrange transportation to and from town; once there, hiking trails abound, and hummingbirds flit on the cool mountain air. At least a couple of nights should be allocated to the Blue Mountains, especially for serious hikers, birders, or coffee connoisseurs.

## ORIENTATION

The parish of Kingston encompasses what is referred to as Downtown, as well as the Palisadoes, a 16-kilometer-long (10-mile) thin strip of land that runs from the roundabout at Harbour View to the tip of Port Royal.

Metropolitan Kingston is often referred to as the Corporate Area and is divided into two regions, referred to by Kingstonians as Uptown and Downtown. The junction at **Cross Roads** forms a dividing line between Downtown and Uptown.

**Downtown Kingston** comprises the old city, which was originally laid out in a grid bound by Harbour, North, East, and West Streets. The city soon overgrew these boundaries with ramshackle residential neighborhoods springing up on every side. Over the years, some of these areas have seen zinc shacks replaced by homes of better stature, as well as government sponsored low income apartments and row houses. Most of the buildings in the area below **St. William Grant Park,** or the **Parade,** as it is known, are commercial, with limited middle-income

housing in high-rise buildings near the waterfront.

**Uptown Kingston** is actually in St. Andrew parish and includes most of the bustling areas of town. Uptown is more of an urban and suburban sprawl with little order, the result of more recent economic development. The two most developed commercial areas are the hubs of **New Kingston,** immediately north of Cross Roads, and **Half Way Tree,** just east of New Kingston. **Hope Road,** where several businesses and sights are located, runs east from Half Way Tree Square, before becoming Old Hope Road in Liguanea and ending at the square in **Papine** on the eastern edge of town.

Half Way Tree Road is also a major thoroughfare; it starts at Cross Roads, turning into **Constant Spring Road** north of Half Way Tree Square, and runs to the northernmost edge of town, where it becomes **Stony Hill Road,** and later turns into the **A3,** leading to St. Mary parish and the North Coast via the town of Junction.

The Blue Mountain foothills flank the entire city, forming a constant backdrop. Along with a handful of high-rises in New Kingston, the hills provide the best natural landmarks for orientation in the city. Kingston's most affluent residential neighborhoods hug the hills.

From Papine, the **B1,** a narrow winding road that often becomes impassable on the descent due to landslides, leads into and over the **Blue Mountains.**

## SAFETY

Kingston is a city of nearly one million people, the vast majority living in poverty. Keep in mind that people will say and do just about anything that gives them the opportunity to eat. While some may use physical intimidation to get what they want, a more common occurrence is for someone to pretend to know you or yell aggressively from across the street, "Come here!" When you get the feeling that an advance of this sort may lead to an uncomfortable situation, go with that instinct. It helps to keep petty cash on hand to

# Metropolitan Kingston

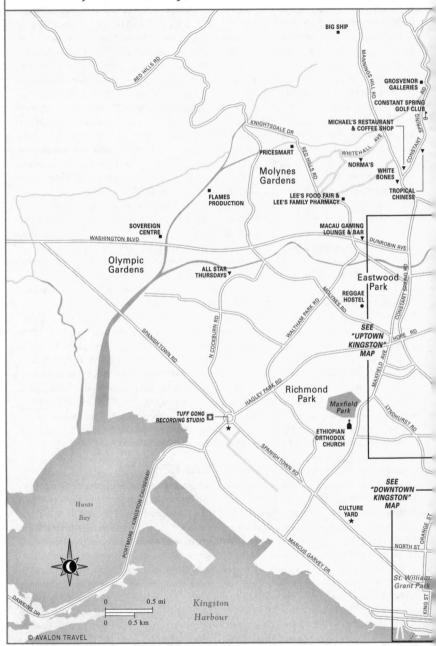

BIG SHIP

RED HILLS RD

MANNINGS HILL RD

GROSVENOR
GALLERIES

CONSTANT SPRING
GOLF CLUB

CONSTANT SPRING RD

MICHAEL'S RESTAURANT
& COFFEE SHOP

KNIGHTSDALE DR

PRICESMART

RED HILLS RD

WHITE HALL AVE

NORMA'S

WHITE
BONES

Molynes
Gardens

LEE'S FOOD FAIR &
LEE'S FAMILY PHARMACY

TROPICAL
CHINESE

FLAMES
PRODUCTION

MACAU GAMING
LOUNGE & BAR

SOVEREIGN
CENTRE

WASHINGTON BLVD

DUNROBIN AVE

Olympic
Gardens

ALL STAR
THURSDAYS

Eastwood
Park

CONSTANT SPRING RD

N COCKBURN RD

WALTHAM PARK RD

MOLYNES RD

REGGAE
HOSTEL

SPANISH TOWN RD

SEE
"UPTOWN
KINGSTON"
MAP

HOPE RD

MAXFIELD AVE

HAGLEY PARK RD

Richmond
Park

Maxfield
Park

LYNDHURST RD

TUFF GONG
RECORDING STUDIO

ETHIOPIAN
ORTHODOX
CHURCH

SPANISH TOWN RD

SEE
"DOWNTOWN
KINGSTON"
MAP

Hunts
Bay

PORTMORE – KINGSTON CAUSEWAY

CULTURE
YARD

NORTH ST

ORANGE ST

St. William
Grant Park

MARCUS GARVEY DR

KING ST

DAWKINS DR

0        0.5 mi

0        0.5 km

Kingston
Harbour

© AVALON TRAVEL

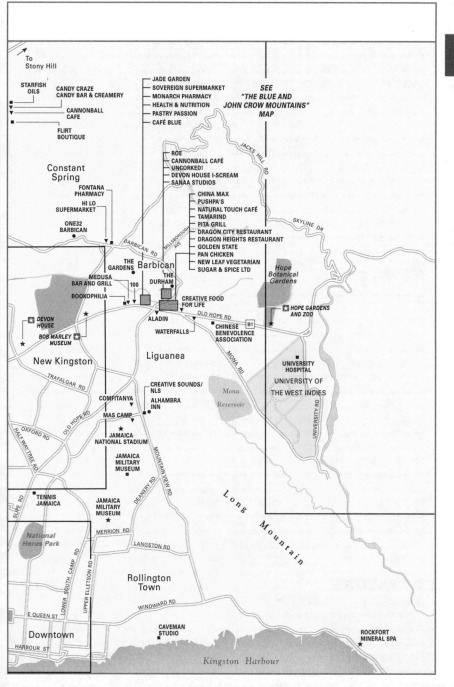

To Stony Hill

STARFISH OILS

CANDY CRAZE CANDY BAR & CREAMERY

CANNONBALL CAFE

FLIRT BOUTIQUE

JADE GARDEN
SOVEREIGN SUPERMARKET
MONARCH PHARMACY
HEALTH & NUTRITION
PASTRY PASSION
CAFÉ BLUE

SEE "THE BLUE AND JOHN CROW MOUNTAINS" MAP

Constant Spring

ROE
CANNONBALL CAFÉ
UNCORKED!
DEVON HOUSE I-SCREAM
SANAA STUDIOS

CHINA MAX
PUSHPA'S
NATURAL TOUCH CAFÉ
TAMARIND
PITA GRILL
DRAGON CITY RESTAURANT
DRAGON HEIGHTS RESTAURANT
GOLDEN STATE
PAN CHICKEN
NEW LEAF VEGETARIAN
SUGAR & SPICE LTD

FONTANA PHARMACY

HI LO SUPERMARKET

ONE32 BARBICAN

JACKS HILL RD

SKYLINE DR

BARBICAN RD

MILLSBOROUGH AVE

THE GARDENS

Barbican

MEDUSA BAR AND GRILL

100

THE DURHAM

BOOKOPHILIA

CREATIVE FOOD FOR LIFE

Hope Botanical Gardens

DEVON HOUSE

BOB MARLEY MUSEUM

ALADIN

WATERFALLS

OLD HOPE RD

CHINESE BENEVOLENCE ASSOCIATION

B1

HOPE GARDENS AND ZOO

New Kingston

Liguanea

TRAFALGAR RD

OLD HOPE RD

OXFORD RD

HALF WAY TREE RD

MONA RD

UNIVERSITY HOSPITAL

UNIVERSITY OF THE WEST INDIES

CREATIVE SOUNDS/NLS

ALHAMBRA INN

COMFITANYA

MAS CAMP

Mona Reservoir

UNIVERSITY RD

JAMAICA NATIONAL STADIUM

JAMAICA MILITARY MUSEUM

MOUNTAIN VIEW RD

DEANERY RD

SLIPE RD

TENNIS JAMAICA

JAMAICA MILITARY MUSEUM

MERRION RD

LANGSTON RD

Long Mountain

National Heros Park

LOWER SOUTH CAMP RD

UPPER ELLETSON RD

Rollington Town

WINDWARD RD

E QUEEN ST

Downtown

HARBOUR ST

CAVEMAN STUDIO

ROCKFORT MINERAL SPA

Kingston Harbour

ease tensions when strategically necessary. If you're driving, there's almost always someone nearby to direct your parking and then volunteer to watch your car. When you return, the helpful volunteer will expect a tip. While you don't need to be intimidated by these everyday occurrences, a bit of change or a small bill will put you in good stead.

Crime and violence certainly exist in Kingston, although visitors are unlikely to encounter it. Don't make the mistake of making political statements or getting involved in any way as a visitor, like wearing an orange People's National Party (PNP) T-shirt while walking through Tivoli Gardens, one of the city's most notorious ghettos and a stronghold for the Jamaica Labour Party (JLP).

These garrison communities can flare up in violence, usually demonstrated by residents barricading the streets in one of the only displays of power they can muster. Should you be unfortunate enough to be caught in Kingston under these circumstances, avoid going downtown and discuss safety with locals. The U.S. embassy is typically the first to sound an alarm, issuing travel advisories anytime such a situation exists.

Generally, foreigners only make crime news when they have tried to exit the country carrying drugs. Stick with the right locals in the right places, and Kingston will be no more dangerous than any other big city in the developing world where wealth and poverty coexist.

# Sights

Kingston's main attractions relate to Jamaica's history, heritage, and culture as opposed to the natural features on the north and west coasts. Most of the historical sights, as well as those associated with the Institute of Jamaica, are located Downtown. The more popular hangouts, as well as most restaurants, bars, clubs, and shopping plazas, are located Uptown. As Jamaica's music scene has decentralized, thanks in large part to technological advances, the Downtown production studios of yesteryear that controlled the industry, like Sir Clement "Coxsone" Dodd's World Disc, or his even more successful Studio One, have been replaced by scores of modern studios scattered around the residential suburbs, often based at the homes of the artists and producers who run them.

## DOWNTOWN

Jamaican art pioneer Edna Manley was honored with a re-creation of her sculpture *Negro Aroused* on Ocean Boulevard along the waterfront at the end of King Street. It's as good as any a place to begin a tour of Downtown. Along Ocean Boulevard, anglers casually

reel in their lines and children jump off big concrete blocks into the choppy waters of Kingston Harbour. It's a great place for an afternoon stroll or to watch sunsets over the Hellshire Hills.

The free **Coin and Notes Museum** (Bank of Jamaica, Nethersole Place, between East St. and Duke St., tel. 876/922-0750, ext. 2108, 9am-4pm Mon.-Fri., free) provides a history of money in Jamaica from the time when goods were bartered to the present. The in-between period saw the circulation of coins from many countries, including Spain and Mexico. Curators have a wealth of knowledge to share with visitors.

For souvenirs, the **Crafts Market** (7am-6pm Mon.-Sat.), at the junction of Ocean Boulevard and Port Royal Street, features some authentic Jamaican crafts as well as an ever-increasing slew of trinkets, T-shirts, and towels imported from China.

## ★ Tuff Gong Recording Studio

**Tuff Gong Recording Studio** (220 Marcus Garvey Dr., tel. 876/937-4216 or 876/923-9383, www.tuffgong.com) operates as living proof that a recording artist can own his music and be in control of his legacy. Bob Marley started as a struggling artist much like the one depicted by Jimmy Cliff in Perry Henzell's film *The Harder They Come.* He was subject to the producer-artist relationship that made voicing the next tune an economic imperative rather than a carefully planned and executed project. When Marley built Tuff Gong Recording Studio, he seeded an empire that continues to earn millions of dollars per year. Today the studio operates as Marley's legacy, with his wife, Rita, and children Ziggy, Stephen, and Cedella in charge. The studio offers a guided tour, where visitors can see the entire music production process. The studio can be booked for recording for about US $40 per hour. A small record shop on-site sells CD, LPs, and other Tuff Gong paraphernalia.

## Culture Yard

A project developed by the Trench Town Development Association, **Culture Yard** (6-8 1st St., off Collie Smith Dr., contact Clifford "Ferdie" Bent, tel. 876/572-4085, 8am-6pm daily, US$10) offers a museum tour based around Bob Marley's former home, deemed a historical site. Visiting Culture Yard is a decent excuse to see the slums of **Trench Town,** which have retained the dire conditions that gave birth to songs like "Concrete Jungle" and "No Woman No Cry," even if the cost for a look-around feels more like charity than value. The area is marked by a large mural of Marley, visible from Spanish Town Road. Visiting Culture Yard is safe, but the communities in and around Trench Town remain explosive, so it's not a good idea to go wandering on your own. **Colin Smikle** (tel. 876/370-8243 or 876/978-5833, colinsmikle@yahoo.com) can arrange community tours around Kingston, including Culture Yard.

A few years ago the Trench Town Development Association was established to carry out projects to benefit the community. Another success has been the **Trenchtown Reading Centre** (Lower 1st St., contact Christopher Stone, tel. 876/546-1559, stonec@kasnet.com, www.trenchtownreadingcentre.com). The center welcomes book donations.

## St. William Grant Park

**The Parade,** also known as **St. William Grant Park,** was a popular congregation ground for a host of labor leaders, including William Grant, Marcus Garvey, and Alexander Bustamante, who spoke regularly before large audiences in the decades

Tuff Gong Recording Studio

# Downtown Kingston

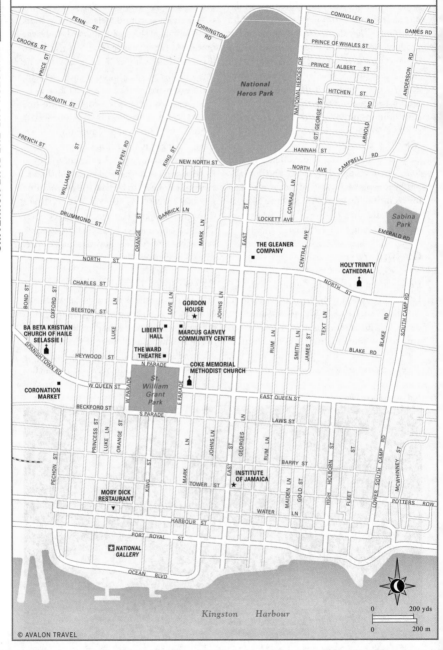

CONNOLLEY RD
DAMES RD
PENN ST
TORRINGTON RD
CROOKS ST
PRINCE OF WHALES ST
PRICE ST
PRINCE ALBERT ST
ANDERSON RD
ASQUITH ST
National Heros Park
HITCHEN ST
GT GEORGE ST
NATIONAL HEROES CIR
ARNOLD RD
FRENCH ST
HANNAH ST
CAMPBELL RD
KING ST
NEW NORTH ST
NORTH AVE
WILLIAMS ST
SLIPE PEN RD
CONRAD LN
DRUMMOND ST
GARRICK LN
LOCKETT AVE
Sabina Park
ORANGE ST
MARK LN
EAST ST
CENTRAL AVE
EMERALD RD
THE GLEANER COMPANY
NORTH ST
HOLY TRINITY CATHEDRAL
BOND ST
OXFORD ST
CHARLES ST
NORTH ST
SOUTH CAMP RD
BEESTON ST
LN
LOVE LN
JOHNS LN
GORDON HOUSE ★
TEXT LN
RD
BA BETA KRISTIAN CHURCH OF HAILE SELASSIE I
LUKE LN
LIBERTY HALL
MARCUS GARVEY COMMUNITY CENTRE
RUM LN
SMITH LN
JAMES ST
BLAKE RD
SPANISH TOWN RD
HEYWOOD ST
THE WARD THEATRE
N PARADE
COKE MEMORIAL METHODIST CHURCH
CORONATION MARKET
W QUEEN ST
St. William Grant Park
W PARADE
E PARADE
EAST QUEEN ST
BECKFORD ST
S PARADE
LAWS ST
PRINCESS ST
LUKE LN
ORANGE ST
LN
JOHNS LN
GEORGES LN
RUM LN
HIGH ST
HOLBORN ST
ST
LOWER SOUTH CAMP RD
McWHINNEY ST
PECHON ST
KING ST
MARK LN
EAST ST
BARRY ST
POTTERS ROW
MOBY DICK RESTAURANT ▼
TOWER ST
INSTITUTE OF JAMAICA ★
MAIDEN LN
GOLD ST
FLEET ST
WATER LN
HARBOUR ST
PORT ROYAL ST
★ NATIONAL GALLERY
OCEAN BLVD

Kingston Harbour

0    200 yds
0    200 m

© AVALON TRAVEL

preceding independence. Originally a parade ground for British soldiers, the park divides King Street into upper and lower regions. The park was recently refurbished to rid it of a sullied reputation after years of neglect, and it is certainly more pleasant today than just a few years ago. Once called Victoria Park, it was renamed in 1977 to honor William Grant for his role in Jamaica's labor movement. Grant was a follower of Marcus Garvey and joined forces with Alexander Bustamante in championing workers' rights. In 1938, both he and Bustamante were arrested for fomenting upheaval among the early trade unions. In the early 1940s, Grant broke with Bustamante's Industrial Trade Union and drifted into poverty and obscurity. Nevertheless he was given the Honor of Distinction in 1974, three years before his death, for his contribution to the labor movement, which paved the way for Jamaica's independence. The "St." preceding his name is for "sergeant," attributable to his service in the military or as a militant member of the United Negro Improvement Association.

**Kingston Parish Church** (tel. 876/922-6888) stands on the corner of South Parade and King Street. It was rebuilt 1911 after the earthquake of 1907, which virtually flattened all of downtown. It is a replica of the original with the addition of a clock tower. The original had stood since reconstruction after the earthquake of 1692. Inside there are several pieces of Jamaican art and a few statues gifted by the Chinese (Our Lady at the High Altar) and Lebanese (Saint Thomas) governments.

**Coke Church** (tel. 876/922-2224), the most prominent building on East Parade, stands on the site of the first Methodist chapel in Jamaica. The present structure was rebuilt after the 1907 earthquake, replacing the 1840 original named after Thomas Coke, who founded the Methodist missions in the British Caribbean. It is one of the few buildings of brick construction in Kingston.

For a guided tour lasting about half an hour, call **Juliet Gordon** (tel. 876/925-8798, cell tel. 876/362-9319, oldejamaica@ yahoo.com, www.oldejamaicatours.com, US$5 adults, US$2 children), who runs **We Jamaica Tours.** She can arrange transportation from anywhere in Kingston and specializes in historical structures around the Corporate Area such as Holy Trinity Church, the Jewish synagogue, St. Andrew Parish Church, East Queen's Street Baptist, Coke Methodist, Cots Kirk, and Spanish Town Cathedral.

The **Ward Theatre** (tel. 876/922-0453 or 876/922-3213, www.wardtheatrefoundation. com, 9am-5pm Mon.-Fri., or for scheduled events) facing the park on North Parade was also a regular venue for Garvey speeches. The theater, like many buildings in town, has gone through many incarnations and hosts occasional events, including its famous pantomime performances, some of which are posted on the foundation's website.

## Institute of Jamaica

The **Institute of Jamaica** (IOJ, Main Bldg., 14-16 East St., tel. 876/922-0620 or 876/922-0626, ioj.jam@mail.infochan.com, www. natgalja.org.jm, admission US$4, free for students with ID) was founded in 1879 by Governor-General Anthony Musgrave to encourage "Literature, Science, and Art," as the letters on the main building's facade read. The institute's several divisions include the National Gallery, National Library, and the Museum of History and Ethnography. The IOJ publishes an excellent series called *Jamaica Journal,* which delves into a range of topics from dancehall music to sea sponges off Port Royal to national heroes. It's a great way to get a glimpse at the introspective side of the Jamaican people.

## ★ NATIONAL GALLERY

The **National Gallery** (12 Ocean Blvd., tel. 876/922-1561, http://about.galleryjamaica.org, 10am-4:30pm Tues.-Thurs., 10am-4pm Fri., 10am-3pm Sat., US$1.15 adults, US$0.55 students and over age 64) is the go-to place for a concise overview of Jamaican art, from Taino artifacts and colonial art dating to Spanish and English rule, to pieces charting the development of Jamaican intuitive and mainstream expression. The works at the National Gallery reflect Jamaica's landscapes and its people. Artists whose work is part of the gallery's permanent collection include Mallica "Kapo" Reynolds, Barrington Watson, Albert Huie, Carl Abrahams, John Dunkley, and Edna Manley.

## THE NATURAL HISTORY DIVISION AND THE MUSEUM OF HISTORY AND ETHNOGRAPHY

The **Natural History Division** is the oldest division of the IOJ and is housed adjacent to the Institute's main building on the ground floor. The **Museum of History and Ethnography** (10 East St., 8:30am-5pm Mon.-Thurs., 8:30am-4pm Fri., US$4 adults, US$3 students, US$1 under age 13) features temporary exhibits at its headquarters ranging from colorful examples of contemporary Jamaican life to historical commemorations of events and movements in Jamaican history.

The **Museum of Jamaican Music** is a new development envisioned as part of the IOJ's museum network and dedicated to conserving Jamaica's musical history. Presided over by the IOJ's Museum of Ethnography under the leadership of director and curator Herbie Miller (cell tel. 876/476-6575), the museum supports research into and documentation of all aspects of Jamaican musical history. A temporary exhibit in the ethnography division of the Institute features a display containing musical memorabilia.

## THE JAMAICA MILITARY MUSEUM

The **Jamaica Military Museum** (Up Park Camp, contact Michael Anglin, cell tel. 876/926-8121, jmmlib@gmail.com, 10am-4pm Wed.-Sun., US$1 adults, US$0.50 children) is a collaborative effort between the Jamaica Defense Force (JDF) and the staff of the Museum of History and Ethnography, showcasing Jamaica's military past, starting with the Taino and the Spanish-Taino encounter, with a few old tanks and uniforms on display from the British period, to the present JDF uniforms and medals.

## LIBERTY HALL

**Liberty Hall** (76 King St., tel. 876/948-8639, www.libertyhall-ioj.org.jm, info@libertyhall-ioj.org.jm, museum 10am-4pm Mon.-Fri., US$1 adults, US$0.50 children) is the latest addition to the IOJ. The rehabilitated building was Marcus Garvey's base of operations in the 1920s and today has a small reference library with a wealth of knowledge related to Garvey and his teachings. Liberty Hall houses a multimedia museum and resource center as well as continuing Garvey's vision with programs for local youth. Garvey's influence on the Jamaican psyche is profound. Liberty Hall, just a few blocks up from St. William Grant Park and the Ward Theatre, a hotbed of Jamaica's labor movement, is the best place to grasp his importance as a founder of pan-Africanism.

## AFRICAN-CARIBBEAN INSTITUTE OF JAMAICA

The **African-Caribbean Institute of Jamaica** (ACIJ, 12 Ocean Blvd., tel. 876/922-4793 or 876/922-7415, acij@anngel.com.jm, 8am-4:30pm Mon.-Thurs., 8am-3:30pm Fri.) has a mandate is to "collect, research, document, analyze, and preserve information on Jamaica's cultural heritage, through the exploitation of oral and scribal sources." The ACIJ has a memory-bank program in which oral histories are recorded around the country and then transcribed, as well as an active publications program featuring the *ACIJ Research Review*. There is a small library at the office where the Institute's top-notch academic publications can be browsed and purchased. The ACIJ has a tradition of collaboration with individual researchers and institutions. Projects have included studies of traditional religions like Kumina and Revival, and research on the Maroons.

who formed the Jamaica Labour Party, and his cousin Norman Manley, who founded the opposition People's National Party. Norman's son Michael Manley, who gave the country its biggest communist scare for his closeness with Cuba's Fidel Castro, is also interred here. Paul Bogle and George William Gordon are honored for their role in the Morant Bay Rebellion, which was at the vanguard of Jamaica's civil rights movement in the post-emancipation period. The most recent icon to be laid to rest at Heroes Memorial is the cultural legend Louise Bennett, referred to lovingly by Jamaicans as "Miss Lou," who died in June 2006.

## Other Sights

**Headquarters House** (79 Duke St., tel. 876/922-1287, 8:30am-4:30pm Mon.-Fri., free) is the home of the Jamaica National Heritage Trust, which oversees the country's heritage sites; it dates from 1755 and is a good example of Georgian architecture. Merchant Thomas Hibbert built the house in a contest to see who could construct the most ornate edifice to impress a local woman. There's a nice gallery on the ground floor with antiquities. It is also called Hibbert House; the Jamaican Parliament was housed here until it outgrew the small confines of the main chamber.

**Gordon House** (81 Duke St., tel. 876/922-0202) was built in 1960 to replace Headquarters House as the meeting place for Jamaica's House of Representatives. There's not much to see, but visitors can drop in and experience Jamaican political wrangling at its most civil in a House of Commons or Senate session. The building is named after labor leader George William Gordon (1815-1865), made a national hero in 1969.

The *Jamaica Gleaner* **Building** (7 North St., tel. 876/922-3400), home to the country's longest-running newspaper, is on North Street, with the cricket grounds of **Sabina Park** a few blocks east. Also nearby, on Duke Street, is Jamaica's only synagogue, the **United Congregation of Israelites,** which dates from 1912. **The Ba Beta**

Paul Bogle is memorialized in National Heroes Park.

## National Heroes Park

National Heroes Park occupies 30 hectares (74 acres) below Cross Roads on Marescaux Road within the large roundabout known as **Heroes Circle.** The roundabout surrounds what was once the city's main sporting ground, later becoming the Kingston Race Course. The park was also the site of several important historical events, including Emancipation Day celebrations on August 1, 1938; the jubilee celebrating Queen Victoria's reign in 1887; and the free Smile Jamaica concert where a wounded Bob Marley offered the people of Kingston a 90-minute performance in defiance of his would-be assassins in 1976. Heroes Park is also said to have been the battleground where warring factions from East and West Kingston would face off in organized skirmishes.

At the southern end of the park, **Heroes Memorial** commemorates Jamaica's most important historical figures and events. Black Nationalist Marcus Garvey rests here, as does labor leader Alexander Bustamante,

**Kristian Church of Haile Selassie I** is on Oxford Street in front of Coronation Market and is worth a visit for its colorful service on Sunday afternoons. Women must cover their heads, wear dresses, and sit on the right side of the aisle. Men should not cover their heads. The church sponsors community initiatives as well as the Amha Selassie basic school located next door.

**Jubilee and Coronation Markets** fuse together starting at West Parade and running along West Queen Street and Spanish Town Road to Darling Street. It's worth a visit to browse the stalls, renowned for touting the best bargains in town on produce and just about anything else. It's not the place for high-end gear, but the experience is gritty Jamaica at its best—with all the accompanying smells. While it's most comfortably enjoyed accompanied by a local, there is no danger to going unaccompanied as long as you can handle unsolicited attention from hagglers seeking a sale. If you're a woman, it's guaranteed the market men will approach you with romantic interest.

**Marcus Garvey Community Center** (69 Church St.) is the present-day venue for meetings of the Marcus Garvey People's Political Party (MGPPP, 6pm-8pm Thurs.), which had a stronger following when its iconic leader still attended. A fish fry is held on the last Friday of even-numbered months, accompanied by a sound system, of course.

**Trinity Cathedral** (1-3 George Edly Dr., tel. 876/922-3335, service 8:30am Sun., mass 5:30pm Mon.-Fri.) has been center stage for several important national events. Archbishop Samuel Carter is buried on the site, and Michael Manley's funeral—attended by Fidel Castro and Louis Farrakhan, among others—was held here. The original mosaic tile on the north wall has been uncovered, and a Spanish restoration team is set to restore the rest of the mosaic walls, which were painted over in white. Caretaker Craig Frazer leads tours of the building and points out interesting details. A generous tip is sure to make the pious young man even more devout.

# UPTOWN
## Emancipation Park

At the corner of Knutsford Boulevard and Oxford Road is **Emancipation Park** (tel. 876/926-6312 or 876/968-9292, emanpark@cwjamaica.com), where two figures stand resolute, cast in bronze, their bodies thick and steadfast, their heads proudly lifted to acknowledge the rectitude of the long struggle for freedom and silently praying for guidance in a new era. The work, titled *Redemption Song*, was the winner of a competition to give the newly constructed Emancipation Park a meaningful headpiece. It was controversial because its creator, Jamaican sculptor Laura Facey (www.laurafacey.com), is light-skinned, also because the figures are naked, and the man could be considered well-endowed. Some people wanted the sculpture immediately removed, and Facey was the talk of the island for weeks. In the end, artistic freedom prevailed, and the sculpture was kept in place.

*Redemption Song* and the controversy that surrounded it reflect the deep wounds slavery left on Jamaica and the rest of the world. Emancipation Park is among the best-maintained public spaces in Kingston, perfect for reflecting on the past, relaxing on one of the many benches, or just taking a stroll. Events are held frequently on a stage at the center of the park and next door at the Liguanea Club or on top of the NHT Building.

## Half Way Tree

Half Way Tree is the capital of St. Andrew, the parish that envelops Kingston. The bustling commercial area seen today is a far cry from its rural days when it was a popular rest stop for travelers between Kingston and Spanish Town. Several historical sites are wedged among the concrete and strip malls. The **clock tower** at the junction of Half Way Tree, Hope, Constant Spring, and Hagley Park Roads was erected in 1913 as a monument to Britain's King Edward VII. It's the symbol of Half Way Tree.

**St. Andrew Parish Church** (free), also called Half Way Tree Church, is one

# Uptown Kingston

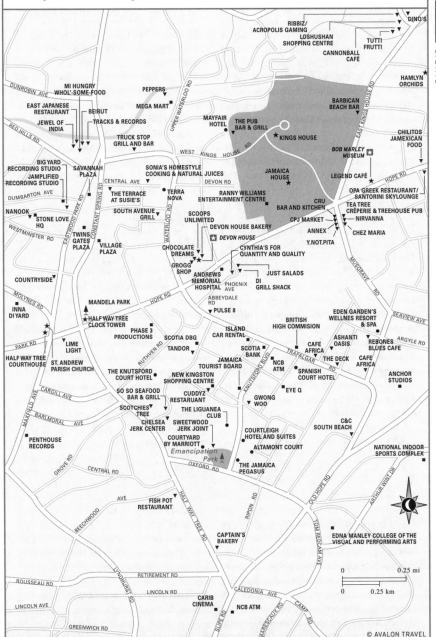

© AVALON TRAVEL

of the oldest Anglican churches on the island. The present church has a foundation that dates from 1692, when the earthquake destroyed the previous structure. One of the first U.S. consuls to Jamaica, Robert Monroe Harrison, brother of U.S. President Benjamin Harrison, is buried here along with his wife. Philip Livingston, a Jamaica-based merchant and son of one of the founding fathers of the United States, was married in the church. Outside there's an old, poorly maintained cemetery.

The **Half Way Tree Courthouse,** adjacent to the Parish Church, is a good example of Georgian architecture, dating from 1807. The front of the building is covered with latticework, presumably to keep out the heat as a form of early air conditioning. The building has been repaired and altered several times to fix storm damage, while it miraculously escaped damage during the 1907 earthquake. The courthouse has seen formerly enslaved people obtaining their certificates of freedom as well as agricultural society meetings, and after 1920 legal proceedings were no longer held here. Until the mid-1980s the building was a branch of the Institute of Jamaica called the Junior Centre, which hosted skills-training courses. The courthouse was listed as a Jamaica National Heritage Trust site in 1957, and in 1985 it was declared a National Monument. Meanwhile the structure suffered neglect and decay.

One important trial held at the Half Way Tree Courthouse was that of Alexander Bedward, a popular folk hero and founder of a Native Free Baptist sect known as Bedwardism, in 1921. Bedward was an early Black Nationalist who spoke out against the religious and government authorities of the day. For this he was committed to Bellevue asylum until his death in 1930.

The **Ethiopian Orthodox Church** (McDonald Lane) was founded in Jamaica in 1972. This is the state church of Ethiopia to which Haile Selassie I belonged. The church has an awkward relationship with Rastafarians in Jamaica; many of them have been baptized as Ethiopian Orthodox, including Bob Marley's children. To this day, the construction remains incomplete, with little more than a foundation in place. Its construction has been held up by a lack of cosmic alignment and a lack of togetherness in the Rasta community, according to Rasta elder Kojo and many others who share his view. Meanwhile, many inside the Ethiopian Church scorn Rastas for considering Haile Selassie a God.

Kingston's **Hindu Temple** (139 Maxfield Ave.) holds events for all the major Hindu holidays, including Ganesh Puja and Diwali. Local Hindus attend in heavy numbers on Sunday morning.

## ★ Devon House

Still one of Kingston's finest homes, **Devon House** (26 Hope Rd., Great House, tel. 876/929-6602 or 876/929-0815, devonhouse-jamaica@cw.com, www.devonhousejamaica.com, guided tours 9:30am-5pm Mon.-Sat., last tour 4:30pm, US$5 adults, US$1.50 under age 12) is a source of pride for the City. The mansion was constructed in 1881 by Jamaica's first black millionaire, George Stiebel, who made his fortune in Venezuelan gold. Some of the city's predominantly white elite of the day were less than happy to be outdone by a black man; it is said that Lady Musgrave—wife of Governor-General Lord Musgrave, who founded the Institute of Jamaica—actually had a road built (Lady Musgrave Rd.) so she wouldn't have to bear the humiliation of passing the spectacular mansion that humbled even her husband's residence. Until 1983 Devon House was home to the National Gallery. Today it is furnished and decorated with a range of English, French, and Caribbean antiques as well as some reproductions. The courtyard behind Devon House is full of boutique shops.

## ★ Bob Marley Museum

Located in Bob Marley's former residence at 56 Hope Road, just north of New Kingston, the house has been turned into the **Bob**

**Marley Museum** (tel. 876/630-1588, www. bobmarley-foundation.com, US$25 adults, US$12 ages 4-12), a shrine to the man and his music, with rooms full of newspaper clippings and personal effects. Tours (9:30am-4pm Mon.-Sat.) last one hour. Around back, there's a gift shop and a gallery with rotating exhibitions. A comfortable, cozy theater is a great place to catch a movie. A presentation on Marley is part of the tour, and the theater is used occasionally for touring international film festivals.

**Legend Café,** on one side of the main gate, has great steamed fish and fresh juices. Marley's Land Rover sits under a protective carport in the other corner of the yard in front of a wall plastered with Wailers photos. Photos are not allowed inside or behind the main building that houses the museum.

## King's House

**King's House** (Hope Rd. at Lady Musgrave Rd., tel. 876/927-6424, fax 876/978-6025, visits scheduled by request) has been the home of the Governor-General since the capital was moved from Spanish Town in 1872. Jamaica's ceremonial head of state is appointed by the British monarch for six-year terms. King's House was formerly the residence of Jamaica's Anglican bishop. The original building was destroyed in the 1907 earthquake and rebuilt in 1909. The grounds have nice gardens that can be toured. Write to The Office of the Governor General or email kingshouse@ kingshoue.gov.jm to schedule a visit. Jamaica House, just south of King's House on the same grounds, is now the location for the Prime Minister's offices and is closed to the public.

## ★ Hope Gardens and Zoo

**Hope Botanical Gardens** (Hope Rd., 6am-6pm daily, free, parking US$1.50) was founded in 1873 and is managed by an NGO, Nature Preservation Foundation. It's a great place to hang out in the shade of a Bombacacea tree or picnic on the grass. The diverse collection of exotic and endemic plants isn't as well labeled as it could be. Hope Gardens were named after Major Richard Hope, who once owned the estate. The gardens span 8.5 hectares (21 acres) on the Liguanea Plain. Visitors to Hope Gardens should make time to tour the magnificent Chinese Gardens, gifted by the Chinese government and completed in 2016. The design adheres to feng shui and is adorned with symbols of Chinese culture, including a massive sculpture made of rare Lingbi stone. Of special note is the sizable lily pond,

Devon House

featuring an island in the shape of Jamaica. Guided tours (US$1) of the Chinese Garden are offered. A band shell features occasional performances, and parties are regularly held on the lawns. **Hope Zoo** (tel. 876/927-1085, 10am-4pm daily, US$15 adults, US$10 ages 3-11) is located within Hope Gardens, boasting a lion, monkeys, a few birds, alligators, and iguanas.

## AROUND KINGSTON

The **University of the West Indies** (UWI, Mona Rd. and University Rd., www.mona. uwi.edu), in the quiet residential neighborhood of Mona, is worth a visit. The campus sits at the base of the Blue Mountains and has extensive rolling lawns with interesting ruins of the old Mona Estate aqueduct and a beautiful mural created by Belgian artist Claude Rahir with the help of UWI students. The cut-stone University Chapel by the main entrance is an excellent example of Georgian architecture. It was transported block by block from Gales Valley Estate in Trelawny at the bidding of Princess Alice, first chancellor of the University. The former sugar warehouse was given a new life at UWI, its interior decorated with materials from all the countries the university has served. The coats of arms of these countries are inlaid in the chapel ceiling.

Along the main Kingston-to-Annotto Bay road (the A3), just over the border from St. Andrew, **Castleton Botanical Gardens** (Castleton, St. Mary, tel. 876/942-0717, free) is still one of the nicest parks in Jamaica, despite having suffered years of neglect and recurring hurricane damage. Castleton was established in the 1860s and planted with 400 species from Kew Gardens in England. It remained an important introduction point for ornamental and economically important species, including scores of palms as well as poincianas and the large Bombay mango variety. One of the most interesting specimens in the gardens is the screwpine (*Pandanus tectorius*), which sends down aerial, or stilt, roots; another is the poor man's orchid, not a true orchid, which has become ubiquitous around the island. Other economically important tree species still growing at the gardens are the Burma teak and West Indian mahogany.

# Entertainment and Events

Many Jamaicans love a good party, or "session," as they call it, and Kingston has the most consistent and varied nightlife to support partygoers and dance enthusiasts. Don't be alarmed if someone approaches within intimate distance for what is known as a slow "wine," or sexually suggestive dance, in a club or at a street dance. But it's not just "wining" that Kingston offers. While still less than cosmopolitan in terms of its entertainment offerings (you won't find an opera house), the city does support a wide array of cultural and artistic forms, from modern dance to art and theater. Of course, music touches everybody, and Kingston's nightclubs deliver a raw celebration of music on dance floors as much as in the streets.

There's no need to hurry in Jamaica, as everything inevitably starts late, especially nightlife. Family-oriented and cultural entertainment generally starts earlier in the evenings, 7pm-10pm. Few people go out to a nightclub before midnight, and clubs don't typically fill up until 2am-3am. Street dances start particularly late and can be quite boring until a sizeable crowd gathers and people start showing off their moves amid pan-chicken vendors, enormous speakers, wafting ganja smoke, and the rising sun. Expensive all-inclusive parties maintain an exclusive crowd with ticket prices in the range of US$100. These parties have become quite popular, with the Frenchman's parties the vanguard of Kingston high society chic for its

a Bacchanal performer at Mas Camp

food and select crowd. UWI and University of Technology campuses host parties somewhat regularly.

## LIVE MUSIC

Hardly a week passes without some kind of concert for an album launch, talent show, or birthday celebration. Young artists following in the footsteps of reggae legend Bob Marley compete to chant down Babylon with the freshest lyrics. Kingston's vibrant nightlife is a world unto itself, with clubs, parties, and stage shows that entertain well into the morning almost any night of the week.

Live music and stage show performances in Kingston are not as frequent or varied as one would expect given the prominent role music plays in Jamaican life and the prolific music production in town. Nonetheless, there are a handful of venues that feature somewhat regular acts. Stage shows are held routinely, and there are large events held during Jamaica's carnival season, known as Bacchanal, at **Mas Camp** on Arthur Wint Drive. Parties begin in

February and continue every Friday until the climax of the carnival season in April.

**Jammin at the Springs** (Constant Spring Golf Club, 152 Constant Spring Rd.) is an open mic and jam session held each Thursday.

**Chinna Smith** (6 St. Andrew Park, tel. 876/631-6927, cell tel. 876/421-1295, earlflute@yahoo.com, US$10 pp contribution is customary) and his Inna Di Yard Band, legendary old school roots reggae artists, welcome visitors to join for rehearsals and host regular jam sessions on Friday.

**Red Bones** (1 Argyle Rd., tel. 876/978-8262, cell tel. 876/879-8262, redbonesmanager@gmail.com, www.redbonesbluescafe.com, noon-11pm Mon.-Fri., 6pm-11pm Sat.) hosts live music on a regular basis, sometimes a few nights a week.

**Kingston Dub Club** (contact Gabre Selassie, cell tel. 876/815-1184, sholintemple@gmail.com, www.rockerssoundstation.co, noon-10pm Wed.-Sat., noon-3am Sun.) began as an informal gathering of "bredren" devotees of roots reggae and dub, preferably emanating from vinyl, and has developed into Kingston's weekly pilgrimage to Skyline Drive, where the home of Rockers Sound Station torch bearer Gabre Selassie is transformed into Kingston's preeminent culture yard. The tiered hillside fills with a motley mix of old school Rastas, young hipsters, and flag-waving disciples, all gathered to relish the fresh and ancient sounds mixed together by the host and his endless entourage of guest selectors and artists. Nowhere can a more authentic scene be found. A few vendors sell books and ital foods. A spacious deck with a bar overlooks Kingston's glimmering lights. The stacked boxes begin pumping early in the evening and don't go quiet until late in the wee hours, when, if you're not moving to the beat, it can get a bit chilly and a sweater or light jacket can come in handy.

**Jamaica Association of Vintage Artistes and Affiliates** (JAVAA, 7-9 Hagley Park Rd., Half Way Tree Entertainment Complex, next to York Plaza, tel. 876/908-4464, www.javaa.com.

jm) hosts occasional concerts at a variety of venues around the city, most notably a weekly free concert (Wed. in Feb.) in the Heart of Half Way Tree during Reggae Month. The organization was formed to bring recognition and financial support to these artists, many of whom participated in the formation of Jamaican popular music, as they reach their golden years. Tickets are available at the JAVAA office.

**Jacob's Place** (shop 15 King's Plaza, cell tel. 876/327-3435 or 876/754-6929, 10am-10pm Mon.-Sat., 2:30pm-10:30pm, bar only open Sun.) is a hole in the wall rum bar and restaurant with a rotating themed menu: Chinese on Mondays, seafood on Tuesdays, stewed dishes on Wednesdays, Curry dishes on Thursdays, seafood again on Fridays with an after work jam featuring VJ, and soup and freestyle dishes on Saturdays. The corner of the plaza that Jacob's is located in heats up with live music on Tuesdays, featuring scheduled acts and occasional open mic nights.

**Comfitanya Lounge & Restaurant** (169 Mountainview Ave on Creiffe Road, tel. 876/978-3517, comfitanya@aol.com, 11am-4:30pm Mon.-Thurs., 11am-11pm Fri.-Sat., bar 2pm-11pm, no food on Sun.) serves local dishes like fried chicken with rice and peas, oxtail, curry goat, and vegetarian dishes like steamed veggies in a low key bar frequented almost exclusively by locals. Live bands perform on Saturdays and holidays from 9:30pm-1am. The bar has a pool table (free on Fridays). A DJ spins on Mondays, Thursdays, and Fridays. Rance Chambers is responsible for keeping the disco ball spinning and the good vibes flowing. A movie night on Tuesdays streams comedy and action films.

**Magnum Kings & Queens of Dancehall,** an annual talent show broadcast on TV, hosts weekly televised competitions on Saturdays at a pop-up set at **D'Entrance** (78-80 Constant Spring Rd.) February through May.

# FESTIVALS AND EVENTS

Several annual events are worth being in Kingston for, including **Bacchanal,** which runs February to April; the **Observer Food Awards,** held in late May; **Caribbean Fashion Week,** in early June; and **Restaurant Week,** typically held the third week in November, when participating restaurants slash prices and feature culinary novelties.

**Jamaica's Girls and Boys Championships,** better known as **Champs,** is an annual track and field meet held in late March that sees Kingston's hotels booked with fans from home and abroad who come out in hoards to watch the competition. The energy at the National Stadium is palpable, with fans screaming and waving for their schools.

**The *Jamaica Observer* Food Awards,** the brainchild of larger-than-life fashionista, food critic, and *Observer* lifestyle editor Novia McDonald-Whyte, was established in 1998 to celebrate excellence in culinary presentation. It affords patrons an opportunity to taste what's new and different in Jamaica's food industry, with over 60 booths showcasing the country's scrumptious offerings, from the tried-and-true jerk sauces, rum, and Blue Mountain coffee to more exotic offerings. Top winners are awarded two full scholarships each year to the Hospitality Department at the University of Technology, with 20-odd awards presented to establishments that have excelled. Dubbed "The Caribbean's Oscar Night of Food," the event is held on the east lawns of Devon House in late May each year. Contact the *Jamaica Observer* (tel. 876/926-7655) for further details and tickets, which usually run about US$100.

Held over the course of a week each year in mid-June, **Kingston on the Edge (KOTE) Arts Festival** (kingstonontheedge@gmail.com, www.kingstonontheedge.org) is a series of exhibits showcasing up-and-coming artistic talent from across the island in a host of art studios and gallery spaces.

**Kingston Restaurant Week,** staged the

# Caribbean Fashion Week

Jamaica's contribution has been central to a bourgeoning Caribbean fashion industry. **Pulse Entertainment** (38-A Trafalgar Rd., tel. 876/960-0049, www.pulsemodels.com, www.caribbeanfashionweek.com), started holding Caribbean Fashion Week (CFW) in 2001, now a wildly successful annual event described by British *Vogue* as one of the most important fashion trends on the planet. Held during the first half of June, the week is filled with fashion shows, parties, and some of the world's most striking women clad in creative attire designed by a young cadre of imaginative talent. It's definitely one of the best times of year to be in Kingston.

Caribbean Fashion Week

Pulse Entertainment has found great success in supporting an ever-swelling corps of young model hopefuls, mostly from Jamaica, and giving them a chance on the world stage. Some of the most successful have been featured in the world's foremost magazines, like *Sports Illustrated* and *Esquire* (Carla Campbell), *Vogue* (Nadine Willis and Jaunel McKenzie), and *Cosmopolitan* (Sunna Gottshalk). At the same time, CFW has provided a forum for established Caribbean designers like Uzuri, Mutamba, and Biggy. Bob's daughter Cedella Marley never fails to create a splash with her proud and tasteful Catch a Fire line.

CFW events are held at numerous venues around the capital but centered mostly at Pulse's stately Villa Ronai in Kingston's uptown suburb of Stony Hill. Fashion Week attendees descend on Kingston amid a tangible buzz created by an invasion of models, fashion media, and increasingly, designers from the United States and Europe coming to catch a glimpse of the latest unabashed creation with the potential to spur a trend reaching far beyond Jamaica.

second or third week in November by *The Jamaica Gleaner* in association with Stephanie Scott's SSCO Event Management (tel. 876/978-6245 or cell tel. 876/564-1700), is one of the best times to be in Kingston for those who love to sample restaurants. Prices are slashed by up to 50 percent, and participating venues offer patrons new creations in an attempt to develop customers who will return throughout the year. The weeklong program has extended to other towns across Jamaica over the years, with participating restaurants now spanning the island, especially in Ocho Rios and Montego Bay.

## PARTIES

**Bikini Sundayz** (contact Maurice Johnson, cell tel. 876/381-1281, marjohno@hotmail.com, US$15, half price for women wearing bikinis) is a monthly beach party held the first Sunday of each month, usually staged at Ultra Beach Club adjacent to Fort Clarence Beach Park. The theme of the party changes according to the season, with Soca Dancehall J'Ouvert crowning the carnival festivities the week after Easter Sunday, kicking off as Road March winds down in Kingston.

## NIGHTCLUBS

**Club Privilege** (14-16 Trinidad Terrace, tel. 876/754-8561, info@clubprivilegejm.com, www.clubprivilegejm.com, 10pm-4am Fri.-Sat., admission US$12) is a slick club located above Treasure Hunt gaming lounge that prides itself on being the most exclusive venue in town. Bottles of champagne and Moët adorn two bars, with lounge furniture in the cordoned-off VIP area overlooking a

# Sound Systems and Street Dances

Sound systems fostered the development of Jamaican music. Starting out as little more than a set of speaker boxes on wheels, the sounds would set up in different places to feed a thirst created by the advent of radio in 1939, which brought American popular music, whetting Jamaica's appetite for new sounds. Jamaica's musicians responded by bringing traditional mento and calypso rhythms to the R&B and pop tunes the people were demanding, ultimately giving birth to the ska, rocksteady, reggae, and dancehall genres. Historically the voice of the street dance, Jamaican sound systems have grown at clubs and stage shows, having replaced the African drums of yesteryear.

A sound generally comprises a few individual selectors (DJs) who form a team to blast the latest dancehall tunes using equipment that ranges from a home stereo at max output, for those just starting out, to the most sophisticated equipment operated by the more established. Street dances like Passa Passa foster the development of DJ artistry, providing a venue for the different sound systems to flex and clash, like the ever popular Stone Love, Renaissance, Black Chiney, or Razz and Biggy. These sounds grew on the coattails of King Tubby, among the biggest sound system personalities of all time. Sound clashes are held often, during which each sound attempts to outperform the other, with the ultimate judge being the crowd, which expresses approval with hands raised in the air as if firing a pistol, accompanied by the requisite shouts of "braap, braap, braap, braap!" or "pam, pam, pam!"

Street dances fill an important role in providing entertainment and an expressive outlet for Kingston's poorest. Dances are held for special occasions, including birthdays, funerals, and holidays. Many started as one-off parties but were so popular they became established as regular weekly events. Typically a section of street is blocked off to traffic and huge towers of speakers are set up. Sometimes the street is not blocked off at all, but the early morning hours when these dances are held see little traffic, and what does flow is accommodated by the dancers—who sometimes use the passing vehicles to prop up their dance partner for a more dramatic "wine."

While clubs across Uptown Kingston assess an admission fee, which varies depending on the crowd they are looking to attract, the street is a public venue where all are welcome. Uptown people might have traditionally preferred a bar setting, but Downtown people have resorted to creating the party on their doorstep. Increasingly, Uptown folks venture down to the poor areas on nights when dances are held to partake in a scene that doesn't exist anywhere else and has come to be acknowledged as an invaluable cultural phenomenon where DJs flex their skills to discriminating crowds.

In the past, noise ordinances became the favorite justification for police raids to "lock off di dance," but today the dances are for the most part tolerated by the authorities as harmless entertainment effective in pacifying the city's poor. Intellectuals like Jamaican poet Mutabaruka, who claims "the more dance is the less crime," have come to endorse and encourage these dances as healthy community events. Even though they are often held in areas obviously scarred with urban

large dance floor. Drinks range from US$5 for a beer to US$750 for a bottle of Ace of Spades champagne.

**Fiction Fantasy** (unit 6, Marketplace, 67 Constant Spring Rd., tel. 876/631-8038, fictionloungeja@gmail.com, www.fictionloungeja.com, 6pm-4am Mon.-Sat., cover usually US$12) is the newest Uptown nightclub in Kingston, with a popular "ladies' night" on Thursday. Call or go online for actual event schedules. Fiction is a magnet for Jamaica's young elite partygoers. It offers a varied bar menu and a wide selection of local and imported liquors, with a cordoned off VIP section and elegant styling.

## BARS

**Puls8** (38-A Trafalgar Rd., tel. 876/906-6465) is an open-air bar at the Pulse Investments complex that hosts a couple of weekly live music nights, including Pepperseed and MVP blight and associated with violence, like Tivoli Gardens and Rae Town, violence is not a part of the street dance. Rather, it is a place where people come to enjoy, decked out in their flashiest clothes (jackets and fancy shoes for men, skimpy skirts and tops for women) to drink a Guinness, smoke a spliff, and catch up on the latest dances.

Regular patrons welcome visitors from Uptown and abroad, but care should be taken to show respect and concede that you are clearly not on your turf. Plenty a "badman" frequent these dances, and they don't appreciate being photographed without granting approval first. Parts of Downtown, especially along parts of Spanish Town Road, can be desolate and unsafe at night, and many drivers use that as an excuse to proceed with caution at red lights rather than coming to a stop.

Street dances struggle under the constant threat from police, who have a mandate to shut down music in public spaces at midnight during the week and at 2am on weekends. Promoters complain that this doesn't allow them to recoup their investment, and that street dances reduce crime by giving the youth a free venue, but such claims have fallen on deaf ears. Despite the challenges, dedicated party promoters keep at it and struggle through, even if they have to change venues or even take their dance on the road, as was the case with Dutty Fridaze. Other dances that began on the street were forced into a club by regular disruptions by the police. Some of the more regular dances around town include:

- **Mojito Mondays** (South Avenue Plaza, Half Way Tree), which attracts serious dancers to bust their moves in the parking lot by Susie's

- **Uptown Mondays** (Savannah Plaza, Half Way Tree, cell tel. 876/468-1742), put on by Whitfield "Witty" Henry

- **Boasy Tuesdays** (10 Balmoral Ave.), run by dancer and promoter extraordinaire, Blazey (cell tel. 876/507-7254 or 876/354-0130)

- **Nipples Tuesdays** (cell tel. 876/488-5062), located in Waterhouse

- **Weddy Weddy Wednesdays** (Stone Love HQ, Burlington Ave., Half Way Tree)

- **All-Star Thursdays** (Olympic Way, Waterhouse)

- **MVP Fridays** (Pulse838-A Trafalgar Rd., tel. 876/906-6465), which features established dancehall and reggae acts of today and yesteryear

- **Wet Sundaze** (Auto Vision car wash, 8 Hillview Ave., tel. 876/968-9952)

- **Kingston Dub Club** (Skyline Dr., tel. 876/815-1184), hosted at the hilltop home of roots reggae selector Gabre Selassie of Rockers Sound Station

Fridays, the latter featuring top contemporary and throwback dancehall and reggae artists.

**Club Escape** (24 Knutsford Blvd., tel. 876/960-1856, open 24 hours daily, US$6 men, US$5 women after 9pm Fri.-Sat.) is an outdoor bar and nightclub that often has heated dominoes games in the early evenings, plus a mix of music that includes hip-hop and reggae. Lunch (11am-4pm Mon.-Sat.) has items like chicken, oxtail, curry goat, and pepper steak (US$3.50-5). Light items like kebabs and grilled and jerk chicken are served until 3am.

**The Deck** (14 Trafalgar Rd., tel. 876/978-1582, richard@thedeck.biz, from 4:30pm daily) is a large venue with a boat motif. Fishing nets hang from what was once the roof of an auto garage. There are a few billiards tables and a decent bar food menu (US$4-15). Friday's after-work jam is popular, and weekend nights are generally busy when music blares and patrons are occasionally inspired to dance.

**C&C South Beach** (2 Bromton Rd., tel. 876/630-4571) is a restaurant, sports bar, and grill, but best considered a bar. Occasional live shows are held in the yard.

**The Pub** (Mayfair Hotel, 4 Kings House Close, tel. 876/926-1610 or 876/926-1612, 10am-midnight Sun.-Thurs., 10am-2am Fri., 10am-1am Sat.) is located poolside. The bar serves burgers, wings, oxtail, shrimp, and other local dishes.

**Nanook** (20 Burlingston Ave., cell tel. 876/512-2005, www.nanookonline.com) is a bar and performance space geared toward creativity that promotes up-and-coming artists as part of its mission to help Caribbean people find a livelihood through art. Live music performances, spoken word, and live art are regular features.

**Countryside Club** (7 Courtney Walsh Dr., tel. 876/920-6645) is an oasis in the city that comes alive on Friday evenings when outside fried fish, oyster, and pastry vendors are invited to set up shop, and live music performances or DJs keep the crowd entertained. The bar and restaurant is open throughout the week. The venue is frequently used for album or event launches.

**Regency Bar & Lounge** (Terra Nova, 17 Waterloo Rd., tel. 876/926-2211, 11am-1am Mon.-Thurs., 11am-2am Fri.-Sat., 11am-midnight Sun.) is one the most popular Uptown bars in Kingston, catering to guests of the Terra Nova hotel and well-heeled locals. It's one of the most expensive watering holes in town, but the scrumptious appetizers are worth splurging for. Try the duck pissaladière or the lobster tempura appetizers. The over-the-top interior, reminiscent of a Victorian noble's lair, is complemented by more modest furnishings in the open-air courtyard surrounded by tropical foliage.

**East Japanese Next Door** (adjacent to East Japanese Restaurant, Market Place, 67 Constant Spring Rd., tel. 876/960-3962) is a bar with turntables, old school reggae in the speakers, and lava lamps, serving Kingston's best Japanese food from the full service sushi bar and restaurant next door.

**Peppers Lounge & Grill** (Upper Waterloo Rd., tel. 876/969-2421 or 876/905-3831), is a second-story bar and grill behind MegaMart with a decent bar food menu (US$4-14), the pepper shrimp being the highlight.

**Macau Gaming Lounge & Bar** (28 Lindsay Crescent, tel. 876/925-6395) has a large gaming lounge on the ground level and an open-air bar upstairs serving dinner.

**Kno Limit Sports Bar** (8 Hillview Ave., tel. 876/285-7775, kitchen 11:30am-9pm Mon.-Sat., bar until late Mon.-Sat.) has a nice outdoor courtyard space with a flat-screen TV behind the bar. Kno Limit is perhaps best known for Passion Sunday (midnight Sun.-3:30am Mon.), a popular street party held weekly. The kitchen serves traditional Jamaican fare, including fried, baked, and roast chicken.

**Medusa Bar and Grill** (96 Hope, behind Treasure Hut shopping plaza, tel. 876/622-6323, 4pm-late Mon.-Sat.), located on a second-story wood deck with a panoramic view of the hills surrounding Kingston, was launched by proprietor Jason Lee in 2005. It's a great spot for an evening drink. The all-you-can-drink night (6pm-midnight Wed., US$10) packs them in.

**Ribbiz UltraLounge and Restaurant** (Inside Acropolis, Barbican Centre, cell tel. 876/410-7637, 12pm-3am Mon.-Thurs., 12pm-5am Fri.-Sun.) is a popular watering hole located within the Acropolis gaming lounge at Barbican Centre. The bar draws a regular crowd of well-watered uptown Kingstonians, some of them such regular patrons they consider it their second home. Proprietor Ribbi Chung is almost always on location nursing a rum and building the vibes. Red Carpet Fridays and Sensation Saturdaze feature selectors like Kurt Riley and DJ Narity spinning hip hop, reggae and dancehall into the wee hours.

**100** (100 Hope Rd., tel. 876/665-3238, contact@islandbet.com, 24 hours daily, kitchen until midnight Sun.-Thurs., until 4am

# The Life and Legacy of "Miss Lou"

The life of Louise Bennett Coverley (1919-2006) spanned an evolution in the identity of the Jamaican people. Born in Kingston, she was raised during the tumultuous time of the growth of Jamaica's Labour Movement, whose leaders were agitating for racial equality. Miss Lou became an outspoken poet, social commentator, and performer at an early age, converting thick Patois—considered at the time the language of the illiterate underclass—into a national art form and a source of pride. Miss Lou began publishing books in Jamaican Creole in the early 1940s before pursuing opportunities in London to further her performance career. She brought Jamaican folk culture to media and stages around the world, giving presence to a nation yearning for independence.

Jamaican folk culture is based overwhelmingly on African traditions, and in bringing her stories and poems into performance and literary forms, Miss Lou validated an integral part of the country's heritage that had for centuries been scorned. While there are still plenty of examples in contemporary Jamaica of shame about the African past, Miss Lou dispelled the taboo associated with this rich heritage with her warmth and lyrical genius. When Jamaica gained its independence in 1962, Miss Lou's popularity was further cemented as an ambassador for the Jamaican identity in the new era. Miss Lou was a founding member of the Little Theatre Movement.

Fri.-Sat.) is a gaming lounge, restaurant, and bar with an open-air nightclub (8pm-2am Fri.) upstairs.

**Waterfalls** (160 Hope Rd., tel. 876/977-0652) is a banqueting facility that does functions and is open as a nightclub (9pm-4am Thurs., US$7) for oldies featuring the Merritone Disco sound of the late, great Winston "Merritone" Blake, carried on by his brother Monty, with a mixture of reggae, Calypso, and hip-hop from the 1960s to modern times. It's one of the few places in Kingston that catches the vibe of an old dance hall straight out of the 1960s, with the crowd skanking to ska, rocksteady, R&B, and reggae classics well into the night. The cover charge includes complimentary soup.

## PERFORMING ARTS
### Theater

Jamaica has a vibrant tradition in theater, pantomime, and spoken word performances, with annual shows and competitions sponsored by the **Jamaica Cultural Development Commission** (www.jcdc.org.jm). Events are held throughout the year but come to a head during the weeks around Emancipation and Independence in early August.

**Little Theatre Movement,** the **Little-Little Theatre,** and the **National Dance Theatre Company** (4 Tom Redcam Ave., tel. 876/926-6129, www.ltmpantomime.com) share a property on the edge of Downtown. The Xaymaca Dance Theatre also performs here in late October. Plays run throughout the year; call for details on performances. Pantomime performances run December 26 to early May, with school plays after that. The National Dance Theatre performs July-August. Henry Fowler, Rex Nettleford, Barbara Gloudon, Louise "Miss Lou" Bennett, Oliver Samuels, and Ken Hill are some of the founding members of the Little Theatre Movement.

**Centrestage Theatre** (70 Dominica Dr., beside New Kingston Shopping Centre, tel. 876/960-3585, performance info tel. 876/968-7529) is a small venue where productions tend to be family-oriented musicals in a mixture of English and Patois. Centre Stage usually holds two annual performance series, August to November and December 26 to late April or early May. For further information, contact Rosie Williams at Jambiz International (tel. 876/754-3877, www.jambizonline.com). The cast usually includes renowned Jamaican comedians Oliver Samuels and Glen "Titus" Campbell.

**Green Gables Theatre** (6 Cargill Ave., off Half Way Tree Rd., tel. 876/926-4966 or 876/929-5315, www.jamaicastages.com) is the venue for Stages Production plays, which typically run at 8pm Wednesday-Saturday and 5pm and 8pm Sunday.

The **Louise Bennett Garden Theatre** and the **Ranny Williams Entertainment Centre** (36 Hope Rd., tel. 876/926-5726, hrd@jcdc.org.jm, www.jcdc.org.jm) host occasional plays and concerts as well as bingo, book launches, and barbecues a couple of times a month.

**Phillip Sherlock Centre for the Creative Arts** (UWI Mona, tel. 876/927-1047) puts on UWI productions, including those of the student dance society. The building that houses the arts center is architecturally impressive.

The **Theatre Place** (8 Haining Rd., tel. 876/908-0040) is Kingston's newest theatrical venue, run by Pablo Hoilett (cell tel. 876/364-4752, themediaplanet@gmail.com). The theater typically puts on comedies and other plays (US$12).

**Ward Theatre** (North Parade, Downtown, tel. 876/922-0360 or 876/922-0453) holds occasional plays, pantomimes, and special events.

**Pantry Playhouse** (2 Dumfries Rd., tel. 876/960-9845, US$12-15) features comical productions throughout the year in a quaint outdoor setting in the heart of New Kingston. Plays usually run for three months, and performances are generally held Wednesday-Sunday. The outdoor amphitheater at

**Edna Manley College of the Visual and Performing Arts** (1 Arthur Winter Dr., tel. 876/929-2350) hosts poetry readings on the last Tuesday of every month starting at 7:30pm; regular dance performances are held in the indoor theater next door.

## Dance

**Ashe Caribbean Performing Art Ensemble & Academy** (call for dates and locations, executive director Conroy Wilson, tel. 876/960-2985 or 876/997-5935, www.

asheperforms.com, asheperforms@gmail.com) has regular performances throughout the year. Ashe is a full-time dance company that travels frequently and does "edutainment" projects in schools across the island.

**Movements Dance Company** (Liguanea, contact director Monica Campbell, cell tel. 876/999-7953, maccsl@cwjamaica.com) was founded in 1981 and has since grown into one of Jamaica's most dynamic and versatile dance companies. Both traditional Jamaican and Caribbean rhythms inform the company's repertoire. The schedule of performances climaxes each year with the annual Season of Dance in November. The company also travels to perform in the United States, the United Kingdom, Canada, and neighboring Caribbean islands.

**Dance Theatre Xaymaca** (dancetheatrexaymaca@gmail.com) is one of Kingston's leading troupes, performing seasonally at the Little Theatre to an ever growing base of fans.

## GAMBLING

Until recently gambling was illegal in Jamaica, while "gaming" was not, as long as you are at least 18. Off-track betting (OTB) is supported by nearby Caymanas Park racetrack with outlets across the island carrying local and overseas races. Video Gaming Machines are found throughout the island thanks mostly to Supreme Ventures, with a few locations in Kingston to play the odds against a computer. Popular gaming lounges include **100** (100 Hope Rd.), **Acropolis** (Loshusan Plaza, 29 East Kings House Rd., tel. 876/978-1299, 1pm-1am Mon.-Thurs., 1pm-3am Fri.-Sat., 10am-1am Sun.), **Monte Carlo Gaming** (Terra Nova Hotel, 17 Waterloo Rd., tel. 876/926-2211, 11am-4am Mon.-Fri., 11am-6am Sat.-Sun.), and **Treasure Hunt Gaming** (14-15 Trinidad Terrace, tel. 876/929-2938, 24 hours daily).

**Caymanas Park** (racing@cwjamaica.com, www.caymanasracetrack.com) horse track is recognized as one of the best in the Caribbean. Races are held on select Wednesdays and Saturdays, with the occasional Monday race, and are usually well attended. Admission ranges US$0.50-4, depending on seating. Caymanas Track Ltd. (CTL) supports a large network of OTB sites around the corporate area, which offer simulcast races from around the world when races aren't being broadcast from Caymanas.

# Shopping

Kingston is full of shopping plazas and strip malls. Half Way Tree has the highest concentration of shops in Jamaica along the stretch of Constant Spring Road running between Hope Road and Market Place.

## ART STUDIOS AND GALLERIES

**Space Caribbean** (10A W. Kings House Rd., tel. 876/622-7327, www.spacecaribbean.com) opened in 2015 under the leadership of curator Rachel Barrett to provide a cutting edge venue showcasing top local and international talent to further its mission of fostering socioeconomic and cultural development through dialogue and engagement with contemporary art through lectures, workshops and events. It is located in the former Kingston residence of legendary Jamaican writer and filmmaker Perry Henzell, and has for decades been an epicenter of creativity in the nation's capital.

**Amai Craft** (shop 27, Red Hills Trade Centre, 30 Red Hills Rd., tel. 876/920-9134, vanasherman@gmail.com, 10am-5pm Mon.-Fri., 10am-2pm Sat.) sells paintings specializing in Jamaican, Haitian, and Cuban intuitive, or self-taught, artists. Belgium-born Herman van Asbroeck, the proprietor, founded the gallery in 2000 but has been living in Jamaica for more than four decades. The gallery is located upstairs from the unassuming framing shop Herman runs on the ground floor.

**Patrick Waldemar** (Shortwood Professional Centre, 40 Shortwood Rd., tel. 876/960-8222, cell tel. 876/824-8222, wald@ cwjamaica.com, www.patrickwaldemar.com), a talented acrylic, watercolor, and digital artist, has a studio gallery where he welcomes visitors for private viewings and wine.

**Grosvenor Galleries** (1 Grosvenor Terrace, Manor Park, tel. 876/924-6684, grosvenorgallery@cwjamaica.com, 10am-5pm Tues.-Sat.) has contemporary art exhibits and occasional craft fairs that bring artists and craftspeople from around Jamaica. A café (11am-7pm Mon.-Fri., 10am-6pm Sat.) on-site serves salads, sandwiches, and smoothies with outdoor seating.

**Island Art & Framing** (Orchid Village, 20 Barbican Rd., tel. 876/977-0318, islandart@ cwjamaica.com, www.islandartandframing. com) sells a wide variety of local and imported arts and crafts and paintings by an array of talented contemporary artists.

**Sanaa Studios** (25 Barbican Rd., behind Burger King, tel. 876/977-4792 or 876/822-7528, info@sanaastudios.com, www.sanaastudios.com, 10am-5pm Mon.-Sat.) offers classes in ceramics, drawing, painting, art photography, and jewelry making. A small gallery has a steady flow of exhibits featuring student art and an end-of-year art bazaar. Drop-in rates are US$40 for three-hour sessions.

An acronym for New Local Space, **NLS** (190 Mountain View Ave., contact executive director Deborah Anzinger, tel. 876/927-7931, cell tel. 876/406-9771, www.nlskingston.org, by appointment only) is a contemporary visual arts gallery associated with recording studio and production house Creative Sounds, on the same premises. It was launched in 2012 to showcase the works of visual artists exploring contemporary issues through collaboration and engagement with the public, with the goal of supporting experimentation and connecting local artists with the global contemporary art community through residencies and a dynamic exhibition program.

**The Art Centre** (202 Hope Rd., across from the University of Technology, tel. 876/927-1608, artcentre.ja@gmail.com, 9am-5pm Mon.-Fri., 10am-4pm Sat., free) is housed in a uniquely designed apartment building commissioned by A. D. Scott in the 1960s. Inside, colorful murals adorn the walls and art is displayed on the upper two levels as part of the building's permanent collection. The gallery uses the ground floor space for occasional temporary exhibits. Paintings start at around US$100.

## DEVON HOUSE SHOPS

The courtyard at **Devon House** (26 Hope Rd., at Trafalgar Rd.) is home to some of the nicest boutique shops in Kingston, in addition to offering tantalizing treats to stimulate your palate. **Starfish Oils** (tel. 876/908-4763, www.starfishoils.com) is one of Jamaica's leading cottage industries, producing soaps, oils, and candles ideal for compact gift items and everyday use. These products are provided by many of Jamaica's best hotels. Starfish also has an outlet in Manor Park Plaza. **T's and Treasures** (shops 3 and 4, tel. 876/632-2961, 11am-7pm Mon.-Sat., 4pm-7pm Sun.) sells books on travel and culture, cultural DVDs, paintings, souvenirs, apparel, and trinkets. **Things Jamaican** (shops 12-14, tel. 876/926-1961, www.thingsmadeinjamaica.com, 9am-8pm Mon.-Fri., 10am-8pm Sat., noon-8pm Sun.) sells a wide array of crafts, books, and creative gift items, all made in Jamaica.

## CLOTHING AND ACCESSORIES

**Sarai Clothing** has a kiosk at vegetarian restaurant Country Farmhouse (3 Deanery Rd., Vineyard Town) where proprietor Sister May (cell tel. 876/372-6265) sells rootsy African and Jamaican apparel, including Ethiopian sharmas and gear for men, women, and children.

**Mutamba** (tel. 876/387-4112 or 876/320-1209, by appointment only), a clothing line developed by outspoken Jamaican Pan-Africanist dub poet Mutabaruka and his

wife, Amber, is very popular for its minimalist chic aesthetic.

**J'adore Boutique** (shop 33, Bargain Plaza, tel. 876/754-8386, 11am-7pm Mon.-Sat.) has clothes imported from Europe, fit for clubbing or going out.

**Flirt Boutique** (shop 12, Lower Manor Park Plaza, tel. 876/931-9332, flirtboutiqueja@gmail.com, flirtboutiqueja.com) has women's apparel for the nightclub or a dinner out.

Prices vary considerably (US$1.50-357) at **Bling Bling** (shop 5, Mid Spring Plaza, 134 Constant Spring Rd., tel. 876/925-3855, 10am-8pm Mon.-Sat.) has all the bling you'll need to flex big at the club or a street dance; Sharon Beckford is the friendly proprietor.

**Bridget Sandals** (1 Abbeydale Rd., opposite Hope Road entrance to Devon House, tel. 876/968-1913, www.bridgetsandals.net, 9am-6pm Mon.-Sat., US$65-120) sells thong, strappy, and open-toe sandals. The unique and tasteful handcrafted leather footwear for women has a tremendous following. Founder Bridget Brown and son Jonathan Buchanan run the shop.

**Lee's Fifth Avenue** (Tropical Plaza, Half Way Tree, tel. 876/926-8280, www.leesfifthavenue.com, 10am-7pm Mon.-Sat., 11am-4pm Sun.) sells quality, trendy, brand-name clothes like Levi's, Puma, and Tommy Hilfiger.

**Brit Bran Fashion** (shop 7, Half Way Tree Mall, tel. 876/929-3849; shop 2, Bargain Mall, tel. 876/906-5615; shop 13, Lane Plaza, tel. 876/906-4086; State Mall, Cross Roads, tel. 876/754-5400; 10am-7pm Mon.-Thurs., 10am-8pm Fri.-Sat.) retails imported designs and accessories from Forever 21 for women and men, from casual to swimsuits and going-out threads.

**Loran-V Boutique** (shop 2, Northside Plaza, 26 Northside Dr., off Hope Rd., tel. 876/977-6450, loran_v_swimwear@yahoo.com, 9am-5pm Mon.-Fri., 10am-2pm Sat.) makes swimwear and light apparel on-site for men and women, with a handful of women at sewing machines churning out well-designed bikinis and trunks.

**Kerry manwomanhome** (18 South Ave.,

tel. 876/929-1969, www.kerrymanwoman-home.com), is one of Kingston's top boutiques for locally produced garments, jewelry, and books for him and her. Kerry-Ann Clarke, the fashion aficionado proprietor, is a graduate of Parsons School of Design.

**Sobelio Boutique Shop** (Sovereign North, cell tel. 876/631-2114 or 876/779-2885, sobelioboutique@gmail.com, www.sobelioboutique.com) sells casually elegant free-flowing dresses dubbed fun, flirty, and fabulous.

## BOOKSTORES

**Bookland** (53 Knutsford Blvd., New Kingston, tel. 876/926-4035, 9am-6pm Mon.-Fri., 10am-5pm Sat.) has the best selection of Caribbean and Jamaican books, and magazines as well as souvenirs.

**Kingston Bookshop** has several locations around town (70-B King St., tel. 876/922-4056; 74 King St., tel. 876/922-7016; Pavilion Mall, 13 Constant Spring Rd.; shop 6, Boulevard Shopping Center; shop 2, The Springs, 17 Constant Spring Rd.) that carry Jamaican and Caribbean titles as well as imports. It's also a major force in Jamaica's textbook market. Downtown stores operate 9am-5pm daily, Uptown stores 9am-6pm daily.

**Sangster's Book Stores** (several locations, 876/758-6840, info@sangstersbooks.com, www.sangstersbooks.com) is another major chain with several locations around town. See their website for their many locations.

**Bookophilia** (92 Hope Rd., tel. 876/978-5248, 11am-8pm Mon.-Thurs., 11am-9pm Fri., 10am-7pm Sat., noon-5pm Sun.) opened in April 2008 with a great selection of books and magazines. There's a small kiosk in the corner of the cozy shop serving Blue Mountain coffee, tea, cookies, and muffins (US$1-3). The signature drink is the Gingerbread Chai Latte (US$3). A worldbeat night is held 6pm-9pm the last Friday of every month. Bookophilia lures first-time customers with a free cup of coffee.

**Bolivar Bookshop & Gallery** (1-D Grove Rd., tel. 876/926-8799) is a nice boutique with a small art gallery and more rare books than can be found at the other bookstores in town.

**Headstar Books and Crafts** (54 Church St., tel. 876/922-3915, headstarp@hotmail.com) is an Afrocentric bookshop run by Brother Miguel.

## JEWELRY

**Swiss Stores** (107 Harbour St., tel. 876/922-8050, www.swissstoresjamaica.com) sells a wide selection of watches and jewelry, duty-free for visitors.

## RECORD SHOPS

**Techniques Records** (99 Orange St., in front of Jamaica Lifestock, contact Winston Riley, tel. 876/967-4367 or 876/858-6407, 9am-7pm Mon.-Sat.) has what is perhaps Kingston's best selection for all kinds of traditional music and oldies, with LPs, 33s, and 45s, as well as the latest singles and CDs.

**Rockers International Records** (135 Orange St., tel. 876/922-8015, 9am-4pm Mon.-Sat.) specializes in reggae, and has CDs and LPs, 33s, and 45s, with the latest domestic singles and imports. The shop is run by Addis Pablo, son of the late great Augustus Pablo.

**Cap Calcini** (58 Dunbarton Ave., Contact Lucas Corthésy, cell tel. 876/268-4651, 8am-6pm Mon.-Sat.) has a great collection of vinyl sold wholesale both 45s and 33s, both vintage and contemporary recordings, leaning toward oldies.

**Music Mart** (8 South Ave., tel. 876/926-4687, www.musicmart.biz, 9:30am-5pm Mon.-Thurs., 9:30am-6pm Sat.) sells CDs, DVDs and instruments, including traditional Jamaican Maroon gumbe and Rasta base, fundeh and akete drums.

**Derrick Harriott's One Stop Record Shop** (shop 36, Twin Gates Plaza, Constant Spring, tel. 876/926-8027, derrickchariothar-riott@hotmail.com, 10am-6:30pm Mon.-Sat.) has a good selection of oldies as well as the latest LPs and 45 singles.

**Tad's International Records** (Unit 40 at The Trade Centre, 30-32 Red Hills Rd., tel.

876/929-2563, tadsrecordinc@cwjamaica. com, tadsdigidis@gmail.com, www.tadsrecord.com) has an extensive catalog of reggae from the early days of Gregory Isaacs, Dennis Brown, and John Holt, and more contemporary Terry Linen, Cecile, Teflon, Anthony B, and Vybz Kartell.

## ARTS, CRAFTS, AND GIFTS

**Craft Cottage** (Village Plaza, 24 Constant Spring Rd., tel. 876/926-0719, 9:30am-5:30pm Mon.-Thurs., 9:30am-6pm Fri.-Sat.) is a good place for authentic Jamaican arts and crafts.

**Market at the Lawn** is held from 10am-5pm the last Sunday of every other month on the north lawn of Devon House (26 Hope Rd.). The open-air market features a variety of food, fashion, art and craft vendors. Contact Kaili McDonnough-Scott (cell tel. 876/585-7233, thelawnkingston@gmail. com) for more information.

**Original Bamboo Factory** (Caymans Estate, Spanish Town, tel. 876/746-9906 or 876/869-6675, hamilton1@cwjamaica.com or bamboojamaica@gmail.com, www.originalbamboofactory.com) has what you need if you're in the market for bamboo furniture or just want to see how it's put together.

# Sports and Recreation

Kingston is not known for its outdoor recreational opportunities. Nevertheless, there are plenty of local options, including diving, hiking, golf, tennis, and even surfing.

The **National Stadium** hosts most important sporting events on the island, including the home games of the national soccer team **Reggae Boyz** (www.thereggaeboyz.com) and track and field events. Next door at the **National Arena** and the **Indoor Sports Centre,** several trade shows and events are held. For more information contact the **Jamaica Football Federation** (20 St. Lucia Crescent, tel. 876/929-0484 or 876/929-8036, jamff@hotmail.com) and ask for press officer Garth Williams.

**Sabina Park,** located Downtown on South Camp Road, hosts some home games for the West Indies cricket team (www. windiescricket.com). The **Jamaica Cricket Association** (tel. 876/967-0322 or 987/922-8423, jcacricket@hotmail.com, www.jamaicacricket.org) based at Sabina, controls the sport on the island.

## TOURS

**We Jamaica Tours,** run by sole operator Juliet Gordon (tel. 876/925-8798, cell tel. 876/362-9319, oldejamaica@yahoo.com, www. oldejamaicatours.com, US$5 adults, US$2 children) arranges sports tours to cricket matches, athletics meets, and training sessions, or to venues like Sabina Park stadium.

## GOLF

Kingston's most reputable golf course is **Caymanas Golf & Country Club** (Mandela Hwy., tel. 876/746-9772 or 876/746-9773, www.caymanasgolfclub.com, greens fees US$50 Mon.-Fri., US$55.50 Sat.-Sun. and holidays, cart US$22.50), west of town. Designed by Canadian architect Howard Watson in 1958, the course features elevated greens with lush fairways cut through limestone hills. The views from the tees are excellent, with Guango trees providing natural obstacles and occasional shade. A restaurant and bar on-site welcomes members and nonmembers alike..

**Constant Spring Golf Club** (152 Constant Spring Rd., tel. 876/924-1610, csgc@ cwjamaica.com, greens fees US$45 Mon.-Fri., US$50 Sat.-Sun., cart US$20) is a more humble par-70 course located in the middle of Uptown Kingston. Built by Scottish architect Stanley Thompson in 1920, the short, tight course is challenging, with an excellent view at the 13th hole. Clubs (US$35) are available from the pro shop (tel. 876/924-5170) and a caddy costs US$13.50. Canadian National Railways built a magnificent hotel just below the course, parallel to the 18th hole fairway, which was long ago converted into the Immaculate Conception High School, one of Kingston's most prestigious.

## RACKET SPORTS

**Liguanea Club** (80 Knutsford Blvd., tel. 876/926-8144, liguaneaclub@cwjamaica.com), across from the Courtleigh Hotel, has squash, billiards, and tennis, plus an outdoor swimming pool. Membership (US$78 per month) is required to use the facilities.

**Tennis Jamaica** (2A Piccadilly Rd., court bookings tel. 876/929-5878 or 876/906-5700, ask for Sheron Quest, www.tennisjamaica. com, 6am-6pm daily, US$4.50 per hour 6am-4pm, US$6.70 per hour 4pm-6pm), formerly the Jamaica Lawn Tennis Association, has courts and can set up partners. The organization sometimes holds tournaments. Heading toward Cross Roads on Half Way Tree Road or Old Hope Road, turn onto Caledonia Avenue at the light and then take a right onto Marescaux Road. After you pass the National Water Commission on the left, take the next right at the front entrance of L. P. Azar, a textile store. The courts are at the end of the road.

The **Jamaica Pegasus** (81 Knutsford Blvd., tel. 876/926-3690, ext. 3023, or ask for the tennis court, US$14 per hour day, US$19 per hour night) has well-maintained, lit courts. Court fees cover a lesson for a single player or the court for you and your partner. Tennis rackets (US$10) are included in some lesson fees.

## POLO

The **Kingston Polo Club** (contact Lesley Masterton-Fong Yee, tel. 876/381-4660 or 876/922-8060, or Shane Chin, tel. 876/952-4370, chinrcpolo@yahoo.com) is located on the Caymanas Estate west of town off Mandela Highway. It can be reached by taking the same exit as for the Caymanas Golf & Country Club, about 100 meters (330 feet) west of the

turnoff for Portmore. The Kingston Polo Club season runs early January-August 7 and is host to some of the highest-handicap polo played on the island, starting with the ICWI international women's team, ICWI 18 goal, and the NCB High International 15 goal tournament in May. Matches are held at 4pm Wednesday and 10am Sunday.

## WATER SPORTS

Though Kingston has a lot of waterfront, it's not put to great use: there are no cafés, restaurants, or bars on Ocean Boulevard, as one might hope. Nevertheless, there are plenty of places around to have a dip, including Port Royal, Cane River Falls east of town, and beaches on Lime Cay and west of town at Hellshire and Fort Clarence. Lime Cay and Fort Clarence have the cleanest stretches of sand in the area.

### Surfing

If you're looking to catch some waves, don't miss **Jamnesia Surf Camp** in Bull Bay, where the most active members of the tight-knit **Jamaica Surfing Association** (tel. 876/750-0103, www.jamsurfas.webs.com) congregate. The association has raised the profile of Jamaican surfing in a commendable fashion, organizing events and contests at home and competing overseas with a national team.

### Boating

The **Royal Jamaica Yacht Club** (Palisadoes Park, Norman Manley Blvd., tel. 876/924-8685 or 876/924-8686, rjyc@flowja.com, www.rjyc.org.jm), located on the eastern side of Kingston Harbor between the Caribbean Maritime Institute and the international airport, holds regular regattas and yacht races. Yachters arriving in Jamaica should stay on their vessel once docked until being cleared by quarantine, customs, and immigration officials.

Slips can accommodate vessels of up to 50 feet, while the visitors' dock can accommodate larger vessels. Fees are US$1.50 per foot for the first six days and US$1 thereafter; electricity, water, and fuel are charged according to usage. If you want to sign on as crew, make your interest known at the club. Yearly membership costs US$350. Visiting boats can moor in the harbor for US$12 per day (for two people, and US$2 for each additional crewmember), to use the club facilities, which include restrooms with showers, a swimming pool, a restaurant and bar, and Wi-Fi.

**Sail Jamaica** (contact instructor Scott Clarke, cell tel. 876/579-5291, scottsailtt@ gmail.com) offers sailing lessons and courses for children and adults on long-term programs (US$250) and weekend learn-to-sail courses (US$120). Tailored lessons and courses can also be arranged for short-term visitors.

### Fishing

Local anglers go out to the California Banks, about 16 kilometers (10 miles) offshore from Port Royal. Nigel Black operates **Why Not Fishing Charters** (tel. 876/995-1142) from Grand Port Royal Hotel, Marina & Spa. Other fishing expeditions can be arranged by inquiring with Anthony DuCasse at **DuRae's Boat Sales** (18 Rosewell Terrace, tel. 876/905-1713, duraes@cwjamaica.com), the best powerboat parts supplier on the island, in business since 1966.

## RUNNING AND CYCLING

**Jamaica Hash House Harriers** (www.jamaicahash.org) is a running group better known as "a drinking club with a running problem" or "the world's largest disorganization." The club welcomes visiting runners and drinkers to join the pack. Contact Emile Finlay (cell tel. 876/997-4700, efinlay@cwjamaica.com). Hash runs take place approximately every two weeks, usually on a Sunday, with occasional holiday hikes and runs scheduled as well.

**Jamdammers Running Club** (info@jamdammers.com, www.jamdammers.com) is a formal organization that celebrates Jamaica's "out of many, one people" motto. Its founding members are Jamaicans from all walks of life that run regularly at the Mona Reservoir, called "The Dam."

**Bikenutz** is a group of cycling enthusiasts (contact Andre Gordon, U.S. tel. 705/321-5628, wheelnutz@gmail.com) that welcomes newcomers.

## SPAS AND FITNESS

The Jamaican hospitality industry is making a concerted effort to brand Jamaica as a premier health and spa tourism destination. In

The Royal Jamaica Yacht Club holds regular regattas and races.

Kingston there are a few good options when it comes to affordable pampering.

**Isabelle's Day Spa** (Orchid Village, Barbican Rd., tel. 876/970-0025, www.isabellesdayspac.club, reservations recommended) is a highly recommended pampering parlor offering rigorous massage therapy as well as nail, skin and makeup services.

**Pandora Day** (23 Haining Road, New Kingston, reservations recommended, cell. tel. 876/553 4720 or 876/787-6333, pandoradayspa@gmail.com, pandoradayspa@gmail.com) offers facials, waxing massage, Blue Mountain Coffee body scrubs, salon and teeth whitening services closer to the corporate hub and business hotels of the city.

**Eden Gardens Spa** (39 Lady Musgrave Rd., tel. 876/946-9981, 9am-6pm daily) offers facials, body massage, full body scrubs and wraps, oxygen therapy, and more (US$60-120).

**Jencare Skin Farm** (82 Hope Rd., tel. 876/946-3494 or 876/946-3497, jencarejender@yahoo.com) is a slightly more upscale day spa that offers complete bodywork, from nails (US$31) to facials (US$43) and massage (US$50). You can also get a haircut (US$7).

**Rockfort Mineral Spa** (Florizel Glasspole Hwy., just west of the Carib Cement factory, tel. 876/938-6551, 7am-5:30pm Tues.-Sun., US$2.50 adults, US$1.50 children) has one of Kingston's few public swimming pools adjoined by a bathhouse. On the remains of a British Fort from which it gets its name, the baths are fed by mineral water from the Dallas Mountains. A large swimming pool outside is complemented by enclosed whirlpool tubs available for 45-minute sessions (US$14-31). The tubs are heated with electric heaters; by 10am, they're hot and ready for use. Additionally, the spa has a stress-management center offering 45-minute massages (US$35) and reflexology sessions (US$25).

# Food

If there's anything to demonstrate that Kingston has a bona fide cosmopolitan side, it's the food. The city's offerings reflect the country's motto, "Out of Many, One People," with Indian, Chinese, and African influences deeply entrenched. Recent Mexican, Cuban, Lebanese, and Japanese immigrants have also made their mark at a few recommendable restaurants. Of course, Jamaica's traditional fare, including jerk meats and seafood specialties, can also be found in abundance in Kingston. The price for a filling meal varies according to the venue, with traditional Jamaican staples available for as little as US$5.

## DOWNTOWN
### Cafés

**Swiss Stores** (107 Harbour St., tel. 876/922-8050, www.swissstoresjamaica.com, 9am-5pm Mon.-Sat., US$9-20) sells watches and jewelry duty-free for visitors and has a refreshing café serving eggs to order and pancakes for breakfast, and for lunch, chicken teriyaki and shrimp salads, soup, and entrées like Italian style pasta dishes, steak, and oxtail.

### Jamaican

**Moby Dick Restaurant** (3 Orange St., corner of Port Royal St. and Harbour St., tel. 876/922-4468, 10am-5:30pm Mon.-Sat.) is a landmark establishment and the best place to grab lunch Downtown. Moby Dick specializes in curry dishes accompanied by roti, with an ambience reminiscent of India: The cashier sits on a raised structure by the entrance with an overseer's view of the dining area. Seafood like shrimp and conch (US$15) as well as terrestrial staples like goat (US$10) are served with fresh fruit juices (US$3).

**M10 Bar & Grill** (6 Vineyard Rd., cell tel. 876/336-6969, US$8-12) is a popular local eatery serving Jamaican staples like curried goat, oxtail, and fried chicken in an informal atmosphere. The menu changes daily.

# NEW KINGSTON
## Cafés

**24/7 Café** (lobby at the Pegasus, tel. 876/926-3690, US$5-10, 24 hours daily) serves rotating soups like fish or red pea, salads, breakfast bagels with smoked marlin or salmon, paninis, wraps, chicken pot pie, and homemade fries. Coffee with scones, cookies, muffins, and cheesecake are sure to satisfy any sweet tooth. Wi-Fi is complimentary for customers.

**Cannonball Café** (Shop 1, 3M Bldg., 20-24 Barbados Ave., tel. 876/754-4486, 7am-6pm Mon.-Fri.) serves coffee, pastries and sandwiches (US$6), and dishes like beef lasagna (US$10), quiche (US$10), and salad (US$6). Try the scones with sweet cream and jam (US$5) with natural juices (US$4) or cappuccino (US$5). The atmosphere is relaxing and cozy; Wi-Fi is complimentary for customers.

**Spanish Court Café** (lobby at the Spanish Court Hotel, 1 St. Lucia Ave., tel. 876/926-0000, 7am-11pm daily, US$5-10) serves pumpkin bisque, salads, sandwiches, paninis, and desserts like brownies, pudding, cheesecake, chocolate cake, and truffles. Wi-Fi is complimentary for customers.

## Jerk

**Sweetwood Jerk Joint** (Emancipation Park, tel. 876/906-4854, sweetwoodja@yahoo.com, 11:30am-10pm Sun.-Thurs., 11:30am-midnight Fri.-Sat.) serves jerk pork (US$20 per pound), sausage, chicken (US$5 per quarter), lamb, conch, and roast fish, prepared on a coal-fired pit smoked with sweet wood and seasoned with Scotch bonnet peppers.

**Chelsea Jerk Center** (7 Chelsea Ave., tel. 876/926-6322, 10am-10pm Mon.-Thurs., 10am-midnight Fri.-Sat.) has decent fast-food-style jerk chicken and jerk pork with rice-and-peas or festival (US$5-7) at affordable prices.

★ **Scotchies Tree** (2 Chelsea Ave., tel. 876/906-0602, 11:30am-10pm Sun.-Wed., 11:30am-11:30pm Thurs.-Sat., US$4-8) serves the award-winning, mouthwatering jerk chicken and pork made famous at the first Scotchies location in Montego Bay, accompanied by sides of festival, roasted bread fruit, sweet potato, and yellow yam. Excellent steam roast fish fillet is also prepared, along with spicy chicken and pork sausage.

## Jamaican

**Cuddy'z Sportsbar** (shops 4-6, New Kingston Shopping Center, Dominica Dr., tel. 876/920-8019, 11:30am-9pm Mon.-Thurs.,

Scotchies Tree serves mouthwatering jerk pork and chicken.

# Nyammings: Food on the Go

While it is sometimes said that Jamaica's national dish is fried chicken from KFC, there are a host of authentically Jamaican fast-food joints to compete for that title, like Tastee Patties, Juici Patties, Island Grill, and Captain's Bakery. In fact, only a few international franchises have been able to survive in Jamaica; both McDonald's and Taco Bell were unable to stay viable. Others, like Domino's Pizza, Pizza Hut, Popeye's, and Subway, do relatively well in a few locations around town. Pan chicken, patties, and loaves have traditionally been the food of choice for Jamaicans on the go.

**Pan chicken vendors** set up all over town from evening until the early morning. Some of the best spots in town for real hot-off-the-grill pan chicken include the line of vendors on Red Hills Road just beyond Red Hills Plaza, heading toward Meadowbrook and Red Hills. You can also whiff the pan chicken as you approach Manor Plaza in Manor Park on the upper reaches of Constant Spring Road in the evenings. A few dependable **jerk vendors** hawk their fare in the evenings on the corner of Northside Drive and Hope Road by Pizza Hut, and they have a devoted following. Jerk pork (US$8.50 per pound) is sold on one side of the plaza and jerk chicken (US$3.50 per quarter) on the other.

11:30am-1am Sat., 2pm-9pm Sun., US$9-18) is owned by Jamaica's favorite cricket star, Courtney "Cuddy" Walsh. Cuddy'z is flush with TVs in the booths and large flat-screen TVs around the bar. An adjoining room has a projector, making it a good place to catch a big game in the presence of a guaranteed raucous crowd. Typical sports-bar fare of burgers and fries (US$6-7) is complemented by Jamaican staples like curry goat and stewed chicken (US$8) or ribs, tenderloin, and shrimp (US$17).

**The Pantry** (2 Dumphries Rd., tel. 876/929-6804 or 876/929-4149, thepantry52@ yahoo.com, noon-3pm Mon.-Fri., US$3-5) is a roadside takeout cook shop popular for lunch among the corporate crowd of New Kingston, serving Jamaican staples like fried chicken, brown stew fish, and curry goat.

## International

**Café Africa** (2 Trafalgar Rd., cell tel. 876/828-4144, cafeafricaja@gmail.com, 9am-9pm Mon.-Thurs., 10am-10pm Sat., 11am-7pm Sun.) specializes in African dishes, both vegetarian and meat. The spot is also the de facto base for the United Negro Improvement Association, now presided over by the restaurant's proprietor, Stephen Golding, on the site of Marcus Garvey's original office of the Pan-African unity organization. A bust of Garvey stands at the site, commemorating the national hero.

## Meat and Seafood

**Phoenix Lounge at So So Seafood Grill & More** (4 Chelsea Ave., tel. 876/968-2397, 11am-midnight Mon.-Thurs., 11am-2am Fri., 11-1 Sat., 2pm-midnight Sun., from US$15) is a seafood joint serving steamed or fried fish, various shrimp dishes, curry or stewed conch, and lobster in season (US$20-23). Finger food is also served. The pleasant ambience with strings of lights and a little waterfall, reggae in the speakers, and good food make So So a definite misnomer, though in Patois the phrase means "mostly." The restaurant hosts a crab night each Wednesday and Campari specials each Friday when a DJ plays music from 6pm.

★ **Red Bones Blues Café** (1 Argyle Rd., tel. 876/978-8262, cell tel. 876/879-8262, redbonesmanager@gmail.com, www.redbonesbluescafe.com, noon-11pm Mon.-Fri., 6pm-11pm Sat.) has great food, ranging from linguine (US$17) to grilled lobster (US$50). The bar and lounge bring the spirit of New Orleans to Jamaica and are a dependable spot for live music. Album and book launches, fashion shows, poetry readings, jazz and reggae performances are frequent.

## Asian

**Gwong Wo** (12 Trinidad Terrace, tel. 876/906-1288 or 876/906-1388, 11am-9pm Mon.-Sat., noon-9pm Sun., from US$7) has excellent fried fricassee chicken and rice, chow mein, curried shrimp and chicken and broccoli.

## Vegetarian

★ **Ashanti Oasis** (12 Braemar Ave., tel. 876/281-8473 or 876/458-9859, ashanti_fine_cuisine@yahoo.com), owned by Yvonne Hope, has affordable vegetarian food. Combo meals are the best value, giving a taste of everything for US$4, or US$3.50 per single serving of any one dish. The menu changes daily and includes items like chili tofu in smoked sauce. Juices (US$1.50) are the best in town. Call to find out what will be on the menu the following day.

**Mother Earth** (13 Oxford Terrace, off Old Hope Rd., just below Oxford Rd., tel. 876/926-2575, 8am-4pm Mon.-Sat., US$4.50-5.50) is an excellent veggie and fish joint owned by Georgia Adams serving pepper pot, fish, and red pea soups and entrées like tofu creole, Chinese veggie steak, and veggie mince balls. Meals are accompanied by roti or rice-and-peas. Fresh natural juices (US$2-2.25) include beet, cane, calalloo, and papaya. Mother Earth serves dishes exemplary of Jamaica's colorful vegetarian, or ital, culinary repertoire, in a down-to-earth, no-frills setting.

**Seven Basics & More,** run by the **Country Farmhouse** (3 Deanery Rd., Vineyard Town, tel. 876/930-1244 or 876/930-1245) is a vegetarian restaurant and deli, retailing Blessed Delights baked products made by **Ngozi** (tel. 876/899-6332), many of which are vegan. Ngozi supplies Legend Café at the Bob Marley Museum and other vegetarian spots around town, like New Leaf further up Hope Road. Her heavenly vegan chocolate cake and gluten free sweet potato pudding are musts.

# HALF WAY TREE
## Cafés

★ **Susie's Bakery & Coffee Bar** (shop 1, Southdale Plaza, behind Popeye's on Constant Spring Rd., tel. 876/968-5030, 8am-10pm Mon.-Sat., 9am-7:30pm Sun.) is an excellent spot for dinner, with outdoor seating and items like seafood penne, steak, and lamb chops (US$20-29). Dinner is served from 6:30pm. Susie's well-prepared entrées, natural juices, and homemade pastries, while not inexpensive, are worth the cost. Indoor seating

Ashanti Oasis offers hearty vegetarian fare.

by the deli and fresh salad bar complement the elegant courtyard seating next to the outdoor bar with a lively schedule of theme nights throughout the week.

**Rituals Coffee House** (shop 5, Village Plaza, tel. 876/754-1992, www.ritualscoffeehouse.com, 7:30am-7pm Mon.-Thurs., 7:30am-7:30pm Fri., 8am-9pm Sat., 10:30am-5:30pm Sun.) is a coffee shop serving espresso, lattes, cappuccinos, tea, pastries, pastas, salads, and sandwiches (US$3-10). The Village Plaza location is the only Jamaican franchise outlet of the Trinidad-based chain.

## Jerk

★ **Jo Jo's Jerk Pit and More** (12 Waterloo Rd., tel. 876/906-1509 or 876/906-1612) does regular Jamaican breakfast starting at 8am and lunch (Mon.-Wed.) with Jamaican staples, a grill day (noon-10pm Thurs.) featuring barbecued ribs, homemade burgers, steaks, lamb and chicken, and the Jerk Pit (noon-10pm Fri.-Sat.) serving jerk chicken, pork, lamb, and conch in addition to soups and sandwiches. The bar is open during regular business hours. Jamaican breakfast is served starting at 8am Sunday, and featuring mackerel rundown.

**Truck Stop Grill & Bar** (18 W. Kings House Rd., 5pm-midnight Sun.-Thurs., 5pm-2am Fri.-Sat., tel. 876/631-0841, www.truckstopjamaica.com) is a popular bar and informal jerk joint with outdoor seating on barrel stools serving jerk chicken or pork (US$4-7); steamed, fried, or roasted fish; and jerk or garlic lobster (US$16 per pound). A beer costs around US$3.

## Jamaican

**Grog Shoppe Restaurant and Pub** (Devon House, 26 Hope Rd., tel. 876/926-3512, www.grogshoppejm.com, 11am-10pm Mon.-Sat., US$17-50) has a broad menu of soups, appetizers, and mains with Jamaican classics and comfort food done right. Try the smoked marlin salad on a fan of papaya followed by oxtail, curry goat or fried escoveitch fish from the local menu or more exotic dishes like

grilled salmon with a brown sugar citrus ginger glaze.

**Sonia's Homestyle Cooking & Natural Juices** (17 Central Ave., tel. 876/968-6267, 7am-5:30pm Mon.-Fri., 7:30am-5pm Sat., 8am-5pm Sun., US$5-7.50) is Half Way Tree's best and most authentic sit-down eatery for Jamaican dishes like fried chicken, curry goat, and oxtail. Natural juices (US$1-2) like guava, cucumber, and soursop vary based on seasonal availability. The menu changes daily.

## International

**Caffé Da Vinci** (Market Place, tel. 876/906-9051, www.caffedavincija.com, 12pm-10pm Mon.-Sat., 1pm-10pm Sun.) is an Italian restaurant and café serving pizza, pasta, coffee, and desserts with indoor and outdoor seating.

## Asian

Just west of the Junction of West Kings House Road and Constant Spring Road, the **Courtyard at Market Place** (67 Constant Spring Rd.) has become the premier international food court in Kingston.

★ **Taka's East Japanese Restaurant** (shops 50-51, tel. 876/960-3962, 5pm-10pm Tues., noon-10pm Wed.-Sun.) has the best sushi in Jamaica at competitive prices (US$25 pp for a full meal) and a very convincing ambience.

**Saffron Indian Restaurant** (shop 37 Market Place, 67 Constant Spring Rd., tel. 876/926-6598, 11:30am-10pm Mon.-Sat., 1pm-9:30pm Sun.) serves North and South Indian dishes as well as Asian fusion, from grilled fish to tandoori shrimp and malai tikka chicken, accompanied by naan and parotha.

**China Express** (shop 53, Market Place, tel. 876/906-9158 or 876/906-9159, noon-9:30pm Sun.-Thurs., noon-10pm Fri.-Sat.) has decent Chinese food in a cavernous setting. Items on the menu range from wonton soup to Cantonese lobster (US$34). It's a popular lunch location.

**Dragon Court** (6 South Ave., tel. 876/920-8506, 11:30am-9:30pm daily) serves decent Chinese food ranging from chicken dishes

(US$7) to lobster (US$29). Dragon Court does the best dim sum.

**Panda Village Chinese Restaurant** (shop 21, Manor Park Plaza, 184 Constant Spring Rd., tel. 876/941-0833, 11:30am-9pm Mon.-Thurs., 11:30am-10pm Fri.-Sat., US$5-8) has dependable Chinese food with chicken, fish, and shrimp dishes.

### Meat and Seafood

**South Avenue Grill** (20-A South Ave., tel. 876/754-1380) serves a blend of Jamaican and American food with an alleged Italian touch. The ambience is relaxing with open-air seating by a reflecting pool. The bar makes a decent margarita. Prices range from inexpensive for a quarter chicken (US$6.50) to a bit pricey for steak or lobster (US$26).

**The Terra Nova Hotel & Suites** (17 Waterloo Rd., tel. 876/926-2211) has an excellent restaurant that does the best regular buffets in town. Sunday Brunch (11am-4pm Sun., US$30), and daily lunch buffets (noon-3pm Mon.-Sat., US$23) with Jamaican dishes.

### Vegetarian

★ **Mi Hungry Whol'-Some-Food** (shop 24A, Market Place, contact I-Wara, tel. 876/908-1771, cell tel. 876/285-4635, www. mihungrynow.com, 8:30am-11pm Mon.-Sat., noon-10pm Sun.) serves raw food renditions of pizza (pleaza), patties or "happies," sweet and savory fruit and vegetable pies, and burgers (US$5-6.50) as well as fresh natural juices (US$3-5).

## HOPE ROAD TO PAPINE
### Cafés

**The Deli at CPJ Market** (71 Lady Musgrave Rd., info@cpjmarket.com, www.cpjmarket.com, 7am-8pm Mon.-Sat.) serves soups and salads, sandwiches, pastries, and coffee with indoor and outdoor seating and complimentary Wi-Fi.

**Cannonball Café** (7am-7pm Mon.-Fri., 8:30am-7pm Sat., 9am-5pm Sun.) has a location at Barbican Centre (shop 5, 29 East Kings House Rd., next to Loshusan Supermarket, tel. 876/946-0983) and at Sovereign North (shop 8, tel. 876/970-1532). The cafés serve sandwiches (US$6) and dishes like beef lasagna (US$10), quiche (US$10), and Greek salad (US$6), in addition to coffee (US$4), pastries, scones (US$5) with sweet cream and jam, and juices (US$4). The atmosphere is relaxing and cozy; Wi-Fi is complimentary for customers.

★ **Café Blue** (shop 1A, Sovereign Centre, tel. 876/978-7790, cafebluesov@coffeetraders.

Taka's East Japanese Restaurant has the best sushi in Jamaica.

com, www.jamaicacafeblue.com, 7am-8pm Mon.-Fri., 8am-5pm Sat.-Sun.) serves Jamaican Blue Mountain coffee, pastries, and light savory food and offers patrons complimentary Wi-Fi. Try the smoked marlin sandwich and rum cake paired with the Blue Mountain Fog (iced coffee with Sangster's Rum Cream).

## Jamaican

**One Love Café** (Bob Marley Museum, cell tel. 876/630-1588, 9am-5:30pm Mon.-Sat., US$6-8) serves sandwiches, meat, fish, veggie burgers, wraps, shakes, and smoothies.

**Lillian's Restaurant** (237 Old Hope Rd., tel. 876/970-2224, lilians@utech.edu.jm, 11:30am-3pm Mon.-Fri., US$6-12) is a training facility at the School of Hospitality and Tourism Management at the University of Technology. It serves dependable food at affordable prices like chicken, pork, lamb, shrimp, pasta dishes, and desserts. An international cuisine series is offered selected Fridays throughout the year, when evening dinners are served. Check with manager Cheryl Smikle for details.

## International

**Chez Maria** (Shop 3, 80 Musgrave Rd., tel. 876/927-8078, cell tel. 876/430-3822, chezmaria@cwjamaica.com, www.chezmaria.webs.com, 11:30am-10pm Mon.-Sat., noon-9pm Sun.) is a Lebanese restaurant that makes its own pita bread and decent Italian staples. Lebanese favorites include tabbouleh salad and hummus as well as entrées (US$9-18) like kebabs, shawarma, filet mignon, shrimp, and lobster.

**Y.not.pita** (71 Lady Musgrave Rd., tel. 876/927-7482, ynotpita@hotmail.com, 8:30am-9pm Mon.-Fri., 9am-9pm Sat., 9am-5pm Sun., US$5-15) serves traditional Lebanese dishes from soups and salads to falafel and hummus with pita chips as well as Jamaican and Mexican-style chicken, jerk, and curried chicken wraps.

**Chilitos** (64 Hope Rd., tel. 876/978-0537, noon-10pm Mon.-Sat., 5pm-9pm Sun.) is a self-described "Jamexican" restaurant serving quesadillas, tacos, and burritos as well as mixed drinks. A 2-for-1 happy hour is 5pm-7pm Wednesday.

★ **Opa! Greek Restaurant and Lounge** (75 Hope Rd., tel. 876/631-2000, cell tel. 876/550-2000, www.opajamaica.com, US$10-30) serves traditional dishes like moussaka, spinach spanakopita, souvlaki meat skewers and lamb shank, as well as inventive dishes mixing in Jamaican ingredients. The restaurant has an extensive wine list, and well-trained staff providing attentive service. Santorini Skylounge is an adjacent bar and lounge where occasional themed parties are held.

**Pita Grill** (Orchid Village, 20 Barbican Rd., tel. 876/970-4571, open 24/7, www.pitagrilljamaica.com) is a Lebanese-leaning fast food joint serving munchie-killers like ham and cheese sandwiches, Philly cheese steak sliders, hot dogs, buffalo wings, along with Middle Eastern traditional fare like beef kibbeh, tabouleh, pita chips, and falafel. Pita Grill's breakfast wraps and pancakes help get the morning started right.

**Aladin** (shop 6, Liguanea Plaza, cell tel. 876/321-4572, 10am-10pm daily, US$10-20) specializes in Lebanese food with falafel, hummus, tabbouleh, and kebabs.

**Tea Tree Creperie** (Unit 2, 80 Lady Musgrave Rd., 876/978-7333, info@teatreecreperie.com, www.teatreecreperie.com) serves sweet and savory crepes, coffee, and tea, as well as spirited concoctions from the **Treehouse Pub.**

## Asian

**Tamarind** (shop 28, Orchid Village, 18-22 Barbican Rd., tel. 876/977-0695 or 876/702-3486, www.tamarindindiancuisine.com, 11am-9:30pm Mon.-Thurs., 11am-10pm Sat., 5pm-9:30pm Sun., US$12-30) is a North Indian-Chinese fusion restaurant with smart, modern decor and a delectable menu prepared by chefs from Delhi. The offerings include mutton biryani, spring rolls, fish Szechuan, noodles, fried rice, fish tikka, and the Tamarind tandoori platter of assorted kebabs.

**China Max** (shop 27, Orchid Village, 18-20 Barbican Rd., tel. 876/927-1888 or 876/927-1388, 11am-9:30pm Mon.-Sat., 12:30pm-9:30pm Sun., US$3-25) is a Chinese restaurant with a typical menu including wontons, soups, shrimp, chicken, pork, fish, and lobster dishes. Try the delish whole crispy fried snapper with rice.

**Jade Garden** (Shop 54-59 Sovereign Centre, tel. 876/978-3476-9, jadegarden.ja@gmail.com 12pm-10pm Mon.-Sat, 11:00am-9:00pm Sun) serves MSG-free Chinese food with dishes like Peking Duck, roast pork, and their signature pimento steak. Cantonese dim sum is a popular house specialty.

**Roe** (unit 5, Sovereign North, 29 Barbican Rd., tel. 876/632-6669 cell tel. 876/784-4770, roebycore@gmail.com, 11am-9:30pm Mon.-Sat., 12:30pm-9:30pm Sun., US$10-30) is a cozy Japanese restaurant with a private dining room and tables inside and outside. Sushi and sashimi dishes are fresh and well prepared.

★ **Pushpa's** (Northside Plaza, tel. 876/977-5454 or 876/977-5858, www.pushpa-ir.com, 11am-10pm daily, US$4-6.50) is by far the best restaurant in the complex and among the best Indian restaurants on the island,

serving a mix of north and south Indian dishes, including *dosas* and *idli* on Sundays. Lunch specials include chicken dishes like *moghlai,* vindaloo, and *kurma;* vegetarian dishes like eggplant curry as well as mutton, shrimp, and fish are served either curried, fried, or vindaloo.

**Tandoor** (11 Holborne Rd., tel. 876/929-3566, cell tel. 876/770-2959, www.pushpa-ir.com, Mon-Fri 11am-9:30pm, Sat 12pm-10pm, Sun 12pm-9:30pm, US$10-30) is the latest spot-on edition to Pushpa's empire, delivering an elaborate menu of authentic Indian dishes closer to the corporate crowd.

## Meat and Seafood

★ **Di Grill Shack** (9-11 Phoenix Ave., tel. 876/968-0125 or 876/960-4210, digrillshack@gmail.com, noon-9pm Mon.-Thurs., noon-10:30pm Fri.-Sat.) is the best place in town for ribs: fingers, tips, spare, and baby back. Chicken, fish, and lobster dishes are also served. The outdoor setting is pleasant for downing a beer with friends. Takeout and delivery are also offered.

Di Grill Shack serves up a mean rack of barbeque ribs.

**Cynthia's for Quantity and Quality**
(Phoenix Ave., tel. 876/960-1612 or 876/920-4740, breakfast 8am-10:30am, lunch noon-4pm Mon.-Sat., takeout only, US$7-10) serves steamed, escoveitch, and brown stew fish, curry goat, curry chicken, and baked or fried fish or pork. Natural juices are also served (US$2).

## Vegetarian

**Just Salads** (9-11 Phoenix Ave., tel. 876/754-6117 cell tel. 876/809-7719, justsalads@cwjamaica.com, 9am-6pm Mon.-Fri., 10am-3pm Sat., 11am-4pm Sun.) serves salads as well as juices.

**Jamaica Juice** (shop 14, tel. 876/620-4066, askdrjuice@jamaicajuice.net, www.jamaicajuice.net, 10am-9pm Mon.-Thurs., 10am-9:30pm Fri.-Sat., noon-8pm Sun., US$3-5) is perhaps the best shop in Sovereign's food court, with fresh juices, smoothies, and food items, most notably chicken or chickpea roti. The mango smoothie is highly recommended.

★ **New Leaf Vegetarian** (shop 6, Lane Plaza, 121 Old Hope Rd., tel. 876/977-2358 or 876/977-5243, newleafvegetarian1@gmail.com, www.newleafvegetarian.com, 11am-6pm Mon.-Sat.) specializes in Trinidadian-style doubles—mild curried chickpeas wrapped in flatbread with spicy sweet cucumber relish and chutney—but the flavor doesn't stop there. Delicious creations include chile sin carne, falafel platter, and ackee bammy pizza, with fresh fruit blends and vegetable juices to wash it down.

**Creative Food for Life** (Cedar Valley Rd. and Old Hope Rd., cell tel. 876/848-9592, 6am-10pm Mon.-Fri., 8am-3pm Sat.-Sun.) is run by Ista Masters, who dishes up turned cornmeal, nut rundown, seafood, and honey moss, naseberry, and soursop juices.

# UPPER CONSTANT SPRING TO STONY HILL
## Cafés

**Cannonball Café** (Manor Centre, Manor Park, tel. 876/969-3399, 7am-7pm Mon.-Fri., 9am-5pm Sat.-Sun.) prepares sandwiches (US$5), beef lasagna (US$9), quiches (US$9), and salad (US$7), in addition to coffee (US$3), pastries, scones (US$3.50), and juices. The atmosphere is relaxing and cozy; wireless Internet is offered free for customers.

## Jamaican
**Michael's Restaurant & Coffee Shop** (141B Constant Spring Rd., tel. 876/969-24037, 9am-7pm Mon.-Sat., 9am-4pm Sun.) serves Jamaican staples for breakfast, lunch, and dinner to a loyal clientele. It's your best bet in town for ackee and saltfish, boiled banana, and yam for breakfast any day of the week. Lunch items include fried or baked chicken, curried goat and oxtail. The menu rotates daily.

★ **Norma's** (31 Whitehall Ave., tel. 876/931-0064, ktapita@gmail.com, 8:30am-4:30pm Mon.-Sat.) is a legendary cook shop with some of the best local fare, serving staples like curry goat, oxtail, and stewed chicken for takeout. You won't find better value; lunches come in small (US$4) or large (US$5-8). Seasonal juices (US$2-3) like carrot and orange, June plum, Otaheite apple, and carrot punch are made fresh daily. Fish and shrimp are sometimes prepared. Call in advance to find out what's on the menu and to make sure it "nah sell-off" yet. The kitchen, around back, is filled with industrial pots and a flurry of activity.

**Country Style Restaurant** (Stony Hill Square, tel. 876/942-2506, 6am-9pm daily) serves typical Jamaican and Chinese dishes that includes curry mutton, stew pork, escoveitch fish (US$4), and curried shrimp (US$10.50).

## Seafood
**White Bones** (1 Mannings Hill Rd., at Constant Spring Rd., tel. 876/925-9502, 11:30am-11pm Mon.-Sat., 2pm-10pm Sun.) has a great setting with fish tanks, nets, and strings of lights, and excellent seafood to match. Appetizers start at US$8.50 and include raw or grilled oysters, soup du jour, and salads. Entrées include snapper fillet (US$20)

# Sweet Spots

## HALF WAY TREE

- **Chocolate Dreams** (shop 2, Devon House, 26 Hope Rd., tel. 876/927-9574, www.chocolatedreams.com.jm, 10am-7pm Mon.-Thurs., 11am-9pm Fri.-Sat., 2pm-8pm Sun.) retails delectable chocolate treats. All the chocolate treats are produced at the Roosevelt Avenue (better known as Herb McKinley Ave.), where there's also a retail store.

- **Scoops Unlimited** (Devon House, 26 Hope Rd., tel. 876/929-7028 or 876/926-0888, 11am-10pm daily, cones US$2-5, containers US$3.50-10), serves Devon House I Scream, which most Jamaicans rate as the country's best. It gets quite busy on Sunday, with a long line out the door into the courtyard.

- **Devon House Bakery** (next to Scoops Unlimited, Devon House, 26 Hope Rd., tel. 876/968-2153, 9:30am-6pm Mon.-Thurs., 9:30am-8pm Fri.-Sat., 11:30am-8pm Sun.) sells cakes, pastries, and taffies.

## HOPE ROAD TO PAPINE

- **Pastry Passions** (Shop 17, Sovereign Centre Food Court, tel. 876/927-9105,

and grilled snapper burger (US$12). The popular all-you-can-eat crab buffet (US$20) is on Thursday.

## International

**Tropical Chinese** (Mid Spring Plaza, 134 Constant Spring Rd., tel. 876/941-0520, noon-10pm daily) serves entrées like chicken (US$8.50), shrimp with cashew nuts (US$16), steamed whole fish (US$28.50), lobster dishes (US$23.50), eggplant (US$7), seafood (US$17), and stewed duck (US$14). Tropical also has a branch at Barbican Centre.

★ **Majestic Sushi & Grill** (Villa Ronai, Old Stony Hill Rd., tel. 876/960-3594 or 876/564-1334, noon-10pm Tues.-Thurs. and Sun., noon-11pm Fri.-Sat., closed Mon., US$12-40) was built on the success of Taka's East Japanese Restaurant and shares the top ranking for Japanese food in Jamaica. Decor and ambiance include low, comfy lounge couches complementing table seating, and a separate dining room next to the sushi bar. Lunch hour tends to be quiet, making it a good venue for business meetings.

# Accommodations

Kingston is not known for its luxury rental villas or five-star hotels. Nonetheless, comfortable and affordable options abound. Most business travelers tend to stay in New Kingston or Half Way Tree for easy access to the corporate district. Spanish Court, The Courtleigh, and Terra Nova are business traveler favorites. For those with more down time, it may make sense to seek quieter options in residential neighborhoods

or on the edge of town. Don't expect a lot of amenities for less than US$100. The higher end of the spectrum pushes US$300 for suites at a few hotels.

The outlying communities of the corporate area in St. Catherine don't have much in the way of inviting accommodations, with a strip of pay-by-the-hour dives along Port Henderson Road, commonly known as Back Road, in Portmore, and a few similar pastrypassionshome@gmail.com, www.pastrypassions.com, 10am-9pm Mon.-Sat., 2pm-9pm Sun.) serves excellent pastries and coffee.

• **Tutti Frutti** (shop 1D, Barbican Centre, next to Loshusan, 29 East Kings House Rd., tel. 876/946-9664, tuttifruttija@gmail.com, noon-10pm Mon.-Thurs., 10am-11pm Fri., 11am-11pm Sat.-Sun.) sells frozen yogurt and sorbet with a world of toppings by the pound in cups and cones.

## UPPER CONSTANT SPRING TO STONY HILL

• **Candy Craze** (Shop 1, Upper Manor Park Plaza, tel. 876/924-4881, sweetmsja@gmail.com, www.mycandycraze.com, 11am-9pm Mon.-Thurs., 11am-10pm Sat., noon-10pm Sun.) sells ice cream and bulk candy.

• **Tutti Frutti** (Manor Centre, tel. 876/924-7077. tuttifruttija@gmail.com, noon-10pm Mon.-Thurs., 10am-11pm Fri., 11am-11pm Sat.-Sun.) sells frozen yogurt and sorbet with a world of toppings by the pound in cups and cones.

establishments in Spanish Town. None of these are recommended for a good night's sleep.

## Under US$100

**Reggae Hostel** (8 Burlington Ave., tel. 876/920-6528 or 876/968-1694, www.reggaehostel.com, from US$25 per person in a shared room) is a favorite among backpackers for its proximity to Half Way Tree, its affordability and the communal vibe where budget travelers meet, hang out, and explore the city. The hostel has private and shared bunk rooms with common kitchen and bath facilities.

**Mayfair Hotel** (4 Kings House Close, tel. 876/926-1610, mayfairjamaica@gmail.com, www.mayfairja.com, from US$70 for 2 single beds or 1 double) tucked away in the heart of Half Way Tree near King's House, has 41 units in a hotel block and in four stand-alone houses, each with five bedrooms sharing a common entrance and living area. Rooms have air-conditioning, hot water, and cable TV. On a large lawn there's a decent-size swimming pool, an independently run Jamaican restaurant, and a bar called The Pub. Nonguests are welcome to use the pool (US$3.50).

## US$100-250

**Jamaica Pegasus** (81 Knutsford Blvd., tel. 876/926-3690, US$171 s or d, US$215 junior suite, includes breakfast) is a favorite for visiting and local bureaucrats and hosts local government and private sector functions in some of the largest conference facilities and ballrooms in town. A beautiful pool, a 24-hour deli, and tennis courts round out this premier New Kingston property.

**Courtyard by Marriott** (1 Park Close, facing Emancipation Park, tel. 876/618-9900, www.marriott.com, from US$219) is a 130-room property catering to business travelers that opened in early 2016. Guest rooms have a king or a pair of queens, desks, flat-screen TVs, air-conditioning, and Wi-Fi. The pool deck and bar are located on the second floor overlooking the park. Meeting rooms, a large open format lounge and dining area, and its central location make the Courtyard an easy sell.

**Liguanea Club** (Knutsford Blvd., tel. 876/926-8144, www.theliguaneaclub.com, from US$140) is a no-frills hotel and racket club in the heart of New Kingston. Rooms have kings, doubles, or twins, air-conditioning, en suite baths, cable, desks, and mini fridges. The courts are in good shape, as is the pool. Court fees are US$5 and after 6pm US$11. The restaurant serves local dishes and is open for breakfast, lunch, and dinner.

**The Courtleigh Hotel & Suites** (85 Knutsford Blvd., tel. 876/929-9000, courtleigh@cwjamaica.com, www.courtleigh.com, US$207 standard, US$550 presidential suite) is a popular business hotel located next to the Jamaica Pegasus and across from the Liguanea Club. Rooms are modern, with mini-fridges, cable TV, air-conditioning, and a 24-hour gym. Wi-Fi and continental breakfast are included.

**Altamont Court** (1 Altamont Terrace, tel. 876/929-4497, altamontcourt@cwjamaica.com, www.altamontcourt.com, from US$142) is a good value. The 57 standard rooms come with two doubles or one king. The Alexander Suite is a spacious and luxurious room with an expansive bath that has a tub and a separate shower. Wi-Fi is included in all the rooms; there's is a computer for guest use in the business center, which has three meeting rooms. A restaurant by the pool serves breakfast, lunch, and dinner.

★ **Spanish Court Hotel** (1 St. Lucia Avenue, Kingston 5, tel. 876/926-0000, www.spanishcourthotel.com, from US$180) is a chic and clean boutique hotel evocative of Miami and with attentive service. Rooms are well appointed, with flat-screen TVs, warm and cozy decor, and comfortable bedding. It's a favorite of visiting businesspeople. The Spanish Court serves coffee, pastries, and light savory fare; the restaurant on the opposite side of the lobby serves well-executed meals for breakfast, lunch, and dinner. Both welcome nonguests.

**The Knutsford Court Hotel** (16 Chelsea Ave., tel. 876/929-1000, www.knutsfordcourt.com, from US$124) is situated within easy walking distance to New Kingston restaurants, bars, and nightclubs. The hotel offers amenities like a 24-hour business center, a gym, meeting rooms, two restaurants, and a bar. The rooms have standard amenities like

phones and cable TV. Two townhouses in the courtyard have the property's best suites.

**Eden Gardens Wellness Resort & Spa** (39 Lady Musgrave Rd., tel. 876/946-9981 or 844/446-3336, US$193-385) is a stylish boutique hotel operating as a bed-and-breakfast with wellness and business facilities conveniently located a few blocks from the bustle of New Kingston in Liguanea. It has large, comfortable suites with broad, functional desks and kitchenettes. Wireless Internet is included, and the property has conference facilities, a pool, and a restaurant.

**Alhambra Inn** (1 Tucker Ave., tel. 876/978-9072 or 876/978-9073, alhambrainn@cwjamaica.com, US$110 for two double beds, US$120 for a king, US$20 per extra person) is a nice boutique hotel with a country feel across Mountain View Road from the National Stadium and a five-minute drive from New Kingston and Downtown. Twenty spacious rooms with comfortable sheets and a lush courtyard make the inn a cool option where the air-conditioning is barely necessary, even in the summer. Bring soap and shampoo. Wi-Fi is available in the courtyard.

**One32 Guest House** (132 Barbican Rd., Tel. 876/969-6439, cell tel. 876/816-5233, one32jamaica@gmail.com, US$120-180) has two cozy self-contained studios, each suitable for up to two guests, and two two-bedroom apartments, accommodating up to four, giving the property maximum capacity of 12. A deck out back has a love seat, a dining table, a jetted tub, and a plunge pool.

**The Gardens** (23 Liguanea Ave., tel. 876/927-8275, mlyn@cwjamaica.com, www.gardensjamaica.com, 1 bedroom US$105, 2-bedroom unit US$200) has seven two-bedroom townhouses in a quiet and green setting in the heart of Liguanea. The townhouses have spacious living-dining rooms and full kitchens on the ground floor, with a master and second bedroom upstairs, each with a private bath. Guests can rent a single bedroom of the two-bedroom units for the lower rate. Wireless Internet reaches most of the property. Air-conditioning and cable TV are in all bedrooms. Owner and manager Jennifer Lyn lives on-site.

## Over US$250

**Terra Nova All Suite Hotel** (17 Waterloo Rd., tel. 876/926-2211, www.terranovajamaica.com) has comfortable rooms (US$207) with two double beds, junior suites (US$261) with minibars, executive suites (US$331) with whirlpool tubs and a bit more space, and three royalty suites (US$686) with balconies. Internet is included. Terra Nova has a great lunch buffet (US$22) with a different theme each day, and it offers one of the best Sunday brunch buffets (US$28) in town with a mix of international and local food. The Regency Bar on the ground level is popular.

# Information and Services

## INFORMATION AND SERVICES

The **Jamaica Tourist Board** (64 Knutsford Blvd., tel. 876/929-9200, www.visitjamaica.com, 8:30am-4:30pm Mon.-Fri.) has a small library with staffers available to assist with information on Jamaica's more popular attractions.

The **Jamaica National Heritage Trust** (79 Duke St., tel. 876/922-1287, www.jnht.com) is located Downtown in the historic Headquarters House. The Trust can provide information on Heritage sights across the island.

The **Survey Department** (23 Charles St., tel. 876/922-6630 or 876/922-6635, ext. 264, patricia.davis@nla.gov.jm) sells all kinds of maps. Contact Patricia Davis in the business office.

**DaVinci Jamaica Vacations** (info@davincijamaica.com, www.davincijamaica.com) is a Kingston-based travel company that specializes in intimate, off-the-beaten-track roaming tours of the island. DaVinci sells all things Jamaican, all places in Jamaica, and the full cast of Jamaican people; if it is safe and legal, and their clients want to experience it, they'll do it. Packages or customized vacations are offered, emphasizing Jamaica's cuisine with a unique food tour of the island and mini-tour weekend packages. Accommodations are arranged based on your budget and taste.

## Post Offices and Parcel Services

**Post Offices** are located Downtown at 13 King Street (tel. 876/858-2414, www.jamaicapost.gov.jm), Cross Roads (tel. 876/364-6316), and Half Way Tree (118 Hagley Park Rd., tel. 876/364-6119).

Shipping services are available through **DHL** (19 Haining Rd., tel. 876/920-0010) and **FedEx** (40 Half Way Tree Rd.; 75 Knutsford Blvd., U.S. tel. 888/463-3339).

### Telephone, Internet, and Fax

The **Jamaica Library Service** offers Internet access free of charge at all branches.

The **Public Library** (Main Branch, 2 Tom Redcam Rd., tel. 876/928-7975 or 876/926-3315, ksapl@cwjamaica.com, http://jamlib.org.jm) has a decent collection and allows visitors to check out books by leaving a deposit. Internet is available free of charge at a handful of computer terminals.

Several locations around Kingston offer free Wi-Fi access to customers with their own devices. These include **Jo Jo's Jerk Pit and More** (12 Waterloo Rd., in front South Ave., tel. 876/906-1509 or 876/906-1612, 7am-6pm Mon.-Fri., 8am-6pm Sat., 8am-4pm Sun.), **Cannonball Café** (20-24 Barbados Ave., behind Pan Caribbean Bank, New Kingston, tel. 876/754-4486; Manor Centre, Manor Park, tel. 876/969-3399, 7am-7pm Mon.-Fri., 9am-5pm Sat.-Sun.; Barbican Centre, 29 East Kings House Rd., next to Loshusan supermarket, tel. 876/946-0983, 7am-7pm Sat.-Thurs., 7am-9pm Fri.), **Pita Grill** (Orchid Village, 20 Barbican Rd., tel. 876/970-4571, 9am-10pm Mon.-Sat., 12:30pm-1am Mon.-Sat., 3pm-midnight Sun.), and **Susie's** (shop 1, Southdale Plaza, behind Popeye's, Constant Spring Rd., tel. 876/968-5030, 8am-10pm Mon.-Sat., 9am-7:30pm Sun.).

**Digicel** (10 Grenada Way, tel. 876/511-5000) offers island-wide wireless cards for laptops on its plans. GSM SIM cards can be bought at the Digicel outlet on Knutsford Boulevard and across the street behind the Tourist Board at Digicel headquarters. Digicel's USB modem costs US$41, with data usage costing US$0.45 per MB.

**Cable & Wireless LIME** (tel. 876/926-9700, U.S. tel. 888/225-5295), which operates in Jamaica as LIME, has a similar 3G USB modem for US$65. LIME offers unlimited prepaid plans by intervals of 24 hours (US$5), weekly (US$15), or monthly (US$45), and plans for US$10 per month for 50MB, US$15 for 100MB, or US$25 for 1GB.

## POLICE AND IMMIGRATION

**Police stations** are located at Half Way Tree (142 Maxfield Ave., tel. 876/926-8184), Downtown Kingston Central (East Queen St., tel. 876/922-0308), and Constant Spring (2-3 Casava Piece Rd., tel. 876/924-1421).

**Immigration** (25 Constant Spring Rd., tel. 876/906-4402 or 876/906-1304) is responsible for granting extensions of stays or processing the paperwork for visas.

## HOSPITALS AND MEDICAL FACILITIES

UWI's **University Hospital** (Papine Rd., Mona, tel. 876/927-1620) has a good reputation and is probably the best public hospital in Jamaica. **Tony Thwaites** (University Hospital, Mona, tel. 876/977-2607) is UWI's private facility. **Andrews Memorial Hospital** is located at 27 Hope Road (tel. 876/926-7401, emergency tel. 876/926-7403). **Medical Associates Hospital and**

**Medical Center** (18 Tangerine Place, tel. 876/926-1400) is a private clinic with a good reputation. It also has a pharmacy at the same location.

**Eye Q Optical** (shop 10, Lower Manor Park Plaza, tel. 876/925-9298; Courtleigh Corporate Center, 8 St. Lucia Ave., New Kingston, tel. 876/906-1493) is the best spot in town to get your eyes tested or pick up a pair of prescription glasses.

### Pharmacies

**Andrews Memorial Hospital Pharmacy** (tel. 876/926-7401, 8am-10pm Mon.-Thurs., 8am-3:30pm Fri., 9:30am-3:30pm Sun.) is at 27 Hope Road. **Liguanea Drugs and Garden** (134 Old Hope Rd., tel. 876/977-0066) and **Lee's Family Pharmacy** (86-B Red Hills Rd., tel. 876/931-1877) are two other local pharmacies. **Fontana Pharmacy** (Barbican Square, tel. 876/946-2630, www.fontanapharmacy.com, 8am-10pm Mon.-Sat., 9am-9pm Sun.) is a large format drugstore filling prescriptions and retailing a wide array of personal care and consumer products and basic grocery items. **Monarch Pharmacy** (Shop 23, Sovereign Centre, 106 Hope Rd., tel. 876/978-3495) fills prescriptions and sells personal care items, household products, and trinkets.

## MONEY

ATM withdrawals are usually the most convenient way to get cash, but foreign transaction charges and poor exchange rates are drawbacks. Depending on the amount you are changing, a few dollars lost in fees and rates can be worth the convenience. All the major banks will cash traveler's checks, but lines are typically long, slow-moving, and overwhelmingly frustrating.

**Western Union** (main office 2 Trafford Place, tel. 876/926-2454) has offices all over the island, including in Kingston (Cross Roads, 20 Tobago Ave., New Kingston); Hi-Lo in Liguanea Plaza; BluMenthal in Lower Manor Park Plaza; and in Pavilion Mall (shop 30 upstairs, and Super Plus downstairs, Constant Spring Rd., Half Way Tree).

## Currency Exchange

**Scotia Investments** (7 Holborn Rd., tel. 876/960-6699 or 888/225-5324, info@scotiadbg.com, 8:30am-3pm Mon.-Thurs., 8:30am-4pm Fri.) and **FX Traders** (U.S. tel. 888/398-7233) offer the best exchange rates. FX Traders has *cambios* at Cross Roads FSC, (13 Old Hope Rd., 9am-5pm Mon.-Sat.); shop 7, Boulevard Super Centre (45 Elma Crescent, 9:30am-5:30pm Mon.-Sat.); King Street FSC, Woolworth Building (83 King St., 9am-5pm Mon.-Tues. and Thurs.-Sat., 9am-3:30pm Wed.); K's Pharmacy, Shop 17, Duhaney Park Plaza (10am-6pm Mon.-Fri., 10am-5pm Sat.); Central Office FSC (20 Tobago Ave., 9am-5pm Mon.-Sat.); Pavilion FSC, Shop 30 Pavilion Mall (Constant Spring Rd., 9am-5pm Mon.-Sat.); Park View Supermarket (7 Chandos Place, Papine, 8:30am-7pm Mon.-Thurs., 8am-8pm Fri.-Sat.).

## Banks

**Scotiabank** has branches with ATMs Downtown (35-45 King St., tel. 876/922-1420), Cross Roads (86 Slipe Rd., tel. 876/926-1530), Liguanea (125-127 Old Hope Rd., tel. 876/970-4371), New Kingston (2 Knutsford Blvd., tel. 876/926-8034), Portmore (lot 2, Cookson Pen, tel. 876/989-4226), Bushy Park (tel. 876/949-4837), and UWI (tel. 876/702-2518). Some Scotiabank ATMs, namely at Barbican Centre and in New Kingston, allow you to withdraw U.S. dollars in addition to local currency.

**First Caribbean** has branches with ATMs in New Kingston (23-27 Knutsford Blvd., tel. 876/929-9310), Downtown (1 King St., tel. 876/922-6120), Half Way Tree (78 Half Way Tree Rd., tel. 876/926-7400; Twin Gates Shopping Centre, tel. 876/926-1313), Liguanea (129 Hope Rd., tel. 876/977-2595), and Manor Park (Manor Park Plaza, tel. 876/969-2708).

**Sagicor Bank** has branches with ATMs Downtown (134 Tower St., tel. 876/922-8195), New Kingston (17 Dominica Dr., tel. 876/960-2340), Half Way Tree (6C Constant Spring Rd., tel. 876/968-4193; Tropical Plaza, 12 Constant Spring Rd., tel. 876/968-6155), and Liguanea (Sovereign Centre, 106 Hope Rd., tel. 876/928-7524).

**NCB** has branches with ATMs Downtown (37 Duke St., tel. 876/922-6710), Cross Roads (90-94 Slipe Rd., tel. 876/926-7420), New Kingston (32 Trafalgar Rd., tel. 876/929-9050), and Half Way Tree (Half Way Tree Rd., tel. 876/920-8313).

# Transportation

## GETTING THERE AND AROUND
### By Air

**Norman Manley International Airport** (KIN, tel. 876/924-8546, www.nmia.aero) is located on the Palisadoes heading toward Port Royal, east of Downtown. Domestic flights leave from a small terminal by the cargo area, reached by taking a left off the boulevard leading to the main terminal before reaching the roundabout. The airport has flights from North America on **Air Canada** (www.aircanada.com), **American** (www.aa.co), **Delta** (www.delta.com), **JetBlue** (www.jetblue.com), **Spirit** (www.spirit.com), and **WestJet** (www.westjet.com), and from Europe on **British Airways** (www.ba.com). The regional carriers flying to Kingston are **Aerogaviota** (www.aerogaviota.com), **Caribbean Airlines** (www.caribbean-airlines.com), **Cayman Airways** (www.caymanairways.com), **Copa Airlines** (www.copaair.com), **InselAir** (www.fly-inselair.com), **InterCaribbean** (www.interCaribbean.com), and **Fly Jamaica** (www.flyjamaica.com).

**AirLink Express** (Domestic Terminal, tel. 876/940-6660, reservation@flyairlink.net, www.intlairlink.net) offers charter service between any two airports or aerodromes in the island. **TimAir** (Domestic Terminal, tel. 876/952-2516, timair@usa.net, www.ti-mair.net) also offers air taxi service to Negril, Treasure Beach, Boscobel (St. Mary), Ken Jones (Portland), and Montego Bay.

## Ground Transportation

The **Knutsford Express** (18 Dominica Dr., tel. 876/960-5499 or 876/971-1822, www.knutsfordexpress.com) is popular with Jamaicans and visitors alike, offering the most comfortable coach service between Kingston, Ocho Rios, and Montego Bay with two or three daily departures from each city. New Kingston-Montego Bay (departs 6am, 9:30am, 2pm, and 5pm Mon.-Fri., 6am, 9:30am, and 4:30pm Sat., 8:30am and 4:30pm Sun., US$20 prepaid, US$23 day of travel) buses run between the parking lot behind New Kingston Shopping Centre and Pier 1 in Montego Bay. The trip lasts four hours, depending on traffic. There's few places you can't get to with the coach service; check the site for the latest destinations, and book online for discounted rates.

**Buses** ply routes around town and between Kingston and major points on the eastern side of the island. The main bus terminals for routes out of Kingston are the **Transport Centre** (tel. 876/754-2610) in the heart of Half Way Tree and the **Urban Transport Centre** (below Coronation Market, Port Royal St. and Water Lane, tel. 876/754-2584). Buses depart throughout the day to Port Royal (US$0.50), Spanish Town (US$1), Bull Bay (US$0.50), Morant Bay (US$1.50), Mandeville (US$3), Port Antonio (US$3), Ocho Rios (US$3), Savanna-la-Mar (US$7), Montego Bay (US$6), and Negril (US$8).

**Route taxis** and **minibuses** depart from Cross Roads, Half Way Tree, by the roundabout on upper Constant Spring Road in Manor Park for destinations due north and at the roundabout in Papine for destinations in the Blue Mountains. Route taxis or minibuses depart for Kingston from virtually every city or town in the surrounding parishes and from parish capitals across the island. Route taxi fares are typically slightly higher than buses

on the overlapping routes, but don't typically connect faraway points.

# GETTING AROUND
## On Foot

Jamaicans who walk around Kingston generally don't do so by choice, day or night, and are ridiculed as "walk foots" by their fellow citizens. It's mainly due to the prestige of driving, and more importantly, the heat that pedestrians suffer. Traffic safety concerns around town are generally exaggerated, and being in a vehicle stopped at a light offers little protection anyway. There is really no better way to get to know the layout of some of the more congested areas like Downtown around the Parade, Knutsford Boulevard's Hip Strip, and around the center of Half Way Tree than to go on foot. Beyond that, route taxis and public buses are the best way for those without a car to get around.

## By Bus

**Jamaica Urban Transit Company** (www.jutc.com, US$1-3) operates buses in and around the Corporate Area. Routes are extensive, but service and schedules can be daunting. Covered street-side bus stops are scattered along all the major thoroughfares throughout the city, and the more people that are gathered, the sooner you're likely to see a bus. This is definitely the most economical way to get around, and the yellow buses even offer service to and from the airport and guided tours to points of interest across the metropolitan area.

## By Taxi

**Route taxis** are the most popular means of transportation across Jamaica, and apart from careening around corners and making sudden stops without using indicators, they tend to be relatively safe; kidnappings or muggings by taxi drivers are unheard of on the island. White Toyota Corolla, known locally as "deportees" or "Kingfish," tend to be used as shared taxis that can be stopped anywhere along their route, provided there's room to squeeze in another passenger. Route taxi rates are regulated (www.ta.org.jm), so drivers don't usually attempt to rip off unsuspecting passengers. Ask another passenger for the fare if you're in doubt.

For trips around Kingston, call a dispatch service rather than trying to charter a route taxi if you're not traveling along a normal route taxi trajectory. Fares with dispatch services are assessed by distance rather than with a meter; ask for the "stamp," or fare, when booking a pickup so you know exactly what the trip will cost.

**On Time Taxi** (12 Burlington Ave., tel. 876/926-3866, cell tel. 876/309-8294 or 876/881-8294, www.ontimetaxijamaica.com) is Jamaica's leading dispatch taxi service, with countless affiliated drivers and usually the quickest response to pickup requests. **Gadgepro Taxi & Tours** (tel. 876/765-0200, cell tel. 876/434-3050 or 876/437-2021, gadgeprotrading@yahoo.com) also offers reliable service in well-maintained vehicles. **City Guide Taxi** (tel. 876/969-5458) is a decent and dependable service, offering airport pickups and service around Kingston and beyond. **Gevani's Transport** (Darlington Ave., cell tel. 876/448-2118, gevanitransportinc@gmail.com) offers VIP service in Wi-Fi enabled Mercedes Benz sedans with premium bars and drivers in a bow tie and jacket.

## By Car

Rental cars tend to be very expensive across the island, but they are unfortunately indispensable when it comes to independently exploring remote areas. For the upper reaches of the Blue and John Crow Mountains, a 4WD vehicle is necessary. Pervasive potholes in the cities don't really warrant a 4WD. Check with your credit card company to see if it covers insurance.

Unlicensed rental operators abound. While they may be cheaper (US$50 per day) than more reputable agencies, there is less accountability in the event that anything goes wrong. These private rentals don't take credit cards, often want a wad of cash up front, and usually don't offer insurance. These informal agencies are best avoided.

Listed rates do not include insurance or the 16.5 percent GCT (sales tax). Insurance is typically US$15-40 daily, depending on coverage. A deposit is taken for a deductible when customers opt for anything less than full coverage. The use of select gold and platinum credit cards obviates the need to purchase insurance from the rental agency. Check with the establishment for their policies.

**Island Car Rentals** (17 Antigua Ave., tel. 876/926-5991; Norman Manley Airport, tel. 876/924-8075, icar@cwjamaica.com, www.islandcarrentals.com) has a wide range of vehicles from a Toyota Yaris (US$44 low season, US$55 high season) to a Suzuki Grand Vitara (US$99 low season, US$109 high season).

**Budget** (53 South Camp Rd., tel. 876/759-1793; Norman Manley Airport, tel. 876/924-8762, U.S. tel. 877/825-2953, budget@jamweb.net, www.budgetjamaica.com, 8am-4:30pm Mon.-Fri., 8am-10pm daily) has a range of vehicles from a Yaris (US$60 low season, US$75 high season) to a VW Passat (US$95 low season, US$120 high season).

**Bowla's Car Rental** (50 Dumbarton Ave., tel. 876/960-0067, bowlasrentacar@cwjamaica.com) offers a wide range of cars, unlimited mileage, and short-term and long-term rentals starting at US$75 per day, and free rides to and from the airport. Bowla's fleet includes Toyotas, Hyundais, Mazdas, and Nissans.

# Around Kingston

Kingston has a great range of accommodations, and there's no reason to base yourself elsewhere if you're exploring the metropolitan area, from Spanish Town to Greater Portmore, the Palisadoes, and even upper and eastern St. Andrew. Spanish Town, once the colonial capital, has an old iron bridge and historic square that are worth a quick visit but little else to keep visitors. The beaches of Greater Portmore, namely Fort Clarence and Hellshire, are the most popular in the Kingston area, the latter known for its seafood shacks and throngs on weekends. A few beachfront venues in the vicinity, like The Boardwalk and Waves Beach, are alternatives offering shade and seaside bars for a small entry fee.

Communities east along the coast include Harbour View and Bull Bay. The Palisadoes, a 16-kilometer (10-mile) stretch from the roundabout at Harbour View to the tip of Port Royal, is home to the Royal Jamaica Yacht Club, the Marine Research Institute, Norman Manley International Airport, Plumb Point Lighthouse, Port Royal, and just offshore, a couple of cays popular with boaters and Sunday bathers.

The community of Harbour View, to the north and east of the roundabout at the base of the Palisadoes, was built on the site of Fort Nugent, originally constructed by a Spanish slave, James Castillo, and later fortified by Governor Nugent in 1806 to protect the eastern approach to Kingston Harbour.

## PORT ROYAL AND THE PALISADOES

Part of Kingston parish, the Palisadoes is a thin stretch of barren sand, brush, and mangroves; it acts as a natural barrier protecting Kingston Harbour, with Port Royal at its western point. After Lord Cromwell seized Jamaica for Britain from the Spanish in 1655, Port Royal grew in importance, as the town's strategic location brought prosperity to merchants based there. The merchants were joined by pirates and buccaneers, who created one of the busiest and most successful trading posts in the New World. Imports included enslaved people, silks, silver, gold, wine, and salmon, while exports were mostly rum, sugar, and wood.

The British collaborated with the pirates as insurance against the Spanish, who were thought to be seeking revenge on the island's new colonial masters. The outpost flourished, with a local service economy growing alongside its bustling maritime commerce until June 7, 1692, when a massive earthquake left 60 percent of Port Royal underwater, immediately killing 2,000 people. Eight hectares (20 acres) supporting the principal public buildings, wharves, shops, and two of the town's four forts disappeared into the sea. Aftershocks rattled the city for months. In 1703 a fire devastated what remained of Port Royal, sending most survivors across the harbor to what soon grew into the city of Kingston. The town also sustained significant damage in the earthquake of 1907, and then again during Hurricane Charlie in 1951.

Sleepy Port Royal is worth a visit. The village is hassle-free and small enough to stroll leisurely around in a few hours. Scuba trips can be arranged from Grand Port Royal Hotel, Marina & Spa. On weekends the square comes alive with a sound system and an invasion of Kingstonians, who come for the fish and beach just offshore at Lime Cay.

### Plumb Point Lighthouse

Protecting the approach to Kingston Harbour, **Plumb Point Lighthouse** was built in 1853 and has gone dark only once, during the earthquake of 1907. Sitting on a point named Cayo de los Icacos, or Plumb Tree Cay (a reference to the coco plum by the Spanish), it is constructed of stone and cast iron and stands

21 meters (70 feet) high. Its light is visible from 40 kilometers (25 miles) out at sea. The beach immediately west is known for its occasional good surf, as is the shoreline between Plumb Point and Little Plumb Point. The area is also known for its strong currents, however, and surfers should use caution. The lighthouse itself is not accessible to the public.

## Fort Charles

The most prominent historical attraction in town and the most impressive, well-restored fort in Jamaica, **Fort Charles** (tel. 876/967-8438, 9am-4:45pm daily, US$10 adults, US$5 ages 3-17) was built in 1656 immediately following the British takeover and is the oldest fort on the island from the British colonial period and one of the oldest in the New World. Originally it was named Fort Cromwell after Oliver Cromwell, who was responsible for designing the strategic takeover of the island meant to give Britain control of the Caribbean. The fort was renamed in 1662 when Cromwell was deposed and the monarchy reinstated under Charles II. Fort Charles sank a meter (3 feet) during the earthquake of 1692.

Admiral Horatio Nelson, lauded as Britain's all-time greatest naval hero for his victorious role in the 1805 Battle of Trafalgar, spent 30 months in Jamaica, much of it at Fort Charles when the island feared a French invasion; he spent the tense period pacing and nervously scanning the horizon from what's now referred to as Nelson's Quarterdeck, a raised platform along the southern battlement. On the inside wall of the fort is a plaque advising those who tread Nelson's footprints to remember his glory.

Also within Fort Charles walls is the Grogge Shop and a very nice little museum managed by the Museum of History and Ethnography, with period artifacts, old maps, and information about Port Royal and its glorious and notorious inhabitants.

## ★ Lime Cay

**Lime Cay** is a paradisiacal islet, just big enough to sustain some vegetation. The beach gets crowded on weekends, especially Sunday, and is worth a visit to take in the local scene. Launches leave for Lime Cay on weekends from Y-Knot Bar or at Grand Port Royal Hotel, Marina & Spa (US$10 pp round-trip); you can also get here any other day, when the boats don't fill up, for a slightly higher price. At times there are launches from the old Ferry Dock area that will do the trip for a bit less,

Fort Charles

especially for small groups. The beach is popular for sunbathing and swimming.

## Other Attractions

**St. Peter's Church,** built in 1725, replaced earlier churches on the site destroyed by the 1692 earthquake and then the 1703 fire that again ravaged Port Royal. On display inside are several period items. In the churchyard is the tomb of Lewis Galdy, one of the founders of St. Peter's, who miraculously survived the 1692 earthquake after being swallowed by the earth and spit out by the sea, where he was rescued. The tomb is inscribed with the complete legend of Galdy, who went on to become a local hero.

**McFarlene's Bar** is the oldest tavern in Port Royal, constructed in the 1800s, and one of the few buildings to withstand Hurricane Charlie in 1951. Unfortunately the pub no longer operates. The **Old Gaol** (jail, Gaol St.) was once a women's prison. **Giddy House** sits half-submerged at an awkward angle in the earth behind Fort Charles. It was built in 1888 as an artillery store by the British Navy, but the earthquake of 1907 left the building skewed as a reminder that dramatic seismic events can humble vicious buccaneers as easily as the world's foremost navy.

The **Old Naval Hospital** is the oldest prefabricated cast-iron structure in the western hemisphere. The hospital was built in 1818 on the foundation of an earlier hospital, using enslaved labor under the direction of the Royal Engineers of the British Army. The hospital went out of use in 1905 before getting a new lease on life as the Port Royal Centre for Archaeological and Conservation Research in 1968. Seventeen hurricanes have not fazed the structure, nor did the earthquake of 1907 do it any harm.

## Food

With two locations, ★ **Gloria's Seafood Restaurant** ("Bottom," 1 High St., tel. 876/967-8066, managed by Cecil; "Top," beachside, 15 Foreshore Rd., tel. 876/967-8220, managed by Angela) is a must for anyone who appreciates seafood (US$10 for a fried fish and bammy). Service can be slow with the crowds that swarm in, especially on Friday evenings and after church on Sunday. Gloria's does some of the most dependable and delicious fried escoveitch fish with Jamaican marinade. Both Gloria's locations have a laidback setting good for unhurried meals with a view of the water.

## Accommodations

**Grand Port Royal Hotel, Marina & Spa** (tel. 876/967-8494, cell tel. 876/833-6321, grandportroyal@gmail.com, www.grandportroyal.com, from US$117 including continental breakfast buffet) is the only accommodation option in Port Royal. It has a mix of recently refurbished and antiquated rooms, all with A/C and cable.

Slip fees at the hotel marina are reasonable at US$1 per foot per day, plus taxes, similar to rates found across the island. Water, electricity, and laundry services are available. The hotel was built on the former naval shipyard. A scene was shot here in *Dr. No*, the film made based Ian Fleming's 007 novel. Small boats depart from the marina throughout the day for Lime Cay (US$10 adults, US$5 children).

## Getting There

**JUTC buses** leave from the downtown bus terminal (route 98, US$1), or hire a **taxi** (US$25). **Route taxis** between Downtown and Port Royal run sporadically, leaving once filled with passengers. The ferry service, which once brought passengers from downtown Kingston to Port Royal, has unfortunately been discontinued.

# BULL BAY

Bull Bay is a quiet fishing community, 15 minutes east of Kingston along the A3. It has a long beach that lacks fine sand but also lacks crowds. It is a nice place for a dip, and the surf is decent for water sports at times. The community is perhaps best known for reggae artist and Jamaican surfing champion Billy "Mystic" Wilmot, who runs an irie surfing guest house on the beach, and as home to the Bobo Shanti (Ashanti) House of Ras Tafari, which has its base at nearby Bobo Hill.

## Sights

About 1.5 kilometers (1 mile) before reaching Bull Bay, a sign for **Cane River Falls** (US$3) marks a left off the main road onto Greendale Road by Nine Mile Square. The attraction is on the right just before a bridge and cannot be missed. The "falls" are not impressive and hardly justify the entrance fee. Nevertheless, it's a nice place to relax and get some food with the sound of the water, which varies from a bubble to a roar depending on recent rainfall.

**Cane River** meets the sea just before Bull Bay at Seven Mile, on the main road east of Kingston toward St. Thomas. The river is formed by the Barbeque and Mammee Rivers, among smaller tributaries that run down the northern slopes of the Dallas Mountains. The falls were once the stomping ground of Three Finger Jack, a legendary Robin Hood-like cult figure who terrorized the planter class with kidnappings for ransom and murder. Almost 200 years later, the falls became a favorite cool-off spot for Bob Marley, who sang "uppa Cane River to wash my dread / upon a rock I rest my head" in the song "Trench Town."

**Bobo Hill** (top of Weise Rd., Nine Mile, Bull, contact Priest Daniel Samuel, cell tel. 876/422-3471) is home to the Bobo Shanti, or Bobo Ashanti, House of Ras Tafari. Known for their militant interpretation of Marcus Garvey's teachings, the Bobo have been popularized by many dancehall artists who proclaim an affiliation. Paramount to Bobo philosophy and lifestyle are the ever-present themes of self-confidence, self-reliance, and self-respect. The Bobo can often be seen around Kingston, their locks carefully wrapped in a turban, peddling natural-fiber brooms, one of their signature crafts. At the center of the Bobo philosophy is the holy trinity between Bobo Shanti founder Prince Emmanuel Charles Edwards, who is said to have carried the spirit of Christ; Marcus Garvey, the prophet of the Ras Tafari Movement; and Haile Selassie I, the Ethiopian emperor who is their King of Kings. Women visiting the camp are asked to wear a dress or skirt below the knees and a head wrap, in accordance with the traditional dress code.

Leonard Howell, recognized as the first Jamaican to proclaim the divinity of Haile Selassie I, founded a commune at the inception of the movement in Pinnacle, St. Catherine, similar to the community found

Bobo Hill

today at Bobo Hill. Despite popular belief to the contrary, the Bobo are among the most open and welcoming of the various Houses of Ras Tafari. While it will not be appreciated if you turn up unannounced to sightsee at their commune, sincere interest is well received, and they routinely open their home and hearth to visitors from around the world. Some visitors stay several days with them to share food and partake in their ritualized lifestyle. To reach the camp, turn left on Weise Road right after a bridge about 1.5 kilometers (1 mile) past the center of Bull Bay. A contribution of at least US$10 pp for the guidance is customary.

## Surfing

Located in the community of Eight Mile, just before reaching Bull Bay, **Jamnesia Surf Club** (look for the surfboard sign right after the driveway beside AB&C Groceries, next to Cave Hut Beach, tel. 876/750-0103, cell tel. 876/545-4591, www.jamnesiasurf.com) is Jamaica's number-one surfing destination. It's run by Billy "Mystic" Wilmot, of Mystic Revealers fame, and his family. They are great hosts for a surf vacation and offer the widest variety of boards for rental, as well as complete surf vacation packages. Rates start from US$15 for two to pitch your own tent. Three camp rooms (US$35 s, US$45 d) have bunk beds and three bungalows have double and bunk beds (US$45 s, US$55 d). Nearby apartments can also be rented through Jamnesia. Six-night packages include room, two meals daily, a surfboard, and a shuttle to the breaks. Breakfast (US$4), lunch (US$6), and dinner (US$8) are offered at Shacks, the rustic restaurant on the property.

Jamaica has two good surf seasons: summer (June-Sept.) and winter (Dec.-Mar.). The fall and spring seasons may or may not have surf, but the room rates are lower off-season and open to negotiation. The property also features a skateboard bowl for when the water is flat, and the kids have set up a gully a short distance away like a skate park.

## Entertainment

**Little Copa** (Eight Miles, contact Ian Hudson, cell tel. 876/845-3418, ianhudson348@yahoo.com) hosts a regular "Young People Tuesday" event as well as occasional functions and parties.

**Wickie Wackie Beach** (contact Ronnie Jarrett, cell tel. 876/864-6188, Nine Mile), is a private home turned live music venue in Nine Mile since the 1940s, when a Night Club stood on the beach. Today the venue hosts occasional parties, like the Fat Tyre Festival and the Wickie Wackie Music Festival (US$10) the first week of December. One room is available for rent to short-term visitors (US$60).

**Jamnesia Sessions** are held at Jamnesia Surf Club starting around 9pm every other Saturday and feature up-and-coming musicians.

# GREATER PORTMORE

With over a million people, the parish of St. Catherine is Jamaica's most populous. Spanish Town, the sedate parish capital, was Jamaica's center of government until the British bureaucrats relocated to Kingston in 1872. Originally founded as Villa de la Vega or St. Jago de la Vega by the Spanish, the city was named Spanish Town after the British takeover in 1655.

Spanish Town and surrounding communities like Old Harbour and Freetown have grown rapidly with housing schemes that respond to demand for low-income housing for first-time homebuyers and are essentially bedroom communities for Kingston. Most activity in Spanish Town today revolves around the two malls and bus park along Burke Road. Mandela Highway has heavy traffic between Kingston and Spanish Town during weekday rush hours (7am-9am and 4pm-7pm).

## Spanish Town

Known simply as "Spain" or "St. Jago" on the street, the city has a rich heritage but has largely been left to decay. The old part of the city is well organized in a grid with Spanish Town Square at its center. There's

# Spanish Town

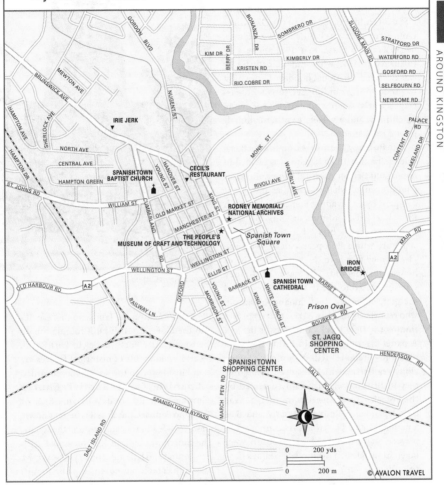

© AVALON TRAVEL

little activity in the historic part of the city; the hustle and bustle is around the commercial plazas along Burke Road and the bus park where route taxis and buses depart for Kingston, May Pen, Mandeville, Linstead, and Ocho Rios.

Still, it has impressive facades and is home to Jamaica's national archives. The oldest Anglican Church outside of England is within a five-minute walk of the square.

## SIGHTS

**Spanish Town Square** was laid out by Jamaica's first colonial rulers as their Plaza Mayor. It's surrounded by the burned remains of the old courthouse on its southern side, Old King's House on the west, the Rodney Memorial, and behind it the National Archives on the north side; the Old House of Assembly, now parish administration offices, on its eastern side, is the only building facing the square that's still in use.

**The People's Museum of Craft and Technology** (tel. 876/907-0322, 9am-4pm Mon.-Thurs., 9am-3pm Fri., US$1.50 adults, US$0.50 children), located in the Old King's House complex on Spanish Town Square, began as a Folk Museum in 1961 and was refurbished in 1997 when Emancipation Day was declared a national holiday. The exhibit has indoor and outdoor sections with carriages, early sugar and coffee processing machinery, and a variety of other colonial-period implements.

The **Rodney Memorial,** on the northern side of Spanish Town Square, was erected in homage to British Admiral George Rodney, who prevented what was seen as imminent conquest by an invading French and Spanish naval fleet led by Admiral de Grasse in 1782. The memorial is housed in a spectacular structure with a European palatial look and gives a nice facade to the National Archives housed just behind. The statue of Rodney was contracted to one of the most respected sculptors of the day, Englishman John Bacon, who reportedly made two trips to Italy before finding the right block of marble for the job. A panel inscribed in Latin inside Rodney's octagonal "temple" tells of Rodney's victorious sea battle, which restored some dignity to Britain, recently badly defeated by the French-American allies in the U.S. War of Independence. Rodney was duly lauded as a national hero. The two brass cannons displayed just outside the statue enclosure were taken from defeated Admiral de Grasse's flagship, *Ville de Paris.*

**Spanish Town Cathedral,** or the Anglican Cathedral Church of St. James, stands on the site of the Roman Catholic Red Cross Spanish Chapel, originally built in 1525 and run by Franciscans. Cromwell's Puritan soldiers destroyed the Spanish chapel along with another on the northern end of town known as White Cross, run by Dominicans. The church has been destroyed and rebuilt several times through a series of earthquakes and hurricanes. It became the first Anglican cathedral outside England in

Spanish Town Cathedral

1843, representing the Jamaican diocese. It's also the oldest English-built foundation on the island, after Fort Charles in Port Royal. Several monuments of historical figures are found inside and in the walled churchyard.

**Spanish Town Baptist Church** (Cumberland Rd. and Williams St.), or Phillippo Baptist Church as it is better known, is located a few blocks northwest of the square. The church was built in 1827 on an old artillery ground and later went on to play an active role in the abolition movement. Abolitionist Reverend James Murcell Phillippo arrived in Jamaica in 1823 and later established the church with help from freed slaves. On the night of emancipation in 1838, when local authorities granted Jamaica's slave population full freedom, 2000 freed slaves were baptized in the church. There is a tablet in the churchyard commemorating the act of emancipation, which was celebrated there after the proclamation was read in front of Old King's House.

The **Iron Bridge** over the Rio Cobre was shipped in prefabricated segments from where it was cast in England and erected on the eastern edge of Spanish Town in 1801. Today it is used as a pedestrian crossing and is in a poor state of preservation. Designed by English engineer Thomas Wilson, it was the first prefab cast-iron bridge erected in the western hemisphere.

**White Marl Taino Museum** is sited on an old Taino settlement, the largest in Jamaica pre-Columbus. The museum had to be moved due to poor security in the area. It features artifacts and displays pinpointing Taino archeological sites across the island and providing information on the lifestyle and practices of these first Jamaicans.

**Mountain River Cave** (caretaker Monica Wright, tel. 876/705-2790), with its Taino wall paintings first uncovered in 1897, is located 21 kilometers (13 miles) due northwest from the roundabout at the beginning of St. John's Road on the western edge of Spanish Town. After leaving an Uptown suburb, St. John's becomes Cudjoe's Hill Road as you pass through red earth hills on the way to Kitson and then Guanaboa Vale, the stomping ground of Juan de Bolas. A few kilometers beyond a beautiful old church, pull over at Joan's Bar & Grocery Shop, marked by a painted facade reading Cudjoe's Cavern.

Monica will indicate the trailhead that leads down a steep hill across the meandering Thompson's River and up the facing bank through cacao and passion-fruit stands to where the small cave is caged in against vandals. The cave itself is shallow and unspectacular, but its paintings are interesting; it's easy to make out a man with a spear, a turtle, some fish, and a few women. The paintings are said to be authentic, given the ash and bat guano mix used, supposedly a typical medium for the earliest Jamaican artists. The highlight of this attraction, apart from the well-preserved petroglyphs, is the beautiful walk through lush forests and Thompson's River, which has a large pool upstream and a waterfall downstream from the crossing, fitting for a cool dip.

**FOOD**
**Irie Jerk Centre** (21 Brunswick Ave., tel. 876/749-5375, 24 hours daily) serves fried and jerk chicken (US$2 per piece, quarter chicken US$4), pork (US$10 per pound), and beer to wash it down (US$2). Irie also cooks curry goat, porridge, and soup.

**St. Jago Shopping Centre** has a small food court with some decent lunch options.

**Tastebuds Delight** (shop 32, tel. 876/769-7002, 7am-8pm Mon.-Sat., 7am-10pm Sun., US$2-4) also has Jamaican dishes ranging from chicken to oxtail.

**Nature's Vitamins, Herbs & Wellness Centre** (tel. 876/984-1305, US$2) serves vegetarian patties, sugar-free pastries and natural juices.

★ **Cecil's** (35 Martin St., tel. 876/984-2986 or 876/984-2404, 10am-10pm Mon.-Sat., noon-8pm Sun., US$4-12) is easily Spanish Town's most-lauded restaurant. The late Cecil Reid was a chef at a number of other restaurants for years before opening his own place in 1983. Menu items have a decidedly Asian lean, with chop suey, chow mein, fried rice, and more typical curry dishes, beef, chicken, and lobster. Beer and fresh juices are US$2.

**SERVICES**
**St. Catherine Parish Library** (tel. 876/984-2356, 9am-6pm Mon.-Fri., 10am-5pm Sat.), across from Spanish Town Cathedral, offers free Internet access on a few computers.

**GETTING THERE AND AROUND**
Spanish Town is served by Kingston's JUTC with **buses** from Half Way Tree Transport Centre and the Downtown bus terminals departing every 10 minutes on routes 21 and 22. Private Coaster buses arrive and depart from bus stops a few paces down Molynes Road, across Eastwood Park Road from the Transport Centre. They charge just over US$1 one-way. **Route taxis** ply all major roads in Spanish Town and can be flagged down, charging anywhere from US$0.75 to US$1.75 around town.

If you're driving, the most direct route to

Spanish Town is along Spanish Town Road or Washington Boulevard to Mandela Highway. Stay to the right at the first roundabout. You'll see the Old Iron Bridge on the right just after crossing the Rio Cobre as you enter town. Take a right at the stoplight at the gas station immediately thereafter to reach the historical sites surrounding Spanish Town Square or to pass through town for Linstead, Moneague, Walkerswood, and Ocho Rios. Heading straight at the stoplight leads to the commercial district after passing Prison Oval.

To reach Old Harbour, head west out of Spanish Town along the bypass, keeping left following well-marked signs at the second roundabout along Old Harbour Road, which leads southwest through vast tracts of sugarcane fields.

## Fort Clarence Beach Park

**Fort Clarence Beach Park** (cell tel. 876/364-3628, 10am-6pm Wed.-Fri., 10am-6pm Sat.-Sun., US$2, US$1 under age 13) is a popular 13-hectare (32-acre) beach with showers, portable toilets, and a ramshackle kitchen cooking up fried fish and soup. The beach has lifeguards on duty and a cordoned swimming area.

## Waves Beach

**Waves Beach** (contact Lisa Golding, cell tel. 876/364-0182, wavesbeach@icloud.com, www.wavesbeachja.com, 10am-10pm Mon.-Fri., 8am-10pm Sat.-Sun., US$2 adults, US$1 under age 13) is a family-friendly private beach a few lots west of Fort Clarence Beach Park, offering a seaside restaurant and full bar with a covered dining area. The restaurant serves a variety of seafood dishes, including conch soup, fried, curry, and brown stew fish, lobster, and shrimp. Patrons are offered complimentary Wi-Fi, showers, and baths as well as secure parking.

## The Boardwalk

**The Boardwalk** (contact proprietor Roger Davis, cell tel. 876/404-0078, US$2 adults, US$1 under age 12) is a restaurant and bar with its own strip of beach a few lots west of Fort Clarence Beach Park. The admission gets you a bit of shade under wooden umbrellas and rustic nailed-together lounge chairs—watch out for the rusty nails. A kitchen on-site serves soup and fish.

## ★ Hellshire

**Hellshire** is a free public beach protected by offshore reefs with small waves where families from Greater Portmore and Kingston congregate on weekends, filling the sea with bobbing bodies and the sand with playing children. Speakers are stacked at Prendry's on the far eastern end of the beach by a rocky breakwater, and party-lovers gather round as the day grows old to dance, with plenty of drinking and smoking.

Fish-frying entrepreneurs are highly competitive as they woo hungry diners, and unsuspecting patrons can easily be scammed in search of lunch. As soon as you drive beneath the arch into Hellshire, men will offer parking spaces, and once parked, they'll direct you to the fish stalls where they receive a commission for bringing guests; it's best to keep walking like you know where you're headed. A handful of dependable and honest restaurateurs offer good value, and the lively beach scene is worth a visit.

The sand and water can be littered, but it's generally clean enough to swim despite the fishermen's habit of scaling their catch at the water's edge, and the locals don't bat an eye at the floating plastic bags. Peddlers of every sort eke out a living at Hellshire, from the man selling customized bamboo vessels to the ganja, jewelry, and bootleg CD vendors and the pony handler who gives tame rides down the short stretch of beach for a couple of bucks. Don't be alarmed by constant solicitations; it's just part of Hellshire's color.

### FOOD

★ **Shorty's** (contact proprietor Judith Ewers, cell tel. 876/586-3623 or 876/323-1915, 9am-10pm Mon.-Thurs., 9am-10pm Fri.-Sat., 6am-11pm Sun.) is highly recommended for dependable brown stew, snapper (US$12 per pound), as well as lobster (US$12 per pound) in season, accompanied by bammy and festival. It's always best to call ahead to put in your order to ensure minimal waiting time.

**Prendy's on the Beach** (cell tel. 876/575-6057 or 876/575-6063, prendysonthebeach@ yahoo.com, 9am-9pm Mon.-Thurs., 8am-11pm Fri.-Sun., US$11-15 per pound) is an honest and dependable seafood restaurant serving fried (US$11 per pound), steamed, garlic, brown stew, roast, curry, and jerk fish, conch, lobster, shrimp, and king crab, with two festival included. A location at Hi-Lo in Portmore Pines Plaza offers prix fixe meals (3pm-10pm Fri.-Sat., US$10). DJ Marlon of Exstasy Sound plays a mix of reggae, dancehall, and hip-hop all day Sunday.

## Two Sisters Cave

**Two Sisters Cave** (tel. 876/999-2283 or 876/953-9238, 9am-6pm Wed.-Sun., US$3 adults, US$2 children), was a regular hangout for the first Jamaicans centuries ago. Two large caves, one with a deep pool suitable for swimming (if you're allowed to by the wardens), are about 100 meters (300 feet) apart down a series of steps. A third, unmanaged cave can be found about 100 (300 feet) meters east of Two Sisters, reached by a footpath descending from the road.

# The Blue and John Crow Mountains

The Blue and John Crow Mountains harbor rich biodiversity and played an important cultural role in history, providing refuge to Taino and enslaved Africans fleeing colonial oppressors, transplanted French-Haitian coffee farmers fleeing revolution, and later to Bob Marley, when he sought safety and seclusion at Strawberry Hill following an attempt on his life in 1976. Today the area attracts visitors for its lush and diverse flora, colorful birdlife, delicious coffee, and crisp mountain air, all of which earned the Blue and John Crow Mountains UNESCO World Heritage Site status in 2015. During much of the year, the peaks cloud over by mid-morning, so it's always a good idea to get an early start for the best views.

Five parishes can be seen from Blue Mountain Peak, Jamaica's highest summit, at 2,256 meters (7,402 feet): Kingston and St. Andrew to the south, St. Thomas to the east, Portland to the north, and St. Mary to the east. The range forms a physical barrier to the northeasterly fronts that typically hit the island, giving Portland and St. Thomas copious rainfall compared to the southern coastal plains, where drought is more common.

Irish Town, Hardwar Gap, and Mavis Bank are great destinations for a quick escape from the city, all within an hour's drive. This is where rural Jamaica is at its coolest. The elevation and lush greenery offer welcome respite from the heat of the city. The road up and the rugged terrain are not for the faint of heart, but the prized Blue Mountain coffee, breathtaking views, diverse vegetation, and abundance of native birds are more than adequate rewards.

## COOPERAGE TO SILVER HILL GAP

Turning left at the Cooperage onto the B3 leads up a series of sharp hairpin turns that can leave passengers nauseated. The winding road first passes through the lower hills and valleys of Maryland before reaching the principal hamlet along the route, Irish Town. **Irish Town** has as its centerpiece St. Mark's Chapel, a quaint little church reached by a 15-minute walk along a footpath.

### St. Mark's Chapel

A beautiful old church that sits on a hilltop in Irish Town, **St. Mark's Chapel** is a great

# The Blue and John Crow Mountains

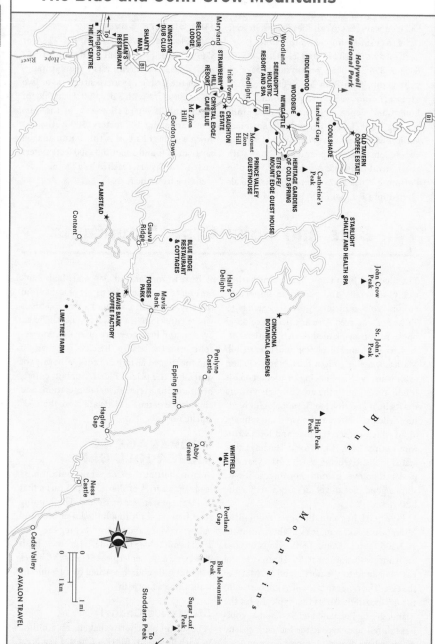

Hope River

To Kingston

THE ART CENTRE

LILLIAN'S RESTAURANT

SHANTY MAN

KINGSTON DUB CLUB

BELCOUR LODGE

Maryland

STRAWBERRY HILL RESORT

CRYSTAL EDGE/ CAFÉ BLUE

CRAIGHTON ESTATE

Irish Town

SERENDIPITY HOLISTIC RESORT AND SPA

Redlight

Woodland

FIDDLEWOOD

WOODSIDE

NEWCASTLE

Mt Zion Hill

Mount Zion Hill

PRINCE VALLEY GUESTHOUSE

EITS CAFÉ/ MOUNT EDGE GUEST HOUSE

HERITAGE GARDENS OF COLD SPRING

Catherine's Peak

Hardwar Gap

Holywell National Park

COOLSHADE

OLD TAVERN COFFEE ESTATE

Gordon Town

FLAMSTEAD

Content

Guava Ridge

BLUE RIDGE RESTAURANT & COTTAGES

FORRES PARK

MAVIS BANK COFFEE FACTORY

Mavis Bank

Hall's Delight

CINCHONA BOTANICAL GARDENS

STARLIGHT CHALET AND HEALTH SPA

John Crow Peak

St. John's Peak

LIME TREE FARM

Penlyne Castle

Epping Farm

Hagley Gap

Abby Green

WHITFIELD HALL

High Peak

Blue Mountains

Ness Castle

Cedar Valley

Portland Gap

Blue Mountain Peak

Sugar Loaf Peak

To Stoddarts Peak

© AVALON TRAVEL

0          1 mi

0          1 km

destination for a short hike. As you arrive at the junction in Irish Town where the driveway to Strawberry Hill leads up to the left, the chapel looms up ahead.

## Mt. Zion Hill

A Rastafarian farming community is based in a squatter settlement known as **Mt. Zion Hill** (to request a visit call Priest Dermot Fagan, cell tel. 876/868-9636). The carefully maintained trail and fence along the path up the hill demonstrates the respect given to Priest Dermot Fagan, referred to simply as "the priest" by his followers, who rank in the range of 50-odd adults and children living at Zion Hill. Fagan has established His Imperial Majesty School of Bible Study and Sabbath Service, with a small yurt-like structure at the entrance to the community serving as its chapel. The small community follows primarily an agrarian life, growing food and herbs and selling roots wine around town to bring in a little cash. There are several people who espouse the school's teaching but live in town rather than on Zion Hill.

It becomes evident when the group descends on Papine Square every Saturday for a Nyabinghi Sabbath Service of singing and drumming that the number of followers is significant indeed. Fagan advocates a total rejection of the system that has separated humankind from direct reliance on our labor and the food we can provide for ourselves. He warns of an even greater divide between man and his sustenance through the impending mass implantation of micro-biochips. The Mt. Zion Hill community has established itself as one of the more colorful, albeit apocalyptic, Houses of Rastafari.

## Strawberry Hill

**Strawberry Hill** (tel. 876/944-8400, www.islandoutpost.com) is a boutique hilltop resort of the Island Outpost hotel group, with an assortment of guest cottages that hug steep hillsides, and a restaurant and bar as the property's centerpiece at its highest point. The property welcomes nonguests (US$15) when not overly busy to enjoy the view, food and drinks, spa treatments, and the gift shop. Don't miss the collection of gold and platinum albums hanging on the walls in the boardroom below the restaurant recalling Island Records and Island Outpost founder Chris Blackwell's illustrious career as a music producer. It's well worth a visit for a luxurious afternoon or evening. The hotel boasts an Aveda concept **spa and wellness**

Strawberry Hill

# Jamaican Coffee: Cultivating an Industry

Coffee is one of 600 species in the Rubiaceae family, understood to have its center of origin in what is today Ethiopia. The plant's beans and leaves are believed to have been chewed by the earliest inhabitants and later brewed by ancient Abyssinians and Arabs, the latter credited with originating the global coffee trade. Jamaica's relationship with the revered bean dates to 1728, when a former governor introduced coffee of the Typica cultivar to his Temple Hall estate in upper St. Andrew. Its cultivation was formalized in earnest with large plantations covering hundreds of hectares established in the nearby Blue Mountains by an influx of planters fleeing Haiti in the years leading up to the neighboring country's 1804 independence. By 1800, there were 686 coffee plantations in Jamaica, with exports totaling 15,199 tons.

These early planters discovered that the intact plantation economy and the cloud forest climatic conditions were conducive to lucrative coffee production. The misty climate allowed the coffee berries to ripen slowly, a process said to grant the end product its smooth, full-bodied flavor, free of bitterness. The bumper earnings of these early plantations were short-lived, however, deteriorating when global demand subsided and competition increased from other colonies imposing lower taxes. The abolition of slavery and emancipation further challenged Jamaica's large-scale coffee plantations; when labor became more expensive, the country's production deteriorated, and the bean's cultivation was soon dominated by smallholders. By 1850 there were only 186 plantations left in Jamaica, with exports falling to 1,486 tons.

Jamaica's Coffee Industry Board, established in 1950, was set up to control the quality of the product and participate directly in the production process. The CIB also regulates the coveted Blue Mountain Coffee registered trademark, allowing its use only by farms certified by the board

center with a holistic approach to rejuvenation, dubbed Strawberry Hill Living.

## Craighton Estate Blue Mountain Coffee Tour

**Craighton Estate Blue Mountain Coffee Tour** (Irish Town, tel. 876/929-8490, cell. tel. 876/292-3774, beddalton@gmail.com, US$25 adults, US$15 children 6-12), owned by Japan-based Ueshima Coffee Company, offers a one-hour tour led by leading Blue Mountain Coffee connoisseur Alton "Junior" Bedward. The tour features a lecture covering coffee history and cultivation and a walk around the working coffee farm and historic great house ending at a hilltop gazebo. UCC is one of the foremost exporters of Jamaican Blue Mountain Coffee to Japan, the leading foreign market for the prized product.

## ★ Old Tavern Coffee Estate

The Twyman family has been growing some of the best Blue Mountain coffee since 1968 at their **Old Tavern Coffee Estate** (contact David Twyman in his Kingston office to arrange a visit, tel. 876/924-2785, cell tel. 876/865-2978, oldtaverncoffee@gmail.com, www.oldtaverncoffee.com, US$20 adults, US$10 children 6-12). The estate is run by David Twyman, son of original owners Dorothy and the late, great coffee farmer Alex Twyman. He offers a coffee roasting and tasting tour with a jaunt through the fields, weather permitting.

The Twymans have a coveted Coffee Board license, which allows them to sell directly to their customers (US$40 per pound) and market their beans as "Blue Mountain Coffee," a closely held trademark belonging to Jamaica. They use integrated pest management in their fields, limiting the use of chemical fertilizers and pesticides while employing traditional fermentation and sun-drying processes. The unique climatic conditions found at the Twymans' estate requires a longer maturation period—the berries remain on the trees for 10 months due to the near-constant mist blanketing the ridge around Hardwar Gap.

Three different roasts are produced from Old Tavern beans: medium, medium in the parishes of St. Andrew, St. Thomas, Portland, and St. Mary, all located at elevations between 610 and 1,525 meters (2,000-5,000 feet).

Obtaining a certification by the CIB as a producer of Blue Mountain Coffee is a challenge, especially for small farms. It can take several years, as certification demands scrupulous implantation of the CIB farming practices and production processes.

Coffee produced at lower elevations can also be of high quality, though it doesn't attract the same attention or price as Jamaica's Blue Mountain coffee. Jamaica Prime, Premium Washed, and High Mountain Supreme are some of the names Jamaican coffee is sold under when not originating from the Blue Mountains. There are notable coffee producers in several parishes around Jamaica, among them farms in Bog Walk and St. Catherine, at Key Park Estate in Westmoreland, at Aenon Park along the Clarendon-St. Ann border, at Clarendon Park, and in Maggoty, St. Elizabeth.

Jamaica's climate is at once a blessing and a curse for the country's coffee farmers. The high altitude mist nurtures the bean to give it its distinct character, but the country's highest peaks are also most exposed and vulnerable to hurricanes and tropical storms, which can destroy several years' work in one night. The lack of insurance for the industry since Hurricane Ivan in 2004 has made production at many small farms a real gamble. Combating disease is also a constant struggle. Nonetheless, today's coffee industry employees some 50,000 Jamaicans and brings in around US$35 million in foreign exchange each year. Retailing at nearly US$40 per pound in Jamaica and US$50 per pound abroad, Jamaican Blue Mountain coffee's high price keeps the coffee industry viable.

dark (Proprietors' Choice), and dark roast. Peaberry beans, odd balls that develop only one side of the normally paired bean, are smaller and have a unique mild flavor that's prized by many.

## Catherine's Peak

Rising to the right as you drive up to Newcastle from Red Light, **Catherine's Peak** quickly becomes visible, easily distinguishable by the clutter of communications antennae at the summit. The peak is a one-hour hike from the Parade ground at Newcastle, where there is plenty of parking. A rough road goes all the way up, but it becomes impassable to anything but a 4WD vehicle. Jamaica Defense Force soldiers stationed at Newcastle restrict access to all vehicles except those carrying the most trustworthy-looking visitors. It's best to hoof it from Newcastle rather than drive part of the way.

## Holywell National Park

**Holywell National Park** (US$5) sits atop Hardwar Gap, affording a view of St. Andrew Parish to the south and St. Mary and Portland to the north. The birding is excellent in the 50-hectare (124-acre) park, which borders Twyman's Old Tavern Coffee Estate on the north side and is a haven for migratory birds in the winter months. Hiking trails lead to a few peaks, and there's also a loop trail. Holywell is home to the **Blue Mountain Music Festival,** held in February.

The graveled 1.2-kilometer (0.75-mile) **Oatley Mountain Loop Trail** is a steep ascent to Oatley Mountain Peak at 1,400 meters (4,593 feet). Three lookout points along the way offer great views of St. Andrew, St. Mary, and Portland. The **Waterfall Trail** is also about 1.2 kilometers (0.75 miles) long, meandering along the mountain edge and then following a stream with a small waterfall at the end. Shorter and less strenuous trails include the 600-meter (2,000-foot) **Shelter Trail,** the 350-meter (1,150-foot) **Blue Mahoe Trail,** and the 630-meter (2,100-foot) **Wag Water/ Dick's Pond Trail.**

## Food

**Shanty Man** (Gordon Town Rd., cell tel. 876/533-3513, US$2-4, 8am-10pm Sun.-Fri.) serves natural juices and cooked ital food out of a little Rasta-colored restaurant along the road between Papine and the Cooperage, just before the turnoff up to Skyline Drive. The menu features tofu, chick peas, pumpkin soup, and sautéed ackee with potato and carrot served with rice-and-peas.

**Café Blue** (Irish Town, tel. 876/944-8918, www.jamaicacafeblue.com, 8am-6pm Mon.-Fri., 8am-8pm Sat.-Sun.) serves Blue Mountain coffee and pastries and retails local sauces, candles, and soaps. Café Blue is owned by the Sharps, who own Coffee Traders and Clifton Mount coffee estate.

★ **Crystal Edge** (next door to Café Blue, Irish Town, contact Winsome Hall, tel. 876/944-8053, 8:30am-4pm Sat.-Sun., 10:30am-4pm Tues.-Fri.) serves excellent Jamaican dishes at Jamaican prices. The menu rotates daily, with starters like crayfish or red pea soup and entrées that include oxtail and escoveitch fish. The restaurant is located just before Irish Town where the road starts to level out, sharing a building with Café Blue.

**Strawberry Hill** (tel. 876/944-8400, www.islandoutpost.com, 8am-10:30am, noon-4pm, 6pm-9pm daily, appetizers US$13-20, entrées US$30-50) has a varied menu of Jamaican and international cuisine and spectacular views from a wraparound porch. By no means a budget eatery, the ambience will leave you with no regrets for having splurged. Reservations are required for guests not staying on the property. On Sunday there is an all-you-can-eat brunch buffet (noon-3pm).

**Bubbles Bar** (contact proprietor Reid, cell tel. 876/773-1134), about halfway between Redlight and Newcastle, is the only watering hole along that stretch, selling basic supplies in addition to beer and rum. The bar marks the turnoff to Middleton down a poor road that falls sharply. The first hairpin to the right descends farther toward the valley floor. Another hairpin turn to the left,

200 meters (660 feet) past a rise in the road over a landslide, leads down toward Prince Valley Guesthouse, run by Bobby "Scorcha" Williams and his wife Jackie, on the opposite side of the hill. A 4WD vehicle is critical to get much beyond the landslide.

**Karen's One Stop** (Settlement-Middleton, cell tel. 876/429-2551, US$5-10, 7am-8pm daily), located just past the hairpin turn on the left, is one of the few cook shops around to get Jamaican staples like fried or barbecue chicken, fish, calalloo, and rice-and-peas cooked to order any time of day. Proprietor Karen Arnold also sells basic foodstuffs.

**Europe in the Summer (EITS) Café** (Mount Edge Guesthouse, just before mile marker 17, approaching Newcastle, tel. 876/944-8151, foodbasketjamaica@gmail.com, www.17milepost.com, 9am-6pm daily, US$5-30) offers a farm-to-table dining experience in a cozy open-air dining terrace overlooking the gardens of Food Basket Farm and the valleys, ridges, and peaks of the Blue Mountains. Entrées include rack of lamb, barrel roasted chicken, and coconut curry veggie stew.

**The Gap Café** (Hardwar Gap, cell tel. 876/399-2406, 10am-3pm Mon.-Thurs., 10am-5pm Fri.-Sun., US$10-18) is a charming restaurant with indoor and outdoor seating serving a rotating home-style menu with items like curried goat, oxtail and beans, and callaloo-stuffed chicken breast. When not shrouded in mist, it boasts spectacular views over Kingston and St. Andrew at 1,280 meters (4,200 feet) elevation. Located three kilometers (2 miles) past the Jamaica Defense Force hill station at Newcastle, the restaurant will stay open longer by reservation. It is said Ian Fleming wrote some of his first James Bond book, *Dr. No*, at the Gap.

**Starlight Chalet** (Silver Hill Gap, tel. 876/969-3070, 7am-5pm daily, later with reservations, US$10-25) serves Jamaican dishes at reasonable prices, bakes cakes and pastries from scratch, and prepares natural juices with whatever fruit is in season.

Book a cabin in Holywell National Park.

## Accommodations
### UNDER US$100

**Mount Edge Guesthouse** (just before mile marker 17, approaching Newcastle, tel. 876/944-8151, jamaicanmountedge@gmail. com, www.17milepost.com, from US$45) has four rustic cottages hanging on the edge of a cliff overlooking the farm with single, double, or king beds. Some share a bath and some have private baths. A central building has two private rooms with a shared bath, living room, and dining room. A third building has bunk beds for four with adjoining baths. Amenities include hot water, Wi-Fi, a small roadside bar, and a trail to the river. Mountain bikes are available.

★ **Prince Valley Guesthouse** (cell tel. 876/892-2365, jaqdes@netstep.net, US$35-40 pp) is located on a small coffee farm in Middleton Settlement. The property is managed by Bobby Williams and has five guest rooms, each with its own bathroom. Linens and towels are provided along with a basic breakfast of coffee and toast. Dinner is

available by request (US$12 pp). A common room has a refrigerator, books, a couch, work table and Wi-Fi. The lodging is ideal for backpackers. Bobby offers pickups from the airport (US$100) or Kingston (US$60), or you can take a route taxi from Papine for about US$3. To get there, take the first right after Mount Edge Guesthouse at Bubbles Bar, followed by another right at the first intersection, and then a left after crossing a little ramp.

**Holywell National Park** provides cabins and tent sites bookable through the **Jamaica Conservation and Development Trust** (29 Dumbarton Ave., Half Way Tree, tel. 876/920-8278 or 876/920-8279, jamaicaconservation@ gmail.com, www.greenjamaica.org.jm). Book at least two weeks in advance for a weekend stay in one of three self-contained cabins. Two one-bedroom units (US$50) have an open layout, one two-bedroom unit is US$70. Campers (US$10) can use the shared showers, toilets, and barbecue pits (US$5) on-site.

**The Gap Café** (Harwar Gap, cell tel. 876/319-2406) offers a one-bedroom rustic apartment (US$60) containing two twin beds, a private bath, a kitchenette, and a small sitting room.

### US$100-250

★ **Belcour Lodge** (Maryland district, contact Robin Lim Lumsden, tel. 876/927-2448, cell tel. 876/383-8942, limlums@gmail.com, US$125) is a beautiful colonial-era home in an enchanting river valley amid citrus groves and orchids. Home of Belcour Preserves (www. belcourpreserves.com), the lodge has a quaint self-contained cottage for a one-of-a-kind retreat. Belcour's sauces, jams, and marmalades are available for purchase.

**Serendipity Holistic Resort & Spa** (Red Light, tel. 876/944-8760, U.S. tel. 305/320-6925, www.serendipityholisticresort.com, US$125-659) is a collection of six one-bedroom cabins, five of them double occupancy and one that can hold up to four on two king beds or a king and two singles. The cabins all have private baths with showers and cable TV, and Wi-Fi covers the whole property; one cabin has a kitchenette. The main house, Rock Stone, has a master bedroom with a king and a second bedroom with a queen or two singles. Both rooms have private baths with shower tubs. Rock Stone has a full kitchen, dining room, and fireplace, and a large flat-screen TV. All have private baths and quality linens, and overhang the banks of the Hope River. Nonguests can make a reservation to dine on property and avoid the day pass fee (US$10) to swim in the river and enjoy the facilities. The spa offers Swedish, deep tissue, and full body massage, as well as manis and pedis, by reservation. The resort opened in 2014.

**Heritage Gardens of Cold Spring** (just below Newcastle, tel. 876/960-0794 or 876/960-8627, b.eleanor@gmail.com, www. heritagegardensjamaica.com, US$100 for 2, US$20 per additional person) is an old coffee estate with large barbecues, the flat areas where coffee is laid out to dry, hinting at its past as a coffee processing estate, established in 1747 by Irish botanist Matthew Wallen, credited with bringing several exotic plant species to Jamaica, including watercress, dandelion, nasturtiums, and bamboo. The cottage on the property sleeps up to six and has a rustic but comfortable feel with hot water and a cool breeze. The gardens are well cared for, and the entire property boasts spectacular views. The cottage makes a good base for hiking in the western section of the Blue Mountains and is a short walk to Newcastle, where the road up to Catherine's Peak begins.

**Starlight Chalet** (Silver Hill Gap, tel. 876/969-3070, cell tel. 876/414-8570, www. starlightchalet.com, US$130, includes breakfast) is a quaint retreat, reached by heading north from Hardwar Gap. Turn right at Section and travel until you reach Starlight Chalet. The 17-room property has several different room layouts, some with one queen, others with two, and two with kings. The original structure, a two-bedroom cottage at the top of the property, has a formal dining room with marble floors, a fireplace, and antique furniture, ideal for small groups looking for a degree of independence. Common areas have satellite TV and Wi-Fi. The kitchen serves a rotating menu of Jamaican fare.

## OVER US$250

★ **Strawberry Hill** (Newcastle Rd., tel. 876/944-8400 or 876/619-7872, reservations@ islandoutpost.com, www.strawberryhillhotel. com, from US$400) is an exclusive hotel operated by legendary record producer Chris Blackwell's Island Outpost hotel group. There are 13 guest cottages, most with double occupancy, three holding up to four guests, spread over 26 acres hugging steep hillsides covered in bamboo.

Inside the wooden cottages, louvered windows open to panoramic views of lush hillsides and Kingston below, its lights twinkling at night, adding to the timeless romance captured by renowned Jamaican architect Ann Hodges in her minimalist, functional design. Canopy king beds are shrouded in mosquito nets, but you'll hardly need them as the windows are well screened. The purposeful absence of television is a welcome escape from screen life to enjoy the scenery. If you need to stay connected, the Wi-Fi works like a charm and a lounge by the restaurant has a big flat screen if you must tune in to the news or football match. Kitchenettes come with a mini fridge and fixings for tea, coffee, and snacks.

The restaurant and bar are located next to a sprawling lawn. A yoga pavilion faces northward towards the southern slopes of the Blue Mountain range and a reflective infinity pool faces south over Kingston. Below the restaurant, a community room is adorned with the golden discs reflecting the acclaim of Blackwell's career as a record producer. The hotel's **Spa and Wellness Centre** pushes Island Outpost's holistic approach to rejuvenation, dubbed Strawberry Hill Living.

The property welcomes nonguests (admission US$15) to enjoy the view, food and drinks, spa treatments, and visit the gift shop. Make a lunch or dinner reservation to avoid the entrance fee—it's well worth a visit for a luxurious afternoon or evening.

★ **Woodside** (tel. 876/977-5020. ext. 253, guangotree@gmail.com, 2-night minimum, 3 bedrooms US$300, 4 bedrooms US$400, 5 bedrooms US$500) is a charming, staffed, colonial-era home on a 12-hectare (30-acre) coffee farm located about 1.5 kilometers (1 mile) past Newcastle, just below Hardwar Gap and Holywell National Park. Woodside is a stylish base for hiking in the park, bird-watching, and exploring the western reaches of the Blue Mountains. The house is impeccable in its old-Jamaica feel and boasts spectacular views, gardens, and a spring-fed pool. There is no better place for a cool escape during Jamaica's hottest months.

**Fiddlewood** (Greenwich, contact Diane McConnell, cell tel. 876/298-5221, dirmcc@gmail.com, www.fiddlewoodlogcabin.com, US$1,200) is a 557-square-meter (6,000-square-foot), 6-bedroom, 6.5-bath log cabin with spectacular views and all the creature comforts of a luxury villa, including a jetted tub, an indoor-outdoor sound system, a fireplace, and full staff. Flat-screen satellite TV is in each room, and Wi-Fi keep guests connected. Billiards, table tennis, and badminton are available.

# MAVIS BANK

Mavis Bank is a sleepy village nestled in a river valley in the shadow of Blue Mountain Peak. Its principal economic foundation for the past century has been the Mavis Bank Coffee Factory, which keeps many of the area's residents employed. The area is a good base for exploring the upper reaches of the Blue Mountains and for birding.

A few homey lodging options around Mavis Bank offer visitors a chance to prepare in relative comfort for the trek up Blue Mountain Peak, a grueling three-hour hike from the trailhead at Abbey Green reachable by 4WD, or alternatively, a nine-hour hike from Mavis Bank.

## Sights

Right off the Main Road as you reach Mavis Bank from Gordon Town, **Mavis Bank Coffee Factory** (tel. 876/977-8005 or 876/977-8013, www.bluemountaincoffee.com, 8:30am-noon and 1pm-3:30pm Mon.-Fri., US$10 adults, US$5 children) was established in 1923 by an English planter, Victor Munn. As the biggest coffee factory in Jamaica, it has been the economic lifeblood of the area since. Reservations are recommended for the tour.

The factory is supplied by six of its own

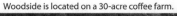
Woodside is located on a 30-acre coffee farm.

plantations and around 5,000 independent farms. Most of the picking is done by local women, who receive about US$50 per box full of berries. Of this, most goes to the farm owner where the berries were picked. The coffee is then left outside to dry for five to seven days, weather permitting, or dried in a giant tumbler for two days if it's too rainy outside. Once dry, the coffee is aged in big sacks for four to six weeks before the outer parchment, or hull, is removed and the beans are cleaned and roasted. The whole process takes three or four months from bush to mug. Four grades (peaberry, 1, 2, and 3) are produced, around 80 percent of which is consumed in Japan, with 5 percent going to the United States and 4 percent to the rest of the world. Mavis Bank processes 1.4 million pounds of green beans per year.

**Cinchona Gardens** (6am-6pm daily) is a former hilltop plantation turned botanical research station, with a sunken garden modeled after London's Kew Gardens. The cinchona for which the gardens were named was brought from Peru in the 1800s to cultivate for quinine to treat malaria, which was afflicting the enslaved population on the sugar plantations below. Visitors will find a wide variety of lilies, dahlias, conifers, eucalyptus and orchid species, making it a magical place with spectacular views.

Cinchona Gardens can be reached by turning left at the Anglican church in Mavis Bank, and then descending to cross the Yallahs River at Robertsfield. Keep left at the fork to Cinchona via Hall's Delight, or take the right at the fork to reach Cinchona via Westphalia. Both roads can only be traveled by 4WD vehicle. The bumpy journey takes about an hour from Mavis Bank. Contact the caretaker, Norman Tait (tel. 876/276-0762, mountainpeak.52@gmail.com) or Brukup (tel. 876/857-7399), who live nearby. There's no admission fee, but given the gardeners' low government wages, it's advisable for visitors to leave a US$5-10 pp tip when presented with the visitors' book for signing. Call the caretaker prior to visiting for weather conditions and the best route, as road conditions are in constant flux and one may be better than another at any given time.

An easier route to Cinchona descends from Section above Hardwar Gap. Turn right at section and descend to St. Peters. In St. Peters turn off the main road to the left toward Chestervale and Clydesdale rather than continuing the decent toward Guava Ridge. At **Clydesdale,** you'll see barbecues used to dry

Cinchona Gardens

coffee beans, a water wheel, and an old great house now in ruins that hints at its more glorious past as a coffee plantation. It's a fitting place for camping for those with their own tent. From Clydesdale, an old road leads to Cinchona that takes about 1.5 hours to walk, or a bit quicker for intrepid drivers with a 4WD vehicle. The views hold more natural beauty on the route down from Section, but it takes quite a while longer to reach Cinchona.

**Flamstead** is a historic estate commanding a strategic view of the approach to Kingston Harbour and was used as a lookout point by Jamaica's colonial overlords. During the Napoleonic Wars it served as a residence for Admiral Rodney, and was used as a base for the British army. Former Jamaican trade ambassador Peter King built a house on the site before he was murdered in 2006. A plaque on the house he built notes that the site helped prove the usefulness of longitude, as first measured using John Harrison's marine chronometer in 1761 by Harrison's son William. The Harrisons would eventually take the prize offered by the British crown for a solution to the problem of measuring longitude in the age of sail.

## Tours
**Jill Byles** (tel. 876/977-8007, cell tel. 876/487-5962, paraisoj@cwjamaica.com), a retired horticultural enthusiast who lives at Guava Ridge near Mavis Bank, offers tour guide services (US$50 per day regardless of group size) on hiking trails in the area. Jill can guide visitors to **Cinchona, Flamstead,** and **Governor's Bench,** a footpath named after Governor Alexander Swettenham, who lived at Bellevue, a great house in the hills now owned by the University of the West Indies that's used for retreats and visitor accommodations.

**Barrett Adventures** (contact Carolyn Barrett, cell tel. 876/382-6384, www.barrettadventures.com) also offers tours in the Blue Mountains from virtually anywhere in Jamaica, including transportation.

**Arrow Head Birding Tours** (cell tel.

876/260-9006, www.arrowheadbirding.com), led by Ricardo Miller, offers excursions to the best birding spots across the island.

## Food
Mavis Bank is not a place for culinary delights or nightlife of any kind. In Mavis Bank square, **By-Way Bar** is a lively local watering hole run by Mr. Haase, with a restaurant upstairs serving home-style Jamaican dishes.

## Services
In the square is the **post office and police station** (tel. 876/977-8004). To venture farther into the mountains, a 4WD vehicle is needed. If you're heading up to Blue Mountain Peak, you can call **Whitfield Hall** (tel. 876/364-0722) to arrange for a 4WD vehicle to meet you at the police station, a good place to leave your car under watchful eyes.

# THE BLUE AND JOHN CROW MOUNTAINS NATIONAL PARK
Consisting of nearly 81,000 hectares (200,000 acres) in the parishes of St. Andrew, St. Mary, St. Thomas, and Portland, the **Blue and John Crow Mountains National Park** (BJCMNP, tel. 876/920-8278, jcdt@cybervale.com, www.greenjamaica.org.jm) covers the highest and steepest terrain in Jamaica. This alpine terrain is the last known habitat for the endangered giant swallowtail butterfly, the second-largest butterfly in the world, which makes its home especially on the northern flanks of the range. Several endemic plant and bird species reside in the park as well, and many migratory birds from northern regions winter there. Among the most impressive of the native birds are the streamertail hummingbirds—known locally as doctor birds—and the Jamaican tody, the Jamaican blackbird, and the yellow-billed parrot. The Blue Mountains generally are the source of water for the Kingston area, one of many reasons it is important to disturb the environment as little as possible. The BJCMNP has the largest unaltered swath of natural

forest in Jamaica, with upper montane rain-forest and elfin woodland at its upper reaches.

## ★ Blue Mountain Peak

The pinnacle of the Blue and John Crow Mountains National Park, **Blue Mountain Peak** can be reached by a variety of means, depending on the level of exhaustion you are willing to endure. Generally, hikers leave before first light from Whitfield Hall at Penlyne, St. Thomas, after having arrived the previous day. For ambitious hikers, there's a 4.5-kilometer (2.8-mile) trail from Mavis Bank to Penlyne Castle, which is pleasant and covers several farms and streams. This option also obviates the need to send for a 4WD vehicle. From Penlyne Castle, follow the road to Abbey Green (3.2 kilometers/2 miles), and from there to Portland Gap (3.7 kilometers/2.3 miles). At Portland Gap a ranger station, sometimes staffed, has bunks, toilets, showers, and campsites. These facilities can be used for US$5 by contacting the JCDT, which asks that visitors register at the ranger station. From Portland Gap to the peak is the most arduous leg, covering 5.6 kilometers (3.5 miles). Warm clothes, rain gear, and comfortable, supportive footwear are essential. Blue Mountain Peak is also a mildly challenging three- to four-hour hike from **Whitfield Hall,** a rustic farmhouse with a great stone fireplace.

From Portland Gap westward along the Blue Mountain range, there are several other lofty peaks along the ridge with far less traffic. These include Sir John's Peak, John Crow Peak, and Catherine's Peak. *Guide to the Blue and John Crow Mountains* by Margaret Hodges has the most thorough coverage of hiking trails throughout the national park. Otherwise, local people are the best resource.

## Accommodations

**Blue Ridge Restaurant & Cottages** (Blue Ridge, tel. 876/562-7580, blueridgeja@gmail.com, www.blueridgeja.com, by reservation) aims high with creative appetizers like bacon wrapped plantain served with cilantro cream sauce, popcorn shrimp and crab cakes, and

The Blue Mountains are a treasure trove of colorful endemic and migratory bird species.

signature entrees like chicken pot pie and Blue Ridge pork chops in guava glaze. Quirky metal ornaments in the shape of larger-than-life birds, ladybugs, and maracas accompany meals as they are served. The spot is very remote and boasts the most spectacular vistas of Jamaica's majestic peaks. The staff is well-trained and attentive.

The property offers guests two cottages on a bed-and-breakfast basis. Peacock Cottage (US$110) sleeps two with a king bed, private bath with hot water and a private balcony. Butterfly Cottage (US$125) sleeps four with a king bed and a sofa bed in the living room. It too has a private bathroom with hot water and a balcony. The cottages are perched on a steep hillside below the restaurant deck surrounded by coffee and fruit trees. The balconies of each cottage face northwest towards the southern slopes of the Blue Mountain range.

A small coffee farm with four tastefully decorated concrete cabins, ★ **Lime Tree Farm** (Tower Hill, cell tel. 876/446-0230, ratcutt@yahoo.com, www.limetreefarm.com,

US$285 per couple, includes 3 meals, alcohol extra) overlooks Mavis Bank with a spectacular view of Portland Gap, Blue Mountain Peak, and the Yallahs River Valley. Owned by English expat Rodger Bolton, the property is all-inclusive, and the excellent meals make Lime Tree Farm one of the best values in Jamaica. Meals are shared in the open-air communal dining area, which gives the place a warm, family vibe. A 4WD vehicle is needed to reach the property; the hosts can arrange transportation. A trained masseuse offers Swedish massage, and a yoga patio faces the ridges and valleys to the north. Lime Tree offers a number of packages that include lodging, food, and excursions to Blue Mountain Peak, Flamstead, and Cinchona Gardens.

A great option for bird-watchers and hikers, especially for groups, is **Forres Park Guest House** (tel. 876/977-8141, reservations tel. 876/927-8275, mlyn@cwjamaica. com, www.forrespark.com, US$105-200). A two-story main house and four cabins are surrounded by a small coffee farm that attracts many endemic and migratory bird species. The large veranda is a great vantage point, as all three of Jamaica's hummingbirds—vervain, Jamaica mango, and streamertail—frequent the bushes all around the chalet-style house. Rooms have a mountain cabin feel. You won't mind the lack of air-conditioning as nights are pleasantly cool. Hot water is appreciated. Two superior deluxe rooms include a suite with a whirlpool tub and a view of the mountains; the other large room below also has a four-poster king bed and a private balcony and opens to a garden.

A few kilometers Past Hagley Gap, just over the border in the parish of St. Thomas, is **Whitfield Hall** (Penlyne, St. Thomas, tel. 876/927-0986 or 876/878-0514, www.whitfieldhall.com, dorm US$20, room US$55, tent with use of indoor facilities US$10), a beautiful old house and coffee farm that offers rustic lodging in a grand setting with a well-appreciated fireplace to fend off the evening chill. Whitfield is the most common starting point for expeditions up to Blue Mountain Peak via Portland Gap, which generally start in the early morning hours to arrive at the summit for sunrise, when there is the best chance at taking in a clear view. As the morning progresses, clouds tend to roll in, often obscuring the peaks and valleys. A guide to the peak (US$36 per party) can be arranged. Penlyne is only accessible by 4WD from Mavis Bank. Transportation can be arranged from any

Lime Tree Farm has stunning views of Jamaica's tallest peaks.

point in Kingston (US$100), Mavis Bank (US$40), or Papine Square (US$65).

**Portland Gap** (booked through JCDT, 29 Dumbarton Ave., off Eastwood Park Rd., Half Way Tree, tel. 876/920-8278 or 876/920-8279, jamaicaconservation@gmail.com, www.greenjamaica.org.jm, US$30-40) has six shared wooden cabins. Foam sleeping mats (US$1 per night) can be rented, but hikers should bring their own sleeping bags. Pit toilets and fire pits are available. A US$1 user fee is assessed at the ranger station or when booking the cabins through the JCDT.

## Getting There and Around

The Blue Mountains are accessible from three points: from Kingston via Papine; from Yallahs, St. Thomas, via Cedar Valley; and from Buff Bay, St. Mary, on the North Coast, via the B1, which runs alongside the Buff Bay River. The B1 route is a very narrow road barely wide enough for one vehicle in many places.

There are two main routes to access the south-facing slopes of the Blue Mountain range. The first, accessed by taking a left onto the B1 at the Cooperage, leads through Maryland to Irish Town, Redlight, Newcastle, and Hardwar Gap before the Buff Bay River Valley opens up overlooking Portland and St. Mary on the other side of the range. The second route, straight ahead at the Cooperage along Gordon Town Road, leads to Gordon Town, and then taking a right at the town square over the bridge, to Mavis Bank.

Continuing beyond Mavis Bank requires a 4WD vehicle, and you can either take a left at Hagley Gap to Penlyne, or straight down to Cedar Valley and along the Yallahs River to the town of Yallahs.

Getting to and around the Blue Mountains can be a challenge, even if keeping lunch down on the way isn't. Only for the upper reaches, namely beyond Mavis Bank, is it really necessary to have a 4WD vehicle; otherwise the abundant potholes and washed-out road is only mildly more challenging to navigate than any other part of Jamaica due to the sharp turns.

A hired **taxi** into the Blue Mountains will cost upward of US$30 for a drop-off at Strawberry Hill, and at least US$100 for the day to be chauffeured around. **Route taxis** travel between Papine and Gordon Town (US$3) throughout the day, as well as to Irish Town (US$4); you'll have to wait for the car to fill up with passengers before it departs.

To reach Whitfield Hall, the most common starting point for hiking up Blue Mountain Peak, 4WD taxis can be arranged by calling Whitfield Hall.

Many travelers find letting a tour operator take care of the driving is the easiest, most hassle-free way to get around the island. One of the most dependable and versatile tour companies on the island is **Barrett Adventures** (contact Carolyn Barrett, cell tel. 876/382-6384). Barrett can pick you up from any point on the island and specializes in off-the-beaten-path tours.

# The South Coast

Look for ★ to find recommended
sights, activities, dining, and lodging.

# Highlights

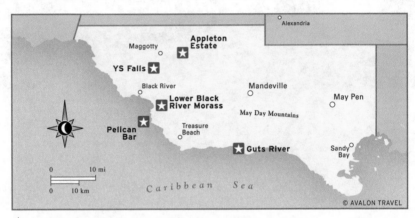

★ **Guts River:** A forlorn stretch of coastal road east of Alligator Pond leads to a seldom-visited one-of-a-kind swimming hole (page 265).

★ **Pelican Bar:** Located on a sandbar about 1.5 kilometers (1 mile) offshore, this is the best place to spend an afternoon snorkeling and eating fresh fish (page 274).

★ **Lower Black River Morass:** As one of Jamaica's largest wetlands, this mangrove and swamp is home to a variety of unique animals and plantlife (page 274).

★ **YS Falls:** The best-managed waterfall attraction in Jamaica offers swimming, tubing, and a heart-thumping zipline (page 276).

★ **Appleton Estate:** Take a rum tour at the distillery of Jamaica's most popular brand (page 278).

The South Coast is the place to get away from crowded tourist hubs and see some of the country's farmland and less-frequented coastline.

Rather than boasting grandiose or glitzy resorts, this region, made up of Elizabeth, Manchester, and Clarendon parishes, offers accommodations with rustic charm and unpretentious luxury, especially in Treasure Beach. And even if unwinding away from it all gets dull, there's still plenty to do: YS Falls is arguably the best waterfall attraction in Jamaica. Appleton Estate welcomes visitors to tour the distillery producing the island's most revered rum. Many swimming holes along the South Coast are visited rarely, even by locals, and languid fishing villages dot the coast from Treasure Beach to Rocky Point.

High above the plains, the cool air of Mandeville has been a draw for centuries. It's often referred to as the "retirement capital of Jamaica" for the number of repatriating Jamaicans who call the small city home. Serious birders will find a warm welcome at Marshall's Pen, and foodies will find a handful of noteworthy restaurants and bars, making it a worthwhile stop for a bite or even an overnight on trips between Kingston and points west. It's not a place that keeps visitors long, though, which makes it an attraction in itself for those seeking the "real" Jamaica.

## PLANNING YOUR TIME

If your goal is to hit the main sights and take in a bit of the South Coast culture, a few days in Treasure Beach and a night in Mandeville is probably sufficient. Treasure Beach is the kind of place many find hard to leave, with a unique feel and windswept natural beauty that gives the area its rough-edged charm. The immediate surroundings of Treasure Beach lend themselves to long walks in Back-Sea-Side, hiking in the Santa Cruz Mountains, boat rides, and cautious swimming.

Most people visiting the South Coast choose Treasure Beach as a base, making easy day trips to surrounding attractions. This is probably the best option given that it has the most varied lodging options, a natural hip vibe, several good beaches, and unique scenery. A few decent lodging options are found farther west in Black River, but it's not

---

**Previous:** YS Falls; boats on the Lower Black River Morass. **Above:** pepper shrimp at Marcia Williams' One Stop.

# The South Coast

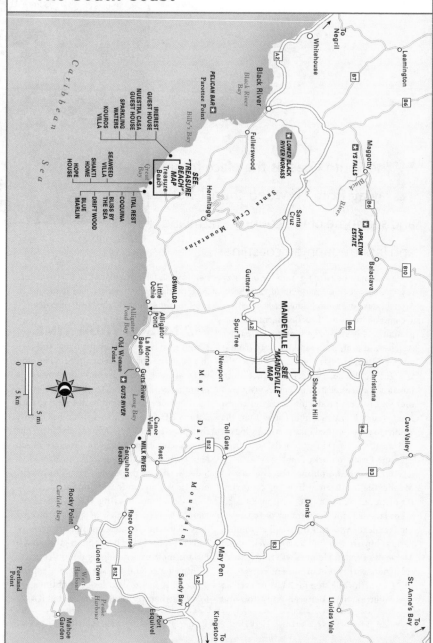

To Negril

Whitehouse

Leamington

A2

B7

B6

Black River

Black River Bay

PELICAN BAR ✚

Parottee Point

Fullerswood

★ LOWER BLACK RIVER MORASS

★ YS FALLS

Maggotty

Black River

B6

★ APPLETON ESTATE

Balaclava

B10

Billy's Bay

Great Bay

GUEST HOUSE
NUESTRA CASA
GUEST HOUSE
SPARKLING WATERS
KOUROS VILLA
IRIEREST

SEE "TREASURE BEACH MAP"

Treasure Beach

Hermitage

Santa Cruz Mountains

Santa Cruz

Gutters

A2

Spur Tree

Christiana

B4

Cave Valley

Caribbean Sea

SEAWEED VILLA
SHAKTI HOME
HOPE HOUSE
ITAL REST
COQUINA
BLISS BY THE SEA
DRIFT WOOD
BLUE MARLIN

OSWALDS

Little Ochie

Alligator Pond

MANDEVILLE

SEE "MANDEVILLE MAP"

Shooter's Hill

Alligator Pond Bay

La Morna Beach

Newport

May

Day

Toll Gate

Old Woman Point

Guts River

★ GUTS RIVER

Long Bay

Canoe Valley

Rest

B12

0   5 km
0   5 mi

N

Milk River

MILK RIVER

Farquhars Beach

Mountains

May Pen

Danks

B3

Rocky Point

Carlisle Bay

Race Course

Lionel Town

B12

Sandy Bay

A2

Lluidas Vale

Portland Point

West Harbour

Mahoe Garden

Peake Harbour

Port Esquivel

To Kingston

St. Anne's Bay

To

a magnetic destination for most. Mandeville also has a smattering of decent hotels, and for those set on getting as much curative power as possible from the hot baths at Milk River, the on-site hotel has basic affordable rooms. Beyond birding, lying low with alligators, and splashing around at Pelican Bar, there's little to keep visitors for more than a day or two in Black River.

## SAFETY

Locals in these parishes are less dependent on tourism dollars, so you will find that there's far less hustling in this area. Nevertheless, travelers are advised to keep their heads up, avoid compromising or vulnerable situations,

not to keep valuables laying around or unattended while swimming, and not to wander alone on forlorn stretches of beach or road at night. Don't draw attention to yourself or trust strangers. When partying, stick with a group.

Beaches along the South Coast are commonly deserted, and swimming alone is not safe, especially at Treasure Beach, where anglers drown every year. The current and undertow in all the bays of Treasure Beach are quite dangerous, and it's wise to ask the locals about conditions before getting too comfortable in the water. It's also advisable to avoid the jackfish, which can produce high levels of toxins, while in the water.

# Mandeville

Manchester is Jamaica's sixth-largest parish, much of it at relatively high altitudes with three mountain ranges: the May Day Mountains, the Don Figuerero Mountains, and the Carpenters Mountains, where the highest peak in the parish stands at 844 meters (2,769 feet). Any approach to Mandeville, the parish capital, entails steep climbs, which fortunately feature some of Jamaica's best-maintained roads. Caution is advised in navigating the sharp turns and heavy grades.

## SIGHTS

Mandeville's historic sights are concentrated around the town square, known as Cecil Charlton Park. These include the **Mandeville Courthouse,** built of limestone using slave labor and finished in 1820. The courthouse had the town's first school on its ground floor. The **Mandeville Jail and Workhouse,** also among the first public buildings in town, is now in use as the police station. Adjacent to the courthouse, the **Mandeville Rectory** is the oldest house of worship and the original Anglican rectory in Mandeville, having once also served as a tavern and guesthouse, to the dismay of many parishioners.

## Bird-Watching at Marshall's Pen

**Marshall's Pen** (contact owner Ann Sutton, tel. 876/904-5454, cell tel. 876/877-7335, asutton@cwjamaica.com) has been a popular spot for serious birding for many years. Birders come especially to see the Jamaican owl, which can often be seen in its favorite, easily accessible tree. Of Jamaica's 28 endemic birds, 23 have been spotted at Marshall's Pen, with a total of 110 species recorded on the property over the years.

Marshall's Pen was built in 1795 at the latest, the exact date a mystery. Originally the estate was about 809 hectares (2,000 acres), whereas today is has dwindled to a still respectable 121 hectares (300 acres). The origin of the name is also ambiguous. The present owner is Ann Sutton, widow of the late Robert Sutton, one of Jamaica's foremost ornithologists, who created an audio catalog of Jamaican bird songs that was released by Cornell University's ornithology department. Robert Sutton also coauthored *Birds of Jamaica,* the island's best bird guide. Ann Sutton is also an ornithologist as well as a conservationist.

Robert Sutton coauthored *Birds of Jamaica*, the island's best bird guide. Ann Sutton, herself an ornithologist and conservationist, welcomes serious birders to Marshall's Pen, where they will find warm hospitality on a tour (by appointment only, US$20 pp, min. 6 persons) of the great house and extensive gardens. Visitors will find orchids, anthuriums, ferns, and other indigenous plants.

## BARS AND NIGHTLIFE

**Paris Ville Nightclub** (Willowgate Plaza, cell tel. 876/881-8215) is the most happening spot in Mandeville, hosting Beer Rave Wednesday, Ladies Night Thursday, Afterwork Jam Friday, Clubbing Saturday, and Karaoke-Retro Sunday. **Stars Among Stars Nightclub & Bar** (33 Ward Ave., cell tel. 876/347-1270), formerly Beavers, is another spot to catch a wine or occasional performance from selectors and deejays.

## SPORTS AND RECREATION

**Manchester Club** (Caledonia Rd., tel. 876/962-2403, manchester_club@hotmail.com) is the oldest golf course in the western hemisphere, dating to 1865. It remains the least expensive course in Jamaica (greens fees US$30, clubs US$12, caddy US$14 per round). The nine-hole course is well maintained, even if it is not the bright green of more popular courses on the island. Beyond golf, the club also offers tennis on three hard courts, the only squash court on the South Coast, table tennis, a swimming pool, and a billiard table in continuous use for over 100 years. The club also hosts barbecues and luncheons. A golf tournament is held every month in which golfers from across the island participate. The All Jamaica Hard Court Tennis Championship is held each summer, attracting over 200 children and adults over a one-week period. There's a resident tennis coach and a golf professional.

## FOOD
### Contemporary

★ **Regie's Bistro** (37 Main St., entrance on Villa Rd., tel. 876/285-6605, 11:30am-10:30pm Mon.-Sat., US$3.50-40) serves creative Jamaican and Caribbean dishes in a cozy second-floor dining room. The top level has a beautiful outdoor bar area suitable for large groups and parties. The menu includes starters like jerk chicken drumsticks, buffalo wings, shrimp bruschetta, and salad. Sumptuous entrées range from prime aged

a Jamaican tody at Marshall's Pen

# Mandeville

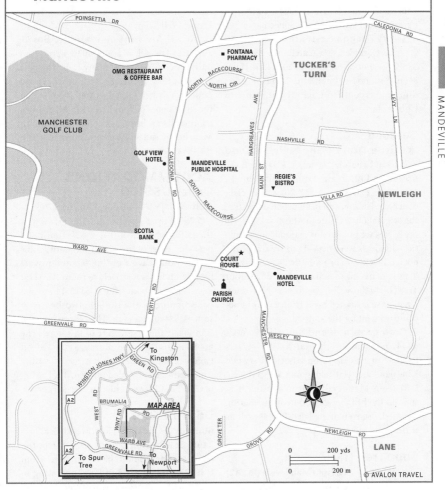

steaks, chops, and ribs to lobster thermidor and coconut shrimp beignets with pepper jelly dipping sauce. Regie's also has one of the area's best international wine lists, including ice wine from Canada.

**OMG Restaurant & Coffee Bar** (1 Brumalia Rd., tel. 876/962-7251, 7am-10pm Mon.-Sat., brunch 10am-3:30pm Sun., dinner 5pm-10pm Sun., US$10-50) is an upscale restaurant with marble tables and a sleek bar. It serves a mix of vegetarian and meat dishes with appetizers like calamari al aioli, shrimp margarita, and spring rolls. Entrées range from snapper cutlet pan fried in caper butter to duckling breast. OMG is located in Cobblestone Professional Centre, the first set of buildings on Brumalia Road on the left coming up from Caledonia Road.

## Chinese

**Bamboo Garden Restaurant** (35 Ward Ave., tel. 876/962-4515, noon-10pm Mon.-Sat.,

1pm-10pm Sun., US$7-30) serves sweet-and-sour chicken, butterfly shrimp, and lobster with butter and cola. The restaurant is located upstairs from Cash & Carry Supermarket.

**Lucky Dragon Restaurant** (shops 9-10 Orange Complex, 5½ Caledonia Ave., tel. 876/961-6544 or 876/867-6720, 11am-10pm Mon.-Sat., noon-10pm Sun., US$2-8) offers dine-in, takeout, and delivery of standard Chinese fare.

## Seafood

★ **Little Ochie Mandeville Seafood Specialist** (beside Nashville Plaza, cell tel. 876/852-6430, 11am-11pm Mon.-Thurs., 11am-late Fri.-Sun., US$7-20) serves fish, conch, and lobster tail in an urban outpost of the original Little Ochie in Alligator Pond. It's the best place in town for seafood, answering the call locals were making for years for the owner, Blackie, to bring Little Ochie to them instead of having to make the trek down Spur Tree Hill to the St. Elizabeth coast. Next door, a vendor sells roasted breadfruit, a favorite accompaniment for the seafood.

**Gran's Seafood and Bar** (tel. 876/603-4254, noon-midnight daily, US$7-17) is located in the Hopeton district between Kingsland and Hatfield, going up Spur Tree Hill from Mandeville. Gran's is the best spot on the hill for seafood items, including steamed, escoveitch, or fried fish as well as shrimp and lobster.

## Spur Tree Hill

The main road west from Mandeville (the A2) rises over Spur Tree Hill and is infamous as a dangerous stretch to drive—the road plunges from around 600 meters (2,000 feet) elevation to sea level in the span of just a few kilometers. It is famous for a couple of sumptuous roadside jerk pits and a noteworthy curry goat hut. From atop Spur Tree Hill, the view of Manchester's lowlands, St. Elizabeth, and Westmoreland is spectacular. To the west, the Santa Cruz Mountains can be seen tapering down to the sea.

**Claudette's Top Class** (Spur Tree Hill,

tel. 876/964-6452, 8am-4pm daily) is a favorite local spot to get curry goat. The little sit-in restaurant is across the highway from Hood Daniel Well Company.

★ **All Seasons Restaurant Bar & Jerk Centre** (tel. 876/965-4030, 8am-11pm daily) is considered by many to be the best jerk spot in Manchester, with other typical Jamaican dishes served as well. Perched on the steep slopes of Spur Tree Hill, All Seasons commands an impressive view of southern Manchester and St. Elizabeth, down to where the sky meets the sea.

# ACCOMMODATIONS
## Under US$100

**Golf View** (5 1/2 Caledonia Rd., tel. 876/962-4477, gviewrosi@hotmail.com, www.thegolfviewhotel.com) is a 62-room hotel near the center of town with standard rooms (US$89) that have a ceiling fan and private baths with hot water. Deluxe room (US$115) and a one-bedroom suite (US$125) have air-conditioning, while the sole two-bedroom suite (US$140) does not. The central location is probably the best feature of this hotel. The hotel claims the same address as the Odeon Cineplex but is actually not adjacent, sitting a bit farther down Caledonia Road at the top of Golf View Plaza, bordering the golf course.

## US$100-250

**Mandeville Hotel** (4 Hotel St., tel. 876/962-2460, reservations@themandevillehotel.com, mandevillehoteljamaica.com, from US$42-103) is the oldest hotel operating in Mandeville. Clean sheets, ceiling fans, air-conditioning and a fridge in select rooms, cable TV, and hot water make this a comfortable option in the heart of town. Bring your own soap and shampoo. Rooms have full, queen, and king beds. There are also junior suites and one- to three-bedroom apartments.

**Tropics View Hotel** (Wardville District, off Winston Jones Hwy., tel. 876/625-2452, tropicsview@cwjamaica.com, www.tropicsview.com, from US$57, includes breakfast) offers Wi-Fi throughout, a pool, a gym, a basketball court, and a restaurant and bar. Standard rooms have queen beds and private baths with hot water. Two-bedroom suites (US$127) are also available. A restaurant and bar (7am-10pm daily) by the front gate on the property serves local dishes. Rooms have ceiling fans and no air-conditioning, but it rarely gets hot in Mandeville. Standing fans are available on request.

## INFORMATION AND SERVICES

### Medical

**Hargreaves Memorial Hospital** (Caledonia Ave., tel. 876/961-1589) is a private clinic, with many of its staff also working at Mandeville Regional. **Mandeville Regional Hospital** (32 Hargreaves Ave., tel. 876/962-2067) is the largest hospital for kilometers around, with a good reputation.

### Money

Both **NCB** (9 Manchester Rd., tel. 876/962-2083; Mandeville Plaza, tel. 876/962-2618) and **Scotiabank** (1A Caledonia Rd., tel. 876/962-2035) have bank branches with ATMs in Mandeville.

### Internet

**Manchester Parish Library** (34 Hargreaves Ave., tel. 876/962-2972, manparlib@cwjamica. com, 9:30am-5:30pm Mon.-Fri., 9:30am-4pm Sat.) offers free Internet access. **Manchester Shopping Centre** has an Internet café, along with a food court with a lot of hole-in-the-wall restaurants.

## GETTING THERE AND AROUND

Mandeville is served by regular **buses** from Kingston and May Pen and regular **route taxis** departing from the square for surrounding destinations including May Pen, Christiana, and Santa Cruz (US$2).

One of Jamaica's best thoroughfares is a stretch of toll road known as **Highway 2000**, or Usain Bolt Highway, as it was renamed in 2009. It begins in Portmore and leads west to rejoin the A2 in Free Town at the Clarendon border. From May Pen, the A2 climbs to the upper reaches of Manchester, passing Mandeville along the bypass before descending to the South Coast and extending as far west as Negril. To get between Mandeville and the North Coast, the most direct route can be found by following signs for Christiana heading east toward Kingston, and then

All Seasons Restaurant Bar & Jerk Centre is a tasty pit stop.

toward Spalding, Cave Valley, Alexandria, and Brown's Town, before hitting the coast in Runaway Bay.

From Mandeville, the drive to Kingston takes about 1.5 hours along the toll road from May Pen, with Treasure Beach within 1.5 hours in the opposite direction. Negril, Montego Bay, and Ocho Rios are all about a 2-hour drive, and Port Antonio is another 1.5 hours east of Ocho Rios along the North Coast.

# North of Mandeville

## CHRISTIANA

A small community near the highest reaches of Manchester Parish, Christiana is a quiet town with one main drag and a single guest house. The most popular attraction in town is **Christiana Bottom,** a gorge located within walking distance of the center of the small village.

### Sights
#### GOURIE STATE PARK
Between Christiana and Colleyville, about three kilometers (2 miles) past Christiana, **Gourie State Park** is a recreational area on government land. Immediately after passing Bryce United Church, take the first left turn and then the first right until reaching the un-manned Forestry Department station and pic-nic area. **Gourie Cave,** the highlight of the park, is not actually inside the park but rather about 400 meters (0.25 miles) down the hill to the left of the park entrance. By the cave entrance is a picnic and camping area with a hut and tables and benches. There is one main trail through the park that leads to the com-munity of Ticky Ticky, with excellent views along the way of the Santa Cruz Mountains, Spur Tree Hill, and the historic Bethany Moravian Church.

Gourie Cave was a hideout for runaway slaves. The cave follows the channels of an un-derground river about one meter (3 feet) deep, depending on how much rain has fallen. If you go north from the entrance and upstream against the current, you end up on the other side of Colleyville Mountain. A different route leads downstream along the underground river, deep into the earth where there are sev-eral caverns along the way. If you're going to be exploring in the cave, you should moni-tor the weather and be aware of any rain in the forecast. It's not wise to venture into the cave alone.

### CHRISTIANA BOTTOM
In **Christiana Bottom,** the Blue Hole is fed from underground streams with two water-falls dumping into the pool. There's another waterfall at William Hole farther down-stream. To get here from Mandeville, turn right immediately after the NCB bank on Moravia Road, then take the first left around a blind corner, and then the first right, which leads to Christiana Bottom. Continue past the first left that leads to Tyme Town, and park at the entrance to the second left, a wide path that leads down to the river. Ask for Mr. Jones for a guided tour (US$20) of Blue Hole and William Hole and his farm, where he grows ginger, yams, potatoes, pineapples, bananas, and sugarcane.

### PICKAPEPPA FACTORY
The **Pickapeppa Factory** (base of Shooter's Hill, beside Windalco plant, call ahead to ar-range a visit, tel. 876/603-3441, pickapeppa@cwjamaica.com, www.pickapeppajamaica.com, US$3 adults, US$1.50 children) offers a half-hour educational tour (8:30am-3:30pm Mon.-Thurs.) that covers the company's founding in 1921 and the process involved in the manufacture of its world-famous sauces. The factory is closed the first two weeks in August and between Christmas and New

Year's, but any other time of year a sampling of the all-natural Pickapeppa sauces is included in the tour.

## SCOTT'S PASS

**Scott's Pass** (between Toll Gate and Porus) is the headquarters for the Nyabinghi house of Rastafari in Jamaica, with the House of Elders based here. The land was bought by Bob Marley and given to the Binghi for that specific purpose. The community members are for the most part welcoming of visitors, but you may get some evil eyes if you fail to recognize their customs for the Binghi celebrations: women must wear skirts or dresses (no pants) and cover their heads, while men must not cover their heads. To arrange a visit or learn about the birthday celebrations or other Nyabinghi events around the island, contact the Rasta in Charge, Paul Reid, known as **Iyatolah** (cell tel. 876/850-3469) or Charlena McKenzie, known as **Daughter Dunan** (cell

tel. 876/843-3227). Arts and crafts are sold throughout the year at Scott's Pass.

**Roy "Ras Carver" Bent** (cell tel. 876/866-7745, rascarver@gmail.com) is a Nyabinghi elder and master drum maker associated with the Scott's Pass order of Rastafari who lives in nearby May Pen. Ras Carver fashions, tunes, repairs, and sells the full line of drums used at Nyabinghi ceremonies. Other important **Binghi celebrations** throughout the year include Ethiopian Christmas (Jan. 7), one during Black History Month (a couple of days in Feb.), commemoration of His Majesty's 1966 visit to Jamaica (Apr. 21), All African Liberation Day (May 25), Marcus Garvey's birthday (three nights around Aug. 19), Ethiopian New Year (3-7 days starting Sept. 11) and Haile Selassie's coronation (Nov. 2).

To get to Scott's Pass, take the first left heading west of the train line in Clarendon Park, where the Juici Patties plant is located. Look for a small bridge crossing the Milk River before reaching Porus.

# South of Mandeville

## CANOE VALLEY WETLAND

**Canoe Valley Protected Area** (contact rangers Devon Douglas, cell tel. 876/578-9456, or Ucal Whyte, cell tel. 876/874-1422) is a coastal wetlands area just west of Guts River full of diverse plant and animal life. The manatees that live in semi-captivity along the river in the park are the highlight. **Rowboat excursions** (US$10 pp) to spot the manatees and snorkel in the surreal crystal blue waters are offered from the ranger station, a few kilometers south of Milk River. The rangers at the station also offer hikes to remote Taino Caves (rates negotiable). Turtles and alligators also share the waters; swimmers are advised to be vigilant.

## ★ GUTS RIVER

**Guts River** is a crystalline swimming hole about 16 kilometers (10 miles) east along the coast into Manchester from Alligator Pond. The Guts River creates a small pool as it emerges from the rocks with cool, crystal-clear waters purported to have medicinal qualities. The deserted beach nearby is great for a stroll. Getting to Guts River requires chartering a taxi if you don't have your own vehicle, or hiring a boat from Treasure Beach or Alligator Pond.

## ALLIGATOR POND

One of the busiest fishing villages on the South Coast, Alligator Pond has a few popular seafood restaurants. To get to Alligator Pond, turn south at the bottom of Spur Tree Hill (a left coming from Mandeville, from Santa

Cruz a right) and continue straight until you reach the coast.

★ **Oswald's** (cell tel. 876/381-3535, 10am-11pm daily, US$10 per lb. for fish, US$20 per lb. for lobster), located on the main fishing beach in Alligator Pond, serves excellent seafood in a casual setting.

**Little Ochie** (tel. 876/610-9692, cell tel. 876/852-6430, little.ochie@yahoo.com, www.littleochie.com, 9am-midnight daily, US$10-30) is a seafood emporium, serving a wide range of dishes like jerk and garlic crab, fish, and lobster. Over 75 seafood recipes are utilized on a daily basis, with lobster cooked 15 different ways, the best of which could very well be the garlic lobster.

The **Little Ochie Seafood Festival** (tel. 876/852-6430, little.ochie@yahoo.com), held the first or second Sunday in July, draws patrons from across the island for the lobster, fish, oysters, and cultural activities that range from traditional dance to popular reggae acts.

**Black Sands** (overlooking the beach, less than a mile out of Alligator Pond heading towards Guts River, cell tel. 876/852-6430, US$50) offers three basic rooms with a single bed in each and A/C. One room has a veranda, another has a patio.

## JUNCTION

A busy stopover point on the way over the Santa Cruz Mountains, Junction is the closest outpost of civilization to Treasure Beach that has supermarkets and banks. Junction Guest House offers basic accommodations, and a few restaurants serve hearty meals.

Just before reaching Junction, next to Lunie's Hot Spot, which is plastered with Heineken posters, ★ **Atlantis Seafood** (Main Rd., contact Shay Sinclair, cell tel. 876/409-3373, 7:30am-9pm daily) serves the best seafood in Junction, with fish, lobster, conch, crab, and shrimp (US$10-20 per pound).

**Junction Oasis Café Restaurant** (Main St., cell tel. 876/508-9802 or 876/312-0116, www.junctionoasiscafe.com, 7am-8pm Mon.-Sat.) serves baked beans and salt mackerel, callaloo and cabbage, kidney and liver, and ackee and saltfish for breakfast and escoveitch fish, curry goat, and chicken prepared many ways for lunch and dinner.

**Althea Lewis** (Dunder Hill, cell tel. 876/340-1460, U.S. tel. 239/257-4960) prepares excellent cookouts with at least 48 hours' notice. Althea specializes in curry goat and fish dishes, bammy, and puddings.

**Heavy's Bar & Grill** (on the way from Junction to Bull Savanna) is the hottest club in the area.

**Junction Guest House** (tel. 876/965-8668, www.junctionguesthouse.com, US$25-100) has basic rooms with fans, private baths, TVs, and air-conditioning. There's also a suite with a kitchen and a veranda.

The **Shopper's Fair** and **Intown Super Save Supermarket** are the best options for groceries. **NCB** (tel. 876/965-8611) and **Scotiabank** (shop 1, Tony Rowe Plaza, tel. 876/965-8257) have branches with ATMs, as does Jamaica National.

# Treasure Beach

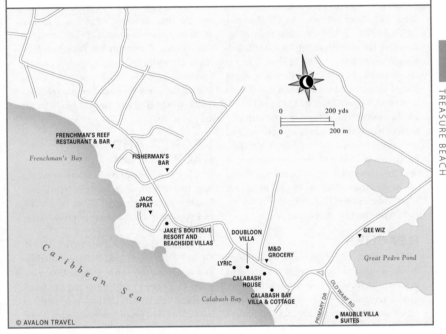

© AVALON TRAVEL

# Treasure Beach

Isolated from the rest of the island by the Santa Cruz mountains, which create the area's distinct coastal desert environment by capturing the westbound rainfall, Treasure Beach is a catch-all name for a series of bays and fishing villages that extend from Fort Charles at the greater community's western edge, to Billy's Bay, Frenchman's Bay, and Great Bay on the eastern edge. Treasure Beach prides itself on offering a different kind of experience than in Jamaica's more built-up tourism centers. Local ownership of the guesthouses and restaurants is more the rule than the exception, and it's impossible not to interact with Jamaicans in a more substantial context than being served your cocktail.

Many of the bays have decent swimming areas, but it's best to inquire with locals about

the safety of jumping in the water at any particular point until you get accustomed to the area. Remain vigilant of riptides and strong currents.

## SIGHTS

As an off-the-beaten-track destination, the main appeal of Treasure Beach is the community itself and the infectious sleepy pace that permeates the area. Despite their laid-back nature, residents of St. Elizabeth pride themselves on being extremely hardworking, from the fishermen who spend days out at sea to the farmers who take great care in mulching and watering their crops to fight the perpetual drought. Despite the lack of sights of interest along the Treasure Beach coast, there are several worthwhile excursions within an hour's drive, many of which are around Black River.

East of Treasure Beach along the coast are also a few notable natural attractions.

**Lovers' Leap** (Southfield, 9am-9pm Mon.-Sat., later on Sun.) is a 480-meter (1,575-foot) drop to the sea less than 16 kilometers (10 miles) east of Treasure Beach along the coast. According to legend, an enslaved couple leapt to their deaths to avoid forced separation by their master, who was lusting after the woman. As the legend has it, an old woman who witnessed their leap said the moon caught them up in a golden net, and they were last seen holding hands, standing on the moon as it sank over the horizon. A lighthouse was built on the point in 1979 and can be seen from 35 kilometers (22 miles) out at sea. Admission is US$3, or support the bar and restaurant in lieu of admission.

## BEACHES

Wherever you go in the water in Treasure Beach, it's best to have a companion and to inquire with locals to ensure it is safe. Many people have fallen victim to the hungry sea, which can have strong currents and undertows. While Treasure Beach doesn't have the high-quality beaches found in other parts of the island, its beaches are picturesque and romantic in a different way.

**Frenchman's Beach** is great for body surfing when the sea is a little rough. There is coral aplenty toward the edges of this beach, even in shallow waters. The safest spot to swim is directly in front of Golden Sands Guest House. **Calabash Bay Beach** is a fishing beach with a large, clear, sandy area good for swimming. The safest spot to swim is in front of Calabash House before you reach the boats. **Great Bay** has the best beach in the area for a dip.

## SPORTS AND RECREATION

People come to Treasure Beach to avoid the busy tourist hubs of Ocho Rios, Negril, and Montego Bay. Swimming, fishing, long walks, and yoga may be the most popular recreational activities.

**Captain Dennis Adventure** (cell tel. 876/435-3779, tel. 876/965-3084, dennisabrahams@yahoo.com), run by Dennis Abrahams, offers excursions and fishing trips to Black River and Pelican Bar (US$140), to just Pelican Bar (US$85 for 2 people), or to secluded white-sand beaches where he'll cook up a private seafood meal. Dennis also offers fishing excursions by the hour (US$60).

Treasure Beach has a picturesque coastline.

## SPAS

**Shirley's Steam Bath** (tel. 876/965-3820, cell tel. 876/827-2447, smgenus@hotmail.com, by appointment daily), run by Great Bay native herbalist Shirley Genus, is a local institution offering 15-minute herbal steam baths along with 30- or 60-minute massage sessions (US$70-90).

**Joshua's Massage & Bodywork** (tel. 876/965-0583, cell tel. 876/389-3698, doctorlee85@outlook.com, US$80 for an hour, US$115 for 1.5 hours), run by Joshua Lee Stein, offers deep and light pressure, gentle movement, and sensitive touch massage therapy on location by appointment.

**Jake's Driftwood Spa** (Calabash Bay, tel. 876/965-3000, jakes@cwjamaica.com, www.islandoutpost.com, US$75-135) offers a mélange of techniques and philosophies from around the world, with treatments that include Swedish, aromatherapy, and tai chi energy massages; coffee, wild ginger, and mint scrubs; mocha rum, wild ginger, and lemongrass wraps; and Jake's signature facials.

## ENTERTAINMENT AND EVENTS

If you're looking for wild all-night parties, Treasure Beach is probably not the best destination. Romantic sunsets and quiet nights are more the norm than live music. Nonetheless, a few venues see regular activity on weekends. Most of these venues operate as restaurants as much as nightspots.

Treasure Beach comes alive for annual events like Calabash Literary Festival and the Hook 'n' Line Fishing Tournament, with bonfires on the beach and roots reggae pumping from sound systems well into the night.

### Nightlife

**Fisherman's Bar** (cell tel. 876/379-9780) is a club open nightly with dancehall and roots reggae booming. A pool table and domino area around back are popular with locals, while the restaurant out front serves typical Jamaican fare at reasonable prices. The venue occasionally hosts live music.

**Wild Onion** (contact Owen Clarke, cell tel. 876/428-5048 or 876/861-4917, 2pm-2am Thurs.-Sun., US$4-7) is a nightclub serving beers and mixed drinks, with indoor and outdoor bars and a billiards table. They also serve light food items like fried chicken, jerk chicken, and soup. There are occasional live shows on a stage outside.

### Festivals and Events

**Calabash Literary Festival** (www.calabashfestival.org) is a fun, free event held the last weekend in May or first weekend in June at **Jake's** (tel. 876/965-0635, www.jakeshotel.com) in Treasure Beach that draws writers and attendees from across the Caribbean and African diaspora, as well as featuring some of Jamaica's own lyricists and authors.

**Jake's Jamaican Off-Road Triathlon and Sunset Run** (contact Tamesha Dyght, tel. 876/965-0748, cell tel. 876/564-6319), held the last weekend in April, consists of a 500-meter (550-yard) swim, a 15-kilometer (9-mile) mountain bike ride, and a 7-kilometer (4.3-mile) cross-country run. It draws Jamaicans from across the island as well as international competitors. The winner typically receives a weekend for two at a sponsoring hotel.

**BREDS** (Kingfisher Plaza, Calabash Bay, contact Sean Chedda, tel. 876/965-0748, www.breds.org, 9am-5pm Mon.-Fri., 9am-1pm Sat.) is a community-based nongovernmental organization engaged in community betterment activities and staging events, currently involved in environmental integrity to keep the community green and sustainable. It is also working to train lifeguards, including those posted at Frenchman's Beach, one of the area's most dangerous. BREDS organizes Jake's Triathlon and Run as well as the **Hook 'n' Line Canoe Tournament** held at the Calabash Bay Beach on Heroes weekend, the second weekend in October. The popular event starts on Saturday and goes into Sunday, when all the boats come in by noon to weigh their catch. Whoever gets the largest fish by weight wins; any species is fair game. Visitors

# Farm-to-Table Dinners at Jake's

The farm-to-table movement hasn't been lost on Jamaica's number-one agricultural community in St. Elizabeth, and the savvy entrepreneurs at Jake's have wholeheartedly embraced the growing interest in reducing the intermediaries between production and consumption. Jake's farm-to-table dinners are held each month at a long communal table on Dool's farm near Southfield.

Each month a different guest chef is invited to create a five-course meal using mostly local ingredients. Not for travelers on a budget, the tantalizing flavors and good company will surely be a memorable highlight of any trip to treasure beach. Check www.jakeshotel.com for upcoming dates.

may participate by renting boats. The entry fee is low (US$7 per boat) to ensure that the event remains decidedly local. The top prize is usually fishing equipment.

## SHOPPING

**Treasure Hunt Craft Shop** (Old Wharf Rd., tel. 876/965-3878, 9am-3pm Mon.-Fri., 9am-1pm Sat.), run by the Treasure Beach Women's Group, makes handcrafted items out of calabash and other local materials. Baskets, gourds, post cards, and the signature Star Light candle holders are nice gift items sold at the shop.

**Callaloo Butik** (Frenchman's District, cell tel. 876/390-3949, www.callaloo-jam. com, 9am-6pm daily) is an upscale craft and souvenir shop run by Sophie Eyssautier, selling clothing, bags, jewelry, beach wraps, baby items, ceramics, and home decor, all of it made in Jamaica.

## FOOD

**Gee Wiz Vegetarian Restaurant** (shop 4, Lazza Plaza, Calabash Bay, cell tel. 876/573-5988, 8am-7pm daily, US$6-15) serves fish and veggie food like curry or tomato chunks, pumpkin in coconut sauce, and broad bean stew. Delroy Brown is the affable proprietor and ital chef.

★ **Jack Sprat** (adjacent to Jake's, tel. 876/965-3583, 10am-10pm daily) is a favorite for fried fish, conch soup, pizza, and Devon

Jack Sprat

House ice cream, with a large outdoor eating area overlooking the sea.

**Frenchman's Reef Restaurant & Cocktail Bar** (tel. 876/965-3049, cell tel. 876/428-5048 or 876/861-4917, 7am-11pm daily) serves seafood and pizza as well as burgers, Chinese dishes, and Jamaican staples. Natural juices and local and international breakfasts are also served. Frenchman's delivers, accepts credit cards, and offers patrons complimentary Wi-Fi. A beachside cocktail bar was added in early 2016.

**Pardy's Coffee Shop** (Frenchman's Bay, cell tel. 876/326-9008, 7am-7pm Mon.-Sat., US$5-20) serves Jamaican breakfast dishes like ackee and saltfish, callaloo and saltfish, and continental favorites like omelets and eggs done to order. Lunch and dinner are prepared to order, with items like fish, lobster, and curry goat. Pardy's serves High Mountain coffee and freshly squeezed OJ in season, and you can also grab a beer anytime.

**M&D Grocery** (7am-8pm Mon.-Fri., 4am-late Sat.), named after proprietors Maureen and Delvin Powell, is a small grocery shop and bar selling basics. Jerk chicken and pork as well as conch and mutton soup are prepared on Friday and Saturday.

**Round the Clock Bar** (Frenchman's Bay, contact owner Charmaine Moxam, cell tel. 876/378-6690, 6am-midnight daily) is a small grocery shop and bar good for basic supplies and drinks, located next to Jake's.

# ACCOMMODATIONS

The popularity of Treasure Beach as an off-the-beaten-track destination has led to a blossoming in the lodging market. Most of the guesthouses are remarkably affordable compared with heavily touristed areas, with a comfortable room for two starting around US$30. Even villas rent for considerably less than in other parts of Jamaica, starting at around US$1,200-2,600 weekly for 2-8 people.

The only time of year it becomes hard to find a room is during Calabash Literary Festival, when those who haven't booked well in advance happily settle for whatever's available, even staying in Black River, Junction, or as far away as Mandeville if necessary. Rebecca Wiersma has over the past decade created a great online presence with her **Treasure Tours** (tel. 876/965-0126, treasuretours@gmail.com, www.treasure-toursjamaica.com) website, subscribed to by most of the accommodations operators in the area with prices and amenities listed. Unless otherwise noted, all the accommodations listed can be booked through Treasure Tours.

## Under US$100

★ **Ital Rest** (contact Frankie and Jean, tel. 876/863-3481, US$40, US$250 weekly) is about as roots as you can get. The property has limited electricity supplied by solar panels to the smart wood cabins, which are an easy walk from several sandy coves. Mosquito nets cover the beds to keep the bugs out at night. There are no fans or air-conditioning, and a kitchen on the property is available for guest use. Vegetarian food can also be prepared by request.

**Nuestra Casa** (Billy's Bay, tel. 876/965-0152, roger@billybay.com, www.billysbay.com, US$45 low season, US$50 high season) is a villa-style guesthouse run by Lillian Chamberlain and her son Roger. It rents three rooms, two with a double bed, and a third with two twin beds. One room has a private bath, while the other two share a bath. Amenities include ceiling and standing fans and hot water. Dinner is prepared by request.

**Dolphin's Villa** (US$50, US$70 with air-conditioning, entire house US$290) is a spacious five-bedroom, five-bath villa with en suite baths with hot water, screened windows in rooms with fans, satellite TV in the common living area, and spacious verandas. The house rents through Treasure Tours.

## US$100-250

**Calabash House** (Calabash Bay, tel. 876/965-0126, US$75 low season, US$85 high season, entire house US$200 low season, US$250 high season) is a four-bedroom villa right on Calabash Bay, one of the best spots for swimming in Treasure Beach. Bedrooms have air-conditioning, with hot water in the baths. A housekeeper tidies up during the day, while a cook can be arranged to prepare breakfast and dinner (additional US$25 daily for four people). Two cute mini cottages were recently added to the yard, where there's also a hammock for lazing the days away and watching the fishermen bring in their catch. Owner Elizabeth Seltzer is an artist who brings a creative vibe to the house and its ambience.

**Marblue Villa Suites** (tel. 876/965-3408, www.marblue.com, US$111-275) is an attractive seafront property located on a quiet, windswept stretch of beach along Calabash Bay offering junior, villa, and honeymoon categories. The well-appointed suites have air-conditioning, CD players, fans, attractive decor, and full, king, or queen beds. Sitting areas with day beds overlook one of two pools on the property from the veranda or pool deck. Rates include breakfast and Wi-Fi.

### Over US$250

★ **Shakti Home** (tel. 876/965-0126, trea-suretours@gmail.com, www.shaktihomeja.com, US$1,750 weekly low season, US$1,950 weekly high season), "your Om away from home," as its owner, Jamaica's leading yoga proponent, Sharon McConnell, puts it, is an airy, well-appointed, and tastefully decorated beach house with mosquito nets and fans in two bedrooms. The house sits beachfront, overlooking Old Wharf, and includes a great cook and caretaker-gardener. The chef specializes in vegetarian cuisine in addition to traditional Jamaican food. Shakti Home has a beautiful yoga deck overlooking the sea that comfortably fits six people, with yoga mats included.

★ **Jake's Boutique Resort and Beachside Villas** (tel. 876/965-3000, cell tel. 876/526-2428, www.jakeshotel.com, from US$95) has taken rustic chic to a new level, pouring on the kind of details sought by those on the prowl for the next "in" spot. To call Jake's rustic is to ignore the plush bedding and elaborate detailing reminiscent of an Arabian love lair. The honeymoon suites have outdoor showers and sunbathing decks on the roof. The most unpretentiously hip room at Jake's is the two-bedroom **Jack Sprat** (US$177 low season, US$230 high season), located right next to Frenchman's Beach with its iconic buttonwood tree. Sometimes described as "shabby shacks," the cottages don't neglect the modern essentials, with solar-heated hot water in all rooms. The Henzells bought the

Enjoy the view at one of Jake's Beachside Villas.

property in 1991 and opened and developed the rooms and cottages little by little. Jake was the owners' pet parrot, but "Jake" is also a generic term to call a white person.

## Villas

**Doubloon Villa** (UK tel. +44/1543-480-612, www.doubloonvilla.com, from US$2,950 weekly) is a comfortable four-bedroom villa with a small pool and deck overlooking the beach on Calabash Bay. One of the area's premier properties, Doubloon amenities include private baths, a well-equipped kitchen, air-conditioning, complimentary Wi-Fi, and three full-time staffers.

★ **Kouros Villa** (gillesnegril@hotmail.com, www.villa-kouros.com, 3-night minimum, from US$480, US$3,000 weekly) is a four-bedroom villa built in the whitewashed style of Greek island homes on a bluff overlooking the sea. The villa has three terraces with sea views and a large outdoor space by the infinity pool for alfresco dining. Inside, the polished cement floors are etched with wistful spirals. Amenities include wicker furnishings, comfortable mattresses, a utilitarian kitchen, Wi-Fi, and an entertainment center in the living room, making Kouros a cozy and welcoming home away from home.

**Sparkling Waters** (Billy's Bay, tel. 876/927-8020, www.sparklingwatersvilla.com, from US$250) is an exquisitely decorated collection of three modern two-bedroom villas that share the grounds, which have a pool, a whirlpool tub, and a gorgeous private beach. The villas have comfortable and inviting baths with hot water plus satellite TV, stereos, and air-conditioning in the bedrooms. Spacious and comfortable living and dining rooms are found downstairs along with the kitchen. The bedrooms are on the second floor at the top of a spiral staircase. Wi-Fi is included.

★ **Blue Marlin Villas** (Great Bay, contact Sandy Tatham, cell tel. 876/855-1122, bluemarlinjamaica@gmail.com, www.bluemarlinvillas.com) is two villas located on a one-hectare (2.5-acre) beachfront property at the western side of the beach in Great Pedro Bay. The villas can be rented together or separately. Wi-Fi covers the property. Blue Marlin (US$2,000 low season, US$2,500 high season) is a four-bedroom, three-bath, single-story villa with air-conditioning and ceiling fans in the bedrooms. Coquina (US$1,900 low season, US$2,300 high season) is a three-bedroom, three-bath, two-story villa with ceiling fans. Staff for both villas includes a cook-housekeeper, maid, and gardener.

## INFORMATION AND SERVICES

The Calabash Bay **post office** (5 minutes' walk east of Southern Supplies, 10:30am-1pm and 2pm-4:30pm Mon.-Fri.) often lacks stamps.

**Treasure Beach Meat Mart & Grocery** (Kingfisher Plaza, cell tel. 876/489-3641, 9am-5pm Mon.-Sat.), run by Marjorie Henry-Somers, sells fresh fruit, vegetables, ground provisions, and frozen fish and meat. **Southern Supplies** (8 minutes' walk north of Kingfisher Plaza, just before the ice factory) is the largest supermarket in Treasure Beach, selling, among other essentials, international phone cards, gift items, and music. The store has an Internet café.

**L. H. Malahoo & Nephews Fishing Tackles** (Kingfisher Plaza, cell tel. 876/409-7305, 10:30am-2pm Mon. and Wed., 10:30am-1:30pm Fri.) is the best bet in the area for fishing gear, but Mr. Malahoo doesn't keep regular hours, so it's best to call ahead.

## GETTING THERE AND AROUND

Treasure Beach is served by frequent **route taxis** from Santa Cruz, direct and via Watchwell (US$2), and from Junction (US$2). If you're driving, there are three routes: From Black River there is a short, direct road along the coast that is rough in places, but still passable with a regular passenger vehicle. Turn off the main toward the sea on a road just east of the communications tower east of Parottee. From Mandeville, take a left at the base of Spur Tree Hill, following signs for

Little Ochie, and take a right at the first four-way intersection following signs for Alumina Partners. At the first junction take a left and pass the bauxite and alumina plant, followed by a right at the stop sign to continue up the hill, passing straight through Junction. From Santa Cruz, turn south toward the sea about 1.5 kilometers (1 mile) west of the stoplight on the west side of town. The turnoff is marked by a sign for Jack Sprat.

# Black River and South Cockpit Country

An important economic center in years past, especially for the export of logwood and mahogany, Black River is today a quiet backwater parish capital, with the main attraction being the river at the heart of town that serves as the entry point into the Great Morass. There are a few popular attractions within a half hour's drive, and plenty of forlorn stretches of mediocre beach just east of town along the coast toward Parottee. A few minutes west, Font Hill offers great swimming on a beautiful small tract of sand surrounded by coral reef. A few interesting buildings around town are worth a look, most notably Invercauld Great House. The accommodations options for staying in Black River are limited. Most visitors come to town just for the day, either from nearby Treasure Beach or from Negril.

## BLACK RIVER
### Invercauld Great House
Along the waterfront between town and the hospital, **Invercauld Great House** is the most striking structure in Black River, with well-preserved Georgian architecture. The great house was built in 1894 by Patrick Leydon. For many years it was a hotel but has fallen out of use and sits idle within its gated compound. Nevertheless it remains one of Black River's architectural gems and is worth a peak from outside the gate.

### Luana Orchid Farm
**Luana Orchid Farm** (contact Dr. Bennett, cell tel. 876/361-3252, US$5) offers formal tours by appointment only to check out the 150,000-odd local and foreign orchid plants at the 0.6-hectare (1.5-acre) farm. Bennett has bred several new varieties himself. The farm is located on the northern outskirts of Black River along the road between Black River and Middle Quarters, opposite Luana Sports Club and quarry.

### ★ Pelican Bar
One of the most exceptional attractions in all of Jamaica, **Pelican Bar** is a ramshackle structure less than 1.5 kilometers (1 mile) offshore on a sandbar off Parottee Point. Run by the charismatic Denever Forbes, known by everybody as Floyde (cell tel. 876/354-4218), Pelican Bar serves drinks and cooks up excellent plates of fish (US$10) and lobster (US$15) accompanied by rice, bammy, or festival. The sandbar is an excellent spot to spend the day relaxing and snorkeling. The best way to reach the bar is by calling Daniel McLenon, known as **Dee** (cell tel. 876/860-7277), who offers round-trip shuttle service in his fishing boat (US$10 pp) from Parottee. Dee leaves from near his yard past Basil's, just after some houses with blue roofs. Turn right and park along a little lane that leads to the beach. Call Floyde before heading out to make sure he's around. Generally he keeps hours starting at 9am until the last customers are ready to leave in the evening. The bar is closed in bad weather.

### ★ Lower Black River Morass
The **Lower Black River Morass** is one of Jamaica's largest wetlands, with 142 square kilometers (55 square miles) of mangrove and swamp providing a rich habitat for a variety

of animals and plantlife. Turtles and crocodiles are still abundant, although manatees, once relatively common around the mouth of the river, are gone. It's the largest remaining undisturbed wetland in the English-speaking Caribbean at 7,285 hectares (18,000 acres). The Black River Morass has 113 species of plants and 98 species of animals. The anchovy pear *(Grias cauliflora)* of the Brazil nut family (Lecythidaceae) grows in the morass. Sawgrass, or razor grass *(Cladium jamaicense),* first described by botanists in Jamaica and thus given the Latin name *jamaicense,* covers about 60 percent of the wetlands area. Sable palm *(Sabal jamaicensis),* or thatch palm, is another wetland plant abundant in the reserve that was first described in Jamaica.

The crocodiles along the Black River are quite accustomed to being around people, to the point that many visitors think the ones sitting on the river's edge next to the restaurant are tame. While it's not recommended, some people swim in the water with the crocs. It's best to respect their space, however, and not give them the chance to prove they are anything but friendly.

The Black River and the Lower Black River Morass are best accessed by taking one of the river safari tours that start in the town of Black River, where three tours are offered from the river banks on pontoon boats.

## Black River Safaris

Charles Swaby's **Black River Safari** (tel. 876/965-2513 or 876/965-2086, jcsafari@hotmail.com, www.jamaica-southcoast.com) has a pontoon boat tour (75 minutes, 9am, 11am, 12:30pm, 2pm, and 3:30pm daily, US$20 adults, US$10 children) up the Black River with a commentary by the captain. Lunch is served at the Bridge House Inn and at Riverside Dock. **St. Elizabeth Safari** (tel. 876/965-2374, cell tel. 876/361-3252, donovan.bennett07@yahoo.com, www.stelizabethsafari.com, US$20 adults, US$10 under age 12) runs on the opposite side of the river, with local businessman Dr. Bennett operating a virtually identical 75-minute tour up the Black River.

**Irie Safari** (12 High St., cell tel. 876/472-4644, 876/834-0262, or 876/877-6222, lintonirie@hotmail.com, www.lostriverkayak.com, 8:30am-5pm Mon.-Sat., 9am-4pm Sun.) offers a narrated Black River Safari tour on pontoon boats (70 minutes, US$20 pp, minimum 2 guests). Irie's kayak tour includes the regular safari tour on pontoon boats before continuing into the upper reaches of the Broad River,

Pelican Bar

which runs east west into the Black River (US$65, single and two person trips).

**Lost River Kayak Adventures** (www. lostriverkayak.com), also run by Lloyd Linton from the Irie Safari location, has two three-seater, four two-seater, and two single-seat kayaks. Tours (2 hours, US$40 pp) venture into the upper reaches of the Black River, where there are blue holes suitable for swimming, birds that wouldn't be seen from a motorized craft, and no crocodiles, thanks to the freshwater.

## ★ YS Falls

By far the best conceived and organized waterfalls destination in Jamaica, **YS Falls** (ysfalls@cwjamaica.com, www.ysfalls.com, 9:30am-3:30pm Tues.-Sun., US$17 adults, US$8.50 children 3-13 years), on the YS Estate, has been operated by Simon Browne since 1991. The YS River changes with the weather—normally clear blue, and brown after rain in the mountains when it swells. A bar and grill on the property serves jerk chicken, and gift shops sell a wide array of books, crafts, and Jamaica-inspired clothing. Lounge chairs surround two swimming pools, one with colder water near the base of the falls and the other slightly warmer by the picnic area.

A **canopy tour** (US$50 adults, US$35 children) with a series of three ziplines traversing the falls, is operated by Chukka Caribbean. The tour is a rush, to say the least, and perhaps the most exhilarating of Chukka's many canopy tours in Jamaica, given the scenery.

The origin of the name "YS" is disputed: One version is that it comes from the Gaelic word "wyess," meaning winding and twisting. The other version is that it comes from the last names of the two men who ran the estate in 1684, John Yates and Richard Scott, who branded the cattle and hogshead of sugar with "YS." The original 3,238-hectare (8,000-acre) property has been reduced to 809 hectares (2,000 acres) today, where champion thoroughbred racehorses are bred and Pedigree Red Poll cattle graze the Guango tree-lined fields. Sugarcane production was discontinued in the 1960s.

The YS River originates in Cockpit Country and is fed by many springs on its way to meet the Black River. A spring on the estate is the original source of water for the town of Black River, 13 kilometers (8 miles) downstream.

## Bamboo Avenue

One of the most beautiful four-kilometer

YS Falls join the Lower Black River Morass.

Howie's HQ

(2.5-mile) stretches of road in Jamaica, running from Middle Quarters to West Lacovia, Bamboo Avenue is also known as Holland Bamboo. The stretch is lined with Jamaica's largest bamboo species, the common bamboo *(Bambusa vulgaris),* brought from Haiti by the owners of the neighboring Holland sugar estate, which once belonged to John Gladstone (1764-1851), father of William Gladstone, who became the prime minister to Britain.

Bamboo Avenue provides shade for several jelly coconut and peanut vendors. On the eastern side of Bamboo Avenue is **Bamboo Ville,** a vibsey jerk center with big pots on open fires.

**Middle Quarters** is a community located at the edge of the Black River Morass that's a favorite pit stop for passing motorists. Women line the road calling out "swimps, swimps!" to advertise their spicy morsels of boiled pepper shrimp.

**Jamaica Zoo** (Burton District, Lacovia, tel. 876/435-9999 or 876/487-3001, jamaica-zoo@cwjamaica.com, www.jamaicazoo.webs.com, 10am-5pm Sat.-Sun., by reservation Mon.-Fri., US$10 adults, US$5 under age 13) has a petting zoo that allows visitors to touch and interact with snakes, baby American crocodiles, iguanas, and birds. A monkey performs tricks, as does a Labrador retriever. The guided walking tour allows visitors to see the llama, a pair of lions, Amazon parrots, and snakes like boa pythons and boa constrictors, among the 20 species on the farm.

## Food

**Northside Jerk Centre** (5 North St., tel. 876/965-9855, 8am-7pm daily, US$2.50-5) aka Alvin's Fish & Jerk Pork Center, serves fried curry, stew, jerk chicken, stew jerk pork, and curry goat as well as steamed, brown stew, and escoveitch fish.

**Tasty Foods** (2 Market St., tel. 876/634-4027, 8am-9pm Mon.-Sat., US$2.50-7) serves ackee and saltfish, salt mackerel, chicken, and fries.

**Basil's Seafood Restaurant** (cell tel. 876/369-2565, 7am-midnight daily, US$6.50-13) in nearby Parottee has excellent fish, conch, and lobster.

★ **Cloggy's on the Beach** (22 Crane Rd., tel. 876/471-7766, www.cloggys.com, 10am-12am daily, US$3-11) is the quintessential beachfront bar and restaurant, serving chicken and seafood dishes, including fish, conch, shrimp, and lobster. This is a great place to kick back and unwind, even if the beach along this stretch out to Parottee Point can get a bit muddied by the mouth of the Black River.

**Pelican Bar** is the most interesting restaurant around, but it requires a boat ride to get there: It's offshore on a sandbar off Parottee Point. Run by Denever Forbes, known as Floyde (cell tel. 876/354-4218), Pelican Bar serves drinks and cooks up excellent plates of fish (US$10) and lobster (US$15) accompanied by rice, bammy, or festival.

**Holland Bamboo Curry Restaurant** (beside the primary school, cell tel. 876/507-3236, 10:30am-5pm daily) serves curry goat, curried chicken and fried chicken, roti, rice and peas or white rice.

**Marcia Williams' One Stop** (cell tel. 876/363-7242, 10am-7pm daily, US$3-7) is a roadside shop painted red, gold, and green. It's a good bet for fresh-out-the-pot swimps, cold beer to wash it down, and fresh fruits and vegetables.

**Howie's HQ** (cell tel. 876/860-5733, 24/7) is a roadside cook shop that serves up Jamaican favorites like fried chicken, curry goat, and oxtail out of huge pots to hungry passing motorists.

### Information and Services

The **post office** (35 High St., tel. 876/634-3769) is open 8am-5pm Monday-Friday. **DHL** (tel. 876/965-2651, 9am-5pm Mon.-Sat.) is at 17 High Street. Both **NCB** (13 High St., tel. 876/929-4622) and **Scotiabank** (6 High St., tel. 876/965-2251) have branches with ATMs.

The **St. Elizabeth Parish Library** (64 High St., 8:45am-5:15pm Mon.-Fri., 8:45am-3pm Sat.) also offers Internet service (US$1.50 per hour).

### Getting There and Around

Black River is easily reached by **route taxi** from Sav-la-Mar in Westmoreland (US$3) or from Santa Cruz in St. Elizabeth (US$2). If you're driving, there's a dodgy but interesting road along the coast to Treasure Beach that's much shorter and not too much more potholed than the long way around. To take the coastal route, head over the bridge east of Black River along Crane Road and turn off the main road toward the water after passing the communications tower east of Parottee. A left turn at a Y intersection leads along the coast to Treasure Beach.

## SOUTH COCKPIT COUNTRY

The interior of St. James, St. Elizabeth, Manchester, and Clarendon Parishes is rugged terrain, much of it forming part of Cockpit Country, which blankets pitted limestone hills full of caves and underground rivers. As the impassible interior descends to the sea, ridged hills taper down around lush valleys, which have proved some of the most fertile land in Jamaica. The YS and Appleton Estates remain prized lands. The **Nassau Valley**, where Appleton Estate is located, is still heavily planted in sugarcane to feed the healthy rum business.

From Maggotty, the main road (the B6) heads east, skirting a large wetland area fed by the upper reaches of the Black River before rejoining the main South Coast "highway" (the A2) just east of Santa Cruz. From Balaclava, a turn to the north (the B10) leads deep into the interior to Troy and then Warsop, passing by Ramgoat Cave before hitting Clarks Town, Trelawny. North of Clarks Town the road emerges on the coast in Duncans. For extreme adventure-seekers, the **Troy Trail** is a challenging traverse of the most rugged part of Cockpit Country. The trail is best accessed with the help of a guide, which can be set up through the **Jamaica Caves Organization** (www.jamaicancaves.org).

### ★ Appleton Estate

One of the most popular tours in Jamaica and well worth a visit, **Appleton Estate** (tel. 876/963-9215 or 876/963-9217, appleton@infochan.com, www.appletonrum.com, tours 9am-3pm Mon.-Sat., US$22, includes a miniature bottle of rum), in Nassau Valley, allows you to sample several grades of rum and to experience the lushest corner of St. Elizabeth and its impressive topography. The distillery is run by J. Wray and Nephew, now a Gruppo Campari company, which makes Appleton's rums and Sangster's Rum Cream, among other popular Jamaican spirits. To get here, turn inland off the A2 toward Maggotty in West Lacovia after passing through Bamboo Avenue from the west or Lacovia from the east. Where the road splits, keep right, following well-marked signs for Appleton Estate.

### Maggotty

**Apple Valley Park** (contact Lucille Lee, cell tel. 876/487-4521, or Andrea, cell tel.

876/572-9996, www.applevalleypark.com, 10:30am-5pm daily, by reservation only, US$5 adults, US$3.50 under age 12) is one of those places where even locals aren't entirely sure whether it's open or not. The park offers pedal-boating around an artificial pond, swimming pools, a cold-water whirlpool tub, and a picnic area. Food can be brought or ordered in advance. Four rustic cabins on the property (US$25-35) have private bathrooms and cold water.

**Apple Valley Guest House** (contact Lucille Lee, cell tel. 876/487-4521 or 876/963-9508) has slightly less basic double-occupancy rooms (US$36) than those at the park, with hot water in private baths and air-conditioning or fans available on request.

## Accompong

Home of the Leeward, or Trelawny, Maroons, Accompong was named after Achumpun, the brother of the most famous Maroon leader Cudjoe (Kojo), who signed a peace treaty with Great Britain in 1738 that granted his people autonomy from the crown. In exchange for their sovereignty, granted 100 years before slavery was abolished in Jamaica, the Maroons were called on repeatedly to assist the British in suppressing rebellions and to capture runaways and insurgent leaders.

The Leeward Maroons are today led by **Colonel Ferron Williams** (cell tel. 876/790-0867 and 876/893-2321, ferronwilliams302@yahoo.com), a retired police inspector who was elected for his first five-year term in 2009 and reelected in 2015. The Colonel will ensure visitors are treated fairly and can arrange community tours (US$20 pp) to important local landmarks, including the cave where the peace treaty was signed in 1738, a burial ground, and the church where English names were doled out to the Maroons after emancipation. A modest maroon museum holds artifacts dating to the 18th century, among them a pistol captured from the British during the 83-year war before the peace treaty was signed.

The best time to visit is for the annual **Accompong Maroon Festival** (Jan. 5-6), when the village comes alive with traditional Maroon music and dance as well as stage shows more typical of the rest of Jamaica. During the rest of the year it's a great destination for getting some fresh air and taking in the spectacular countryside from a seldom-visited corner of St. Elizabeth.

Appleton Estate

# The Unconquered Maroons

Jamaica's Maroons date back to the Spanish settlement of the island, when it became accepted that a fraction of the people brought from Africa would perpetually resist enslavement. These so-called "runaways" were termed Cimarrones by the Spaniards, a name later translated into English as Maroon. To name these warriors "runaway" is to diminish the fact that they claimed land in the most remote and mountainous regions of the island and held it against assault. The Spaniards ultimately gave up trying to conquer the Maroons, many of whom it is said descended from the warrior Ashanti people of West Africa. The British would also eventually sign a peace treaty with the Maroons in 1738, the legacy of which has left the Maroons with their sovereignty to this day.

Large Maroon settlements grew in Accompong, St. Elizabeth; in Moore Town in the Rio Grande River Valley; above Buff Bay in Charles Town, Portland; and in Scott's Hall, St. Mary. Today the Maroons are still courted by elected officials who have Maroon lands within their constituencies. While the communities themselves have largely been diluted since emancipation, their warrior spirit has permeated Jamaican society at large, influencing social movements like the Rastafarians, who draw on their experience as rebels against the status quo to present an alternate worldview based on principles that can be traced through the Maroon heritage to Africa.

## Santa Cruz

A bustling transportation hub more than a destination, Santa Cruz can get congested during the day; if you're passing through, the bypass around the town center saves a lot of time. Arriving from the east, veer right off the main road at the Y where the road splits at the Total gas station before town. Take the third left to rejoin the main road at the stoplight on the western edge of town. Arriving from the west, follow the reverse route: a left at the first stoplight, and then a right until the road meets the main road at the Total station on the eastern edge of town. The dusty bus terminal parking lot in the heart of Santa Cruz is a good place to catch a route taxi for Treasure Beach, Black River, or Mandeville.

### FOOD

**Grills & Frills** (New River Rd., 10am-10pm Mon.-Sat., US$3-4.50) serves Boston-style jerk chicken and pork and roast fish, as well as other Jamaican staples.

**Hinds Restaurant & Bakery** (Santa Cruz Plaza, tel. 876/966-2234, 7:30am-5pm Mon.-Thurs., 7:30am-7pm Fri.-Sat., US$4-6) has decent Jamaican dishes liked fried, stewed, and baked chicken, as well as oxtail, curry goat, stew pork, and escoveitch fish.

### ACCOMMODATIONS

**Chariots Hotel** (Leeds, tel. 876/966-3860, US$40-75) has a pool, a Jamaican restaurant, and a bar. Heading west through Santa Cruz, turn left at the stoplight onto Coke Drive, pass RBTT bank and then NCB, four kilometers (2.5 miles) from Santa Cruz on the road to Malvern. All rooms have private baths, cable TV, air-conditioning, and either two doubles or one king. The more expensive rooms have hot water. It's a well-kept place.

**Kool Rooms Guest House** (just west of the last stoplight in Santa Cruz, cell tel. 876/883-8838, tel. 876/387-9417, vernon-bourne@yahoo.com, www.thekoolrooms-guesthouse.com, US$50) has four rooms with two queens or two doubles in each room with air-conditioning, cable TV, and en suite baths with a tub and shower. Run by roots rock reggae singer Vernon Bourne, aka Singing Vernon, the guesthouse is a good place for young travelers looking to unwind in the countryside. You're likely to "buck up" other popular reggae artists during your stay.

### SERVICES

**NCB** (7 Coke Dr., tel. 876/966-2204) and **Scotiabank** (77 Main St., tel. 876/966-2230) have small branches with ATMs.

# Background

# The Landscape

Jamaica enjoys widely varied topography for its small size, ranging from tropical montane regions in the Blue and John Crow Mountains to temperate areas at the higher elevations of Manchester, lush tropical coastline along much of the coast, and near-desert conditions south of the Santa Cruz Mountains in St. Elizabeth. No other island in the Caribbean can boast natural features and attractions in such abundance and close proximity. The most expansive wetlands in the Caribbean, the Lower Black River Morass, for example, is a popular wintering ground for birds from across the continent, while Jamaica's various mountain ranges create distinct ecosystems that support high levels of endemism.

Land use in Jamaica was historically framed in the context of the colonial plantation economy, where overseers would control vast tracts of land on behalf of absentee landowners and enslaved people would not be granted title. The plains were coveted for growing sugarcane, while the more mountainous regions produced timber and spices. The birth of the banana industry in the Northeast opened up large new areas to plantation agriculture, before a plague virtually wiped out the crop.

After the abolition of slavery, migration made towns into cities, and a cultural aversion to agriculture and rural life persists today. As you drive across the island you still see vast cane fields in many parishes, with banana and citrus plantations in others. But farming as a way of life has fallen out of fashion, and much agricultural land is left unfarmed.

When the Jamaica Labour Party came to power in 2008 after being in the opposition for 18 years, a renewed emphasis was placed on agriculture as a sector vital to the country's growth and development. Nonetheless, Jamaica has struggled to bring its land-use policies into the modern era to encourage productive use of land, and squatting continues to be a problem. In the Kingston area, subdivisions are claiming old cane fields as urban sprawl continues to fan outward from bedroom communities like Old Harbour, Spanish Town, and Portmore.

## GEOGRAPHY

Jamaica is a relatively small island: 235 kilometers (146 miles) long and 93 kilometers (58 miles) at its widest point, covering an area of 10,992 square kilometers (4,244 square miles), slightly smaller than the state of Connecticut. Distances in Jamaica can seem much greater than they really are thanks to mountainous terrain and poor roads.

## CLIMATE

Jamaica has a tropical climate along the coast and lowlands, with average annual temperatures of 26 to 32°C (79-90°F). In the mountains, temperatures can drop down near freezing at night at the highest elevations. Jamaica has two loose rainy seasons: between May and June and then later, with heavier, more sustained rains coinciding with hurricane season from July to October.

---

**Previous:** Passionfruit grows from incredible flowers; Doctors Cave Beach in Montego Bay.

# Plants and Animals

In terms of biodiversity, Jamaica is surpassed in the Caribbean only by Cuba, a country many times its size. What's more, Jamaica has an extremely high rate of endemism, both in plant and animal life. Perhaps most noticeable are the endemic birds, some of the most striking of which are hard to miss. The national bird is the red-billed streamertail hummingbird, also called the doctor bird, ubiquitous across the island. Other endemic birds, like the Jamaican tody, are rarer—requiring excursions into remote areas to see.

## PLANTS

While agriculture has diminished in importance as bauxite and tourism have taken over as Jamaica's chief earners, the country still depends heavily on subsistence farming outside the largest cities and towns, where many houses still have mango and ackee trees in the yard. Coffee remains an important export crop, the Blue Mountains varieties fetching some of the highest prices per pound in the world. In recent years, a growing number of entrepreneurs have begun developing cottage industries based on key agricultural crops.

The market for Jamaica's niche products is strong both domestically and abroad. It helps that prices within the country are buoyed by heavy reliance on imported foodstuffs, which, while posing a challenge for consumers, means producers can get a fair price for their goods at home. Some of the most notable of these cottage industries based on natural products of Jamaica are Walkerswood, Starfish Oils, Pickapeppa, and Belcour Preserves. Look out for these in crafts shops and specialty supermarkets across the island. Many of these enterprises offer tours of their production facilities.

Jamaica's flora consists of a diverse mix of tropical and subtropical vegetation. Along the dry South Coast, the landscape resembles a desert, while mangrove wetlands near Black River provide a sharp contrast within relatively close proximity. In the highlands of Manchester, temperate crops like carrots and potatoes, known as Irish, thrive.

## Fruits

**Ackee** (*Blighia sapida*) is a small to midsize tree native to West Africa, introduced to Jamaica in 1778 when some plants were purchased from a slave ship captain. It is said to have been present earlier, however, owing to a slave who wouldn't relinquish the fruit across the Middle Passage. Ackee is Jamaica's national fruit.

**Apple** in Jamaica is a generic term that could refer to any number of fruits, starting with the delicious Otaheite apple. Other apples include star apple, custard apple (sweetsop, soursop), mammee apple (*Mammea americana*), crab apple (also known as coolie plum), golden apple (*Passiflora laurifolia*), velvet apple (*Diospyros discolor*)—also known as the Philippine persimmon—and rose apple (*Syzygium jambos*), used as a windbreak and for erosion control. The imported American or English apple, the common apple of the United States, has unfortunately slowly been taking over from the more exotic varieties on fruit stands in recent years due to its exotic appeal.

**Avocado** (*Persea americana*) is known commonly in Jamaica as "pear." Avocado is a native of Mexico, from where it was taken by the Spaniards throughout the Americas and much of the world. The Spanish name, *aguacate*, is a substitute for the Aztec name, *ahucatl*. Avocados are in season in Jamaica from August to December with a few varieties ripening into February. Alligator, Simmonds, Lulu, Collinson, and Winslowson are some of the varieties grown on the island.

**Banana** (*Musa acuminata* x *balbisiana*) is the world's largest herb (nonwoody plant); it became an important Jamaican export in the post-Emancipation period, 1876 to 1927. Jamaica was the world's foremost producer of the fruit during the period, with Gros Michel and later Cavendish varieties. The banana trade gave rise to Caribbean tourism when increasingly wealthy shippers began to offer passage on their empty boats returning to Jamaica from New England, where much of the produce was destined. In this way Portland, an important banana-growing region, became the Caribbean's first tourism destination with the Titchfield Hotel, built by a banana baron, exemplifying the relationship between the fruit and the tourism economy that would come to replace it in importance. Several varieties of banana are still grown in Jamaica, including plantain, an important starch; boiled bananas are a necessary accompaniment in the typical Jamaican Sunday breakfast of ackee and saltfish, callaloo, and dumpling.

**Jimbalin,** the Jamaican name for what is known in the United States as starfruit *(Passiflora edulis* var. *flavicarpa),* has one of the world's most beautiful flowers and a delicious fruit not commonly seen fresh in northern countries.

**Ugli fruit** is a hybrid between grapefruit *(Citrus paradisi)* and tangerine *(Citrus reticulata)* developed at Trout Hall, St. Catherine. It has a brainy-textured thick skin that is easily removed to reveal the juicy, orange-like fruit inside. A few large citrus estates, most notably Good Hope in Trelawny, make this an important export.

## Trees, Shrubs, and Flowers

**Agave** *(Agave sobolifera)* is a succulent, its broad leaves edged with prickles, notable for its tremendous 5- to 10-meter (16-33-foot) flower shoots February to April. Bulbils fall from the shoots to develop into independent plants.

**Anatto** *(Bixa orellana)* is an important dye and food coloring, and was once an important Jamaican export, likely lending its name to Annotto Bay in St. Mary, which was a center of production and export.

**Antidote caccoon** *(Fevillea cordifolia),* known as sabo, segra-seed, and nhandiroba, is a perennial climbing vine whose fruit has been used for its medicinal and purgative qualities.

**Arrowroot** *(Maranta arundinacea)* was brought from South America by pre-Columbian populations and used medicinally. Later it was grown on plantations and used as a starch substitute and thickener.

**Barringtonia** *(Barringtonia asiatica)* is a

Otaheite apples, cacao, and grapefruit

large evergreen originating in Asia. Its large coconut-like fruit will float for up to two years and root on the shore where it lands. Known locally as the duppy coconut, the tree has been naturalized in Portland, and 220-year-old trees grow at Bath Gardens in St. Thomas.

**Bauhinia** *(Bauhinia spp.),* known locally as "poor man's orchid," is a favorite of the streamertail hummingbird, or doctor bird, which visits the orchid-like flowers. It grows as a shrub or mid-size tree with pinkish flowers.

**Blue mahoe** *(Hibiscus elatus)* is a quality hardwood of the Malvaceae family. It grows native in the Blue Mountains and is the national tree.

**Ironwood** *(Lignum vitae)* is an extremely dense tropical hardwood that produces Jamaica's national flower.

**Kingston buttercup** *(Tribulus cistoides)* is a low, spreading plant with bright yellow flowers. It's known commonly as "Kill Backra" because it was thought to have caused yellow fever, which killed many European settlers. It's also called "police macca" because of its thorns, and turkey blossom.

**Madam Fate** *(Hippobroma longiflora)* is a poisonous perennial herb with a five-petaled, star-shaped flower used in Obeah and folk medicine. Found along pastures or on riverbanks, it's commonly called star flower or horse poison.

**Mahogany** *(Swietenia mahagoni)* is still highly valued for its timber and has accordingly been unsustainably harvested since the Spanish colonial period, resulting in dwindling numbers today. Mahogany can still be seen growing, albeit sparsely, along the banks of the Black River, which was originally called Rio Caobana (Mahogany River) by the Spanish.

**Sorrel** *(Rumex acetosella)* is a cousin of the hibiscus whose flowers are boiled to make a drink popular around Christmas time.

**Wild basil** *(Ocimum micranthum)* is a wild bush used in folk medicine and in cooking, popularly called barsley or baazli.

## Mammals

The **coney** or Jamaican hutia *(Geocapromys brownii)* is Jamaica's only surviving indigenous land-dwelling mammal, the only other being bats. Conies are nocturnal and thus seldom seen. The animal is basically a large rodent with cousins inhabiting other Caribbean islands like Hispaniola. Its meat was prized by the Taino centuries ago, while it is still a delicacy for the mongoose today, which is blamed for pushing it toward extinction. Another threat is loss of habitat, owing to encroaching urbanization of its principal habitats in the Hellshire Hills and Worthy Park of St. Catherine. It is also found in the John Crow Mountains in Portland and St. Thomas.

**Mongooses** are a common animal seen scurrying across the road. Widely regarded as pests, it is said that all mongooses in the western hemisphere are descendants of four males and five females introduced to Jamaica from India in 1872 to control the rat population on the sugar estate of one William Bancroft Espeut. They soon went on to outgrow their function, eventually being held responsible for killing off five endemic vertebrates and bringing Jamaica's iguanas to the verge of extinction.

## Bats

In Jamaica, the term *bat* typically refers to moths. Jamaica has 23 species of bat, known locally as rat bats. Many species of the Bombacaceae family are bat-pollinated, including the baobab, cottonwood, cannonball, and night cactus trees. Bats also go for other pulpy fruits like sweetsop, banana, naseberry, and mango. *Noctilio leporinus,* a fish-eating bat, can be seen swooping low over harbors and inlets at twilight.

## Birds

Of the 280 species of birds that have been recorded in Jamaica, 30 species and 19 subspecies are found nowhere else. Of these 30, two are extinct. There are 116 species that use

Jamaica as a breeding ground, while around 80 species spend the northern winter months on the island. The Jamaican tody, the ubiquitous "doctor bird" (Jamaica's national bird, properly called the red-billed streamertail), and the Jamaican mango hummingbird are especially colorful species to watch for.

## Reptiles

Jamaica has 26 species of lizards, including the island's largest, the iguana, now protected in the Helshire Hills and in slow recovery after near extinction due to slaughter by farmers and mongooses. The *Anolis* genus includes seven of the most common species, often seen in hotel rooms and on verandas, their showy throat fan extending to attract females. The largest *Anolis* is the garmani, which prefers large trees to human dwellings. All Jamaica's lizards are harmless.

Six of Jamaica's seven snake species are endemic, and all of them are harmless. Mostly found in remote areas like Cockpit Country, snakes have fallen victim to the fear of country folk, who generally kill them on sight, and to the introduced mongoose, famous for its ability to win a fight with the cobras of its native India. The island's largest snake is the yellow snake, with yellow and black patterns across its back. The snake is a boa constrictor, known locally as nanka, which can grow up to 3.5 meters (11 feet) in length. The nanka is seldom seen, as it is only active at night when it emerges from hiding to feed on bats and rats. Other less impressive snakes include three species of grass snake of the *Arrhyton* genus and the two-headed or worm snake *(Typhlops jamaicensis)*, which burrows below ground with its tail end virtually indistinguishable from its head. The black snake is considered an extinct victim of the mongoose.

Crocodiles are Jamaica's biggest reptiles, and are often referred to on the island as alligators. The American crocodile *(Crocodylus acutus)* is found across the island in swampy mangrove areas like Font Hill Wildlife Sanctuary and the Lower Black River Morass. This is the same species of croc found in Florida and other coastal wetlands of the Caribbean. Crocodiles have a long tapering snout, whereas alligators have a short, flat head.

# Endangered Fisheries

The **spiny lobster** is one of Jamaica's most prized culinary delicacies, often prepared grilled, with garlic sauce, or with a curry sauce. Lobsters fetch US$10-20 per pound at local grills and restaurants, and as high as US$40 per plate in many tourist establishments. The sustainability of lobster harvesting depends on allowing the creatures a safe period for reproduction, which has been acknowledged in Jamaica by the Ministry of Agriculture and Land with a ban on harvesting between April 1 and June 30. It is crucial that visitors to the island respect this ban to ensure sustainable lobster populations for the future. Some establishments serve what they say is frozen lobster during the closed season, but it's best to avoid ordering altogether. **Conch** *(Strombus gigas)* is also protected from overfishing and has a closed season from July 1 through October 31.

Jamaican waters are also becoming severely overharvested where **finned fish** are concerned. It's best to avoid buying fresh fish smaller than 15 centimeters (6 inches) unless it's a type of fish that doesn't grow to a larger size. The median size of the catch brought in from traditional line fishing and spear fishing in waters close to Jamaica's shores has decreased noticeably over the past decade. The situation becomes clear when snorkeling along Jamaica's coastal reefs, as few large fish can be seen today, and snapper, once common, are increasingly scarce.

# SEALIFE
## Marine Mammals

Jamaica has no large native mammals on land. The largest mammals are instead marine-based, namely dolphins and manatees, the latter known locally as sea cows. Manatees are endangered and now protected under wildlife laws after having seen their population dwindle due to hunting.

## Turtles

Of the six sea turtle species known worldwide, four were once common, and now less so, in Jamaican waters: the green turtle *(Chelonia mydas)*, the hawksbill *(Eretmochelys imbricata)*, the leatherback *(Dermochelys coriacea)*, and the loggerhead *(Caretta caretta)*. Turtle meat formed an important part of the diet of the Taino and was later adopted as a delicacy by colonial settlers. In keeping with Taino practice, they kept green turtles in large coastal pens known as turtle crawles to be killed and eaten at will.

# History

## EARLY INHABITANTS AND SPANISH DISCOVERY

Jamaica was first inhabited by the Taino, sometimes referred to as the Arawak, who arrived from the northern coast of South America in dugout canoes around AD 900. The Taino practiced subsistence agriculture to complement hunting, fishing, and foraging activities, forming mostly seaside settlements from where travel by dugout canoe remained an important mode of transportation.

Upon his arrival on the island in 1494, Italian explorer Christopher Columbus claimed the island on behalf of his financiers, King Ferdinand and Queen Isabella of Spain—in spite of the presence of a large Taino population with whom the Europeans engaged in an easily won battle. The exact point of his arrival is contested; it is likely the explorer landed in Rio Bueno, on the border of present-day St. Ann and Trelawny, where there is freshwater, rather than in Discovery Bay, which he named Puerto Seco, or Dry Harbour, because it lacked freshwater—something historical observers say would have influenced where explorers chose to make landfall.

Jamaica was not deemed of much importance to the Spanish Crown due to its relatively rugged terrain, and more importantly its lack of gold. Spain was more concerned with exploits in Mexico and Central and South America. Neighboring Hispaniola had more gold and was thus deemed more worthwhile, while Cuba, 145 kilometers (90 miles) to the north, was also more important to Spaniards, as its vast arable flat lands were easily settled, and it held a strategic position as the key to the Gulf of Mexico. While Cuba became increasingly important as a transshipment point for gold and other goods from the New World to Europe, Jamaica remained a backwater left largely under the control of Columbus's heirs. Within 50 years of "discovery," the indigenous Taino population, estimated to have been as high as one million at time of contact, was virtually annihilated through forced labor and European diseases to which they had no immunological defenses.

Four early Spanish settlements are known to have been established at Melilla, somewhere on the North Coast; at Oristan, near present-day Bluefields, Westmoreland; at Spanish Town, which grew into the principal city of Santiago de la Vega; and in Yallahs, near today's border of St. Andrew and St. Thomas. These settlements were mainly focused on cattle ranching, while horse breeding was also an important endeavor. Jamaica became a regular provisions stop for Spanish galleons heading to Colombia, among other important goldfields. While a few inland routes were carved out of the tropical rainforest, transportation around the island remained almost entirely sea-based, with the long and navigable Martha Brae River becoming an important route between the North and South Coasts.

The lack of a centralized strategy for settlement and defense left Jamaica extremely vulnerable to attack from other early colonial powers, ultimately leading to an easy takeover by England's naval forces during the rule of Oliver Cromwell. While it was the Spanish who first brought many of the plants that would become key to the island's economy in subsequent centuries, including bananas, sugarcane, and indigo, it was the English who created an organized plantation system—key to effectively exploiting the land and establishing lucrative trade with Europe.

## THE ENGLISH TAKEOVER

In 1655, during the rule of Oliver Cromwell, English naval forces invaded Jamaica and easily captured Spanish Town, the colonial rival's capital. The Spanish colony had virtually no defense strategy in place, a fact known and exploited by the English, who distributed vast tracts of land to the officers as a reward for their service. These land grants would form the first plantation estates of the English colony. The former Spanish rulers, led by the last governor, Cristóbal Ysassi, were loath to abandon the island, waging guerrilla warfare and reprisal attacks on the English with the help of loyal Maroons. The Spanish fled to the North Coast or left the island altogether for Hispaniola or Cuba.

Soon after their forces seized Jamaica, the English began a policy of legitimizing the activity of pirates—in effect gaining their allegiance in exchange for allowing them to continue their raids on mostly Spanish ships as privateers instead of buccaneers. The alliance made Port Royal, at the tip of the Palisadoes in Kingston harbor, into a boomtown, fueled by bustling trade in enslaved people and rum in addition to commerce in luxury goods, some imported from England and beyond, others plundered from victim ships.

While the slave trade had been established on the island under Spanish rule, it wasn't until the English set up vast, well-organized sugarcane plantations that enslaved laborers were imported en masse from Africa. Jamaica became the Caribbean's primary transshipment point for enslaved people to other parts of the New World, including the United States.

## PLANTATION CULTURE AND THE SLAVE TRADE

As an incentive to see Jamaica reach its full potential as a plantation colony, the English offered land not only to those who had been involved in the successful takeover, but also to people from England and other English colonies, most notably Barbados. Vast estates covered thousands of hectares, with many absentee landowners installing overseers to take care of business on the island while reaping the benefits from quiet England. The cultivation of sugar expanded during the 1700s to the point where Jamaica was the world's foremost producer and England's most prized colony. But the economic boom was far from equitable, relying heavily on the slave trade, set up first by the Portuguese and later by the Dutch and English along the Gold Coast, now Ghana, and the Slave Coast, in today's Nigeria. Slavery was not a new phenomenon in Africa, but with the arrival of European traders it was formalized, and raids into the interior began to supplement the prisoners of war who were first exported as slaves. The slaves brought to Jamaica were a mix of different ethnicities, including Coromantee, Ibo, Mandingo, Yoruba, and Congo. Slaves of different ethnic backgrounds and languages were intentionally put together to complicate any potential resistance.

Enslaved laborers were not only used in the fields on the plantations, but also as domestic workers, carpenters, masons, and coopers. The tendency for women around the plantation to give birth to children of lighter complexion helped loosen the hold of the slave system as the moral high ground assumed by the English eroded and the boundaries of race increasingly blurred.

# RUMORS AND REBELLION

The 1700s saw Jamaica rise to be the world's greatest producer of sugar and rum, with large estates covering the island's arable land worked by thousands of enslaved people. The runaway slaves, or Maroons, consolidated their autonomy in the country's rugged highland interior, while overseers managed the large estates for their mostly absentee masters.

But the plantation system could not be taken for granted by the British, with a series of slave uprisings stirring the foundations of their booming economy. The rumors of freedom began with Tacky's War in 1760, in which a Coromantee chief known as Tacky, a driver on Frontier Estate in St. Mary, orchestrated an uprising that spread to neighboring estates, and had as its objective the overthrow of the colonial masters throughout the island. Even while the Maroons maintained, and still maintain, aloofness when it came to how they viewed enslaved Africans who accepted their lot, their parallel existence in free communities served as a constant reminder on the plantation that slavery was not unshakable. Free people of color, meanwhile, helped maintain the status quo, breeding a culture of superiority related to their complexion, which is retained in Jamaican society to this day.

With fellow slaves in North America earning or buying their freedom in increasing numbers following the War of Independence, the nonconformists in Jamaica took added encouragement. In 1783 one such freed slave, the Baptist reverend George Liele, arrived in Jamaica to establish a ministry in Kingston that would give birth to the Baptist nonconformist movement on the island as he proceeded to baptize enslaved people in scores. These early Baptists, like nonconformist Methodists, Moravians, and Congregationalists, struck a chord with the masses with their antislavery stance. Liele sought patronage from the Baptist Ministry Society of Great Britain, which responded by sending the first British Baptist Missionary in 1814. For the next 20 years, anti-slavery rumblings grew until Sam Sharpe's rebellion, known as The Baptist War, broke from its intent of carrying out a peaceful strike with several plantations burned to the ground. While the uprising was suppressed by the plantocracy's militia and a British garrison, the British Parliament held inquiries that would lead to abolition two years later.

# EMANCIPATION AND THE FALL OF COLONIAL RULE

The abolition of slavery in 1834 preceded a four-year period of "apprenticeship" designed to integrate newly freed slaves into more "sophisticated" jobs, and more importantly, allow the plantation economy to adapt to a labor force that required compensation.

Following the apprenticeship period, however, the plantation owners soon found it difficult to secure workers, as many left the countryside for town in search of alternative livelihoods far from the memory of chains. Soon after emancipation, Jamaica's plantocracy, along with cane growers in places like Trinidad, Guyana, and Suriname, resorted to the importation of indentured Indian and Chinese laborers to work their fields beginning in 1845 through 1921.

The period following emancipation was the cradle for the modern identity of the Jamaican people. It was by no means an easy time, as Jamaica continued to be wrought with oppression and injustice, as evidenced by the Morant Bay Rebellion of 1865. Continued repression and oppression in Jamaica led many ambitious and frustrated young men to seek their fortunes overseas, whether in Panama, where the canal would be built between the late 1800s and the early 1900s, thanks in part to Jamaican labor, or to the United States, where a similar cultural identity was being formed as uprooted Africans became African Americans. Many of these fortune seekers, among them Marcus Garvey, George Stiebel, and Alexander Bustamante, returned with wealth, which afforded them a voice in society that they used to advance the cause of the worker, and ultimately, an independent Jamaica. Suffrage was tied to land ownership until it was universally declared in 1944, one of the many reasons for the ongoing struggle throughout the post-emancipation period. Jamaica's dark history of forced labor was a natural hotbed of resistance leading to the rise of the country's vibrant labor movement.

## "INDEPENDENT" JAMAICA

Jamaica's road to independence was trod with baby steps. In 1938, Norman Manley founded the People's National Party, and Alexander Bustamante formed the Jamaica Labour Party five years later. The first elections with voting rights for all were held in 1944. World War II had a significant impact on Jamaica, with widespread shortages adding to the urgency of rising social and political movements. The 1950s saw waves of emigrants leave Jamaica for England, with the tendency for emigrants

to head for the United States increasing when Britain restricted immigration following independence. Many old folks in Jamaica still bemoan the country's independence, recalling the good old days when schools were better and society more proper under the British.

The past several decades have been characterized by a young nation, still under the Commonwealth system, experiencing growing pains and still dependent as ever, albeit on different external forces. The flow of remittances from Jamaicans abroad, the health of the global economy, approval of multilateral financial institutions, maintenance of bilateral trade agreements, and uninterrupted royalty payments from foreign mining companies are all vital for Jamaica's economic welfare today. Until Jamaica becomes a net exporter of goods and services, it will have a difficult time being truly independent, as today it relies little on its own productivity for survival.

# Government and Economy

## GOVERNMENT

The Jamaican central government is organized as a constitutional monarchy and member of the British Commonwealth with Queen Elizabeth II as its official head of state. On the island, the queen is represented by the governor-general, who signs all legislation passed by the bicameral Jamaican Parliament. Parliament comprises a Senate and a House of Representatives, known as the Upper and Lower Houses, respectively. Representatives are elected for five-year terms, one from each of the island's 60 constituencies. Of Jamaica's 50 senators, 21 are appointed by the governor-general, 13 on the advice of the prime minister, and eight by the opposition leader. The cabinet consists of the prime minister and a minimum of 13 other ministers, including the minister of finance, who must also be an elected representative in the house, with not

more than four cabinet ministers selected from the members of the senate.

Beyond the national government, Jamaica has been organized into parishes of ecclesiastical origin since the arrival of the British, who installed the Church of England as their watchdog and pacifier. The Church of England later became the Anglican Church, whose rectories are still some of the most impressive buildings in rural areas across the island. The 60 federal constituencies are subdivided into 275 electoral units, each of which has a parish councilor in the local government. The Corporate Area, as metropolitan Kingston is known, combines the parishes of Kingston and St. Andrew into one local government entity known as the Kingston and St. Andrew Corporation.

Local representation dates to 1662, when the Vestry system was installed to manage local affairs across the island. The Vestry was composed of clergy members and lay magistrates of each parish and was in effect indistinguishable from the Church of England as far as governance and policy were concerned, as it operated almost exclusively for the benefit of the landed elite. The ruling class of the planters, clergy, and magistrates became known as the plantocracy. After 200 years of the Vestry system, it was abandoned in favor of a system of Municipal and Road Boards following the Morant Bay Rebellion of 1865. During the period when Jamaica was ruled by the Vestry system, the number of parishes increased from seven at the outset to 22 by the time it was abandoned. In 1867, the number of parishes was reduced to the 14 recognized today. In 1886, a new representational system of local government was installed consisting of Parochial Boards, which merged the operations of the Municipal and Road Boards into one entity. A general decentralization occurred during the intermittent period before the Parochial Boards were established, leaving local governments in charge of public health, markets, fire services, and water supply. Following implementation of the Parochial Board system, the oversight of building regulations, public beaches, sanitation, slaughterhouses, and streetlights was also assigned to the local government bodies.

## Political Parties and Elections

Jamaica's two political parties, the People's National Party (PNP) and the Jamaica Labour Party (JLP), were founded by cousins Norman Manley and Alexander Bustamante. Bustamante was a labor leader who came to some degree of wealth through his travels around Latin America before exploiting the anticolonial sentiment of the day to push for greater worker rights and ultimately Jamaican independence. The PNP held power since the 1980s, instating Portia Simpson-Miler in 2007 before the JLP's Bruce Golding toppled her in 2008. Five years later Sister P was back, beating shoe-in Andrew Holness. Simpson-Miller held power until February 2016, when

her party lost by a thin margin and Andrew Holness became prime minister once more.

Election time tends to be tense and tumultuous in Jamaica, when memories of the political violence of the 1970s become fresh again. Kingston's poor neighborhoods bear the brunt of the tension and are often barricaded during elections to prevent opposition loyalists from entering with their vehicles to stage drive-by shootings.

# ECONOMY

Jamaica's economy is supported by agriculture, bauxite, tourism, and remittances (in order of increasing importance). The financial sector is closely tied to other English-speaking Caribbean countries, most significantly Trinidad and Tobago, with large regional banks and insurance companies dominating the market. Jamaica has a serious balance of payments problem owing to high external debt dating back several decades. Austerity measures imposed by International Monetary Fund (IMF) restructuring during the political reign of Edward Seaga left little money for education and social programs, a situation which persists today. A new IMF arrangement was brokered in 2010 that imposed a heavy burden on the country, with a two-year public sector wage freeze accompanied by large government job cuts. Universal education has inched nearer with the removal of school fees, but the quality of schools varies widely from district to district, and many old-timers claim education was better under British rule. Failure to guarantee universal education is a serious shortfall of both political parties and has directly impacted productivity. The flip side of the coin sees the country's best educated leaving for higher-paid jobs overseas.

## Agriculture

Agriculture remains an important part of Jamaica's economy, if not in sheer numbers then for its role in providing sustenance. Cultivation of provisions as established during slavery persists to some degree in rural areas today, where most households grow some kind of crop, even if it is limited to a few mango and ackee trees.

Sugar production is still ongoing on a handful of large estates across the country, but the end of preferential pricing for Jamaican sugar in England has affected the crop's viability just as it dampened the prospects for Jamaica's banana industry. Apart from sugar, important export crops include coffee, the Blue Mountain variety fetching some of the highest prices in the world, papaya, yam, peppers, ginger, coconut, pimento, and citrus, including oranges and Ugli fruit.

## Mining

Bauxite mining and processing in Jamaica is dominated by foreign entities like Russia's RUSAL, Noble Group of Hong Kong, and U.S.-based Noranda. Bauxite is mined across the island, leaving gaping red holes as the telltale sign. Bauxite is converted into alumina before being smelted into aluminum, both processes requiring huge amounts of energy. Jamaica has a serious energy problem in that it is overwhelmingly dependent on imported oil for generating electricity. High global energy prices combined with the global recession and low aluminum prices paralyzed the bauxite and alumina industry in 2009, eliminating a large royalty revenue stream earning foreign exchange for the government. Jamaica remains one of the most important bauxite sources in the world, once ranked third in production of bauxite ore and fourth in alumina production globally, but it requires high aluminum prices and low energy prices to be viable. At its peak, the bauxite industry accounted for 75 percent of the country's export earnings.

Other less important mineral resources found in Jamaica include gypsum, limestone, marble, silica sand, clay peat, lignite, titanium, copper, lead, and zinc. The export of crushed limestone, or aggregates, and limestone derivatives is an important growth industry with several players across the island.

## Tourism

Tourism continues to be the primary driver of economic growth in Jamaica. Tourism development in recent years has taken the form of megaprojects that employ large numbers at low wages and keep foreign exchange and profits offshore. There seems to be little interest in seeing tourism dollars distributed more evenly among the population, with the government apparently happy just to collect its general consumption tax for each guest that passes through the mass-market all-inclusive resorts. Despite the government's lack of effort to see tourism revenue benefit more Jamaicans, entrepreneurial Jamaicans see great benefits from tourism, with a slew of niche attractions created and developed to serve this market.

## Remittances

As a percentage of GDP contributed by remittances, Jamaica is ranked seventh in the world and fourth in the Caribbean—after the Dominican Republic—with nearly US$2 billion entering the country each year. The "Jamaican Dream," pursued by many who are able, consists of leaving the country to pursue a career abroad for however long it takes to make it, and then returning to Jamaica to live well. Sometimes the required time lasts generations, especially when those left back home are reliant on remittances. In tough economic times, Jamaica is more dependent than ever on expatriates, with large concentrations living in Toronto, New York, Florida, and London.

## Distribution of Wealth

Some say there are two Jamaicas, made up of the haves and the have-nots. While the truth is more complex, the fact is that there is a serious cash-flow problem in Jamaica. Competition is strong in larger cities for resources that might otherwise be picked from a tree. Even more overwhelming than the price of local produce from the market are imports, which cover everything else.

With jobs hard to come by for youth, there is a desperate situation for many, especially as prices for groceries and other basic goods keep rising. Add in the fact that it is not uncommon for a man to have several children with more than one woman, and the role of what's termed "social capital" becomes clear. If it weren't for the way Jamaicans help each other out—raising children belonging to a niece or nephew, employing a man around the house who really doesn't do much gardening but clearly has no other prospects—Jamaica would find itself in a far worse state.

This cycle of too many mouths to feed with too little to go around maintains a steep class divide on the island. Education costs money for school fees, books, and uniforms, and with competing interests vying for the limited resources in many cash-strapped homes, school can be a low priority. Without proper education, youth become stuck doing menial jobs or nothing at all, and the cycle continues.

# People and Culture

## RACE AND CLASS

Jamaica's national motto, "Out of many, one people," reflects the tolerance and appreciation for diversity promulgated from an institutional level. Meanwhile, individuals and communities of Jamaica's myriad ethnic groups keep old prejudices and stereotypes very much alive, usually without malice but still with names that are considered derogatory in other parts of the world. If you find yourself the victim of this kind of stereotyping, try not to be offended. Ethnic divisions and cultural prejudices in Jamaica are a result of a history steeped in confrontation and oppression. Rarely, if ever, do these prejudices lead to conflict or violence.

Historically, race in Jamaican society has been of utmost importance in maintaining the strict class structure, while in contemporary society everything boils down to money. Nonetheless, complexion and ethnic background still often form the basis of an individual's perception of self and place in society. While the island has an overwhelming black majority, other minority groups play an important, even dominant role in the local economy. Chinese and Indians who were brought to the island as indentured laborers following the abolition of slavery became and remain prominent members of society as shopkeepers and traders, even in the smaller communities. Lebanese Jamaicans have also played a significant role in business as well as in national politics. White Jamaicans still own some of the most beautiful and expansive estates.

The British established the precedent of "complexionism" by putting lighter-skinned, or "brown" Jamaicans—often their own progeny—in managerial positions, a self-perpetuating phenomenon that continues today in the nepotism that pervades the political and economic elite. The Maroons, who initially put up fierce resistance to the British colonial government and forced a treaty giving them autonomy and freedom from slavery long before abolition, have been an important source of pride for Jamaicans, even while the issue of their collaboration with the British in suppressing slave rebellions remains something of a cultural taboo.

Today Jamaica's African heritage is celebrated in popular music enjoyed across social and economic classes.

## RELIGION

Jamaica holds the Guinness Book World Record for most churches per capita. Virtually every religion and denomination on earth is represented on the island, with churches everywhere you turn. A common sight on weekends is large tents set up across the countryside for the open-air services preferred by the evangelical denominations. Only those churches that are unique to Jamaica or have played an important role in the country's history are described here, with listings in the destination chapters for those of historical or architectural significance.

## Revival

Born as a distinctly Jamaican fusion between Christian and African beliefs during the Great Revival of 1860-1861, Revival today is composed of two different branches: Pukkumina (Pocomania or Poco) and Revival Zion, the former closer toward the African end of the spectrum, the latter incorporating more obviously Christian beliefs and practices. Revivalists wear colorful robes and turbans during energetic ceremonies, during which trancelike states are reached with drumming, singing, and a wheeling dance that is said to induce possession by spirits. Revival has its roots in the Native Baptist and Myal movements that lie at the margins of Jamaica's more prominent Anglican and Baptist churches. Baptist churches were early venues for the emergence of what would become known as the Revival faith. Morant Bay rebellion leader Paul Bogle's church in Stony Gut was one such Native Baptist church, where elements of African worship were incorporated into more typical Baptist practice. Today Revival is closely associated with the Pentecostal denomination, and practitioners will generally attend one of the established churches in addition to observing Revival practices.

Core to Revival philosophy is the inseparability of the spirit and physical worlds. It is based on this belief that Revivalists can be possessed and influenced by ancestral spirits. Revivalists reinterpreted the Christian theme of the Father, the Son, and the Holy Spirit, placing emphasis on the last, which manifests as the "Messenger" attending services and possessing believers.

## Baptist Church

Significant in Jamaica for its role in fomenting abolitionist sentiment and fueling revolt, the Baptist church was first brought to the island by a freed American slave, Reverend George Liele, in 1738. Liele was baptized in Savannah, Georgia, before receiving a preacher's license and being ordained a minister. He brought his ministerial prowess to Jamaica, where he attracted large numbers of converts with his abolitionist rhetoric that would prove indispensable in firstly attracting followers and ultimately in bringing about emancipation with the help of the British Baptist Mission, which arrived on the island in 1814. After emancipation, the Baptist Church was instrumental in organizing the free villages that allowed the former slaves a new start after leaving the plantation. The church was also important in promoting education among the former slaves. Three of Jamaica's seven national heroes were Baptists, including rebellion leaders Sam Sharpe and Paul Bogle. Today Baptists remain one of Jamaica's strongest religious groups following their separation from the British Baptists in 1842.

## Hinduism

Brought to the island by indentured Indians, Hinduism is still practiced but maintains an extremely low profile within tight-knit and economically stable Indian communities. There is a temple on Maxfield Avenue in Kingston that holds regular service on Sunday.

## Judaism

The first Jewish people arrived in Jamaica early in the colonial period during the Spanish Inquisition, when they were expelled by King Ferdinand and Queen Isabella and found refuge in Jamaica—in spite of not being officially allowed in the Spanish colonies. Many of these Jews outwardly converted to Catholicism while continuing to practice their own religion in secret. When the British arrived in 1655 to capture the island from the Spanish, they were aided by the Jews, who were subsequently free to practice their religion openly after the conquest. Sephardic Jews of Spanish, Portuguese, and North African descent were the first arrivals, followed in the 1770s by Ashkenazi who left Germany and Eastern Europe.

## Ethiopian Orthodox Church
Brought to Jamaica in 1972, the Ethiopian Orthodox Church was the official state church of Ethiopia. Following Haile Selassie's visit to the island in 1966, he instructed the establishment of a church in Kingston in an attempt to legitimize the Rastafarians with a bona fide institution. Many Rastafarians were drawn to the church, even while it does not recognize Selassie as a divine person beyond his own affiliation with the church and the divinity that would convey.

## Obeah
Essentially the Jamaican version of Voodoo, Obeah plays an important role in Jamaica, evoking fear even among those who don't believe in it. The mysticism and use of natural concoctions that help bridge the physical and spiritual worlds has similar African roots as Santeria or Voodoo found in neighboring Cuba and Haiti. While there are few who practice Obeah as priests or worshippers, its casual practice is a widespread phenomenon evidenced by markings and charms strewn about many Jamaican homes.

## Rastafari
The name of Ethiopian Emperor Haile Selassie I prior to his coronation was Ras Tafari, Ras meaning Prince, and Tafari Makonnen his given name at birth. When Leonard Howell, a Jamaican follower of Marcus Garvey, saw Ras Tafari Makonnen crowned as Emperor Haile Selassie I on November 2, 1930, he viewed the coronation as the fulfillment of biblical prophecy, more so given the emperor's title, King of Kings, Lord of Lords, Conquering Lion of Tribe of Judah. The original prophecy that foretold of a black man rising in the East is attributed to Black Nationalist and Jamaican national hero Marcus Garvey, who had written a play performed in support of his movement in the United States, from which the now-famous line, "look to the East for the crowning of a black king" was supposedly gleaned. It is interesting to note that Garvey never viewed Selassie as a god or claimed his coronation a fulfillment of prophecy at any point during his turbulent life, but this did not stop Leonard Howell from making the proclamation, which fell upon eager ears among his own followers in rural Jamaica and sparked a global movement that continues to grow today.

Leonard Howell chose an opportune time to proclaim Selassie's divinity. Disillusionment by the masses of blacks descended from slaves was high in the 1920s and 1930s, fueling Jamaica's labor movement and the establishment of the two political parties. The Harlem Renaissance of the 1920s gave blacks in the United States a confidence that was exported to the Caribbean in the form of bold ideas that came to a people that never really forgot Africa. Thanks to the important role Jamaica's Maroons played in preserving African belief systems, and the persistence of Revivalist and Obeah religious practices even within the many Christian denominations that were established on the island, select segments of the Jamaican population were well primed for the proposition that the divine had manifested in an African king.

Nevertheless, these select segments were predominantly poor blacks, essentially social outcasts seen as the dregs of society. Dreadlocks, as the hairstyle became known to the chagrin of many adherents who scorn the fear and criminality the term "dread" implies, predate the Rasta movement and were effectively a natural occurrence for those who neglected to use a comb. With the conversion to the Rastafarian philosophy among many up-and-coming reggae musicians during the 1960s and 1970s, the faith gained traction in Jamaica, and as the island's music became an increasingly important export, Rasta soon became almost synonymous with reggae, and the philosophy spread around the world.

The Rastafarian movement can be traced directly to the recognition of the divinity of Selassie upon his coronation in 1930, but most

Rastafarians assert their faith is far more ancient, going back at least to the Nazarenes mentioned in the Old Testament from whence they derive their aversion to razors and scissors, as well as to the eating of flesh. King Selassie has become the head of the movement by default as the most recent manifestation of divinity on earth, despite his own disagreement with being viewed as a god. But the line is traced straight back to the divine theocracy of the Old Testament, Selassie himself said to be the 225th descendant of King Solomon and the Queen of Sheba. Rastafarians essentially claim the Hebrew lineage as their own and have reinterpreted the Old Testament by identifying Africans as the Israelites of modern times, having been enslaved just like the Jews in Babylon. In effect, Rastafarians espouse a natural lifestyle free of the contamination and corruption of modern society. Repatriation to Africa, whether spiritual or physical, forms a central theme.

Along the movement's course of development, charismatic leaders carved out the many "houses," or denominations, that can be found today across the island, including the Nyabinghi, Bobo Ashanti, and the Twelve Tribes of Israel.

The Nyabinghi invoke the warrior spirit of the African empress Iyabinghi; drum ceremonies that last for days around important dates are a central feature.

The Bobo Ashanti, or Bobo Shanti, is a group based at Bobo Hill in Nine Mile, just east of Kingston along the coast. The Bobo live a ritualized lifestyle away from society, putting emphasis on the teaching of Marcus Garvey and founder Prince Emmanuel. Themes of self-reliance and self-confidence are central to the Bobo philosophy. The group has gained as converts many contemporary dancehall reggae musicians including Sizzla and Capleton.

Perhaps the most international house of Rastafari is the Twelve Tribes of Israel, founded by the late Vernon Carrington, known by his brethren as Brother Gad. Members of the Twelve Tribes are found across the world with the denomination having crossed social and economic barriers more than other houses, perhaps due to its Christian lean. The Twelve Tribes of Israel embraces Christianity and views Haile Selassie I as representing the spirit of Christ.

Another important force within the Rastafarian movement has been that of Abuna, or Rasta priest Ascento Fox, who has made strong inroads in society by establishing churches in Kingston, London, and New York. These churches are used as a base for maintaining a presence in the community and providing an alternative for convicts in the prison systems, where the group does a lot of work.

Rastafarians in Jamaica and "in farin" (abroad) are viewed with a combination of respect and fear to this day. Many Rasta colloquialisms have become everyday parlance in Jamaican society as reggae music grew to a global force recognized and appreciated far beyond the Caribbean, with phrases like "one love," "blessed," and "irie" used commonly even by those who don't claim the faith as their own. Use of marijuana, or ganja, has been legitimized to some degree in society at large thanks to the important role it plays for Rastas as a sacrament.

## LANGUAGE

In Jamaica, free speech is held as one of the foremost tenets of society. Nevertheless, using the wrong language in the wrong place can cause scorn, embarrassment, or even murder, and knowing how to speak under given circumstances defines a Jamaican's identity and the reveals the layers of a highly classist society. Language use ranges from thick patois to the most eloquent queen's English and generally suggests to which tier of society the speaker belongs. Nevertheless, those raised in Jamaica to speak an impeccable form of English will often flip in mid-conversation to outwardly unintelligible patois. The rich flavor of Jamaica's language is the most apparent expression of feverish pride based on a 400-year struggle that spanned the country's anti-slavery, black power, and independence movements. The rise of the island as a cultural hotspot owes not disparagingly to the influence of Indians, Lebanese, Syrians, Jews, and Chinese, and a remaining smattering of the old white plantocracy.

## MUSICAL HERITAGE

Music has been an integral element of Jamaican society for centuries—from use of song on the plantation to mitigate the torturous work, to funeral rituals that combine Christian and African elements in the traditional nine nights. Most of the instruments used in Jamaica have been borrowed or adapted from either European or African traditions, while some Taino influence surely occurred before their cultural annihilation.

Today music remains as important and central to Jamaican culture as ever. From the beach resorts to the rural hills, sound systems blare out on weekends into the early dawn hours, with a wide variety of genres appreciated on the airwaves.

### Jonkunnu

Pronounced "John Canoe," Jonkunnu is a traditional music and skit-like dance performed primarily at Christmas. The Jonkunnu rhythm is played in 2/2 or 4/4 time on the fife, a rattling drum with sticks, bass, and grater. Dancers wear costumes and masks representing characters like Pitchy Patchy, King, Queen, Horse-Head, Cow-Head, and Belly Woman that act out skits and dance.

The origin of Jonkunnu is revealed in the word's etymology: Jonkunnu is an adaptation of the Ghanaian words *dzon'ko* (sorcerer) *nu* (man), derived from secret societies found on the African mainland. Among the costumes found in Jonkunnu are pieced-together sacks similar to those seen in the Abakua, a secret society in neighboring Cuba that also uses dance and drumming.

In Jamaica, Jonkunnu became associated with Christmastime likely because it was the only real holiday for the slaves in the whole year, during which they would tour the plantation with their music, dance, and skits, typically with headgear consisting of ox horns. At the height of the British colonial period, plantation owners actively encouraged Jonkunnu, and it took on European elements, including satire of the masters, Morris dance jigs, and polka steps. The importance of Jonkunnu declined as it was replaced by the emergence of "set girls" who would dance about to display their beauty and sexual rivalry. Later, following emancipation, nonconformist missionaries suppressed Jonkunnu and the mayor of Kingston banned the Jonkunnu parade in 1841, leading to riots. In the years leading up to Jamaican independence, as the country's cultural identity was being explored, Jonkunnu gained the support of the government, which still sponsors the folk form in annual carnival and other events.

### Kumina

The most distinctly African of Jamaica's musical forms, Kumina was brought to Jamaica after emancipation by indentured laborers from Congo and remains a strong tradition in Portland and St. Thomas. Kumina ceremonies are often held for wakes and burials, as well as for births and anniversaries, and involve drumming and dancing.

### Mento

Jamaica's original folk music, mento is a fusion of African and European musical elements played with a variety of instruments that were borrowed from plantation owners and fashioned by the slaves themselves as the genre developed. A variety of instruments have a place in mento, from stick and hand drums to stringed instruments, flutes, and brass, along with the crucial rumba box, the precursor to the upright bass and bass guitar. Mento was one of the most important foundations for ska, which gave birth to reggae.

### Ska and Rocksteady

The origins of ska date to the early 1950s, when Jamaicans began to catch on to popular music from the United States that reached the island via the radio and U.S. military

# Crucial Reggae

The following selections are not intended as an exhaustive list of reggae releases but are a few essentials for any reggae fan's collection and some of the author's favorites. In the United States, the best source for reggae albums is Ernie B's (www.ebreggae.com), which has an excellent online catalog of full albums and singles.

## ROOTS

The Congos, roots reggae icons

- Abyssinians, *Satta Massagana*
- Burning Spear, *Marcus Garvey/Garvey's Ghost*
- The Congos, *Heart of the Congos*
- Culture, *Two Sevens Clash*
- Dennis Brown, *Milk and Honey*
- Desmond Decker, *Israelites*
- Freddie McGregor, *Bobby Babylon*
- Gladiators, *Dreadlocks The Time Is Now*
- Gregory Isaacs, *Night Nurse*
- I Jah Man, *Marcus Hero*
- Israel Vibration, *Power of the Trinity*
- Jimmy Cliff, *Wonderful World Beautiful People*
- John Holt, *Stealin'*
- Ken Boothe, *Everthing I Own*
- Lee Scratch Perry, *Roast Fish Collie Weed & Corn Bread*
- Max Romeo and, *War Ina Babylon*
- Peter Tosh, *Legalize It*
- Third World, *96° in the Shade*
- Toots and the Maytals, *Pressure Drop*
- Bob Marley and the Wailers, *Songs of Freedom*

personnel stationed here following World War II. Popular American tunes were played by mobile disc jockeys, the predecessors of today's sound systems, before being adopted and adapted by Jamaican musicians. The emphasis on the infectious upbeat was carried over from mento and calypso, with the trademark walking baseline sound borrowed from jazz and R&B. The birth and popularity of ska coincided with an upbeat mood in Jamaica at the time of independence, and the lyrics of many ska classics celebrate the country's separation from England. Spearheaded by pioneering producers like Prince Buster, Duke Reid, and Clement "Sir Coxone" Dodd, the genre became a hit, especially among Jamaica's

## CONTEMPORARY ONE DROP

- Chronixx, *Dread & Terrible*
- Protoje, *Ancient Future*
- Buju Banton, *Till Shiloh*
- Capleton, *Still Blazin*
- Damian Marley, <CI>*Welcome to Jamrock*
- Fanton Mojah, *Haile H.I.M.*
- Garnett Silk, *Gold*
- Gyptian, *My Name is Gyptian*
- I-Wayne, *Lava Ground*
- Jah Mason, *Love & Wisdom*
- Luciano , *Messenger*
- Richie Spice, *In the Streets to Africa*
- Sizzla, *Praise Ye Jah*
- Tanya Stephens, *Rebelution*
- Tony Rebel, *If Jah*

## DANCEHALL

- Beenie Man, *Undisputed*
- Bounty Killer, *The Warlord Scrolls*
- Busy Signal, *Step Out*
- Mavado, *Gangsta For Life*
- Sean Paul, *Dutty Rock*
- Vybz Kartel, *King of the Dancehall*
- Alkaline, *New Level Unlocked*
- Shaggy, *Mr. Lover Lover*

working-class masses. The genre was popularized and taken international by bands like Byron Lee and the Dragonaires, Derrick Morgan, and Desmond Decker.

As ska's popularity began to wane by the late 1960s, the rhythm was slowed down, making way for the syncopated base lines and more sensual tone of rocksteady. A series of hits representative of the genre brought artists like Alton Ellis and Hopeton Lewis to fame with songs like "Girl I've Got a Date" and "Tek it Easy." Made for dancing, rocksteady continued to adapt popular American hits, with rude boy culture and love dominating the lyrics.

## Reggae

Most people know Jamaica by its legendary musical king, Bob Marley. Marley brought international attention to the island. Yet apart from Marley, Jamaica's music has had limited impact beyond the country's expatriate communities in London, Toronto, New York, and Miami. Only recently has dancehall reggae become mainstream internationally, thanks in part to crossover artists like Shaggy and Sean Paul. The genre has its roots in ska and rocksteady of the 1950s and 1960s, when radio brought American popular music to Jamaican shores and the country's creative musicians began to adapt American tunes to an indigenous swing.

After a decade of slackness in reggae during the late 1980s and early 1990s, several talented artists have managed to capitalize on a resurgence of conscious music by launching successful careers as "cultural" reggae artists in the one-drop subgenre, sometimes using original musical tracks, sometimes singing on one of the more popular rhythms of the day or the past. These include I-Wayne, Richie Spice, Fantan Mojah, and more recently a young cadre comprised of Chronixx, Jesse Royal, Kabaka Pyramid, Jah9, and Protoje.

Dub, a form of remixed reggae that drops out much of the lyrics, was an offshoot of roots reggae pioneered by King Tubby and others, that led to the dub poetry genre, whose best-known artists include Mutabaruka and Linton Kwesi Johnson. The most accomplished new artist of the dub-poetry genre is DYCR.

## Dancehall

Clearly the most popular genre of music in Jamaica today, dancehall refers to the venue in which it was first enjoyed. Dancehall music is born of the street, with themes typically reflecting struggle, defiance, and relationships with women. Bounty Killer, Agent Sasco, Voicemail, TOK, Busy Signal, Mavado, Vybz Kartel, Elephant Man, Mr. Vegas, Popcaan, Alkaline, Tifa, and Spice have led the pack in popularity and influence in modern dancehall, while Beenie Man still claims the title,

"King of Dancehall." Lady Saw is still regarded by many as "Queen of the Dancehall," having inspired the emergence of other female artists of the genre like Lady G, Macka Diamond, Spice, and Tifa.

# FINE ART

The Jamaican art world can be classified broadly into folk artists, schooled artists, and self-taught or intuitive artists. Folk art has been around throughout Jamaica's history, as far back as the Taino, whose cave paintings can still be seen in a few locations on the island. European and African arrivals brought a new mix, with the planter class often commissioning works from visiting European portrait painters, while enslaved Africans carried on a wide range of traditions from their homeland, which included wood carving, fashioning musical instruments, and creating decorative masks and costumes for traditional celebrations like Jonkunnu. The annual Hosay celebrations, which date to the mid-1800s in Jamaica, as well as Maroon ceremonies, are considered living art. Folk art had a formative influence on Jamaica's intuitive artists.

The century after full emancipation in 1938 saw deep structural changes and growing pains for Jamaica, first as a colony struggling to maintain order and then in the tumultuous years leading up to independence. Jamaican art as a concerted discipline arose in the late 1800s, and culminated with the establishment of formal training in 1940. In the early years, sculpture and painting reflected the mood of a country nursing fresh wounds of slavery, with progressive, renegade leaders and indigenous Revival and then Rastafari movements giving substance to the work of self-taught artists.

Edna Manley, wife of Jamaica's first prime minister, Norman Manley, is credited with formally establishing a homegrown Jamaican art scene. An accomplished artist, Edna Manley was born in England in 1900 to a Jamaican mother and English father and schooled at English art schools. On arrival in Jamaica, Manley was influenced by Jamaica's early intuitive sculptors like David

Miller Sr. and David Miller Jr., Alvin Marriot, and Mallica Reynolds, a revival bishop better known as "Kapo." Edna Manley's 1935 sculpture *Negro Aroused* captured the mood of an era characterized by cultural nationalization, where Afrocentric imagery and the establishment and tribulations of a black working class were often the focus. Manley began teaching formal classes in 1940 at the Junior Centre of the Institute of Jamaica, giving the structure necessary for the emergence of a slew of Jamaican painters, including Albert Huie, David Pottinger, Ralph Campbell, and Henry Daley. Her school later developed into the Jamaica School of Art and Crafts, which was ultimately absorbed by Edna Manley College. Several other artists who did not come out of Manley's school gained prominence in the early period, including Carl Abrahams, Gloria Escofferey, and John Dunkley. Dunkley's works consistently use somber shades and clean lines with dark symbolism reflective of serious times, making them immediately recognizable.

Jamaican fine arts exploded in the fervent post-independence years along with the country's music industry, fueling the expansion of both the National Gallery as well as a slew of commercial galleries, many of which still exist in Kingston today. The post-independence period counts among its well-recognized artists Osmond Watson, Milton George, George Rodney, Alexander Cooper, and David Boxer. Black Nationalism and the exploration of a national identity remained important topics for artists like Omari Ra and Stanford Watson, while many other artists, like the ubiquitous Ras Dizzy or Ken Abendana Spencer, gained recognition during the period for the sheer abundance of their work, much of which celebrated Jamaica's rural landscape. In the late 1970s, the National Gallery launched an exhibition series called the Intuitive Eye, which brought mainstream recognition to Jamaica's self-taught artists as key contributors to the development of Jamaican art. Some of the artists to gain exposure and wider recognition thanks to the Intuitive Eye series include William "Woody" Joseph, Gason Tabois, Sydney McLaren, Leonard Daley, John "Doc" Williamson, William Rhule, Errol McKenzie, and Allan "Zion" Johnson.

The Institute of Jamaica and its various divisions continues to bring new exhibition space into use, notably opening a gallery in late 2006 on the top floor of the Natural History building.

# Sports

The sporting arena has seen many achievements that have been etched in the hearts of Jamaicans, becoming a part of the country's national identity. Jamaica has come to embody the sporting adage of "punching above one's weight," echoed in the local expression "we likkle but we tallawa" (we're little but we're strong), and this has been shown most emphatically on the sprinting track in recent times, but also historically on the cricket ovals, boxing arenas, and, to add a bit of pizzazz to the diverse accomplishments, with bobsledders and aerial skiers competing in the Winter Olympics.

## Athletics

For an island nation with modest sporting infrastructure, track and field events have always been a mainstay in schools and communities with participants in organized events as young as primary school age. In fact, arguably the biggest and best attended annual sporting event in the island's calendar would be the Boys and Girls Championships held at the National Stadium for the various high schools, known popularly as Champs. It is this background that fostered the likes of Merlene Ottey, Juliet Cuthbert, Veronica Campbell-Brown, Shelly-Ann Fraser-Pryce,

Asafa Powell, and, of course, the inimitable Usain Bolt. Many gold medalists who have run for other nations were also born and raised in Jamaica, including Linford Christie, Ben Johnson, and Donovan Bailey. The excitement is palpable on the island when its fastest citizens are set to race in a meet anywhere in the world.

## Soccer

Though lacking in any major historical exploits preceding qualification to the 1998 FIFA World Cup, the "Reggae Boyz," as the country's national men's team are affectionately called, are viewed with expectant hopefulness by Jamaican sport lovers. Having in recent times vanquished longstanding rivals such as the US and Mexican national teams, supporters anticipate victories in the next World Cup.

## Boxing

Champion boxers who have raised the Jamaican flag include Mike McCallum, Trevor Berbick, and Glen Johnson, while noted boxers Lennox Lewis and Frank Bruno, although representing Great Britain, speak fondly of their Jamaican roots.

## Cricket

A nostalgic remnant of British colonialism, cricket is still an ubiquitous sporting activity on any level field throughout the island. Jamaican cricketers play on the regionally federated West Indies Cricket Team (affectionately called "the Windies"), which joins the other island nations of the Caribbean sharing a British colonial past. Though the fortunes of the Windies have drastically fallen since the turn of the 21st century, there was a time when they were the unmistakable rulers of the sport. West Indies cricket did not lose a single international Test series for 15 years from the mid-1970s to the early 1990s. Notable Jamaican cricketers include former Windies captains Michael Holding, Jimmy Adams, and Courtney Walsh, as well as current bad boy of the sport Chris Gayle.

Cricket is Jamaica's national sport.

# Essentials

# Getting There and Around

## ARRIVING BY AIR

Airlines with regular flights from the United States and Canada to Kingston's Norman Manley International Airport include Air Jamaica, Spirit Airlines, JetBlue, Air Canada, American, and Delta. Virgin Atlantic and British Airways offer flights from London to Montego Bay and Kingston. Sangster International Airport in Montego Bay is the most popular entry point for visitors to Jamaica.

Within the Caribbean, Caribbean Airlines offers service to St. Kitts, Barbados, Trinidad and Tobago, and St. Lucia, while Cayman Airways offers service between Jamaica and Grand Cayman. Copa is the only option direct from Latin America, with flights connecting through Panama City from most countries in the region.

Most accommodations can provide transportation from either airport, and the more remote hotels and villas often make an extra effort to help provide transportation for guests.

## ARRANGING TRANSPORTATION

Public transportation is readily available and very affordable for those who are patient and adventurous. Buses run between major cities and towns, and route taxis run between even the smallest villages and their closest transport hubs. The inevitable drawbacks include blaring music, long waits, ripe body odor, and reckless drivers. Car rentals, JUTA charters, and internal flights are expensive but worth it in the right circumstances.

Nothing compares with the freedom of a rental car, and for two or more people looking to explore the island, it can be reasonably affordable. Many visitors are thrown off by the fact that vehicles drive on the left, and if that weren't confusing enough to pose a challenge, abundant deep potholes and dodging the ubiquitous white route taxis careening around every corner leave little time to enjoy the scenery.

Chartering a car and driver is also very expensive; the standard rate of US$100 for the one-hour trip between Montego Bay and Negril is a good indication of typical charges island-wide. A comfortable and affordable coach service, the Knutsford Express, runs twice daily between Kingston and Montego Bay with one-way fare around US$20. Apart from the multiple internal flights that serve the route for US$70, the Knutsford Express is the best option. Public buses and route taxis are the mass transportation option used by most Jamaicans who don't have their own vehicle.

## PUBLIC TRANSPORTATION

It can be challenging to get around Jamaica on public transportation, and you will likely arrive at your destination a bit frazzled by the congested route taxis and buses, dangerously fast driving, and the inevitably loud R&B or dancehall blasting from the speakers. It's important to keep reminding yourself that this is all part of Jamaica's charm.

In and around Kingston, the public bus system is quite functional—with bus stops along all the main roads and the fare under US$1. The two hubs in Kingston are the Half Way Tree Transport Centre and a similar transport center Downtown, south of Coronation Market.

---

**Previous:** rafting on the Martha Brae River; riding horses on the beach.

## Route Taxis

Arriving with luggage or backpacks to hike up to the road and hail down a route taxi is perfectly feasible in Jamaica, even if it does provide amusement for local people. Most taxis will want to be chartered, however, when you are carrying luggage, and others won't stop. This makes chartering a taxi a good idea.

Route taxis are typically white Toyota Corolla station wagons with the origin and destination painted in small letters on the side by the front doors. These cars can be flagged down from the side of the road anywhere along their route, and when not operating as route taxis, will generally offer private charters at greatly inflated rates. Haggling is a must when chartering a car, while routes have fixed rates that are not typically inflated for visitors except in highly touristed areas like Negril or Ocho Rios, or at night, when fares increase.

## Internal Flights

A few airlines operate internal flights around the island that are an affordable option between Kingston and Montego Bay (US$70 one-way) if time is a concern. Routes to smaller, less trafficked destinations are significantly pricier, but for an extended stay with a small group, a charter from Negril to Port Antonio can make sense.

## RENTING A CAR

For those who can afford it and have the confidence and experience, a rental car is by far the best way to get around the island, most importantly for independence. Rentals are expensive by international standards and you should expect to pay no less than US$60 per day for a compact car, plus insurance and fuel. Options for different car rental agencies are included in the destination chapters.

# Visas and Officialdom

U.S. citizens now require a passport to reenter the United States after visiting Jamaica. U.S., Canadian, and EU citizens do not require a visa to enter Jamaica and can stay for three to six months, although the actual length of stay stamped into your passport will be determined by the customs agent upon entry. For extensions, visit the **immigration office** (25 Constant Spring Rd., tel. 876/906-4402 or 876/906-1304) in Half Way Tree.

## EMBASSIES AND CONSULATES

- **Britain** 28 Trafalgar Rd., Kingston 10, tel. 876/510-0700, fax 876/511-0737, bhckingston@cwjamaica.com (general), consular.kingston@fco.gov.uk (consular), ukvisas.kingston@fco.gov.uk (visa)
- **Canada** 3 West King's House Rd., Kingston 10, tel. 876/926-1500 or 876/926-1507, fax 876/511-3491, kngtn@international.gc.ca

- **Cuba** 9 Trafalgar Rd., tel. 876/978-0931 or 876/978-0933, fax 876/978-5372, embacubajam@cwjamaica.com
- **Dominican Republic** 4 Hacienda Way, Norbrook, tel. 876/931-0044, fax 876/925-1057, domeb@cwjamaica.com
- **European Union** 8 Oliver Rd., PO Box 463, Kingston 8, tel. 876/924-6333 or 876/924-6337, fax 876/924-6339
- **France** 13 Hillcrest Ave., tel. 876/978-1297 or 876/978-4881, fax 876/927-4998, frenchembassy@cwjamaica.com
- **Germany** 10 Waterloo Rd., Kingston 10, tel. 876/926-6728 or 876/926-5665, fax 876/929-8282, germanemb@cwjamaica.com
- **Mexico** PCJ Bldg., 36 Trafalgar Rd., tel. 876/926-6891 or 876/926-4242, fax 876/929-7995, embmexj@cwjamaica.com
- **Panama** 34 Annette Crescent, Spanish

Court, Suite 103, tel. 876/924-5235, fax 876/960-1618, embpanamajamaica@mire.gob.pa

- **Spain** 6th Fl., Courtleigh Corporate Centre, 6-8 St. Lucia Ave., tel. 876/929-5555, fax 876/929-8965, jamespa@cwjamaica.com, emb.kingston@mae.es

- **St. Kitts** 11-A Opal Ave., Golden Acres, PO Box 157, Kingston 7, tel. 876/944-3861, fax 876/945-0105, clrharper@yahoo.com

- **Trinidad and Tobago** 60 Knutsford Blvd., tel. 876/926-5730 or 876/926-5739, fax 876/926-5801, kgnhctt@cwjamaica.com

- **United States** 142 Old Hope Rd., tel. 876/702-6000, consularkingst@state.gov (visa/consular), opakgn@state.gov (general)

- **Venezuela** PCJ Bldg., 36 Trafalgar Rd., tel. 876/926-5510 or 876/926-5519, fax 876/926-7442

# Food

Jamaican food is reason enough to visit the island. Home-cooked meals are generally best, so it's worth seeking out an invitation whenever possible. The traditional dishes were developed during the era of slavery and typically include a generous, even overwhelming, serving of starch, and at least a token of meat or seafood protein known historically as "the watchman." In recent years pan-Caribbean fusion has caught on as a new culinary trend, with creative dishes added to the traditional staples.

**Ackee** is a central ingredient of the national dish, ackee and saltfish. The fruit contains dangerous levels of toxic amino acid hypoglycin A until the fruit pods open naturally on the tree, or "dehisce," in horticultural terminology, at which point the yellow fleshy aril surrounding the glossy black seed is safe to eat. Ackee has the consistency and color of scrambled eggs and is generally prepared with onion and rehydrated saltfish. Dried codfish was the original ingredient, which made an important dietary contribution during slavery, when it was shipped from its abundant source off Cape Cod, Massachusetts. Today cod has become scarce and very expensive as a result of overfishing, and the fish is most often

a traditional dish with sautéed ackee, steamed callaloo, boiled yam, fried breadfruit, ripe plantain, and avocado or "pear"

imported from Norway or replaced altogether with other saltfish substitutes.

**Bammy** is derived from the Taino word *guyami,* which was a staple for the Taino. Bammy is made from cassava, or manioc, known in many Spanish-speaking countries as *yuca.* In Jamaica, bammy is either steamed or fried and usually eaten as the starch accompaniment to fish.

**Bun,** or Easter Bun, is a tradition that has become popular enough to last throughout the year, so much so that by Easter there is little novelty left. Bun is typically eaten with yellow cheddar cheese.

**Bulla** is a heavy biscuit made with flour and molasses.

**Callaloo** is a spinach-like green often steamed and served for breakfast, either alone as a side dish or sometimes mixed with saltfish.

**Curry** was brought to Jamaica by indentured Indians and quickly caught on as a popular flavoring for a variety of dishes, most commonly curry goat, but also including curry chicken, conch, shrimp, crab, and lobster. Curry rivals ganja as the most popular contribution from India to Jamaican culture.

**Dumpling** is a round doughy mass that's either boiled or fried, generally to accompany breakfast. When boiled, at the center there is little difference from raw dough. **Spinners** are basically the same thing but rolled between the hands and boiled with conch or corn soup.

**Fish tea** is similar to mannish water except it is made with boiled fish parts.

**Festival** is another common starchy accompaniment to fish and jerk meals, consisting basically of fried dough and corn flour shaped into a slender cylindrical blob.

**Food** refers to any starchy tubers served to accompany a protein, also known as "ground provisions." The term has its roots in the days of slavery when provision grounds were maintained by slaves to ensure an adequate supply of food.

**Jerk** is a seasoning that goes back as far as Jamaica's Taino. The most common jerk dishes are chicken and pork, optimally barbecued using pimento or sweetwood, which gives the meat a delicious smoky flavor complemented by the spicy seasoning that invariably contains hot scotch bonnet pepper.

**Mannish water** is a popular broth with supposed aphrodisiac properties made of goat parts not suitable for other dishes (the head, ears, testicles) and cooked with green banana, spinners, and seasoned with pepper and sometimes rum.

**Oxtail** is a popular dish.

**Provisions** are an inexpensive and important part of the Jamaican diet. The most commonly consumed starches include rice, yam, cassava, breadfruit, dumpling (fried or boiled balls of flour), boiled green banana, or fried plantain.

**Rice-and-peas** is the most ubiquitous staple served with any main dish. "Peas" in Jamaica are what the rest of the English-speaking world refers to as beans and usually consist of either kidney beans sparsely distributed among the white rice, or gungo peas, cooked with coconut milk and seasonings.

**Saltfish** was originally codfish that was shipped from New England in large quantities, with salt used as a preservative. It became a protein staple that helped sustain the slave trade. Despite the widespread use of refrigeration today, saltfish continues to be a sought-after item, even as the stocks of cod have been depleted from the Grand Banks of the North Atlantic and other salted fish has been substituted in its place.

Fresh seafood is readily available throughout Jamaica, though fish, shrimp, and lobster are typically the most expensive items on any menu. Fish is generally either red snapper or parrot fish prepared steamed with okra, escoveitch style, or fried. **Escoveitch** fish comes from the Spanish tradition of *escaveche,* with vinegar used in the preparation. In Jamaica, scotch bonnet pepper and vinegar-infused onion is usually served with fried escoveitch fish.

The most common Jamaican lobsters are actually marine crayfish belonging to the family Palinuridae *(Palinurus argus)*. Commonly known as the spiny lobster, two species are widely eaten, and, while noticeably different, are every bit as delicious as lobster caught in more northern waters.

Popular breakfast items include **hominy porridge** and **beef liver** in addition to ackee and saltfish, typically eaten on Sunday.

## COFFEE

Jamaican coffee is among the most prized in the world, Blue Mountain Coffee being the most coveted variety on the island. The Jamaica Blue Mountain Coffee name is a registered trademark, and only a select group of farmers are authorized to market their beans with it. Some of the best Blue Mountain Coffee is grown on Old Tavern Estate. Mavis Bank Coffee Factory sells under the Jablum brand and is also of good quality.

Jamaica's coffee industry dates to the Haitian Revolution, when many farmers in the neighboring island fled to Jamaica out of fear for Haiti's future prospects. The cloud forests of the Blue Mountains were found to provide ideal growing conditions that allow the beans to mature slowly, giving the coffee its unique, full-bodied flavor.

## RUM

Since the days of old when pirates stormed from port to port pillaging and plundering their way to riches, Jamaica has been an important consumer of rum. Rum production in Jamaica was an important component of the colonial economy under the British, and Jamaican rum is still highly regarded today. There are two varieties of Jamaican rum, white and aged. Aged rum has a reddish-brown tint and is smoother than white rum. Jamaica's high-end brand is Appleton Estate Jamaica Rum, owned by Italy's Gruppo Campari and produced by J. Wray & Nephew in the parish of St. Elizabeth and at its Kingston distillery. Worthy Park Estate in St. Catherine has been attempting to rival J. Wray & Nephew's White Overproof Rum with its Rum Bar Rum brand in recent years.

It is said that the number of rum bars in Jamaica is matched only by the number of churches, the two institutions equally ubiquitous in even the smallest hamlets across the island.

## SAUCES AND SPICES

Jamaica has for centuries been a great producer of spices, from pimento, known commonly as allspice, to scotch bonnet peppers and annatto. The island's historical reputation as a source of flavorings gave birth to several successful brands sold the world over, from Pickapeppa Sauce, produced in Shooters Hill, Manchester, to Busha Browne's Jamaican sauces, jellies, chutneys, and condiments, made in Kingston, and Walkerswood Jamaican Jerk Seasoning, produced in St. Ann. Belcour Blue Mountain Preserves continues this tradition with delicious sweet and savory product to spice up virtually any dish.

# Conduct and Customs

## ETIQUETTE

Manners are taken very seriously in Jamaica, although there's a lot of variation when it comes to individual concern over proper etiquette. Some people have impeccable manners while others have none. To a more exaggerated extent than elsewhere in the world, etiquette, and speech in Jamaica are perceived as directly correlated to upbringing, socioeconomic class, and social status. It's therefore important to be aware of the impression you make, especially with language. Cussing, for instance, is scorned by many educated Jamaicans, especially devout Christians. Meanwhile, many people couldn't care less about the impression they make and speak quite freely and colorfully.

Photographing people in Jamaica can be rude and should be done only after asking permission. That said, media professionals are highly respected, and if you are walking around with a camera, people will often ask you to take their picture regardless of whether they will ever see it. It makes a nice gesture to give people photos of themselves and is a great way to make friends. Photographing people without asking permission will often result in a request for monetary compensation. Asking permission often gets the same response. If the picture is worth it, placate your subject with whatever you think it's worth. Money is rarely turned down.

## TIPPING

Tipping is common practice in Jamaica to a varying degree of formality, depending on the venue, from leaving a "smalls" for the man who watched or washed your car while you were at the club, to more serious sums for the staff at your villa.

Many of the more formal restaurants include a service charge in the bill, in which case any further tip should be discretionary based on the quality of service provided. At inexpensive eateries, tipping is rare, while at the more upscale restaurants, it is expected. The amount to leave for a good meal at a mid-range to expensive restaurant follows international standards, between 10 percent and 20 percent depending on the attention you received.

Most all-inclusive hotels have banned tipping to discourage the soliciting that makes their guests uncomfortable. Where no-tipping policies are in place, it's best to adhere to them. At lodging-only hotels, a US$5-10 tip for the bellhop is a welcome gesture.

Staffed villas usually state that guests are to leave the staff a tip equal to 10-15 percent of the total rental cost. This consideration should be divided equally among the staff who were present during your stay and given to each person individually.

Tipping is also common practice at spas, where a US$20 bill on top of the cost of treatment for the individual who provided the service will be well received. Tour guides at attractions, even when included in the cost of the tour, greatly appreciate a token tip.

# All-Inclusive Resorts

Jamaica was a pioneer in the all-inclusive formula, which has since spread the world over. The all-inclusive phenomenon has only accelerated in recent years with the arrival of several new chains, including Iberostar, Secrets, Excellence Resorts, Fiesta Group, Riu, Karisma, Meliá, Zoetry, and Principe. The well-established home-grown options include Butch Stewart's Sandals and Beaches Resorts, Lee Issa's Couples Resorts, and his cousin John Issa's SuperClubs brand Hedonism.

Many smaller options have started offering all-inclusive packages that make sense if you're not looking to explore the different food options in the area you're visiting, and most villas offer an all-inclusive option as well. At the right place, a package deal can certainly be worth it.

Smaller all-inclusive accommodations include the Island Outpost properties, as well as some of the island's best cottages and villas. Small properties that offer an all-inclusive plan are indicated in the listings. All of the all-inclusive resorts offer multiple pricing options within each location, which typically start at around US$150 pp per day and go up to US$400 pp for the high-end properties in the winter season.

Here's a look at some of the most popular options:

## COUPLES

Easily at the top of the all-inclusive options, Couples Resorts benefits from Lee Issa's hands-on approach and the exquisite taste of his wife, Jane, who has been instrumental in ensuring tasteful decor and excellent food. Couples operates under the motto, "Couples who play together stay together," and plenty of options are offered for "play," including nude beaches at the Sans Souci and Couples Tower Isle properties. The other two properties, Couples Swept Away and Couples Negril, are within a few miles of each other, on Long Bay and Bloody Bay, respectively. Lee Issa is the son of Abe Issa, who pioneered Jamaica's tourism industry in the late 1940s and founded the first Couples Resort in 1978.

## RIU

If the Spanish retained any bitterness about losing the island to the British in the 17th century, perhaps it is in the 21st century when they will have their revenge on the established all-inclusive resorts. Spanish hotel group Riu aims to undercut across the island. Its owners entered the market by setting up hotels beside Sandals properties in Ocho Rios, and virtually taking over the whole of Bloody Bay in Negril. A fourth Riu Resort was built in Montego Bay adjacent to Sandals Royal Caribbean.

Riu offers some of the most competitive all-inclusive rates in Jamaica, attracting principally cost-minded U.S. tourists. Unfortunately the quality of food at Riu Resorts leaves something to be desired in the "fine dining" à la carte restaurants, with long lines in the morning just to reserve a table. The American-style fare in the buffet dining areas is mediocre at best. Rooms at Riu are well appointed and comfortable.

## SANDALS AND BEACHES

Owned by Gordon "Butch" Stewart, the Sandals chain attracts couples, and the Beaches resorts cater to families. Newly built or refurbished properties like Sandals Whitehouse in Westmoreland and Sandals Royal Caribbean in Montego Bay contrast with the more mid-range properties in Montego Bay, Sandals Carlyle and Sandals Montego Bay. The quality of each varies with the price point, some serving premium brand liquors and others offering a more basic package. Be sure to know what to expect, as the baseline of quality varies greatly among locations.

Royal Caribbean is easily the best Sandals property, with a small private island just offshore and easy access to Montego Bay and its attractions. Sandals Whitehouse is the newest property, but it is also the most remote, and many guests find themselves too isolated for comfort when it comes to seeing Jamaica beyond the walled compound.

# Travel Tips

## VOLUNTEER OPPORTUNITIES

While work is often the last thing on people's minds on a trip to Jamaica, volunteering can be an immensely rewarding experience. It inevitably puts visitors in direct contact with real working people as opposed to the forced smiles associated with the tourism industry. Several church groups offer volunteer opportunities, while there are also several secular options.

**Dream Jamaica** (contact programs director Adrea Simmons, programs@dreamjamaica.org, www.dreamjamaica.org), one of Jamaica's best volunteer programs, operates summer programs in Kingston that brings volunteer professionals from abroad and connects high school students in career-driven summer programs with the local business community. Dream Jamaica seeks local professionals who can commit four hours per month to mentoring high school students, and program coordinators and assistance from Jamaica or abroad for full-time volunteer work over the six week program each summer.

**Blue Mountain Project Jamaica** (contact service learning program coordinator Haley Madson, U.S. tel. 920/229-1829, www.bluemountainproject.org) is a volunteer organization focused on the Hagley Gap community in the Blue Mountains that places visitors to Jamaica in homestays and coordinates volunteer work in any number of socioeconomic development projects it oversees, like establishing health clinics, art camps, adult education, basic infrastructure, and ecological projects embodying the group's "Educating and Empowering" tag line. Volunteers pay US$79 per night for a minimum of a week, which covers lodging, meals, and transportation. Longer volunteer stints are rewarded with discounted rates.

The **U.S. Peace Corps** (www.peacecorps.gov) is quite active in Jamaica but generally requires an extensive application process, offering no opportunity for spontaneous or temporary volunteer work on the island. Nevertheless, Americans looking to make a contribution to sensible development programs have found Jamaica a challenging and rewarding place to work with the Peace Corps.

## ACCESS FOR TRAVELERS WITH DISABILITIES

Travelers with disabilities should not be turned off by the lack of infrastructure on the island to accommodate special needs, but it is important to inquire exhaustively about the facilities available. Most of the all-inclusive resorts have facilities to accommodate wheelchairs and the like, but outside developed tourist areas, a visit will not be without its challenges.

## TRAVELING WITH CHILDREN

Despite the stereotypes associated with Jamaica, seen by many who have never visited as a hedonistic party land or a gun-slinging Wild West, the island is a fascinating and engaging place for children. Beyond the obvious attraction of its beaches, Jamaica has a wealth of attractions that make learning fun, from rainforest and mountain hikes teeming with wildlife to farm tours that offer visitors a sampling of seasonal fruits. The activities available to engage children are endless. What makes the island an especially great destination for families is the love showered on children generally in Jamaica. Nannies are readily available virtually everywhere and can be easily arranged by inquiring at any lodging, not just at those that tout it as a unique service.

## WOMEN TRAVELERS

Jamaica is a raw and aggressive society, with little regard for political correctness and little awareness of what is considered sexual harassment in the United States and Europe. Flirtation is literally a way of life, and women should not be alarmed if they find they are attracting an unusual degree of attention compared with what they are used to back home. On the street, catcalls are common, even when a woman is accompanied by her boyfriend or husband; in nightclubs women are the main attraction, and dancing can be very sexual. Both on the street and in the club it's important to keep your wits about you and communicate interest or disinterest as clearly as possible. It is more the exception than the norm for men to persist after women have clearly communicated disinterest.

Jamaica depends overwhelmingly on the tourist dollar, and the authorities generally make an extra effort to ensure visitor safety. Nonetheless, if you are a woman traveling alone, it's best to exercise caution and avoid uncomfortable encounters. Suitors will inevitably offer any and every kind of enticing service: Accept only what you are completely comfortable with, and keep in mind that local men might make romantic advances because they're motivated by financial interest.

## GAY AND LESBIAN TRAVELERS

Jamaica is notoriously and blatantly anti-gay. Many Jamaicans will defend their antigay stance with religious arguments, and many reggae artists use antigay lyrics as an easy sell, often instigating violence against gay men both metaphorically and literally. Some of these artists—like Buju Banton, who had a hit that suggested killing gay people—have toned down their rhetoric following tour cancellations abroad owing to their prejudice, while others, like Sizzla, continue undaunted.

On the whole Jamaica is a tolerant society, but it is best for gay and lesbian travelers not to display their orientation publicly as a precautionary measure. Many all-inclusive resorts have recently altered their policies to allow for gay travelers, and still other high-end resorts have a noticeably gay lean.

# Sustainable Tourism

## COMMUNITY TOURISM

The most important thing to remember on any visit to a foreign country is that your money is your most substantive demonstration of support. Jamaica is an expensive place to live, and foreign currency is the chief economic driver. The benefit, or lack thereof, that tourism brings to the island is dependent on where the incoming money ends up. Though rock-bottom all-inclusive packages are an easy way to control your vacation spending, it should be noted that the money that flows to these businesses is not widely distributed and typically ends up lining the pockets of a few individuals. What's more, large resorts often pay their workers a pittance.

Jamaica has gone through several different eras of tourism development dating back to the booming banana trade in the late 1800s.

Until the 1960s, Jamaica remained a niche destination for the early yacht set, which later became the jet set. In the late 1960s and early 1970s the hippie movement discovered Jamaica, and large groups would tour around on motorbikes, reveling in the laid-back lifestyle and plentiful herb. Montego Bay was the upscale destination on the island, with Port Antonio the playground of movie stars and Negril a newly discovered fishing beach only just connected by road to the rest of Hanover parish. In those days the numbers of visitors were low and, outside Montego Bay, the environmental impact of tourism was negligible.

Then came the all-inclusive resorts, the largest of which, Sunset Jamaica Grande, had 750 rooms by 2006. Since then, several new hotels have been built along the North Coast with over 1,000 rooms. The water resources required by these facilities puts a huge strain on the environment, as does wastewater, which is often poorly or minimally treated before being dumped into the sea. The enormous demand for food at these establishments generally is insufficiently met by local producers. These hotels cite inconsistency in the local market as a factor in their heavy reliance on imported goods.

Perhaps the best way to make a positive impact on a visit to Jamaica is by promoting "community tourism" by staying in smaller, locally run establishments and eating at a variety of restaurants rather than heeding the fear tactics that keep so many visitors inside gated hotels. Treasure Beach in St. Elizabeth parish is a mecca for community tourism, where the few mid-size hotels are far outnumbered by boutique guesthouses and villas, many of which are locally owned.

# ENVIRONMENTAL ISSUES

In the past 10 years the Jamaican government has opened the country to an incursion from multinational hotel groups that are some of the most blatant culprits of environmental destruction. Ever-larger all-inclusive resorts are covering what were a few years ago Jamaica's remaining untouched stretches of coastline. The absence of beaches has not inhibited developers from making their own, at incalculable environmental cost to the protective coral reefs and marinelife they support along much of the coast. When scuba diving and snorkeling along Jamaica's reefs, make your impact minimal by not touching the coral.

## Bauxite Mining

The bauxite industry is an important foreign exchange earner for Jamaica, but the environmental costs are clear. The Ewarton Aluminum Plant in St. Ann is noticeable by its stench for kilometers around, and from the heights of Mandeville several bauxite facilities visibly scar the landscape. Discovery Bay and Ocho Rios have important export terminals, as does Port Kaiser in St. Elizabeth

with another bauxite port, and Rocky Point in Clarendon and Port Esquivel in St. Catherine.

## Litter

Environmental education in Jamaica is seriously lacking. Environmental awareness has only recently been directly linked to the island's tourism economy by some of the more responsible tourism groups. The difference in sanitation and upkeep between the leisure destinations frequented principally by Jamaicans rather than foreign travelers is marked. Choice spots like Salt River in Clarendon are littered with trash, while other popular local spots like Bluefields Beach Park in Westmoreland make greater efforts to clean up after their patrons. Regardless of how senseless it may seem to take a green stance when it comes to litter in the face of gross negligence on the part of Jamaicans themselves, it's important to be aware of the fact that Jamaicans watch visitors very carefully: Make a point of not trashing the country, even if you seem to be up against insurmountable odds.

## Water Table Salination

Several coastal areas suffer salination of the water table when water is extracted more rapidly than it is replenished. While Jamaica is fortunate to have high rainfall in the east and abundant water generally, there will likely be an increasing problem in drier northwest coast areas, where new all-inclusive resorts are being built. Wherever you end up staying, the best way to lessen your impact on finite water resources is by not taking long showers and by heeding the requests made at many of the more responsible and proactive hotels to reuse towels during your stay.

## Deforestation

Despite the known harm it causes and the ensuing potential for erosion, slash-and-burn agriculture remains the predominant means of smallholder cultivation in rural areas. While significant portions of land have been designated as protected areas across Jamaica, pressure on the environment, especially around tourism boom towns like Ocho Rios, where little planning preceded the influx of workers from other parishes, is leaving the water supply under threat and causing erosion where forestlands on steep inclines are cut for ramshackle housing settlements.

# Health and Safety

## HEAT

Jamaica is a tropical country with temperatures rising well above 38°C (100°F) in the middle of summer. Sensible precautions should be taken, especially for those not accustomed to being under the hot sun. A wide-brimmed hat is advisable for days at the beach, and a high-SPF sunblock is essential. Being in the water exacerbates rather than mitigates the harmful rays, creating a risk for over-exposure even while swimmers may be unaware of the sun's effects—until the evening, when it becomes impossible to lay down on a burned back. While many hotels offer air-conditioning, just as many have been constructed with cooling in mind to obviate the need for air-conditioning. Louvered windows with a fresh sea breeze or ceiling fan can be just as soothing as air-conditioning while not putting strain on Jamaica's antiquated and inefficient electrical grid. In the summer months, air-conditioning is a well-appreciated luxury, especially for sleeping. If you are traveling between June and September, consider spending some time in the Blue Mountains, where there's a cool breeze year-round.

## SEXUALLY TRANSMITTED DISEASES

Jamaican culture celebrates love, romance, and intimacy. Keeping multiple sexual partners is common, and infidelity is generally treated as an inevitable reality by both men and women. The obvious danger in this attitude is reflected in a high incidence of STDs on the island, including underreported figures on HIV infection and AIDS. If you engage in sexual activity while in Jamaica, like anywhere else, condoms are indispensable and the best preventative measure you can take.

## CRIME

Unfortunately, criminal acts are a daily reality for a large number of Jamaicans, from the petty crimes committed by those who find themselves marginalized from the formal economy to high-rolling politicians and drug dons who control the flow of capital, illegal substances, and arms on the island. In sharp contrast to other developing nations with high poverty rates, and perhaps contrary to what one might expect, random armed assault on individuals and muggings in Jamaica are quite rare. The crime that is most ingrained and more or less the order of the day is devious, petty thievery. Almost everybody who has stayed in Jamaica for any length of time has experienced the disappearance of personal items, a wallet or perfume or a cell phone, one of the most prized items. Stay vigilant and take every possible precaution, and you will likely have no problem.

## BRIBERY

Officially bribery is illegal, and people offering a bribe to an officer of the law can be arrested and tried. It's generally quite obvious when a police officer is seeking a payoff. Phrases like "Do something for me nuh," "Gimme a lunch money," or "Buy me a drink" get the message across. Do not try to bribe police when it is not solicited; there are officers who will take offense or use it to compound the severity of the offense or the required bribe.

Within the Jamaican police force, the **Office of Professional Responsibility**

(OPR, tel. 876/967-1909, 876/967-4347, or 876/924-9059) is tasked with routing out corruption. The office is based in Kingston but has officers across the island. Be sure to take note of the badge number of the officer in question if you are planning to make a report.

## DRUGS

Jamaica has a well-deserved reputation as a marijuana haven. Contrary to what many visitors might believe, marijuana is classified as an illegal drug. Practically speaking, however, marijuana use is not criminalized and it's impossible to walk through Half Way Tree in Kingston or Sam Sharpe Square in Mobay without getting a whiff of ganja, as the herb is known locally.

Marijuana has been decriminalized and possession is not an arrestable offense, though possession of up to 55 grams (2 ounces) carries a civil fine of about US$10. Police have been known to prey on travelers who are not familiar with the law and threaten arrest if a handsome bribe is not paid. Should you experience such intimidation, remain calm and explain that you are familiar with the laws covering marijuana possession. It's not generally a good idea to entertain bribes, but some travelers caught in this situation have found that US$20 can go a long way in preventing discomfort for all parties involved. Possession of over 55 grams (2 ounces) is considered dealing and is still a criminal offense subject to arrest and arraignment. All other drugs are illegal and you will be arrested if caught.

Beyond ganja, Jamaica also has a well-deserved reputation as a transshipment point for cocaine originating in Colombia. Crack addiction has been a problem in some coastal communities where cargo has inadvertently washed ashore. While marijuana use is tolerated on the island due to its widespread consumption and the Rastafarian culture, which incorporates its use into religious practices as a sacrament, there is no valid reason to use cocaine or any other hard drug in Jamaica, despite offers that will inevitably arise on a walk along Seven-Mile Beach in Negril.

# Information and Services

## MONEY

Prices throughout the book are converted to U.S. dollars as the best indicator of cost. Most establishments not heavily trafficked by travelers perform most, if not all, transactions in Jamaican dollars. In tourist hubs like Negril, Montego Bay, and Ocho Rios, as well as in establishments catering exclusively to travelers, menus will show prices in U.S. dollars. The U.S. dollar tends to be more stable and is worthwhile as a currency of reference, but most establishments will not use the official or bank exchange rate and set their exchange rate considerably lower as a means of skimming a bit more off the top. It usually pays to buy Jamaican dollars at a *cambio,* or currency trading house, for everyday transactions. While walking around with large amounts of cash is never advisable, carrying enough for a night out does not present a considerable risk. Credit cards, accepted in most well-established businesses, typically incur heavy foreign-transaction fees that will show up on your statement as a percentage of every transaction, and can quickly add up.

The best way to access funds in Jamaica is by using an ATM with your normal NYCE, Maestro, or Cirrus debit card. "Express kidnappings" (where victims are taken to a cash machine to withdraw the maximum on their accounts) are not especially common in Jamaica, and the little effort involved in canceling a debit card makes the ease of 24-hour access well worth the risk of losing it or getting it stolen. Traveler's checks are a good back-up option and can be cashed at most hotels for a small fee. Taking large amounts of cash to Jamaica is not advisable, as it is likely to disappear. Scotiabank offers Jamaican or U.S. currency from many of its ATMs, although foreign bank fees can run as high as 6 percent of the amount withdrawn.

## ELECTRICITY

Jamaica operates on 110 volts, similar to the United States, and uses U.S.-style plugs and sockets, but electricity is at 50 hertz, which shouldn't matter unless you bring a device with a motor. Most electronics are designed to adapt automatically. Power outages are frequent in some areas, but seldom at the resorts. Most tourism establishments have backup generators.

## COMMUNICATIONS AND MEDIA
### Telephones

Fixed-line telephony in Jamaica was until recently a monopoly controlled by Cable & Wireless (C&W). As the Internet has become more widely available, voice over Internet protocol (VoIP) telephony has become increasingly important as a means of communicating with the outside world. Many households now enjoy this inexpensive way to keep in touch with family members abroad.

C&W was the first mobile phone provider before it was challenged by Digicel, which competes aggressively in mobile, broadband, and TV. Both C&W and Digicel operate on GSM networks and sell prepaid SIM cards. The country's two mobile operators have roaming agreements with select carriers in the United States; roaming fees often are such that it makes sense to buy a prepaid SIM card locally (US$5). Prepaid phone credit is sold in different increments, starting at about US$0.50.

The cellular providers penalize customers when calling outside their own network, so many Jamaicans carry both C&W and Digicel phones to avoid out-of-network calling. Similarly, calling landlines from cell phones is more expensive, as is calling cell phones from landlines.

The 876 country code is never dialed for calls within the country; to call abroad, dial 011 and then the country code, area code, and number.

### Radio

Kingston has some of the best radio stations anywhere, and it's not just reggae you'll find on the airwaves. Reggae developed with the help of radio, as young musicians were inspired by American music of the 1950s and 1960s, adapting the songs with a distinct Jamaican flavor. Radio stations of note include RJR, Power 106, Irie FM (which has been referred to as the daily soundtrack of the island), Fame FM, and Zip FM. Radio West broadcasts from Montego Bay, while KLAS FM is based in Mandeville and Irie FM in Ocho Rios. Radio Mona (93 FM) broadcasts from the University of the West Indies at Mona. Hits 92 FM is a good station in Kingston for a wide range of contemporary music, from dancehall to hip-hop and R&B.

Radio broadcasting in Jamaica dates from World War II, when an American resident, John Grinan, gave his shortwave station to the government to comply with wartime regulations. From wartime programming of one hour weekly, the station quickly expanded to four hours daily, including cultural programming. Radio had a key impact on the development of Jamaican popular music in the 1940s and 1950s as the only means of disseminating new musical styles coming mainly from the United States.

### Television

Jamaica's main television stations are Television Jamaica (TVJ, www.televisionjamaica.com), formerly the Jamaica Broadcast Corporation (JBC); CVM (www.cvmtv.com); Reggae Entertainment Television (RETV); and Jamaica News Network (JNN, www.jnnntv.com). In 2006, TVJ acquired both JNN and RETV, consolidating its leadership in both news and entertainment programming on the island. Hype is an entertaining competitor to RETV with music video countdowns, artist interviews, and the latest happenings in the local music industry.

## MAPS AND VISITOR INFORMATION

GPS devices provided by car rental agencies and apps like google maps and Open Street Maps generally afford the best directions and orientation, though some of the more obscure roads may not appear or be incorrectly identified. The city maps sold by the National Land Agency are less detailed and lack many road names. The Land Agency does have good topographical maps, sold for a hefty US$7 per sheet. Twenty sheets cover the whole island, and the maps can be obtained on CD. Handy tourism-oriented business brochures are available free of charge at the chamber of commerce offices in Ocho Rios, Montego Bay, and Negril.

## WEIGHTS AND MEASURES

One of the most frustrating things in Jamaica is the lack of a consistent convention when it comes to measurements. On the road, where the majority of cars are imported from Japan and odometers read in kilometers, many of the signs are in miles, while the newer ones are in kilometers. The mixed use of metric in weights and measurements is also a problem complicating life in Jamaica, with "chains" (20 meters/66 feet) used commonly when referring to distances, liters used at the gas pump, and pounds used for weight.

## TIME

Jamaica is on Greenwich mean time minus five hours, which coincides with North America's Eastern standard time in winter and the central time zone in summer. Given the nominal difference in day length throughout the year at Jamaica's latitude, the country doesn't observe daylight saving time.

# Resources

## Glossary

Jamaican Patois is a creative and ever-evolving English dialect rooted in the mélange of African and European cultures that together make up Jamaica's identity. Irish, English, and Scottish accents are clearly present, as is the influence of Spanish, with many words also of African origin. Patois carries a thick and warm lilt that can be very difficult to understand for those unaccustomed to hearing it. After relaxing your ears for a few weeks, however, Jamaican talk begins to make perfect sense.

**Babylon:** used by Rastafarians to refer to any evil and oppressive system; also used to reference the police

**badman:** a thug or gangster

**badmind:** corrupt mentality; a scheming person, as in, "dem badmind, e-e-eh?" (can be used as a noun, adjective or verb)

**bakra:** a plantation overseer, often used to express resentment toward someone acting in an authoritarian manner

**baldhead:** used by Rastafarians to refer to non-Rasta black persons, in a derogatory sense if they consider them anti-Rasta

**bangarang:** when hell breaks loose

**bankra:** basket (of West African Twi origin)

**bare:** uninhibitedly, solely; as in, "That boy is giving me attitude, bare attitude."

**bashment:** a party; celebration; any form of excitement

**batty:** backside or derriere

**battyman:** a gay man

**big up:** used to show respect; a shout-out, as in, "big up to all mi fans." (used mostly as a verb but also as a noun)

**blenda:** blender; a mixed-up situation rife with confusion

**blessed:** can be used as a greeting, shortened from proclamations like "Blessed love!"

**blood:** used as a greeting between close friends considered like family, as in "wha'apen blood?"

**blouse and skirt:** an exclamation, similar to "Wow!"

**bly:** a chance or opportunity; to be let off the hook

**bombo claat:** an expletive; sometimes used without the "claat" as a less vulgar exclamation

**boops:** a man or woman who is only in a relationship for material gain; a user (as in, "boops you out")

**boots:** condom

**brawta:** an extra something thrown into a deal when the haggling is done, a bonus

**bredda:** brother. Used in referring to a close friend, as in "Yes, mi bredda!"

**bredren:** brethren, used when referring to a close friend, as in "mi bredren dem."

**brownin:** a light-skinned black woman

**buck up:** meet or run into someone

**buddy:** male genitalia

**bruk:** broken or broke, meaning not having any money

**bruk out:** to let loose and be free

**bulla:** a heavy biscuit made with flour and molasses

**buss:** burst or bust out, as in a career break

**bway:** a boy

**cha:** a versatile exclamation that can indicate disgust or astonishment; also written "cho"

**chalice:** a water pipe used to smoke ganja

**clash:** a battle; often used in the context of a sound clash, where different sound systems or artists face off

**chi chi:** a termite

**collie:** marijuana

**copacetic:** usually shortened to copacet: cool, nice, criss

**cotch:** to rest or lean up against; to brace something, as in the tire of a car to keep it from rolling; also used to say where you stay or spend the night

**craven:** greedy

**crawle:** pen, likely derived from the corral where animals were kept, such as a hog crawle or turtle crawle

**criss:** nice (crisp)

**dads:** used as a show of respect, as in "Yes, mi dads"

**dawta:** when used my Rastafarians, can refer to any young woman

**deejay:** a dancehall rapper

**degge-degge:** small or flimsy, as in "$5 for this degge-degge roll?!"

**deh:** to be at, as in "wheh yuh deh?"

**deh pon:** doing or thinking about doing, as in "Mi deh pon a part-time work"

**dehso:** there; over there

**don:** from the Italian usage, a honcho or area leader

**downpress:** to suppress (a play on the word oppress, where the "op" which sounds like up is changed to "down")

**dread:** a derogatory term used for someone who wears locks; also used to describe hardship, as in "The time getting dread."

**duppy:** a ghost

**e-e-eh:** an inflection used at the end of a phrase to denote a casual query of consensus, as in "It's pretty, e-e-eh . . . " ("It's pretty, isn't it?")

**endz:** a home or somewhere where someone spends a lot of time, like a hang-out spot, as in "Mi deh pon di endz."

**face:** to demonstrate interest

**flex:** used negatively, to show off or profile; used positively, to relax or take a trip

**forward:** come or arrive, as in "Mi soon forward."

**front:** genitalia

**galist:** a womanizer

**ginnal:** a con artist or hustler, either male or female

**give bun (burn):** to cheat (on your spouse)

**grind:** pelvic gyrations central to popular dance; also interchangeable with having sex

**groundation:** a Nyabinghi session of drumming that can last for days, usually held around a significant date in the Rasta calendar, such as Selassie's birthday or Ethiopian Christmas

**gwaan:** go on, as in "wha gwaan?" ("What's going on?")

**gweh:** go away, as in "Gweh nuh, tek weh ya self!"

**gyal:** girl; tends to be construed as somewhat derogatory

**haffi:** have to, must

**herb:** marijuana

**higgler:** a trader in the market; also small-scale importers who bring goods to sell in Jamaica from Panama

**high-grade:** top-quality marijuana

**hush:** an expression of sympathy

**I and I:** the Rastafarian substitute for "me," referring to the individual's inseparability from the divine creator

**idren:** used like "bredren"

**irie:** to feel nice or high

**ital:** natural, derived from "vital"

**jacket:** a child born outside an established relationship that is obviously from a different father

**Jah:** Rastafarian term for the Almighty, derived from Jehovah in the Old Testament

**John Crow:** turkey vulture, buzzard *(Cathartes aura)*

**jook:** to stick; to prick; to knock; a jooking stick is used to knock ackee or mangoes off a tree.

**junjo:** mold or fungus; also a type of mushroom once used as a meat substitute

**leggo:** let go; leave alone

**likkle:** little, as in "a likkle more" for "See you later."

**lyme:** to hang out; also used as a noun for a laid-back gathering or party

**macca:** thorn, as in "Di macca jook mi." ("The thorn pricked me.")

**mampy:** a heavy-set woman

**massive:** shortened formed for a large gathering of people or a collective, as in "the Kingston massive"

**mawga:** meager; skinny; thin

**medi or medz:** meditation, as in to "hold a medi" or "hold a medz"; to ponder or meditate on something

**"Mi credit run out":** what people will say when they place a phone call before hanging up so that the recipient will have to call back and pay for the call

**natty:** a person who wears dreadlocks in their hair

**nuff:** enough, or a lot

**nyam:** to eat, as in "Mi a nyam some food" ("I'm going to eat"); thought to be derived from a West African word

**Obeah:** Jamaican black magic or Voodoo

**par:** hang out with, shortened from spar

**pickney:** a child; children; derived from piccaninny

**pop-down:** tired; destroyed; shabby; disheveled, referring to a place or person

**pum pum:** female genitalia

**raahtid:** an exclamation, such as "Wow!"

**ragamuffin:** a serious dude, used in referring to a true soldier, Rasta thug, or rude boy

**ramp:** a Jamaican pronunciation of romp; to play with, as in "Mi nah ramp wid dem people!"

**ram-up:** rammed or ram-packed with people

**raas:** a versatile expletive, referring to your behind

**ras:** from Amharic, meaning "prince," as in Ras Tafari

**rat-bat:** a bat; *bat* alone usually refers to a moth.

**reason:** to converse; hold a discussion; a reasoning

**red:** used in reference to people of a ruddy complexion, typical of the people in St. Elizabeth parish

**respect:** a greeting or acknowledgment of appreciation

**riddim:** rhythm

**roots:** used about drinks, refers to herbal tonics and potions; used about music, refers to

something original: roots reggae is the early form of the music considered the most traditional and authentic.

**rude boy:** a badass, as popularized by Jimmy Cliff's character in the film *The Harder They Come*

**runnings:** the way things operate, as in "Him don't understand di runnings roun' yahso."

**selector:** a disc jockey

**sell-off:** exclamation derived from *sold out,* as in something in high demand; used in the context of something that's immensely popular, as in "Di dance sell-off!"

**screw face:** an expression of bitterness

**sensi, sensimilla:** marijuana, adapted from Spanish *sin semilla,* meaning without seeds

**session:** party

**set girls:** rival groups of female dancers who would sing and dance and compete in matching costumes against other such groups during the colonial period

**sistren:** a sister, the female version of "bredren" (brethren)

**skank:** to dance, especially to ska music

**skettel:** a prostitute

**skylark:** to laze away one's days rather than work or go to school

**slack:** loose; degrading; debauched, as in "pure slackness a gwaan."

**soon come:** used to say, "I'll be there in a bit" or "I'll be back in a bit." This is a very loose phrase, and could mean in a few minutes, days, or years.

**sound system:** often referred to as simply a "sound"

**spliff, skliff:** a marijuana cigarette or joint

**stageshow:** a musical concert typically featuring performances by many artists

**stoosh:** snooty, uptown

**swims:** shrimp

**tek:** to take

**tun up:** turn up, meaning "great" or "on fire"

**unnu:** you (plural), "one" in the third-person sense

**up:** a term used to voice solidarity or support

**vex:** (can sound like "bex" in the Jamaican pronunciation) upset, angry

**wine:** wind; gyrating, sexually suggestive pelvic motion at the heart of the bumping and grinding seen in a typical dance club

**wood:** male genitalia

**wuk:** work, as in "wuk mi a wuk." Also used in a sexual sense, as in "you wuk mi out."

**wutless or wukless:** worthless

**yard/yaad:** home, as in "Mi deh mi yard" ("I'm at home"); also used to refer to Jamaica

**yahso:** here, as in "Yahso mi deh." ("I am here.")

**yuzimi:** "you see me?" as in "Do you understand?" or "Do you see what I'm saying?"

**Zion:** the holy land, as referred to by Rastafarians

# Suggested Reading

## HISTORY

Besson, Jean. *Martha Brae's Two Histories: European Expansion and Caribbean Culture-Building in Jamaica.* The University of North Carolina Press, 2002.

Bryan, Patrick E. *Jamaica: The Aviation Story.* Arawak Publications, 2006. An interesting account of aviation and the role air travel has played in Jamaica's modern history.

Buckley, David. *The Right to Be Proud: A Brief Guide to Jamaican Heritage Sites.* Neil Persadsingh, 2005. This book covers select sites from those listed by the Jamaica National Heritage trust. It is a good coffee-table book with interesting details.

De Lisser, Herbert G. *White Witch of Rose Hall.* Humanity Press, 1982. A fantastic account of Annie Palmer, rooted in much historical truth. This is a great quick preparatory read for a visit to Rose Hall Great House near Montego Bay.

Goldman, Vivian. *The Book of Exodus: The Making and Meaning of Bob Marley and the Wailers' Album of the Century.* Three Rivers Press, 2006. An excellent account of the years surrounding Bob Marley's launch into international stardom with great anecdotes and lots of good context on the tumultuous 1970s.

Gottlieb, Karla. *The Mother of Us All: A History of Queen Nanny, Leader of the Windward Jamaican Maroons.* Africa World Press, 2000. The story of Nanny, Jamaica's most prominent Maroon leader and only national heroine.

Pariag, Florence. *East Indians in the Caribbean: An Illustrated History.* An illustrated look at the arrival of East Indians in the Caribbean basin, focused on Jamaica, Trinidad, and Guyana.

Price, Richard. *Maroon Societies: Rebel Slave Communities in the Americas.* Johns Hopkins University Press, 3rd ed., 1996. An interesting look at the parallel development of Maroon societies in a number of Latin American countries.

Senior, Olive. *An Encyclopedia of Jamaican Heritage.* Twin Guinep Publishers, 2003. An A-to-Z of things, people, and places Jamaican and their historical relevance. An indispensable quick reference for scholars of Jamaica.

## LANGUAGE

Adams, L. Emilie. *Understanding Jamaican Patois.* LMH Publishers, 1991. An introductory guide to Jamaican Patois and phrases.

Christie, Pauline. *Language in Jamaica.* Arawak Publications, 2003. An academic examination of the significance of language in Jamaica as it relates to history, class, and prejudice.

Reynolds, Ras Dennis Jabari. *Jabari Authentic Jamaican Dictionary of the Jamic Language, Featuring Patwa and Rasta Iyaric, Pronunciation and Definitions.* Around the Way Books, 2006.

## LITERATURE

Banks, Russell. *Rule of the Bone.* Minerva, 1996. An engaging novel that traces the growth of a somewhat troubled American youth who ends up in Jamaica.

Bennett, Louise. *Anancy and Miss Lou.* Sangster's Book Stores, 1979. A must-have among Miss Lou's many printed works. The Anancy stories are folk tales rooted in Jamaica's African heritage. Miss Lou brings them to life in a book appreciated by children and adults alike.

Figueroa, John. *Caribbean Voices: An Anthology of West Indian Poetry: Dreams and Visions.* Evans Bros., 1966. This book is a good representative of Figueroa, one of the grandfathers of Jamaican literature.

Henzell, Perry. *Cane.* 10a Publications, 2003. A novel about a white slave from Barbados who becomes a member of the planter class and owner of the largest plantation in Jamaica. While the book is fiction, it accurately portrays class dynamics and gives an excellent sense of the brutal reality that characterized the colonial period.

Kennaway, Guy. *One People.* Canongate Books, 2001. A hilarious look at the idiosyncrasies of the Jamaican people.

McKay, Claude. *Selected Poems.* Dover Publications, 1999. Many of McKay's poems are written in colorful dialect ranging in theme from clever critiques on political and economic ills to love poetry.

McKenzie, Earl. *Boy Named Ossie: A Jamaican Childhood.* Heinemann, 1991. Earl McKenzie, who grew up in the years leading up to independence, is one of Jamaica's most respected literary figures.

Mutabaruka. *The First Poems/The Next Poems.* Paul Issa Publications, 2005. Mutabaruka's definitive collected printed works, spanning many years of his career.

## NATURE AND THE ENVIRONMENT

Fincham, Alan. *Jamaica Underground.* University Press of the West Indies, 1998. An essential guide to the sinkholes and caves of Cockpit Country. Diagram and plates of cave layouts complement anecdotal accounts and exploration logs.

Hodges, Margaret. *Guide to the Blue and John Crow Mountains.* Natural History Society of Jamaica. Ian Randle Publishers, 2nd ed., 2007. Edited by expert naturalist Margaret Hodges with chapters written by several members of Jamaica's Natural History Society, this book improves on the much-in-demand and out-of-print first edition, *Blue Mountain Guide,* published in 1993. This is an essential guide for travelers looking to get intimately acquainted with Jamaica's most spectacular national park, for which the Jamaica Conservation and Development Trust is seeking UNESCO endorsement. The book is divided into six regions, making it especially practical for devising day-trip excursions.

Iremonger, Susan. *Guide to the Plants of the Blue Mountains of Jamaica.* University Press of the West Indies, 2002. A handy guide to the flora of the Blue Mountains.

Lethbridge, John, Harvey, Guy, and Carter, David. *The Yachtman's Guide to Jamaica* Cruising Guide Publications, 1996.

## BIRDING

Downer, Audrey and Robert Sutton. *Birds of Jamaica: A Photographic Field Guide.*

Cambridge University Press, 1990. A good guide to Jamaica's birds.

Raffaele, Herbert, et al. *Birds of the West Indies*. Princeton University Press, 2003. This is the best bird guide for the Caribbean basin, with excellent plates.

## FOOD

Burke, Virginia. *Eat Caribbean Cook Book*. Simon & Schuster, 2005. Easily among the best Caribbean cookbooks on the market. Burke makes essential recipes easy to put together with widely available ingredients.

Lumsden, Robin. *Belcour Cookbook: Jamaican, French and Chinese Family Recipes for Entertaining*. Belcour Preservatives, 2014. This autobiographical culinary masterpiece can't be recommended enough, tracing one of Jamaica's most prominent families across oceans and generations in food.

Quinn, Lucinda Scala. *Jamaican Cooking*. Wiley, 2006. A selective cookbook with some excellent recipes for those seasoned in Jamaican cooking.

## SPIRITUAL

Barrett, Leonard E. *The Rastafarians*. Beacon Press, 20th anniversary ed., 1997. A comprehensive study of the Rastafarian movement.

Bender, Wolfgang. *Rastafarian Art*. Ian Randle Publishers, 2004. Bender covers the contribution of Rastafarian philosophy to Jamaican contemporary art.

Bethel, Clement E. *Junkanoo*. Macmillan Caribbean, 1992. An in-depth look at Jonkunnu, a fascinating dance and music style closely associated with Jamaica's folk religions and performed for a few celebrations throughout the year, notably at Christmastime.

Chevannes, Barry. *Rastafari: Roots and Ideology*. University of West Indies Press, 1995. One of the best assessments in print of the Rastafarian movement, Chevannes is the top academic authority in Jamaica on the faith, having studied and lived amongst Rastas throughout his career.

Hausman, Gerald. *The Kebra Negast: The Lost Bible of Rastafarian Wisdom and Faith from Ethiopia and Jamaica*. St. Martin's Press, 1st ed., 1997. Considered the Rasta bible by many adherents, this is a must-have resource book for those with deep interest in the faith.

## ESSENTIAL PERIODICALS

*Jamaica Journal*, published by the Institute of Jamaica (IOJ), is a great easy-to-read academic publication highlighting different aspects of Jamaican culture and heritage.

*The Jamaican Magazine* is an excellent periodical published by the University of Technology. Each edition highlights a different parish.

# Internet Resources

## TRAVEL INFORMATION

**Jamaica Tourist Board**
**www.visitjamaica.com**
The official website of the Jamaica Tourist Board, smartly designed and easy to navigate.

## NEWS

**The Jamaica Gleaner**
**www.jamaica-gleaner.com**
Jamaica's most widely circulated daily, aligned center-left.

**The Jamaica Observer**
**www.jamaicaobserver.com**
The island's second most popular, pro-business newspaper, owned by Gordon "Butch" Stewart.

**The Star**
**www.jamaica-star.com**
Jamaica's daily entertainment tabloid, published by the Gleaner Company, is chock full of gossip and trash talk, making for good entertainment and little news.

**Loop Jamaica**
**www.loopjamaica.com**
A news portal owned by mobile phone carrier Digicel.

## FLIGHT INFORMATION

**Norman Manley International Airport**
**www.nmia.aero**
Norman Manley is the Kingston's international airport. The site has useful information, including airlines and flight schedules.

**Sangster International Airport**
**www.mbjairport.com**
Montego Bay's international airport receives the majority of the island's visitors. The airport's website provides complete travel information from arrivals and departures to shopping and food options.

## ECOTOURISM

**Jamaica Environment Trust**
**www.jamentrust.org**
Education, advocacy, and conservation are the pillars of this crucial NGO. The membership organization welcomes volunteers and contributors for projects aimed at protecting Jamaica's natural resources.

**Jamaica Caves Organization (JCO)**
**www.jamaicancaves.org**
JCO is the most active scientific exploratory organization on the western side of the island, researching the caves and sinkholes of Cockpit Country on a continual basis. The JCO sells maps and can arrange guides for those with an interest in serious exploring through Jamaica's deepest caves and backcountry.

**Jamaica Conservation and Development Trust (JCDT)**
**www.jcdt.org.jm**
The JCDT is in charge of the Blue and John Crow Mountain National Park and is the go-to organization for matters related to hiking and staying at the park.

**Southern Trelawny Environmental Agency (STEA)**
**www.stea.net**
A regularly updated site dedicated to coverage of the activities of the STEA, which include the annual Yam Festival. The site also contains resources for exploring the Trelawny interior and contracting guide services.

## MUSIC AND ENTERTAINMENT

**Irie FM**
**www.iriefm.net**
Jamaica's most popular reggae station, Irie broadcasts on 107.5 and 107.9 FM as well as over the Internet.

**Sun City Radio**
www.suncityradio.fm
104.9 FM is the voice of Portmore, representing "fi di Gaza" with music, information, news, artist interviews and more.

**Muzik Media**
www.muzikmedia.com
A New Jersey-based website that runs the top 10 music videos of the week as well as archiving and contemporary classic videos.

**Jammin Reggae Archives**
www.niceup.com
A U.S.-based site with information on reggae artists and upcoming performances.

**Skkan Media**
www.skkanme.com
An entertainment site covering parties across Jamaica.

**Bob Marley**
www.bobmarley.com
The official Bob Marley family website, with bios on individual family members, merchandise, and news. Most of the Marley progeny have their own sites as well.

**Reggae Entertainment**
www.reggaeentertainment.com
A site dedicated to the reggae industry with entertainment news and downloads.

**Ernie B's**
www.ebreggae.com
One of the best catalogs available for purchasing reggae on vinyl, both classics and new releases. Based in California.

# ART AND CULTURE

**Afflicted Yard**
www.afflictedyard.com
A counterculture site that reflects the pulse of popular edgy Jamaica, with enticing visuals and selected writing by the late founder of the site, artist par excellence Peter Dean Rickards. He sadly died in 2015, but his work and legacy live on.

**Panache**
www.panachejamagazine.com
A Caribbean fashion, beauty, and lifestyle magazine with print and online editions.

**Buzz Caribbean**
www.buzzzmagazine.com
A lifestyle and entertainment magazine with an online edition mirroring its print copy.

# Index

**332**

INDEX

# List of Maps

# Photo Credits

# Acknowledgments

This book would not have been possible without the support of my parents, Maria del Pilar Abaurrea and William Blaine Hill, whose wanderlust inspired my own. My parents nurtured my curiosity from day one, instilling a desire to see more, learn more, and travel the world. They taught me the virtue of appreciating how people live beyond our borders and the joy of indulging in new cultures, hearing fresh music, and tasting exotic foods. Most of all, my parents taught me to make every encounter a positive one.

I am grateful for the support and hospitality I was offered in my travels around Jamaica and am honored to consider many I had the pleasure of meeting in the course of this project not merely as professional and respectable colleagues, but also as friends and compatriots in a common cause.

Countless individuals facilitated the logistics behind the 7th edition of *Moon Jamaica* and generously offered their time and assistance, chief among them Robin and Mike Lumsden, who've shared their slice of paradise and enlightened vision for more than a decade; Carolyn Barrett, who knows how best to enjoy the island and its waters; Yvonne Blakey, with the best links in Portland; Mary Phillips, who wrote the book on how to entertain with class; Lee and Paul Issa, true torch bearers of Jamaican hospitality; Ed Bartlett, a stellar tourism minister full of well-guided energy and a consistent supporter; Essie Gardner and Paul Pennicook at the JTB, whose endorsement helped open many doors; Tammy and Blaise Hart, who continue to reinvent Good Hope and build value for Jamaica; Christopher Issa, who leads by example at the Spanish Court in Kingston, and now in Montego Bay; the Melville family, for demonstrating how to build a successful people business in tune with nature; and Jeffrey Jensen, for his undying appreciation for the real Jamaica and insight into its hidden gems.

For their gracious hospitality and support, I would also like to extend my sincerest gratitude to Jenny Wood of Island Outpost; Keressa Page of Hammerstein Highland House; Vickie Luetscher and Jean Lawrence at Silent Waters; Carol Slee of Sunset at the Palms; Nicky and Stefan at Wharf House; Sarah and Tabetha at Blue Ridge; Rodger Bolton at Lime Tree Farm; Dorothy and David Twyman at Old Tavern Estate; Elise Yap at The Blue House; Simon Browne at Y.S. Falls; Mike Drakulich of Mystic Mountain; Andrea and Axel at Marblue; Sandy Tatham of Blue Marlin and Coquina; events marketing guru Marcia McDonnough; the Burrowes family at Dolphin Cove; Elizabeth Seltzer of Calabash House; Sally, Justine, Laura and Jason Henzell of Jakes; Karin and Richard Murray at Tensing Pen; Debbie, Braxton and Houston Moncure of Bluefields Villas; Linda Chedester at the Luna Sea Inn; Shauna Vassel of Starlight Chalet; Christine Cohen at the Spa Retreat; Lloyd Edwards at Pimento Lodge; Jennifer Chatelain of Blue Hole Gardens; Kevin Robertson of Coyaba Beach Resort, now Zoëtry Montego Bay; Rosalie and Marvin Goodman of Goblin Hill; the Wallace brothers in Negril; Nora Perez of Villa Kelso; Maria Esther Zugasti and Rafael Echevarne for their fresh insight; Brian Nejedly, photographer extraordinaire for his generous contributions; and to the many others who I've failed to mention by name, thank you.

Lastly, but certainly not least, I need to acknowledge my editor Rachel Feldman, production coordinator Sarah Wildfang, and map editor Albert Angulo, as well as the entire team at Avalon Travel who made the publishing process virtually painless and set the bar for best practices in putting this book together.

# Also Available

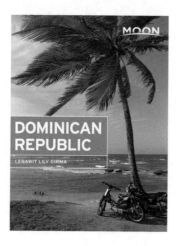

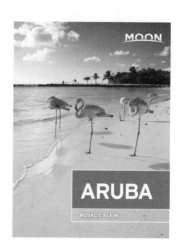

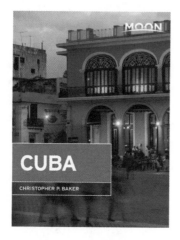

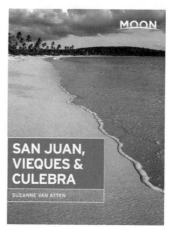

# MAP SYMBOLS

| | | | | | | | |
|---|---|---|---|---|---|---|---|
| ≡≡≡ Expressway | ○ City/Town | ✈ Airport | ⚲ Golf Course |
| ═══ Primary Road | ◉ State Capital | ✗ Airfield | 🅿 Parking Area |
| ─── Secondary Road | ⊛ National Capital | ▲ Mountain | ⬟ Archaeological Site |
| ⋯⋯ Unpaved Road | ★ Point of Interest | ✛ Unique Natural Feature | 🛢 Church |
| ─── Feature Trail | • Accommodation | | 🛢 Gas Station |
| - - - Other Trail | ▼ Restaurant/Bar | 🦅 Waterfall | ◠ Glacier |
| ⋯⋯ Ferry | ■ Other Location | ⚑ Park | ▨ Mangrove |
| ═══ Pedestrian Walkway | ▲ Campground | ⬛ Trailhead | ◡ Reef |
| ▥ Stairs | | 🎿 Skiing Area | ▦ Swamp |

# CONVERSION TABLES

°C = (°F – 32) / 1.8
°F = (°C x 1.8) + 32
1 inch = 2.54 centimeters (cm)
1 foot = 0.304 meters (m)
1 yard = 0.914 meters
1 mile = 1.6093 kilometers (km)
1 km = 0.6214 miles
1 fathom = 1.8288 m
1 chain = 20.1168 m
1 furlong = 201.168 m
1 acre = 0.4047 hectares
1 sq km = 100 hectares
1 sq mile = 2.59 square km
1 ounce = 28.35 grams
1 pound = 0.4536 kilograms
1 short ton = 0.90718 metric ton
1 short ton = 2,000 pounds
1 long ton = 1.016 metric tons
1 long ton = 2,240 pounds
1 metric ton = 1,000 kilograms
1 quart = 0.94635 liters
1 US gallon = 3.7854 liters
1 Imperial gallon = 4.5459 liters
1 nautical mile = 1.852 km

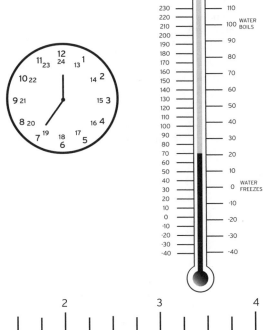

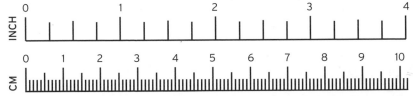

**MOON JAMAICA**
Avalon Travel
a member of the Perseus Books Group
1700 Fourth Street
Berkeley, CA 94710, USA
www.moon.com

Editor: Rachel Feldman
Series Manager: Kathryn Ettinger
Copy Editor: Christopher Church
Graphics Coordinator: Darren Alessi
Production Coordinator: Sarah Wildfang
Cover Design: Faceout Studios, Charles Brock
Interior Design: Domini Dragoone
Moon Logo: Tim McGrath
Map Editor: Albert Angulo
Cartographers: Karin Dahl and Brian Shotwell
Indexer: Rachel Kuhn

ISBN-13: 978-1-63121-383-0
ISSN: 1088-0941

Printing History
1st Edition — 1991
7th Edition — November 2016
5 4 3 2 1

Front cover photo: © Greg Johnston | Getty Images
Back cover photo: © Oliver Hill

Printed in Canada by Friesens